NARRATIVES OF TRANSMISSION

Narratives
of
Transmission

BERNARD DUYFHUIZEN

Rutherford • Madison • Teaneck
Fairleigh Dickinson University Press
London and Toronto: Associated University Presses

Associated University Presses
440 Forsgate Drive
Cranbury, NJ 08512

Associated University Presses
25 Sicilian Avenue
London WC1A 2QH, England

Associated University Presses
P.O. Box 39, Clarkson Pstl. Stn.
Mississauga, Ontario
L5J 3X9 Canada

The paper used in this publication meets the requirements of the American National Standard for Permanence of Paper for Printed Library Materials Z39.48–1984.

Library of Congress Cataloging-in-Publication Data

Duyfhuizen, Bernard, 1953–
     Narratives of Transmission
  / Bernard Duyfhuizen.
          p.   cm.
     Bibliography: p.
     Includes index
     ISBN 0–8386–3472–9 (alk. paper)
     1992   91–58803
                                                       CIP

PRINTED IN THE UNITED STATES OF AMERICA

for Tricia

Contents

Acknowledgments

Portions of this study have appeared previously in different form in *Comparative Literature, Novel, New Orleans Review, The Texas Review*, and *Why the Novel Matters: A Postmodern Perplex*, edited by Mark Spilka and Caroline McCracken-Flesher. I would like to thank the editors of these journals and Indiana University Press for their permission to reprint those materials here. Additionally, I want to thank the editors of *Novel, Papers on Language and Literature*, and *Critical Texts* for assigning me reviews on books related to this study. I also want to thank Keith Odom, Marianna Torgovnick, and Peggy McCormack for giving me the opportunity to present portions of this work at both the Modern Language Association and South Central Modern Language Association conventions; the Society for the Study of Narrative Literature for an opportunity to present a section at its 1987 narrative conference; the Language and Literature Society at the University of Wisconsin-Eau Claire for an opportunity to present a section at one of its meetings; and especially Joseph Wiesenfarth at the University of Wisconsin-Madison, who gave me an opportunity to present my ideas to the English department there and whose support of my work will always be appreciated.

I would like to acknowledge the Office of Research at the University of Tulsa for two grants that aided me in my research effort and the Office of Research and the School of Arts and Sciences at the University of Wisconsin-Eau Claire for support to attend conferences at which I was presenting my work. Also, I want to acknowledge Princeton University Press for permission to reproduce the figure on page 34.

My intellectual debts are many, but I particularly want to thank Tzvetan Todorov and E. D. Hirsch, Jr. for helpful preliminary discussions at the 1981 session of the School of Criticism and Theory. This study had its genesis in my doctoral thesis at the University of Tulsa, and I want to thank Gordon O. Taylor and Darcy O'Brien of my committee for reading early drafts of the complete text and providing their support for my work. I also want to thank Khachig Tölölyan, Hugh Kenner, Richard Pearce, and Tim Raser for discussing my work with me in its formative stages. In my work's later stages, Daniel R. Schwarz, Martin Wood, Elizabeth Preston, Blagoy Trenev, and especially Robyn Warhol provided helpful guides to revision—to them I express my appreciation. By far my largest debt is owed to Joseph Kestner, whose encouragement and involvement with this project from the outset, both as thesis advisor and as a friend, has enabled me to see my way clearly when the path seemed impenetrable. Whatever mistransmissions remain are, of course, my own.

Reginald Martin, John Yozzo, Sharon Jessee, Richard Sullivan, John M. Krafft, Ninette Maples, and my colleagues at the University of Wisconsin-Eau Claire have also provided me with the necessary encouragement and friendship during the course of my research, writing, and revision. Of course my parents, Duffy and Louise, and my aunt, Dr. G. M. J. Duyfhuizen, deserve more thanks than I can ever give them. A special thanks goes to my daughter Kate, whose editorial restraint kept the many drafts of the text crayon-free. And lastly, I dedicate this work to my wife Tricia, without whom this study could not have been written; she provided not only support and patience, but a keen editorial eye and sense.

NARRATIVES OF TRANSMISSION

Introduction

> The reader must begin this book with an act of faith and
> end it with an act of charity. We ask him to believe in the
> sincerity and authenticity of this preface, affirming in re-
> turn his prerogative to be skeptical of all that follows it.
> —Barth, *Giles Goat-Boy*

IN HIS CLASSIC WORK *Mimesis*, Erich Auerbach states that each
event Homer "narrates is for the time being the only present, and
fills both the stage and the reader's mind completely."[1] For instance,
when Odysseus narrates his adventures during his attempts to return home, the reader supposedly suspends his or her awareness of
the epic singer and makes present in the reading experience the very
voice of Odysseus. Near the middle of *The Odyssey*,[2] at the close
of book 12, however, there occurs a rare moment in Homer's narrative: the illusion of immediacy breaks down while Odysseus explains
to the Phaiakians how he came to know certain details included in
his story. He had been telling his listeners of how he and his crew
had been stranded on Thrinakia, the island of the god Helios, the
place prophecized as the site of the last disaster to befall his crew
on their long journey home. After a month of waiting on the island's
shores for a shift in the winds, Odysseus traveled into the interior of
the island "'to pray to the gods, if any of them might show [him]
some course / to sail on'" (334–35). He left behind his starving crew,
who gazed hungrily on the oxen that according to Teiresias's and
Circe's prophecies they were forbidden to eat. But as Odysseus related later, the gods "'shed a sweet sleep on my eyelids'" (338), and
while he slept, Eurylochos made a speech convincing the crew that
violating the sacred law and chancing destruction at sea were pref-
erable to starving to death. Odysseus then awakened and returned
to his ships, only to smell "'the pleasant savor of cooking meat.'"

> 'And I cried out my grief aloud to the gods immortal:
> "Father Zeus, and you other everlasting and blessed

gods, with a pitiless sleep you lulled me, to my confusion,
and my companions staying here dared a deed that was monstrous.'"
(370–73)

Odysseus then tells his rapt audience that "'Lampetia of the light robes ran swift with the message / to Hyperion [Helios] the Sun God, that we had killed his cattle'" (374–75), and that Helios demanded retribution from Zeus and, if he did not get it, threatened an even more "monstrous" transgression: "'"I will go down to Hades' and give my light to the dead men"'" (383). Zeus judged swiftly how to punish Odysseus's crew, and assured Helios, "'"I will strike these men's fast ship midway on the open / wine-blue sea with a shining bolt and dash it to pieces"'" (387–88). Zeus's thunderbolt fulfilled the prophecy—the already written fate of Odysseus's crew.

In focusing on this moment in the narration of *The Odyssey*, I have retained (as Richmond Lattimore, Homer's translator, has) the quotation marks indicating that Odysseus's narration is always the reported speech of a character embedded in the epic singer's act of narrating. As Auerbach's notion of immediacy suggests, we seemingly forget that Odysseus has an entranced audience following his every word; we too are entranced by a storyteller. But in the scene I have retold, the frames that mark narrative transmission suddenly appear. Odysseus's narrating is invaded by the voices of Eurylochos, Helios, and Zeus that Odysseus could hardly have heard. First, he was asleep when Eurylochos spoke, and secondly, the words of the gods were spoken far away on Olympus. How does Odysseus know exactly what they said, particularly the speech of the gods? He tells the Phaiakians in a quite matter-of-fact way:

'All this I heard afterward from fair-haired Kalypso,
and she told me she herself had heard it from the guide, Hermes.
'But when I came back again to the ship ...'
(389–90)

It is an extraordinary moment. Hardly missing a beat, Odysseus picks up the thread of his narrative, and the problem of transmission is cleaned up like so much spilled wine in the Phaiakian great hall.

This little bit of narrative housekeeping is easily ignored; after all, we hear such formulae nearly every day in common gossip. Yet at the same time, this brief account of narrative transmission underscores Odysseus's double position in *The Odyssey*—he is both a character and one of its narrators (a doubling made problematic by Odysseus's occasional disguises and false narratives of origin, journey, and "self"). Indeed, at this moment Odysseus is the very emblem of transmission, standing between gods and men, Troy and Ithaca, the suitors and Penelope, Laertes and Telemachos, the beginning of Homer's epic and its end. Ultimately, *The Odyssey* is a "narrative of transmission" on many formal and thematic levels. Odysseus's special relationship with Athena makes him the mediator, as we have just seen, between the transgressive acts of men and the retribution of the gods. On the physical plane his journey home is a transmission of body and plunder from Troy to Ithaca. While Troy is sacked by the Greeks, Ithaca is being sacked by the suitors. Penelope keeps them at bay by maintaining the image of Odysseus's presence through the stories of her husband that travelers tell her. In addition to threatening Penelope's fidelity, by their plots to kill Telemachos and usurp his birthright, the suitors threaten the genealogical imperative of transmission. Hence, the epic opens in the charged atmosphere of the suitors' plots and closes with the final victory of Laertes, Odysseus, and Telemachos over the families of the dead suitors. The line of transmission and authority, marked and mediated by the figure of Odysseus, has been restored. Lastly, this short allegory of transmission inscribes the problem of authority that obtains in the entire oral tradition of epic poetry and the troubled history of textual transmission that has attended the Homeric epics since their first transcription.

The richness of transmission has often been obscured. For example, consider Angus Calder's 1975 advice to readers in his introduction to the Penguin edition of Walter Scott's *Old Mortality*: "If you have never opened this novel before—and especially if you have never before read one of the Scottish novels of Walter Scott—you should certainly not bother yet with this introduction. You should vault over the intervening pages, ignore, besides myself, the rather tedious Cleishbotham and perhaps even the interesting Pattieson, and begin at once with Chapter 2."[3] Although we may follow Calder's advice as far as vaulting over his own introduction, we must pause at his suggestion of likewise leaping over the first chapter of *Old Mortality*. For Calder, Scott's "novel" has significance primarily as a mimetic depiction of Scottish life and history. He ignores the fact that Scott's "novel" also has significance because of its complex narrating situation that marks the very difficulty of Scott's project to represent the life and history of his nation. As Joseph Kestner comments on the "extreme recession of the frame" in Old *Mortality*: "Each generation adds a frame surrounding the previous one, so that history becomes a process of *telling in context*: the teller of a new account was the receiver of a previous account. History is thus a series of narrated codes which the next listener deciphers, integrates, and transmits."[4]

In his essay "Discourse in the Novel," Mikhail Bakhtin reminds us that "behind the narrator's story we read a second story, the author's story; he is the one who tells us how the narrator tells stories, and also tells us about the narrator himself.... If one fails to sense this second level, the intentions and accents of the author himself, then one has failed to understand the work."[5] Applying this idea to Calder's advice to readers, we see that to vault over the problematic narrative of transmission with which Scott frames his tale is to read incompletely. We would fail to see that Scott's depiction of this moment in Scottish history (the turmoil of the Covenanting period in the seventeenth century) is also a narrative about the ruptured transmission of Scottish political power, a theme that is the focus of Scott's Waverley novels. Calder's notion of how to read Scott demonstrates a process of text reception that privileges the thematic aspects of prose fiction at the expense of its communicative aspects—its modes and processes of transmission. Calder neglects the acts of telling that both articulate and produce the historical content of the "novel." Like Homer, Scott weaves the narrating with the narrative, in a symbiosis of composition and transmission.

In the last two paragraphs, I placed the term "novel" in quotation marks because in examining the narratives of transmission in countless texts I have become aware of how slippery terms such as "novel" can be. For my purposes here, the term "novel" only refers to the "literary instance" of the published book, transmitted from the actual author to his or her readers. This definition distinguishes between the acts of transmission associated with the published book and those that occur within the text's fictional universe. The narratives of these latter acts of transmission are the main focus of this book. Here at the outset, let me also stipulatively define three terms that are easily confused: narrating, narration, narrative.

By "narrating" I refer to the activity of telling itself, the essential action in a text's narrative of transmission. Narratology commonly distinguishes between events the characters experience and a narrator's tale of those events. To communicate a sense of a character's experience, the narrator must translate experience and the character's discourse into a language that is intelligible to the listener and appropriate to his or her position in the narrating situation. The stories of transmission occur within this social construct of communication, and therefore the means and occasion for producing a tale, along with the occasion and conditions of its reception, are primary to the study of transmission. In the novels and short stories examined in the later chapters, the activity of narrating—whether letter writing, diary writing, memoir writing, or oral recounting—and the activity of reading or listening or transcribing are palpably represented within the text. They not only mark the text's form but also contribute to its themes and our acts of reading and interpreting those themes.

By "narration" I refer to the verbal construct that results from a particular narrator's act of narrating. With this term we are able to conceptualize the boundaries delimiting the different narrating acts within a text, and to see, as Bakhtin does, that "discourse lives ... on the boundary between its own context and another, alien, context."[6] Spatial vocabulary—like the word "boundaries"—has been a part of narrative theory since the first discussions of "point of view." Within the present inquiry the most prevalent metaphors are those of "levels" and "frames" of narration. The spatial analogies used throughout are intended to serve as conceptual models for identifying different narrations and their relationships within a given text or group of texts being compared. These spatial designations, however, beg the question of their role in our interpretive conventions. How are our acts of interpreting overdetermined by spatial hierarchies that seek to distinguish between narrations as to their truth claims and reliability? Like such spatially problematic paintings as René Magritte's series *La Condition Humaine*, the structures of narrative transmission are provisional at best, and capable of dissolving at any moment.

It could be said that every narration is a narrative, but it is necessary to distinguish between these terms. "Narrative" has become a catch-all term in critical discourse about prose fiction; it may refer to the story told by a narrator, to the narration, or to the act of narrating. Because of this confusion I use "narrative" to refer to the signified story articulated by a narration (the signifier—to complete the Saussurian analogy). The study of transmission is concerned with acts of narrating and the narrations produced, but in addition to the narrative that the narration articulates, there is a second narrative that obtains within the process of narrating and that is marked within the narration. This second narrative I call the "narrative of transmission." The present book may be said to represent yet another narration: a telling of the narrative of my having read certain texts that make acts of narrative transmission essential parts of the texts' narrative strategies.

By examining these distinctions I want to show how the narrative process of prose fiction intersects with thematic elements, just as the narrative process of epic poetry intersects with thematic elements in Homer's *Odyssey*. The contribution such an inquiry makes to narrative study is both theoretical and interpretive. The theory of narrative transmission has been developing slowly in the works of such theorists as Seymour Chatman, Franz Stanzel, Gérard Genette, Susan Lanser, Mikhail Bakhtin, and Peter Brooks. In these works, however, transmission makes up only a part of different narratological inquiries. Here, I will attempt to weave these theoretical threads into a coherent tapestry. To achieve this end, I will turn often to texts that stage narratives of transmission. I hope the discussion will contribute to the understanding of particular texts, but my more general purpose is to show how transmission must be seriously considered during the structuration of reading and during the interpretive analysis of theme. The textual analysis of transmission focuses on how, during the act of reading, structure and theme intersect in variously intended discourses. But as Roland Barthes observes, "Textual analysis does not attempt to describe the structure of a work; it is not a matter of recording a structure, but rather producing a mobile structuration of the text (a structuration which shifts from reader to reader throughout history), of staying within the signifying volume of the work, within its *significance*."[7]

After an initial chapter in which I outline and synthesize some of the theoretical issues in narratology relating to narrative transmission, the remainder of the study examines a broad sampling of ways the narrative of transmission is articulated and can be interpreted. Chapter 2 concentrates on the double narrative of transmission and transgression that occurs in three epistolary novels. By charting the interplay between the discursive practices of transmission and the codes of a dialectics of desire in these texts, we see how a formal/thematic logic obtains in systems of transmission that represent and reproduce stories of social/sexual transgression. Chapter 3 explores diary narratives that raise issues of narration and the representation of the "self" as both characterized subject and narrating agent. By focusing on the codes of transmission in the diary text, we see not only the composition of the dichotomy between the experiencing self and the narrating self, but we also see the emergence of a "reading self" necessary to complete the solipsistic system of transmission in diary narrative. Extending the principles established in chapters 2 and 3, chapter 4 examines the transmission strategies deployed when letters or diaries are inserted into other narrating forms, producing a structuration of intertextuality in the reader's response. Also, chapter 4 discusses some hybrid narratives of transmission that merge different forms of narration to produce a multitexted novel.

Chapter 5 shifts the inquiry to transmission strategies in fictional prefaces by editors who "frame" and seek to overdetermine the texts they introduce. By examining these "paratextual" narrators, we begin to locate the first site of the structuration of reading and the interpretive struggle over the reader's production of meaning. Chapter 6 extends the issue of the editor's role in both the structuration of reading and the production of meaning to another genre of transmission: the "found memoir" of a now-absent narrator. This inquiry reveals a "contact character" who moves between the narrative worlds of the editor and the absent narrator, and who both authenticates and problematizes the questions of authority and authenticity posed by the editorial frame. Chapters 7 and 8 explore the narrative of transmission that operates in texts that represent the transcription of oral narrations. These encased narratives stage a complex play of framing that makes clear the dialogic structure of narration and raises questions of how a reader negotiates different narrating acts in seeking the truth of the tale transcribed. Chapter 7 focuses on two French novels that stage narrative contracts for the transmission of stories of sexual transgression, and chapter 8 examines two British novels that further examine questions surrounding the motivations of the narrating agents in the production of texts.

Ian Watt, in his famous study *The Rise of the Novel*, once identified the aspects of fiction my inquiry focuses on as techniques of "formal realism."[8] Watt's identification, although critically valid in regard to the novel, does not adequately account for the structuration of reading such devices as letters, diaries, editorial prefaces, and transcriptions. These devices are not merely *mimetic* conventions (and therefore easy to dismiss, as Calder does with Scott's narrative techniques); they also function as the medium of the narration. By their particular textuality, they influence the narrating and, by extension, the narrative produced. Rather than static formal devices, these documentary techniques are active forces producing the unique fictional universe of any given text. As John T. Matthews observes, "The nature of narrative is all frame and framing, the articulation of thresholds meaningful as they conduct our passing through them, and not our passing by or over them."[9] In all instances of narrative, we enter and condition the society of the narrative utterance by engaging the text's narrative of transmission. In this engagement we enter a dynamic and transformatory process of text production, a process that resembles the narrative of transmission that occurs in each of our individual existences. We live by our stories, our plots, our frames, our letters, diaries, and documents; to see them only as static forms or to ignore their modes of transmission is to miss the patterns of civilization that influence and even control our everyday actions. "Transmission" is a pervasive process that occurs fundamentally in acts of narrating and reading, and dialogically within the literary text and in the critical discourse that comes to surround the text. The narrative of transmission is both a metaphor for processes of continuance in literature and life, and a metonymy—a constituent part of that process.

Tzvetan Todorov has written of the need to find the "sense" of narrative structures so that we can apply it to the "interpretation" of literary texts.[10] To this same end I have tried to weave together perspectives drawn from literary theory, textual examples, practical demonstrations of the "sense" of transmission, and interpretations of individual works. My work here is intended as a beginning, a start to our understanding of transmission and the way it operates in the intersections of stories and lives. By recognizing these fields of intersection, we see that transmission is the process at the heart of systems of preservation, exchange, accumulation, and loss. It models itself on the give-and-take struggles that underwrite all literary plots and is, therefore, at the basis of all narratives. Transmission functions in plots of history, heredity, economics, politics—in plots of the continuation of human existence. Moreover, transmission is a site of power in narrative. To control the lines of transmission is to have power in the fictional universe. The study of transmission can lead us to see the analogous lines of power outside the narrative and literary instance. If we are to understand the historical, hereditary, economic, and political plots that operate in our own lives, we must learn to attend to the lines of transmission that perpetuate power and our relations to power. The task now for studies of transmission is to turn attention to the larger social and cultural questions that an examination of the narrative of transmission could illuminate. If this text succeeds in its own transmission, then in its own way it will contribute to the ongoing human inquiry into the processes of social existence, into the processes by which we frame our lives.

My main intention in *Narratives of Transmission* is to show how particular documentary techniques are necessary elements in the way a narrative constructs an image of a fictional universe. Whether letters, a diary, a memoir, a hybrid collection of documents arranged by an editor, or a transcribed oral narration—each document marks the "will" of its writer to control the transmission of (the reader's "inheritance" of) his or her life story by textually encoding its elements: characters, setting, plot, and dénouement. The document seeks to capture and control the discourse of the other, to channel and make transmissible the narrative of the narrating subject's own existence. Yet every textualized attempt at control presupposes its converse. The discourse of the other marks another narrative of transmission, and the competition of texts, voices, discourses, and plots constitutes the motivating force of narrative. To explore the narrative of transmission is to explore a fundamental article in the reader's contract with the narrative text.

This focus on the transmission process, however, is only one among many possible focuses in narrative analysis. And although I do assert its necessity in interpretation, I would not claim privilege for my readings over others. Moreover, this study is not an exhaustive literary history of narratives of transmission. Because every narrative text exemplifies some aspect of transmission, I had to impose some arbitrary constraints and limitations on this study. Readers will recall texts they would have included, and I hope the present work will encourage others to provide readings of those missing narratives of transmission.

1 | *Toward a Transmission Theory of Narrative*

I was standing one day in the Alcaná, or market place, of Toledo when a lad came up to sell some old notebooks and other papers to a silk weaver who was there. As I am extremely fond of reading anything, even though it be but the scraps of paper in the streets, I followed my natural inclination and took one of the books, whereupon I at once perceived that it was written in characters which I recognized as Arabic. I recognized them, but reading them was another thing; and so I began looking around to see if there was any Spanish-speaking Moor near by who would be able to read them for me. It was not very hard to find such an interpreter, nor would it have been even if the tongue in question had been an older and a better one. To make a long story short, chance brought a fellow my way; and when I told him what it was I wished and placed the book in his hands, he opened it in the middle and began reading and at once fell to laughing. When I asked him what the cause of his laughter was, he replied that it was a note which had been written in the margin.

I besought him to tell me the content of the note, and he, laughing still, went on, "As I told you, it is something in the margin here: 'This Dulcinea del Toboso, so often referred to, is said to have been the best hand at salting pigs of any woman in all La Mancha.'"

No sooner had I heard the name Dulcinea del Toboso than I was astonished and held in suspense, for at once the thought occurred to me that those notebooks must contain the history of Don Quixote. With this in mind I urged him to read me the title, and he proceeded to do so, turning the Arabic into Castilian upon the spot: *History of Don Quixote de la Mancha, Written by Cid Hamete Benengeli, Arabic Historian.* It was all I could do to conceal my satisfaction and, snatching them from the silk weaver, I bought from the lad all the papers and notebooks that he had for half a real; but if he had known or suspected how very much I wanted them, he might well have had more than six reales for them.

The Moor and I then betook ourselves to the cathedral cloister, where I requested him to translate for me into the Castilian tongue all the books that had to do with Don Quixote, adding nothing and subtracting nothing; and I offered him whatever payment he desired.

He was content with two arrobas of raisins and two fanegas of wheat and promised to translate them well and faithfully and with all dispatch. However, in order to facilitate matters, and also because I did not wish to let such a find as this out of my hands, I took the fellow home with me, where in a little more than a month and a half he translated the whole of the work just as you will find it set down here....

If there is any objection to be raised against the veracity of all this, it can be only that the author was an Arab, and that nation is known for its lying propensities; but even though they be our enemies, it may readily be understood that they would more likely have detracted from, rather than added to, the chronicle. So it seems to me, at any rate; for whenever he might and should deploy the resources of his pen in praise of so worthy a knight, the author appears to take pains to pass over the matter in silence; all of which in my opinion is ill done and ill conceived, for it should be the duty of historians to be exact, truthful, and dispassionate, and neither interest nor fear nor rancor nor affection should swerve them from the paths of truth, whose mother is history, rival of time, depository of deeds, witness of the past, exemplar and adviser to the present, and the future's counselor. In this work, I am sure, will be found all that could be desired in the way of pleasant reading; and if it is lacking in any way, I maintain that this is the fault of that hound of an author rather than of the subject.

Momentarily, the reader of the passage just quoted may have wondered, "What a strange opening for a book of literary criticism!" Quickly, I am sure, the reader recognized the passage as coming from Miguel de Cervantes Saavedra's classic novel *The Ingenious Gentleman: Don Quixote de la Mancha* (I, 1605; II, 1615).[1] However, for readers whose memory of the text is slightly rusty, it may come as a surprise to recall that the passage comes from chapter 9 (pt. 1) instead of from the prologue. One interpretive problem any reader of *Don Quixote* confronts is its unstable authorship and textual origin. We have first the "prologue author," who denies "fathering" the text—preferring to see himself as *Don Quixote*'s "stepfather." This prologue author gives way to a narrator who reveals at the end of chapter 8 (pt. 1) that all along he has been presenting another author's text. In a quandary about how the story will continue , the reader comes upon the narrative of text discovery, in which the narrator stumbles upon a history of Don Quixote de la Mancha written in Arabic by Cid Hamete Benengeli, a text which now must be translated so the narrator may conclude the adventure of Don Quixote's battle with the Biscayan. This play of authors and texts is never settled through the course of the novel, and it calls into question authorial genealogy. The text is the offspring of the author's active pen, and to deny authoring/fathering the text is to illegitimize the sign, to detach it from its origin in full presence, as truth, and to relegate it to a trope within a rhetorical universe. As Ralph Flores has shown, Don Quixote's narrative is constructed on a paradox: "apparently rhetorical writing is deemed 'truer' than apparently nonrhetorical writing which for the same reason becomes troped. Any 'truth of the story' (to use a recurrent phrase) is itself a story, any norm by which 'rhetoric' or 'authorship' might be assessed is itself rhetorical or authorial. If the stepfather-author can never quite be aligned with his hero or text..., the text's own authors, too, are always fissured by supplementarity: each author—'first' or 'second'—becomes secondary to the other."[2]

This nonalignment makes problematic the authority of the narrating voice and the textual margin in which that voice speaks to the reader. The author/narrator's gloss on the narration is always a marginal act that marks the boundary between discourse and story, but when such glosses cannot be fixed in any certain way, the narrated text loses (forgets) its referential frame. "Truth" becomes a trope within a rhetorical construct; however, speaking truth is not necessarily knowing truth—as the character Don Quixote continually demonstrates. For Don Quixote it is never what he actually does that matters; what matters is the rhetorical conception of his deeds before he undertakes them and the rhetorical explanation of how his triumph and glory has been stolen (troped away) by an enemy "enchanter." Because rhetoric is so important, the narrator who discovers Benengeli's text laments its lack of any "praise of so worthy a knight." From his reading of chivalric romances to his explanation of Mambrino's helmet, Don Quixote places his belief in rhetoric rather than experience. As Flores observes, Don Quixote needs (as does the text itself) an "author" who will recount his adventures and make clear the enchantments he has suffered, and who will provide him with an acceptable "genealogy" so that he might be worthy— on the basis of hereditary right—of a fair princess' hand in marriage. Such a genealogy would, as well, establish the validity and value of the textual inheritance to be handed down in legend.

Of course, if Don Quixote requires an author to discover (concoct) a genealogy to establish his "legal eligibility and right" to marry a princess (who is always only a rhetorical construct in his imagination [see pt. 1, ch. 21]), then the question of truth and fiction, as it arises both in Don Quixote's experience and in *Don Quixote*, becomes hopelessly blurred and inextricably bound to language and rhetoric. Consider Dulcinea del Toboso, whose existence depends on both Don Quixote's need for a "fair lady" to whom he can dedicate his exploits and his belief that those opponents he vanquishes will visit her to proclaim his knightly superiority. Flores comments that it is as if he expects "that the more completely he becomes a knight, the more completely she can become a princess."[3] As we know from the novel, Don Quixote's attempt at realizing his imaginary construct is bedeviled by enchanters (who, of course, are also imaginary constructs) who defeat his desire to "know" that Dulcinea exists in a form compatible with his descriptions of her beauty and nobility. Ultimately, one "enchanter" is Sancho Panza, but we see his enchantment of Dulcinea for what it is: a rhetorically motivated fiction that will please its audience (Don Quixote) yet protect the truth ("Dulcinea's" rhetoricity).

The question of Dulcinea's existence as only a rhetorical construct extends our questions about textual authority and mimetic grounding to the characterized acts of reading enclosed in the narrative. For instance, embedded in the narrative of text discovery quoted earlier was a marginal note. The translator's laughing response to this note opened the channel by which the narrator discovered that this text was about his hero, Don Quixote. The marginal note, the product of an even earlier reader of the text's pages, both lends veracity to the narrative (the particular issue of which we are unaware) and takes it away by the qualifier "is said to"—by whom and in what other narrative construction of the tale? Likewise, consider that Cervantes has the first part of the history (published in 1605) appear as a book in the second part of the novel (published in 1615), where it is read by many of the characters. In addition, a spurious sequel to Don Quixote's tale had been published (both in actuality and in the fictional universe), filled with "fictional" adventures that the "real" Don Quixote is anxious to prove are lies. When in part 2, chapter 78, he meets Don Alvaro Tarfe, a character in the spurious version, Don Quixote makes him declare before witnesses that the "real" Don Quixote and Sancho Panza are not the same as those presented in the already published sequel. These witnesses, it is assumed, are intended to transmit this confession, and thus become additional "authors" of Don Quixote. As Robert Alter has commented, Don Quixote's meeting with Don Alvaro Tarfe "is almost enough to induce ontological vertigo—a fictional character from a 'true' chronicle confronting a fictional character from a false one in order to establish beyond doubt his own exclusive authenticity."[4]

What I have been trying to show is the playfulness and intricacy of narrative transmission in *Don Quixote*, the text often credited as the first genuine novel. I have also tried to suggest indirectly that within this text there exists a *narrative of transmission* that we must confront. Jorge Luis Borges has asked, "Why does it disquiet us to know that Don Quixote is a reader of the *Quixote*?" The "disquiet" in our reading of *Don Quixote* and in our reading of many of the other narratives examined in the present book, stems from the estranged narrative transmission. The estrangement is caused by the reader's overdetermined awareness of the narrating situation structured between the narrated events and the text s/he reads. Borges answers his own question by suggesting, "If the characters in a story can be readers or spectators, then we, their readers or spectators, can be fictitious."[5] We can infer from Borges's statement that the reader of *Don Quixote* risks his or her ontological wholeness if s/he comes in full contact with the textual system and tunes in completely to the different contact channels of narrating that constitute the text. Yet *Don Quixote* saves the reader from such a fate by being critical of its own transmission. It stages the text's difficulty in getting told— reminding us through its process of narrative transmission that we are just reading a novel. We are saved from the fate of Don Quixote: we do not become mad because of our reading.

"TRANSMISSION" has been around for as long as there has been discourse. In literary contexts the word is most often applied to the oral tradition (particularly that of epic poetry) and to the biblical tradition of multiple authors of the Bible. In those exchanges are the cultural histories of peoples and the creative spark of the imagination that remade the poem at each performance and rewrote the sacred stories to fit contemporary structures of religious and political power. Transmission also has a meaning outside of poetic and religious contexts. Western society depends on transmission, and especially textual transmission, to record and pass on legal codes, business records, marriage, birth, and property records. We live in a world built of texts and held together by the processes of transmission that establish, maintain, and perpetuate the documents of our existence. It is little wonder, then, that the establishment of texts—the task of the first generation of scholars, scribes, and publishers—should be mirrored in codes of narrative transmission that are so prevalent in prose fiction and that represent *narratives of transmission* within texts. This book is about these narratives of transmission, and it asserts that the narrative of transmission, though often slighted as a mere convention, should be an essential part of the reader's processes for understanding of any text.

Narrative transmission, then, is not a singular event; instead, it constitutes the entire textual system when viewed as the narrative of transmission. The narrative of transmission includes the communicational structure of narrating (the situation of telling the story), narration (a particular narrator's version of the story), and narrative (the interplay of the narrated events with the narrating situation and the narration produced). It also includes the formal thematics binding the telling with the tale and (in this study) the formal mimetics of the text as represented document (letters, diaries, memoirs, and transcribed narrations). Although these transmission situations are largely *intra*textual, *inter*textual contact between and through other texts containing narratives of transmission also occurs. This intertextuality significantly relates to genre considerations: both synchronic (existing simultaneously, outside historical change) formal structures and conventions and diachronic (existing in a historical relationship of change) transformations of techniques and their applications to specific themes such as transgressive love, self-discovery, inheritance and genealogical transmission, and erotic contracts. To understand the systems of narrative transmission and the narratives of transmission these produce, we must examine some of the theories of narrators, readers, and narrative textuality operating in contemporary narratology, and we must examine the narrating act and the transmission/reception process *staged in the text*. Our task, then, is to establish operating procedures for reading the signs of transmission encoded in the narrative text.

Theories of narrators and theories of readers have led to two essential perceptions about the writer and the reader in the text: (1) Readers and narrators are encoded entities—even if only linguistic signs—within the textual system. Narrators address readers or listeners during their narrations to signify the act of reception and to validate the act of transmission. (2) Narrators and readers characterized in narrative texts are engaged in a mirror act of transmission with actual authors and readers; and these textual surrogates function significantly in the narrative transmission system and thereby influence the actual reader's acts of interpretation. Moving from these two perceptions, we can postulate an addresser and an addressee within a schema of transmission levels possible for any given text. To explore the function of narrative levels on transmission, I will now turn to the astute contributions of Franz Stanzel, Gérard Genette and Susan Lanser.

Franz Stanzel has developed a typology of "narrative situations" for the purpose of classifying novels on the basis of the predominant narrating style. He designates Henry James's *The Ambassadors*, for instance, as the model of a "figural narrative situation" in which the character's consciousness is the filter through which the narrative must pass. This figural narrative situation connects the authorial or third-person narrative situation (e.g., *Tom Jones*) and the first-person narrative situation (e.g., *Moby Dick*) in a triadic model. Together they constitute the dominant narrative orientations in the history of narrative fiction.[6] A difficulty with such typologies is that novels tend to mix the different narrating situations. They experiment and test the limits of language and narrative textuality to create new aesthetic perspectives for the transmission of narrative. Moreover, we must recognize that this model distinguishes more on the level of character representation than narrator or reader functions.

In his later work, *A Theory of Narrative*, Stanzel examines closely the issue of narrative transmission. He appears to have first derived the term (as I have) from Seymour Chatman's 1975 essay "The Structure of Narrative Transmission," which was the foundation for Chatman's major study *Story and Discourse*. Chatman wrote in that essay: "A central consideration for the theory of narrative is the transmitting source which is postulated. By 'transmission' I simply mean the class of kinds of narrative presentation which includes as its two subclasses showing and telling."[7] On the surface it appears that Chatman has actually created only a synonym for narration, and Stanzel substantiates that view when he writes, "Chatman undertakes a systematic description of the forms of 'narrative transmission,' by which he means essentially the forms of rendered mediacy in narration."[8] Stanzel here adds a third term to this synonymic matrix: "mediacy" (*Mittelbarkeit*). "Mediacy," Stanzel insists, "is the generic characteristic which distinguishes narration from other forms of literary art."[9] By this he means the presence of a narrator (either a first-person or authorial "teller-character" or a figural "reflector-character") who mediates through a narrative situation the presentation of the fictional universe (the narrated world and the actions of its characters) to the reader. Stanzel sees transmission in terms of narration-as-textual-speech-act; as a result, all narrating situations for Stanzel are moments of transmission and the evaluative narrative critic can only determine whether the literary artist has achieved the "appropriate form for the transmission of each story."[10]

Stanzel's concept of the transmission process in narrative is particularly significant because it redefines an essential element in narrative theory: the traditional separation of narration into diegesis and mimesis. Strictly speaking, "narration" should refer only to that part of the text told by the narrating voice; but with the development of figural techniques, the reader's sense of mediacy (diegesis) decreases and the sense of "scenic presentation" (mimesis, even of consciousness) increases to such a degree that the narrator almost seems to disappear. Transmission, therefore, serves as a broader category of narrative communication.

Although I clearly agree with most of Stanzel's ideas about transmission, he makes one assertion I consider questionable: "While the authorial narrator and the first-person narrator can be differentiated according to their position in regard to the represented world of the characters, *they cannot be distinguished according to their relationship to the apparatus of narrative transmission.*"[11] By dismissing the "apparatus of narrative transmission," Stanzel overlooks a crucial feature in those narratives that purport to present other written documents to the reader. Within *A Theory of Narrative* Stanzel only alludes briefly to epistolary or diary fictions, or to fictional letters or diaries that occur in narratives. Stanzel is correct when he states, "Point of view and narrator are ... the two most important concepts for the critical and theoretical analysis of the transmission process in narrative."[12] But other narrating situations, especially those that involve fictional production and reception within the narrative text, need to be examined before any comprehensive theory of transmission is possible.

Essential to Gérard Genette's operating procedure in *Narrative Discourse* is the distinction between the "literary instance" and the "narrating instance."[13] Stanzel has also made this distinction: "The process of production, the genesis of a narrative text (deep structure) [the literary instance of the actual author] must ... be distinguished from the process of transmission, 'a tale that has been told' (surface structure) [the narrating instance within the fictional text]."[14] For the purposes of formal analysis, Genette excludes from consideration the actual author and any construct of the implied author. The "narrating instance," therefore, is confined to the narrating acts within the textual universe that may represent but do not contain the actual author's act of composition. Genette establishes three fundamental levels within the narrating instance: (1) extradiegetic, (2) diegetic or intradiegetic, and (3) metadiegetic.

The extradiegetic level (first-degree narrating addressed to either a general or specific narratee) is the discourse level in the narrative text closest to the reader It can feature an overt characterized narrator (who is either involved in or detached from the narrated events) or, as in fully developed figural narratives, a covert narrator (who seemingly only filters and presents "objectively" the perspective of a focalizing character). It must be remembered that such "objectivity" is always an illusion produced by the text's process of narrative transmission.

For the characterized narrator, the events narrated constitute the intradiegetic level, the story told by the extradiegetic narration. However, if intercalated or embedded within the intradiegesis is a character who narrates yet another story (either about him/herself or about something other), then we have an intradiegetic narration of a metadiegetic story. To explain his schema Genette uses the example of the narrating instance in Abbé Prévost's *Manon Lescaut* and its relationship to the larger work in which it is contained—*Les mémoires et aventures d'un homme de qualité qui s'est retiré du monde*:

> We will define this difference in level by saying that *any event a narrative recounts is at a diegetic level immediately higher than the level at which the narrating act producing this narrative is placed.* M. de Renoncourt's writing of his fictive *Mémoires* is a (literary) act carried out at a first level, which we will call *extradiegetic*; the events told in those *Mémoires* (including Des Grieux's narrating act) are inside this first narrative, so we will describe them as *diegetic*, or *intradiegetic*; the events told in Des Grieux's narrative, a narrative in the second degree, we will call *metadiegetic*.* In the same way, M. de Renoncourt as "author" of the *Mémoires* is extradiegetic: although fictive, he addresses the actual public, just like Rousseau or Michelet; the same Marquis as hero of the same *Mémoires* is diegetic, or intradiegetic, and so also is Des Grieux the narrator at the "Lion d'or," as well as the Manon noticed by the Marquis at the first meeting in Pacy; but Des Grieux the hero of his own narrative, and Manon the heroine, and [her] brother, and the minor characters, are metadiegetic. These terms (metadiegetic, etc.) designate, not individuals, but relative situations and functions.[15]

As Genette's description of the "relative situations and functions" makes clear, the narrative text of *Manon Lescaut* marks a transmission process through two acts of narrating: Des Grieux's oral narration and M. de Renoncourt's transcription of Des Grieux's narration. Such cases of double narrating produce significant interpretive questions; moreover, as we shall see in later chapters, more than two levels can exist in the textual universe. Unfortunately, Genette's description of diegetic levels confuses the levels of reading that obtain in literary narrative. He says that M. de Renoncourt as "author" of *Les mémoires* is extradiegetic, but M. de Renoncourt does *not address* "the actual public" as Genette says he does. As I will make clear in the following discussion of Susan Lanser's work and in the next chapter, the reader of an extradiegetic narrating situation is extradiegetic first and resides within the narrating instance of the text. No matter how much their images may seem to coincide such a reader is distinct from the reader postulated for the literary instance of the text. Nevertheless, as Robyn R. Warhol observes, when a novel has an avowedly social message, the narrator may be such an "engaging" advocate for the author's position that the line between the narratee and the actual reader intentionally disappears.[16]

Genette's next step is to define the relationship between the narrator and his or her narrative. Following time-honored tradition in narrative theory, he isolates two "relationships of the narrator to the story": (1) "heterodiegetic," a "narrator who is absent from the story" s/he tells; and (2) "homodiegetic," a "narrator present as a character in the story" s/he tells.[17] Within the category of homodiegesis is the subcategory "autodiegesis"—the narrator who is the protagonist of his or her own narration. Combining these categories with the narrating levels just outlined (i.e., "extradiegetic" and "intradiegetic") provides a flexible schema of narrator status that allows us to distinguish between different narrators and, by extension, different readers in the text. Although guilty of the sin of jargon, Genette's terminology is more precise than such traditional terms as "first-person" or "third-person," which designate the grammatical representation of character in the narrative rather than the narrating agent.

In Genette's more recent study, *Seuils*, he extends his inquiry from the narrative proper to consider the various "paratexts" that surround the narrative and therefore influence the structuration of reading. Among the items he inventories are title pages, epigraphs, dedications, editorial prefaces (fictional and actual), and editorial notes that are inside the text. Defining an element of the paratext, according to Genette, consists in determining its placement in the text relative to the narrative; the date when it was added (Was the paratext part of the original edition or added at a later date, as in the case of a preface to a collected edition?); the mode of its existence, whether it is part of the text's language field or whether it belongs to the "facts" of the text or author outside the text (the author's gender, for instance); the characteristics "de son instance de communication, destinateur et destinataire"; and lastly, the function of the paratext's message in the full text and the structuration of reading.[18] As we will see in chapters 5 and 6, paratextual elements play a crucial role in the narrative of transmission—what Genette might call the "instance of communication," the interaction of addresser ("*destinateur*") and addressee ("*destinataire*").

Susan Lanser has made some interesting modifications to Genette's theory of situations and functions. In *The Narrative Act*, Lanser attempts to articulate a "poetics of point of view" by examining three elements of point of view: (1) *status*, the textual speaker's relationship to the literary act; (2) *contact*, the interactions between narrators and the audience; and (3) *stance*, the attitudes of the textual personae toward the represented world.[19] Each element's different aspects are then analyzed to see how point of view operates. Using Genette's descriptive terminology—heterodiegetic, homodiegetic, and autodiegetic—Lanser sets up a continuum for measuring the narrator's relationship to the story. Thus in moving from heterodiegesis to autodiegesis there obtains a spectrum of possible narrator relationships: the uninvolved narrator (no place in the story), uninvolved witness, witness participant, minor character, co-protagonist, sole protagonist.[20] Although readers may have difficulty distinguishing between a witness participant and a minor character, the relationships represent, from the second position on, different degrees of homodiegesis.

For Lanser the elements of status, contact, and stance obtain at every level of the process of narrative transmission—both in the literary instance and the narrating instance—and for each position on the addresser pole there is a conjunction of elements producing and affecting the transmission of the narrative. Lanser diagrams this structure of narrative transmission as shown on the following page. Lanser's approach to the levels of narrative transmission does not separate the narrating instance from the literary instance, and it thereby stresses the links connecting textual statements, the author's ideology, and the extrafictional contexts of its reception. Moreover, her system of classification allows for one or more of these levels to be absent or for two or more to overlap in a given text (particularly public versus private narrators). Lanser's schema will become clearer if we flesh out her theoretical designations through an example.

Emily Brontë is, of course, the historical author of *Wuthering Heights*, and we as readers constitute part of her historical audience. Although we now construct an image of *her* extrafictional voice, the first readers of *Wuthering Heights* conceived of this voice as masculine: Ellis Bell's. The extrafictional or implied reader might be characterized as familiar with Gothic novels but not the environment of the Yorkshire Moors or of the extremes of passion experienced by Catherine and Heathcliff. The extrafictional reader might also bear some affinities with the public narrator, Lockwood, whose manners and mode of understanding are alien to the world of the Heights. Lockwood's public narratee(s) would probably include that circle

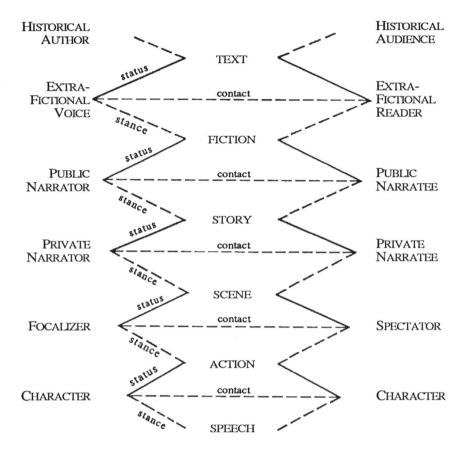

Fig. 1 Susan Lanser's diagram of narrative transmission; from Susan Lanser, The Narrative Act: Point of View in Prose Fiction. *Copyright © 1981 by Princeton University Press. Reprinted by permission of Princeton University Press.*

of his acquaintances who would have access to the pages of his journal where the story is transcribed. Much of the story comes from Nelly Dean, the private narrator, who tells Heathcliff's story to Lockwood, the private narratee (Nelly, likewise, is narratee to many embedded narrations). Nelly also is the primary "focalizer" for most of the scenes, although within her narration other characters assume the role of focalizer at times. Nelly is able to take both the private narrator and focalizer positions because of the temporal distance between her act of narrating (the STORY) and the events narrated (the SCENE). Other minor characters, such as Joseph, fulfill the role of spectators to the action. Lastly, we come to Heathcliff and Catherine, the objects or characters of the narrative situation. Their speech acts reflect the final position—the narrative center—in the addresser/ addressee system.

I will return in chapter 8 to a more extended reading of *Wuthering Heights*. Nevertheless, it should be observed that *Wuthering Heights* is an exceptionally good case for illustrating Lanser's levels of narrative transmission. Narratives with six perfectly distinct levels are a rare occurrence, and even the levels in *Wuthering Heights* soon become intermixed. A common narrating situation is for the last four levels to become almost indistinguishable. An autodiegetic narration, such as Jacques Revel's in *L'emploi du temps* by Michel Butor, might combine the last four levels into a single public/private narrator focalizer character. This is not to say that careful narratological and linguistic analysis of the text's discourse systems and internal dialogism could not distinguish different levels in Jacques Revel's narration or his address to his narratees, but the task would be made difficult because there is only a single character in the text. However, even though some addresser levels can combine in one character, a similar combination does not necessarily take place on the addressee side of narrative transmission. Even when the number of addresser figures is limited, the number of addressees usually increases from a small number of encoded addressees to an infinite number of actual readers.[21] This relationship between the addresser and addressee brings us to the question of *contact* and its place in the process of narrative transmission.

COMMENTING ON Roland Barthes's landmark narrative analysis *S/Z*, Jonathan Culler notes that "the absence of any code relating to narration (the reader's ability to collect items which help characterize a narrator and to place the text in a kind of communicative circuit) is a major flaw in Barthes's analysis."[22] In 1973, Barthes himself addressed this shortcoming in a demonstration of his operating procedures in the essay "Textual Analysis of a Tale by Poe." In this essay Barthes isolates the "code of communication":

> The code of communication could also be called the code of destination. *Communication* should be understood in a restricted sense; it does not cover all *signification* in a text, still less its *significances*; it designates only those relations in the text which are uttered as forms of *address* (as in the case of the "phatic" code, responsible for accentuating the relationship between narrator and reader), or *exchange*

(the narrative is exchanged for truth, for life). In short, *communication* should be here understood in an economic sense (the communication, the circulation of goods).[23]

In the crucial interplay between "address" and "exchange," Barthes locates the channel necessary for the structuration of reading, for the process by which textual meaning is produced. Barthes goes on to observe that "there is a *field of listening* in a written narrative; meaning's mode of presence (except perhaps for actional sequences) is not development, but *bursting-forth*: calls for contact and communication, the positing of contracts and exchanges ..."[24] We might provisionally rename this code the "code of transmission." To examine the code of transmission in narrative we need first to establish its location in the communication structure of literary text, keeping in mind, as Barthes does, that "codes are merely associative fields, a supra-textual organization of notations imposing a certain idea of structure."[25]

In his influential essay "Linguistics and Poetics," Roman Jakobson outlines the constitutive features in any communication event. He diagrams these features as follows:[26]

<pre>
                        CONTEXT
                        MESSAGE
ADDRESSER_____ADDRESSEE
                      C O N T A C T
                        CODE
</pre>

Based on this schema of constitutive features, Jakobson then draws a corollary between each feature and a particular language function. Hence, the schema for the language functions in a communication event would be:

<pre>
                      REFERENTIAL
                        POETIC
EMOTIVE   CONNATIVE
                        PHATIC
                      METALINGUAL
</pre>

According to Jakobson, "each of these six factors determines a different function of language. Although we distinguish six basic aspects of language, we could, however, hardly find verbal messages that would fulfill only one function. The diversity lies not in a monopoly of some one of these several functions but in a different hierarchical order of functions. The verbal structure of a message depends primarily on the predominant function."[27]

Although Jakobson's schema is at the foundation of most contemporary theories of narrative and its fundamental logic is still valid, subsequent literary theory has demonstrated that this model is somewhat simplistic. As a result, certain features and functions (particularly contact and the phatic function) have been neither completely explored nor satisfactorily deployed in textual analysis. "CONTACT"—the "physical channel and psychological connection" that an addresser uses to communicate a message in a shared code about a known context to an addressee—has been largely overlooked in studies that focus on the author/narrator/addresser, hermeneutics of the message, linguistic structures of the code, referentiality of the context, or reception by the reader/narratee/addressee. Some critics discount contact entirely. Raman Selden, in a 1985 handbook of contemporary critical theories, uses Jakobson's diagram of linguistic communication to situate the orientations of various critical movements, but states that "we may omit the 'contact' for the purpose of discussing literature; it is not of special interest to literary theorists, since contact is usually through the printed word."[28] In a 1986 study, Wallace Martin likewise denies that contact has any significant role in narrative communication when he observes that "writers and readers ... do not exchange information about contact and code to ensure the accuracy of transmission."[29] Both Selden and Martin appear to associate contact only with the literary instance of the printed and published book. Yet over and over again in narrative texts, the phatic functions of contact are presented, and they can be organized into a code of transmission that reveals a narrative of transmission structured between the addresser and the addressee.

In a more comprehensive account of literary communication, Robert Scholes asserts that "we sense literariness in an utterance when any of [Jakobson's] six features of communication loses its simplicity and becomes multiple or duplicitous."[30] This duplicitous quality can occur whenever discourse of one sort is "translated" into another sort. Let me give some examples. In *Don Quixote* the adventures of a Spanish knight-errant are recounted in an Arabic text that must be literally "translated" before it can be presented by the narrator. The multiplication of texts in Cervantes's novel marks its fictionality and its literariness, thereby warning the reader away from a naïve chivalric reading of the tale. In *Wuthering Heights* Isabella's letter is read by Nelly to Lockwood, who then transcribes it in his journal. In *L'emploi du temps* Jacques Revel begins to recognize parallels between his journal and a novel, *The Bleston Murder*. "Contact," as Lanser points out, "is a powerful conditioner for the degree of receptivity to the message which the audience will choose to bestow, and co-determines the way a message will be understood."[31] Without contact, narrative transmission would be skewed at best and interpretation would be impossible.

In *The Narrative Act*[32] Lanser expands the theoretical concept of contact, setting forth some of the ways in which contact is made manifest in narrative. She examines first the very substance of the text we hold; second, the psychological contact constituted by addresser and addressee attitudes toward one another; third, the phatic comments to the addressee embedded in the text; and lastly the "pretextual factors" that determine the attitude of the addresser and addressee. We can extend Lanser's list by including the contact that obtains through genre identification of a particular communication. The text's contact then goes beyond the intratextual constraints of the single text and enters the intertextual universe of literariness that connects all texts. Moreover, the textual contact between addresser and addressee changes within ideological and historical matrices. This makes possible gradations, inversions, and even ruptures in the homology between the idiolect of the fictional world and the sociolect of the real world. If the plots of most novels center on the successes and failures of human contact among characters, on the individual's contact with society or self or nature, then there should exist correlatives for these actions in the formal mimetics and the formal thematics of the narrating situation.

Lanser gives her most detailed description of contact in the section of *The Narrative Act* entitled "Modes of Contact: The Narrative Transaction."[33] Discussing the contact "the narrator establishes with the textual readership," she examines the distance and interaction between the narrating "I" and a "you" recipient,[34] the kind and degree of narrative self-consciousness in the narration, the attitudes and relationship the narrator expresses toward the narratee (measured in terms of confidence, power, and intimacy), and the kind and degree of narratee activity in the text. Lanser's modes of contact are certainly important for distinguishing the characters and their functions within the narrative of transmission, but ultimately her system of modes comes up short. It never addresses adequately the question of the contact channel itself, and the fact that it makes a *difference* whether the channel is comprised of letters, a journal, a memoir, or an oral narration transcribed by an other. These channels/ genres for the narrating situation must not be overlooked if we are going to have a transmission theory of narrative.

This need to consider the channel's genre brings us back to Jakobson's communication concept of contact. Jakobson's definition—"a physical channel and psychological connection between the addresser and the addressee, enabling both of them to enter and stay in communication"—appears to mimetically ground contact and to make it as problematic as any other concept in narrative theory. However, a broader understanding of the concept of contact can be derived from the work of Mikhail Bakhtin and Peter Brooks, and their formulations extend the theory of textuality and transmission into a more complete poetics of narrative.

THE FIRST STEP in a theory of transmission and textuality is to understand "contact" as both a process and a thing. If we see "contact" as merely the channel for a particular message, its function in any theory will be narrow. As Tzvetan Todorov writes of the difference between Mikhail Bakhtin's and Jakobson's ideas about communication, "It would be inconceivable for Bakhtin to isolate 'contact' as a factor among others; *the entire utterance is contact* but in a much stronger sense than is to be found in radiotelegraphy or even electricity."[35] As a process of human discourse rather than merely a "factor," contact engages the activities of sending, receiving, coding, referring, and meaning that occur in any communication. Moreover, as process, contact is aligned with Bakhtin's concepts of dialogism and intertextuality. Contact is the channel through which discourses synthesize in a dynamic structure that marks the profoundly social nature of every utterance. This dynamic structure Bakhtin terms "heteroglossia":

> Authorial speech, the speeches of narrators, inserted genres, the speech of characters are merely those fundamental compositional unities with whose help heteroglossia can enter the novel; each of them permits a multiplicity of social voices and a wide variety of their links and interrelationships (always more or less dialogized). These distinctive links and interrelationships between utterances and languages, this movement of the theme through different languages and speech types, its dispersion into the rivulets and droplets of social heteroglossia, its dialogization—this is the basic distinguishing feature of the stylistics of the novel.[36]

Bakhtin's concept of heteroglossia focuses our attention on the matrix of forces operating in a given utterance. These forces include stylizations, ideological constructions, everyday speech, literary and non-literary texts, etc. Significantly, by recognizing the dialogic, multi-discoursed quality of novelistic texts, our sense of literary language is directed back out into the world of its production. The focus of study then becomes the modes of transmission that incorporate and seek to stratify this diversity of voices, speech types, and inserted literary and semiliterary genres. Transmission, therefore, becomes a multivalent process organizing and conveying the discourses of other speakers and writers, of society, and of literature. The importance of dialogism and heteroglossia for a critical theory of narrative transmission lies in the way they help us to understand how the different voices and documents in a text are a composite of other discourses. The result of this multi-voicing is most obvious in hybrid constructions that readers recognize as irony (i.e., dialogism in a character's speech) or as parody (i.e., dialogism in authorial discourse). Particularly significant aspects of dialogism occur when we recognize that a narrator is unequal to the narrating task (e.g., Lockwood in *Wuthering Heights*). Yet this multi-voicing is only possible because of a narrative text's inherent dialogism: the text signifies both narrating and narrative simultaneously. One text must signify a matrix of discourses that are interpenetrated.

Drawing on the processes of everyday speech—where "every conversation is full of transmissions and interpretations of other people's words"[37]—Bakhtin explains how "a speaking person's discourse in the novel is not merely transmitted or reproduced; it is, precisely, *artistically represented*."[38] Bakhtin sees "transmission" as inextricably linked with interpretation—one can hardly pass on another's words verbatim because heteroglossia forces the transmission to undergo some degree of transformation through contextualization.[39] The indissoluble interplay between the means of transmission and that transmission's contextualized framing (interpretation) of another's discourse constitutes a major feature in the narrative of transmission. Transmission, ultimately, marks both the appropriation of another's discourse and the attempts to recontextualize that discourse so that it produces effects other than those originally intended by the speaker or writer.

I add the concept of written discourse to Bakhtin's ideas about speech because within the context of this study (in which one might say Bakhtin's discourse is transmitted and recontextualized) the fictional narratives examined imitate documents composed in the fictional universe. This imitation exposes the activities of discourse and transmission associated with these genres; therefore, we read the narrative of transmission not as merely the mechanical passing on of texts but as a dialogic process in which written form and its modes of transmission dynamically interact with a dialogized set of reader expectations. These expectations result from the artistic representation of the document (letter, diary, etc.) within a secondary formulation—the narrating instance of the literary text. Transmission becomes dialogized as it functions both metonymically (through the fictional transmission of documents) and metaphorically (through its self-representation and its locus as a plot-generating device). As Bakhtin reminds us, "the novel always includes in itself the activity of coming to know another's word, a coming to knowledge whose process [transmission and interpretation] is represented in the novel."[40]

Taking a different angle, Peter Brooks, in *Reading for the Plot*, demonstrates how the process of "coming to knowledge" can be extended from questions about the discourse processes of a text to questions about how narrative plots mirror the narratives of transmission articulated in the text. Brooks contributes to our understanding of contact and narrative transmission with his notion of "transference," the site of exchange in the narrative contract between narrator and narratee. Using a Freudian model of analysis to describe the process of plot-making that obtains in narrative, Brooks shows how "contact" becomes "contract" in a transformatory process that significantly affects both the narrator and narratee. Yet while transmission describes the means toward psychic transference, the costs of this narrating situation are often the transgression of social patterns and the undermining of the narrator's authority to establish determinant meanings for his or her text. Brooks moves beyond a merely narrational sense of transmission in his work. He sees transmission as a constituent aspect of narrative plotting when it concerns genealogic imperatives such as inheritance, legitimate birthright, and the economic exchanges of property or money. Moreover, this thematizing of transmission extends to social and cultural rituals, to values, to belief systems, to political and domestic power, and to sexuality. Brooks uses the "metaphor of transmission" to indicate the deep matrix of narrative plotting:

> One could perhaps claim also that the result aimed at by plotting is in some large sense ever the same: the restoration of the possibility of transmission.... The nineteenth-century novel in particular will play out repeatedly and at length the problem of transmission, staging over and over again the relations of fathers to sons (and also daughters to mothers, aunts, madwomen, and others), asking where an inheritable wisdom is to be found and how its transmission is to

be acted toward. If in [Walter] Benjamin's thesis,... "death is the sanction of everything that the story teller can tell," it is because it is at the moment of death that life becomes *transmissible*. The translations of narrative, its slidings-across in the transformatory process of its plot, its movements forward that recover markings from the past in the play of anticipation and retrospection, lead to a final situation where the claim to understanding is incorporate with the claim to transmissibility. One could find some of the most telling illustrations of this claim in the nineteenth century's frequent use of the framed tale which, dramatizing the relations of tellers and listeners, narrators and narratees, regularly enacts the problematic of transmission, looking for the sign of recognition and the promise to carry on, revealing, too, a deep anxiety about the possibility of transmission, as in Marlow's words to his auditors in *Heart of Darkness*: "Do you see the story? Do you see anything?"[41]

In this conceptualization of transmission's thematic force, Brooks deftly aligns form with content to produce a dynamic (and dialogic) matrix undergirding narrative literature. He sees that narrative "seems ever to imagine in advance the act of its transmission, the moment of reading and understanding that it cannot itself ever know," and that "more sophisticated narrative fictions tend to embed fictive readers within the text, and to stage efforts at decipherment and interpretation."[42] To uncover the moment of reading, the effort at decipherment, the analyst of narrative must focus on the points of contact signaled in the text. Precisely at these moments the reader is most forcibly reminded that narrative is text—discourse, a reconstruction in language—and that reading is a process of structuration rather than simple consumption. The transmission of narrative is thus always a frame that contains, invades, and is invaded by the story in a dynamic process that pulls readers, through their various avatars in the text, into the narrative universe, into the effort at decipherment.

Brooks makes one of his most direct references to the idea of contact in discussing Faulkner's classic novel of transmission *Absalom, Absalom!* He writes of Judith Sutpen's evocation of narrative as a loom or a tombstone or a letter passed on to a stranger: "Judith's statement concedes the evanescence or even the impossibility of the 'referential' and 'metalinguistic' functions of language (in Roman Jakobson's sense) while arguing the continuing pertinence of and need for the 'phatic'.... She makes a claim neither for story nor for plot, but rather for narrating as, in Genette's terms, the narrative act productive of plot and story."[43] Brooks discovers an urgency in the narrating that traces the phatic quality which under-writes all transmission: the desire of the addresser to be heard or read, for the life narrated to be relived, to be reconstructed by an addressee. Only by attending to the narrative of transmission coded in the text will we uncover the secret springs motivating the narrating act.

Therefore, by the term "transmission" neither Bakhtin nor Brooks nor I want to bring the traditional notions of author and narrative authority back in through the back door to a place of monologic privi-lege; transmission must include the dialogic and transformational imperatives of discourse and reception for any full definition of pro-cess and contact in literary texts. Narrative, and the novel in par-ticular, presents a opportunity to observe transmission occurring. All narratives include a "narrating," a "narrated," and a "reception." But again, process rather than product most concerns me here, for tell-ing is never a simple or innocent task. The thing told is a product of language (heteroglossia) and thus always in a condition of becom-ing rather than being, and reading or listening to a narrative actively constructs a text that is often markedly different from the one in-tended by the author, denoted or connoted by the language, or read by any number of other readers. This constructed text can never be a totalization of the narrative—although, as we have all seen, such totalizations are often the goal of interpretive readings. To produce "a reading" is to try to eliminate the transmission process of read-ing by constraining the text within a limited and exclusionary range of interpretive structures.

Yet every reading is also another transmission. Transmission in its fullest sense is a process that brings a text into momentary being, though never into a finally determinant form. A reason for this es-sential indeterminacy is that transmission incorporates a theory of textuality which recognizes the plurality and equivocality of trans-mission processes. The text undergoing transmission is never an autonomous artifact; instead, by its intertextuality, the text includes all previous and later texts within its universe of possible significance and potential meaning. The transmission process rejects those intertexts that appear irrelevant, but it never banishes them totally. This last point is significant because in opening texts to the play of transmission there is, theoretically, a risk that by considering every-thing as meaningful we end up with everything being meaningless. In actuality, of course, readers always select those aspects of their reading experience that contribute to meaning. The aim of a trans-mission theory in the poetics of fiction is to understand how the transmission process is motivated by and maintained in the reading of narrative texts.

To make what I am proposing a bit more concrete, consider again *Don Quixote,* a novel overwhelmingly concerned with questions of literature's relationship to reality and the process of transmission and textuality. Throughout his adventures, Quixote tests literary mimesis as he attempts to live the chivalric life he has read about in books. In so doing, he actively tests the limits of the truth of their discourses. His actions also mark an attempt to reanimate a dead tradition, knight-errantry, but his effort to reassert the transmissibility of the chivalric code fails because he cannot read the totality of his age's degeneration. Similarly, the profusion of narrators, historians, and translators makes any assumption of textual authority yet another fiction, built on the one already in the novel's narrative of transmission. *Don Quixote* asks us not to suspend our disbelief but to maintain it and to enjoy fully the narrative process as it unfolds. That we can feel for Quixote yet simultaneously recognize the narratorial games of the text and our own shifting perception between the narrating and the narrated is, indeed, a unique experience.

Whatever sense a reader has of Don Quixote at a particular moment is conditioned by literary and linguistic experience, particularly experience with novels and critical commentary. To deny this is to create a pure fiction of reading. We are always learning to read texts differently (sometimes for better, sometimes for worse), and if a theory of transmission is to have a valid place in any poetics of fiction, it must contribute to (and remain dynamic and flexible within) this ongoing process for communicating fictional texts. Thus narrative transmission can neither have a single focus nor depend on a fixed center always already present in readers. By broadening the theoretical horizon for a transmission theory of narrative, we can attend to questions—such as gender, ethnicity, and ideology—which are now facing the theory of interpretation. The questions facing a theory of transmission focus on where in the process large scale differences or categories of response can be located. Efforts at a theory of narrative poetics have produced finer and finer tools of analysis, yet our goal may still be as elusive as Dulcinea is to Quixote. The significance of any analysis is in its process of engaging textuality and transmission in a dynamic play of reading.

2 | *Epistolary Narratives of Transmission and Transgression*

> Instead of throwing your first letter into the fire or taking it to my mother, I dared open it. This was my crime and all the rest followed. I tried to force myself not to answer these nefarious letters which I could not prevent myself from reading.
>
> —Rousseau, *Julie, ou la nouvelle Héloïse*

> Your real mistake is in allowing yourself to enter into a correspondence. I defy you now to foresee where this will lead you.
>
> —Laclos, *Les liaisons dangereuses*

ALL EPISTOLARY NOVELS contain a double narrative: a narrative of the events and a narrative of the letters that precipitate or report the events. This double narrative is produced within a textual society formed for the reader by the private correspondence of its members. Even before the novel, the letter had already marked its double nature in drama. For instance, in Euripedes's *Hippolytus*, Phaedra's letter, written in a vengeful attempt to satisfy her repulsed desires for Hippolytus, usurps the spoken voice of reason and truth, substituting the written confession of a sexual transgression that never occurred. Her suicide is a signature that validates the letter's untruths. Shakespeare also understood the power of letters. In *King Lear* Edmund's plans to usurp the power of his father and brother hinge on a forged letter that attempts to discredit his brother Edgar with his father. Then, Edmund uses the knowledge unwittingly given him by Gloucester to reveal to Cornwall and Regan the location of a secret treasonous letter. But his designs on the succession come undone. A love letter from Goneril is intercepted by Regan, and after Edgar acquires the letter, he uses it to convince Albany of the plots made against him by his wife and Edmund. Likewise, one can recall Hamlet's love letters to Ophelia, and his interception and alteration of Claudius's warrant for his death; or the counterfeit letter in *Twelfth Night*; or the undelivered letter at the end of *Romeo and Juliet*.

As opposed to drama, in which only a limited number of letters can effectively motivate the plot without appearing contrived, the epistolary novel allows for a more fully developed *textual* society. The most complex textual societies exist in letter-exchange novels such as *Clarissa*, *La nouvelle Héloïse*, and *Les liaisons dangereuses*, distinctive features of which are an exchange of letters among multiple correspondents (as opposed to the single correspondent of *Pamela* or the unexchanged letters of *Humphry Clinker*) and an editorial framework to transmit the letters to the reader.[1] In a letter-exchange novel the narrative techniques for exchanging letters complicate the sequence of events by keeping the characters unequally informed, while the reader has access to every letter published by the editor. In the case of Samuel Richardson's *The History of Clarissa Harlowe* (1747),[2] Jean-Jacques Rousseau's *Julie, ou la nouvelle Héloïse* (1761),[3] and Pierre Choderlos de Laclos's *Les liaisons dangereuses* (1782),[4] the correspondence represents as well a narrative of sexual transgression within the textual society, a society "lettered" by the epistolary activities that constitute its narrative of transmission and facilitate its narrative of transgression.

Clarissa is a novel of transgression, deception, isolation, and redemption. By secretly corresponding with Lovelace, and by refusing an arranged match with Mr. Solmes, Clarissa Harlowe transgresses the marriage code of her family's social and economic class. Hoping to escape through the help of Lovelace, she falls prey to a calculated deception that results in her brutal rape and ultimate isolation. Yet in her self-imposed isolation Clarissa redeems her stolen dignity and transcends, in death, the social and economic consequences of her fall. *Julie* is a novel of transgression, separation, contrition, and redemption. The love between Julie and Saint-Preux transgresses the standards accepted by her family and society. This transgression, early in the novel, leads to their separation for many years, during which the lovers correspond secretly until Julie's marriage. As Mme de Wolmar, Julie begins the task of contrition necessary to make her worthy of her husband. After years at sea Saint-Preux returns; they are reunited, and through Wolmar their love ascends to a higher plane, a platonic redemption of their earlier relationship. *Les liaisons dangereuses*, by contrast, is a novel of deception, seduction, retribution, and isolation. In effecting their plans of seduction, the Marquise de Merteuil and Valmont variously deceive the other characters. Eventually, however, they turn their jealousies and vengeance upon each other; they each seek retribution for sins against their "*gloire*." The base scheming beneath the correspondents' shells of propriety and social acceptability is exposed, and there is a rapid descent into social isolation of everyone in the textual society.

These novels all transcribe seductions, but Rousseau presents Julie's submission early in the text, thereby abandoning the process of seduction as a plot device. Clarissa's seduction, more centrally developed, issues from lies rather than love; and instead of articulating a narrative sequence of submission-followed-by-love-and-marriage, the novel depicts the violent violation of Clarissa's sexual autonomy. *Les liaisons dangereuses* presents numerous seductions employing various seductive strategies, leading to the Présidente de Tourvel's submission to Valmont. Another strain of difference within the similarities connecting these novels is the way the separation of the lovers is conceived. In *Julie* this is a necessary stage in their redemption, while in *Les liaisons dangereuses* separation is necessary to exploit the seductive power of letters. However, when separation ultimately isolates a character from the textual society, as in Clarissa's desperate escape from Lovelace or in the disintegrated character relationships in *Les liaisons dangereuses*, the isolation becomes, as Joseph Kestner suggests, an existential removal of the self from both the textual society and society in general.[5] But where is one to go?

When Clarissa escapes the repressive society of her family, her escape becomes an abduction, and the refuge Lovelace provides is a brothel, a place where the male aristocracy exercised its power by "ruining" the naïve daughters of the middle class. Saint-Preux, possibly recalling Richardson's London and anticipating Laclos's Paris, writes to Julie: "Shall we be better moralists than those crowds of philosophers with which London and Paris are peopled, who all laugh at conjugal fidelity and consider adultery as a game?" (*J* pt. 3, 16). Saint-Preux damns the loose morals of Paris, and consequently elevates the retirement of Clarens as the perfect milieu for pure love. The escapist utopia Wolmar establishes on his estate, to which the main characters eventually return, is a second Eden where honest affection may reside. In *Les liaisons dangereuses* Mme de Rosemonde's country house is a debased parody of Wolmar's vision—though enough vestiges of the vision remain to color Valmont's feelings for Mme de Tourvel with some genuine sentiment. But the return to Paris for the seduction's dénouement fulfills Saint-Preux's conception of Paris as a city where "adultery [is] a game."

Les liaisons dangereuses is a direct, if somewhat mutated, descendant of *Clarissa* and *Julie*. Twice Mme de Merteuil refers to "*Héloïse*" (*L* 10, 33), twice Valmont quotes from this earlier work (*L* 110), and Laclos takes his epigraph—"J'ai vu les moeurs de mon temps, et j'ai publié ces Lettres" (I saw the customs of my times, and I published these Letters [my translation])—from *Julie*'s preface. More to the point in *Les liaisons dangereuses* are the references to *Clarissa*

(*L* 107, 110). We can see their intertextual influence in this passage from Valmont's letter about Mme de Tourvel's choice of *Clarissa* and a prayer book for guidance: "For the past week I have been turning over in my mind every stratagem known to me, everything I have ever gleaned from novels…. There would be no difficulty in finding my way into her house, even at night, nor yet again in putting her to sleep and making another Clarissa [*une nouvelle Clarisse*] out of her" (*L* 110). The dialogic conjunction of the titles from the two precursor texts in the original French—"une nouvelle Clarisse"—solidifies the intertextual matrix that connects these novels' narratives of transmission and transgression.

As Jacques Derrida observes in "The Law of Genre," texts, particularly novels, usually contain unmistakable marks indicating their genre.[6] These marks may refer to particular books or to a mode of discourse, such as Valmont's gleanings from "novels." Their textual function, however, exceeds mere allusion: they constitute intertextual extensions of the narrative by investing the text with a second narrative matrix, already determined, creating a palimpsestic relationship of narrated events. Thus references to earlier epistolary novels establish an analogous textualization (lettering) of the events, which are in some degree overdetermined by the anterior text; moreover, the reader's response is also in some degree overdetermined.

References to the "novel" or "romance" raise more complex epistemological questions because a fictional discourse is being used to measure truth within another fiction. These generic references are often metatextually significant both in constructing and in deconstructing the illusion of reality necessary for a sympathetic response to the textual society, just as the existence of real literary works in a fictional universe gives that universe credibility and opens to question the fiction's system of representation. Another means of genre marking is the use of specific formal conventions, and here epistolary novels have developed an extensive repertoire of transmission devices. As Alan D. McKillop observes, "The writing of the letters is only the beginning; they are copied, sent, received, shown about, discussed, answered, even perhaps hidden, intercepted, stolen, altered, or forged."[7] In addition to McKillop's catalog, four particular categories of transmission conventions obtain significantly in letter-exchange novels that document transgression: reflexivity, enclosure, intermediary transmission, and the confidant.

Letters are *reflexive* when they quote or recall previous letters in the correspondence. In *Clarissa* the quoting of letters is particularly important. The initial transgressive correspondence between Clarissa and Lovelace, at first only partially given to the reader, is presented almost exclusively in the correspondence between Clarissa and Anna

Howe, and Lovelace and Belford (only 6 of the 537 letters in *Clarissa* are between Lovelace and Clarissa). This reflexive quoting mediates and frames Lovelace and Clarissa's relationship—each letter is double-read, coming to the reader as an already interpreted text. Reflexivity can also show a change of feeling or perspective, as in *Julie* when Julie informs Saint-Preux of her marriage and quotes from letter 24 of part 1 (*J* pt. 3, 18). The quoted letter from Saint-Preux was written before Julie's submission, when he was trying to establish the honor and character of their relationship. By quoting this letter after her marriage, Julie rereads the text of their earlier relationship, no longer regarding it as one of innocence and bliss, but rather as one of blindness and error. In *Les liaisons dangereuses* reflexivity occurs in the semantic cat-and-mouse game played by Valmont and Mme de Merteuil, which climaxes with Valmont's declaration of war (*L* 153). This novel also presents a perfect example of parodic reflexivity when Valmont uses Émilie for a "desk upon which to write [his] fair devotee" (*L* 47). The letter and its double reading, given to Mme de Merteuil, are juxtaposed in the novel, and together they demonstrate both Valmont's duplicity and epistolary reflexivity. Without letter 47 to Mme de Merteuil, letter 48 to Mme de Tourvel would appear an example of contrived sentimental drivel.

An epistolary protagonist's double reading of another character's letters (a convention that predates *Clarissa*) raises the issue that Tzvetan Todorov calls "repetitive narrative"[8] and the indeterminacy of meaning. In most epistolary narratives some intratextual commentary occurs; however, the repeatability of the message becomes problematic as each receiver becomes a sender and commentator as well. Epistolary transmission's temporality forces the signifiers within a particular epistolary system (e.g., the correspondence between Valmont and Mme de Tourvel) to slip among different signifieds as the correspondence continues. Mme de Tourvel's inability to regain control of the sign system in her correspondence with Valmont makes vain her hope of regaining her original purity and virtue. Each letter's reflexivity undermines its ability to posit specific and unchanging meanings; the letter becomes the site for dialogism to enter the novel and motivate its plots of seduction. Valmont's strongest weapon of seduction is Mme de Tourvel's confusion over the meaning of his words, which are routinely double-read within the Valmont-Merteuil correspondence. Thus acts of transmission are also acts of transformation because a letter's original meaning and intention are never completely received.

Reflexivity—by quotation, transmission, and double reading—is one form of repetitive narrative; *enclosure* is a second. The enclosed letter is a standard transmission device in letter-exchange novels, but Rousseau employs it differently than Richardson and Laclos. Generally, Rousseau uses enclosure to forward a letter through an intermediary (this forwarding is discussed below under "intermediary transmission") or as a joint communication from two writers or meant for two readers (see *J* pt. 3, 2–3, 9–10). In *Les liaisons dangereuses* and *Clarissa* enclosure becomes a device for shared information through the *re*transmission of particular letters, especially those from Mme de Tourvel that Valmont sends to Mme de Merteuil, or those from Clarissa that Lovelace sends to Belford. Enclosure for retransmission gives the new reader special "reader's rights," extending his or her power within the textual society. To be granted reader's rights in any novel is to become what W. Daniel Wilson calls a "characterized reader," a narratee within the story who reads some or all of the text eventually transmitted to the reader of the novel.[9] Epistolary novels present a special case, since every receiver of a letter is a characterized reader; therefore, we need to distinguish different kinds of "characterized reading acts" to understand the characterized reader's function in the double narrative of transmission and transgression.

We distinguish characterized reading acts by the intentionality of their occurrence. Characterized reading can be intended (the receiver reads a message written for him or her) or unintended (the receiver obtains access to a message not written for him or her). Lovelace and Valmont, for instance, appropriate letters addressed to others, and this makes their characterized reading acts different from those of the intended receivers. A further distinction can be drawn by considering whether the *response* generated by the characterized reader actively influences the sequence of events. Thus four possibilities obtain in epistolary fiction:

Intended Characterized Reading Acts

Passive   mostly unrealized in letter-exchange novels, but
            exemplified by Mariana's lover in *Les lettres portugaises*

Active   most epistolary characters

Unintended Characterized Reading Acts

Passive   mostly unrealized, but exemplified by Mme de
            Rosemonde

Active   Lovelace, Clarissa, Belford, Anna Howe; Julie's mother
            and Wolmar; Mme de Merteuil, Valmont, and Danceny

A passive, unintended characterized reading act is usually only realized temporarily: a character may read a message meant for someone else without responding immediately. Passive nonresponse must be distinguished from a conscious decision (as best we can interpret it as such) not to respond. For instance, at the conclusion of *Les liaisons dangereuses*, Mme de Rosemonde reads many letters not originally intended for her eyes, and when Mme de Volanges wants to know the truth about Cécile, Mme de Rosemonde does not accede to her friend's request.

An epistolary character could possibly perform all four characterized reading acts (though only one can be performed at a time). A single letter, such as Clarissa's allegorical letter (*C* pt. 7, enclosed in 75),[10] can generate more than one kind of response, whether from a single reader or many; but different responses, like the linear ordering of linguistic signs, occur in sequence. This is true even with confused responses, as when a character becomes indecipherable. Also, the different kinds of characterized reading acts have different degrees of narrative potential for affecting plot. Clearly active unintended reading acts have the most potential, and Laclos offers many examples. For example, Mme de Merteuil creates and manipulates readers, and when she shows Danceny a selected group of Valmont's letters recounting Cécile's seduction (*L* 162), she molds a reader into an agent of revenge: Danceny's interpretive response is to kill Valmont. From our perspective, this deadly response reiterates the dialogism and indeterminacy inhering in any transmission. Valmont's letters intended only for Mme de Merteuil are shown to an unintended reader, and although the text of the letters is unchanged, the secondary transmission with its new interpretive context generates a different response.

Intermediary transmission requires a third party, a "contact character," who participates in the correspondence. This can be an arrangement foreknown by all parties or an unexpected occurrence such as Valmont's interception of Mme de Tourvel's letters. *Julie* is not a novel of treachery; therefore, the intermediary transmissions are straightforward. Early in the novel Claire sends Julie a letter via Saint-Preux, and there is no indication that he reads it (*J* pt. 1, 7). During Julie and Saint-Preux's separation, Claire marries, forcing Julie to find an address to substitute for hers. She first thinks of Fanchon Anet, and writes, "she indeed is the safest intermediary we could choose" (*J* pt. 2, 18). The letter goes on to discuss other possible addresses. This use of the intermediary to hide the transgression from Julie's parents is innocent when compared to the treachery that accompanies the intermediary's role in *Les liaisons dangereuses*. The supreme example of intermediary transmission in *Julie* is Julie's deathbed letter to Saint-Preux, which she gives to Wolmar saying, "I am giving it to you open ... so that after having read it you may decide to send it or suppress it" (*J* pt. 6, 11). Here the power of transmission is given trustingly to the intermediary in an overlapping of intended and unintended characterized reading. In *Les liaisons dangereuses*, Valmont assumes this power and more. After Danceny and Cécile have been separated, Valmont first becomes the intermediary for their correspondence, but then seizes the "power of opportunity" (*L* 96). He exceeds the intermediary role to become both sender and receiver, transmitter and transgressor:

> Having found your pupil yesterday busy writing to him, and having first disturbed her in this agreeable task to put her to a still more agreeable one, I asked to see the letter; discovering it to be cold and constrained, I made her see that this was not the way to console a lover, and persuaded her to write another to my dictation: in which, imitating her little babblings as best I could, I tried to encourage the young man's love by giving him more certain expectations. The little creature was quite delighted, she told me, to find herself writing so well: from now on, I shall be in charge of her correspondence. What shall I not, in the end, have done for Danceny? I shall have been at once his friend, his confidant, his rival, and his mistress! (*L* 115)

As Valmont observes, the intermediary, the contact character, is often also a *confidant*. But equally often, as in *Clarissa*, the distinction between these roles is blurred. Richardson constructs his novel around two parallel correspondences (Clarissa and Anna, Lovelace and Belford), each marking a system of "confidence." Janet Altman has observed that the systems of confidence and confidants that obtain in epistolary fiction establish two related oppositions—confidence (candor) and coquetry (dissimulation), friend and lover—within the context and subject of the speech act. The relationship between the correspondents aligns both oppositions in a system of confidence that would normally pair candor with friendship and coquetry with love.[11] In the pattern of these schematic oppositions, the paired relationships in *Clarissa* exhibit confidence systems predicated on candor and friendship. However, early in the novel Lovelace uses Anna's confidence to learn about Clarissa and to plead his case through Anna's candid letters. Lovelace knows that Anna will report his visits in detail and that his words will assume a value of truth when recounted through her trusted pen. Later in the novel, Belford divides his confidence between Lovelace and Clarissa, and by the end, Belford's allegiance is completely with the wronged Clarissa as he endeavors to protect her from contact with his other confidant.

In *Clarissa*'s two confidence systems, a third party added to the original system (Clarissa and Anna plus Lovelace, Lovelace and Belford plus Clarissa) establishes an intermediary system of contact and transmission that both marks and facilitates the sparse correspondence between the two main characters. François Jost has distinguished two fundamental letter types in epistolary narrative: "*la lettre-confidence*," which narrates events the receiver did not take part in, and "*la lettre-drame*," which constitutes a specific action meant to prompt a reaction from the receiver (e.g., a request for sexual favors).[12] As noted earlier, the letters between Clarissa and Lovelace nearly always come to the reader "double-read" in the context of a letter of confidence; therefore, the full dramatic effect of Clarissa and Lovelace's discordant relationship is displaced by the reflexive filtering of letters through other letters. But, as we will see, much of this filtering is controlled by the narrative Clarissa constructs from the letters.

Jost's distinction between confidential letters and dramatic letters exposes a difference between *Clarissa* and its two French descendants: in these two later texts both Laclos and Rousseau present a greater proportion of dramatic letters. Written within a Puritan literary tradition, Clarissa's letters function as a confessional diary for the writer's self-analysis. This is even true for Lovelace, whose letters inadvertently confess the shallowness of his self-analysis of his actions. Still, confidential letters can reveal more about the letter writer than dramatic letters, and Rousseau and Laclos do not neglect to present many confidential letters or to examine closely the crucial choice of a confidant.[13]

In examining the formal characteristics of confidence systems, Altman has shown that Laclos's novel blurs the natural relations and oppositions of confidence systems to produce dangerous new permutations. For instance, Danceny sees Valmont as a friend and candidly tells him about his love for Cécile, but Valmont uses friendship and its presupposition of candor to effect and to hide Cécile's seduction. Building on this example and others, Altman offers a forceful reading of the more important Valmont-Merteuil confidence system. Valmont sees Mme de Merteuil as both friend and a past-and-potential lover, but what he confides with candor is his growing love for Mme de Tourvel. Although he assumes each letter to Mme de Merteuil is a love letter, he alienates himself from any love relationship with her by overwriting his "bulletins" about Mme de Tourvel. Mme de Merteuil, in contrast, always attempts to keep

Valmont's desire at a distance, and ultimately she betrays their pact of confidence, dissimulating when she promised candor, by keeping secret her liaison with Danceny. Each betrays the other's expectations, dissolving their relationship and their correspondence.[14] Unlike other characters, Mme de Merteuil and Valmont have only each other to confide in; once that bond is severed, their letters of confidence become weapons of revenge.

Because the geographic separation fundamental to letter writing encourages lovers to become confidants, a blurring of the oppositions by which a letter may be identified as confidential is common in letter-exchange novels. Conversely, a confidant who takes an active role in the events can become for the confiding lover an image of the beloved. Essentially, this is how Rousseau constructs the confidence systems in *Julie*. Julie and Saint-Preux easily move beyond their conflictual relationship as lovers to become confidants, although, once Julie's marriage separates them, they never regain all their former candor. Despite Wolmar's absolute trust, Julie and Saint-Preux cannot attain a purified intimacy that equals their original transgressive intimacy. Also significant is Claire's role as an image of the beloved. Claire, because she is confidante to both lovers, becomes for each emblematic of the absent lover, whose secrets she shares in each confidential letter. At the novel's close, Julie offers Claire as a potential wife for Saint-Preux. In Rousseau confidence is part of a dialectic inquiry into the manifestation of feeling.

"The epistolary confidant," Altman writes, "is most fundamentally an archivist";[15] and if a novel in letters is to exist, the act of transmission must include its inverse: the act of retaining or collecting. Therefore, one part of the narrative of transmission in a letter-exchange novel, if not its first purpose, is the story of the collection—how the letters became available to an "Editor." *Julie* has two primary correspondents: Julie and Saint-Preux. Their letters to each other are joined by those of Claire, Lord Bomston, and Wolmar (plus some minor characters). Who collects these letters over the many years comprising the time of the novel? The first hint of a collection comes from Saint-Preux, when he writes in a letter that he is undertaking to reassemble the letters she has written to him. His letter to Julie continues:

> Although there is not one of them which I do not know by heart— and know well by heart, you can believe me—I still like to reread them ceaselessly, were it only to see again the characters of that dear

hand which alone can constitute my happiness. But the paper wears away imperceptibly, and before they are in pieces I intend to copy them all in a blank book which I have just chosen expressly for that purpose. It is rather thick, but I am thinking of the future, and I hope I do not die young enough to be limited only to this volume. I am setting apart my evenings to this charming occupation, and I shall proceed slowly in order to prolong it. This precious collection will never leave me during my life. It will be my manual in the world I am about to enter; it will be the antidote for me against the maxims that are inhaled there; it will console me in my misery; it will prevent or correct my mistakes; it will instruct me during my youth: it will edify me always—and to my knowledge these will be the first love letters ever put to this use. (*J* pt. 2, 13)

And so, Saint-Preux collects a substantial portion of the correspondence. Moreover, because of his devotion, marked both erotically and philosophically in the passage, the reader can be assured that every letter from Julie will be transcribed.

Saint-Preux's letters to Julie have a more colorful history and plainly show a collection's plot potential. Julie has had Claire keep Saint-Preux's letters, but Claire's marriage threatens this archive. Julie writes to Saint-Preux: "From this consideration, I have already found pretext for taking back your letters that fear of surprise made me give to her. She returned them to me with an oppression of the heart which my own made me perceive and which convinced me that I had done what was necessary" (*J* pt. 2, 18). Yet finding a safe archive proves impossible, as the final letter in part 2 makes clear: "All is ruined! All is discovered! I no longer find your letters in the place where I had hidden them. They were still there yesterday evening. They could have been taken away only today. My mother alone can have found them. If my father sees them, it means my life! Oh, what good would it be if he did not see them, if I must renounce … Oh God! My mother sends for me."

The collection's discovery (an active unintended characterized reading act) hastens the death of Julie's mother. But "she die[s] with the fatal secret" of Julie's transgression undisclosed (*J* pt. 3, 7), and the immediate fate of these letters is unclear. After the long temporal gap between parts 3 and 4, however, and after Julie reunites with Saint-Preux, the letters resurface. This time, rather than driving the lovers apart, the letters become the foundation of Wolmar's trust: "Then [Wolmar] led us into his study where I all but fell in a faint to see him take from a drawer, along with copies of some of [Saint-Preux's] accounts that I had given him, the very originals of all the letters that I thought I had once seen Babi burn in my mother's room" (*J* pt. 4, 12). This method for preserving the text and lettering Julie and Saint-Preux's new relationship is certainly melodramatic, yet the lovers are expected to transcend the documents delimiting their earlier transgressive love and to reach a higher plateau of virtue. This virtue can be achieved only through honesty and a forthright separation of their present from their past. The erotic narrative of transgression encoded in the early correspondence is now retransmitted; however, the original transmission system—still traced in the epistolary discourse—has been disrupted beyond repair. This passage reveals Wolmar as an active unintended characterized reader, and although he acts passively in influencing Julie and Saint-Preux, his rationale is based in a hermeneutics of accommodation rather than jealousy.

Apparently all of the characters and their letter collections finally reside at Wolmar's estate. If so, then Rousseau has established the necessary archive to create an illusion of reality around the text's compilation, but as the "collector" of the published letters, he writes in the novel's preface: "As for the truth of these facts, I certify that having many times been in the country of the two lovers, I have never heard talk of Baron D'Etange, his daughter, M. d'Orbe, Lord Bomston, or M. de Wolmar. I also give notice that the topography is crudely falsified in many places, either to better take in the reader, or that in reality the author might not know anything about it. That is all I am able to say about this. Let each consider how it will satisfy him [my translation]." This statement suggests an inherent indeterminateness between fiction and reality in Rousseau's text. In a literary era when many novels were prefaced with editorial assurances of their truth, Rousseau presents an editor who refuses to claim his own authority over the text or the authenticity of the collection, leaving its origin a mystery.

The moral nature of Rousseau's text precludes full exploitation of the letter collection device, but in Laclos, where the letter becomes a weapon in the skirmishes of seduction, the power of the collection is formidable. Early in *Les liaisons dangereuses* Valmont characterizes Mme de Merteuil as a trusted archivist: "trustee of all my inmost secrets" (*L* 4).[16] But Mme de Merteuil, foreshadowing her own doom, expresses her fear of collections: "Having fixed upon this line of proceeding as the best, I have decided to hurry the girl a little, as you [Valmont] will see from my letter. This makes it very important to leave nothing in her hands that might compromise us, and I beg you to take care of that" (*L* 106). Danceny echoes Mme de Merteuil in another letter: "If I am to believe you [Merteuil], I shall receive no reply from you. This very letter will be the last. We are to deny ourselves a correspondence which, according to you, is dangerous and for *which there is no necessity*. Of course I shall believe that, if you insist" (*L* 150). And late in the text Valmont reminds Mme de Merteuil of their mutual power: "No lengthy arguments are necessary to establish that each of us is in possession of all that is necessary to ruin the other, and that we have an equal interest in behaving with mutual caution" (*L* 153).

As these statements suggest, letter collections are feared weapons primarily because they document transgressive behavior. Saint-Preux makes his collection to protect his memories from decay; in *Les liaisons dangereuses* it guards one's existence. Mme de Merteuil makes Danceny an active unintended characterized reader to protect herself; before his death, Valmont will retaliate by giving Danceny his letter collection and authorizing the publication of Mme de Merteuil's most self-damning letters (81 and 85) to expose her hypocrisy. As vital as these two acts of unintended transmission are to the story, my concern here is the collection of more inclusive bundles of letters—among them three collections whose stories can be traced through to their transmission to Mme de Rosemonde, the novel's final archivist.

The first collection Mme de Rosemonde receives is Mme de Tourvel's, sent to Mme de Rosemonde by Mme de Volanges (*L* 165) and containing Valmont's letters of seduction. Valmont borrowed this collection once (*L* 44) to discover Mme de Tourvel's confidante. At that time, Valmont discovered the "Dijon Letter" (*L* 36), which Mme de Tourvel had torn to pieces, "carefully put together again." The Dijon Letter was torn up for two key narrative reasons: to emphasize Mme de Tourvel's obsession with Valmont—repairing the letter suggests a desire for collection and, as Valmont reads it, for the sender—and to reinforce the idea that Valmont prepares drafts of his letters (see *L* 34). But to finish with Mme de Tourvel's: she transports her collection to Paris, storing it in her desk (*L* 107), takes it to the convent when she leaves society, and finally, on her death-bed, gives it to Mme de Volanges for transmission to Mme de Rosemonde.

The second grouping is Valmont's collection, the repository of Mme de Merteuil's and Mme de Tourvel's letters to him, along with drafts of his own to Mme de Merteuil. Of these letters, Mme de Tourvel's function materially as a snare, aiding Valmont in consummating her seduction (*L* 124, 125). As long as she believes her letters will be returned, her desire is to "treasure" them, condemning herself "to reading them every day until my tears have obliterated every word [*les dernières traces*]. His own I shall burn for being tainted with the dangerous poison that has eaten into my soul" (*L* 124). But Valmont never surrenders this "precious collection" (*L* 125), and Mme de Tourvel does not burn his letters, of which the final one, delivered to her convent sanctuary, helps precipitate her death. Although the letters he receives are intrinsically important, the narratological significance of Valmont's collection rests in the drafts he retains of letters he has written. Valmont is an ardent archivist: "This morning I [Mme de Rosemonde] went into my nephew's room. I found him writing, surrounded by various heaps of papers which seemed to be the object of his labors. He was so preoccupied that I was in the middle of the room before he turned around to see who had come in" (*L* 122). Although it may seem a minor point, Laclos must establish that Valmont's drafts exist. If they did not, the Valmont-to-Mme de Merteuil letters would presumably have disappeared with her—hence, the Dijon Letter appears in the novel from a draft enclosed and double-read in letter 34 to Mme de Merteuil. Moreover, as Danceny describes the collection a dying Valmont gives him: "The number of letters it contains in the original would seem to prove the authenticity of those which are merely copies" (*L* 169). After reading the collection and probably extracting his own letters to Cécile, Danceny sends it to Mme de Rosemonde.

The third collection contains the Danceny-Cécile correspondence held by Danceny.[17] Part of this collection, like Julie's collection of Saint-Preux's letters, was discovered by Cécile's mother (this discovery necessitated Valmont's becoming an intermediary). Mme de Volanges sends the discovered collection to Danceny instead of destroying it, but he refuses to return Cécile's letters. In the end, however, Danceny also places his collection in Mme de Rosemonde's hands (*L* 174). As noted earlier, Mme de Rosemonde is mainly a passive unintended characterized reader during the time of the story, but beyond closure she becomes *active* by causing the letters to be published. Indeed, only after the deaths of Valmont and Mme de Tourvel, and the self-exiling of Mme de Merteuil, Danceny, and Cécile, can the entire collection become transmissible and serve to rewrite the characters' image in the public memory—the stories society inherits require a full accounting.

These three collections account for nearly every letter in the novel, and the reader can assume that the unaccounted-for Cécile-to-Sophie letters were accessible. But nine letters to Mme de Merteuil are problematic.[18] To accept the illusion of reality associated with the epistolary novel, every letter must be made available to the editor. Some of these nine letters could reasonably be expected to exist in drafts, but letter 97, in which Cécile tells Mme de Merteuil of her sexual initiation (rape) by Valmont, is loaded with phatic signs of one-time composition: "How shall I tell you? How shall I say it? ... I must speak to someone ... my hand trembles as you see. I can scarcely write.... Every time I thought of him my tears came twice as fast.... I do even now, and you see the result: my paper is quite sodden." Gérard Genette infers that despite the distress Cécile's subject may cause her, she writes thie letter a day after the fact and is thus detached from the event she describes.[19] Cécile's letter, however, suggests a deep psychic wound that infects her ability to articulate clearly her experience. Her need to transmit an account of her experience reinforces the inextricable link in these novels between transgression and transmission—a link underwritten by Cécile's pregnancy and Valmont's musings on the illegitimate lines of transmission that will obtain in Gercourt and Cécile's marriage: "I await the period for the confirmation of my hopes, and the assurance that I have fully succeeded in my enterprise. Yes, my love, I have already had the first indication that my schoolgirl's husband shall run no risk of dying without posterity, and that the house of Gercourt shall in the future be an offshoot of the house of Valmont" (*L* 114; see also 145). With this in mind, we read her eventual miscarriage (letter 140) as breaking the counterfeit line of transmission and as a symbol of the broken epistolary contracts of confidence. Yet the problematic nature of letters such as letter 97 only surfaces when one considers the narrative of transmission in the published text of the collections.

In *Les liaisons dangereuses* and *Julie* the letters and the work of the editor are clearly distinguished: little awareness is shown within the letters of their ultimate publishability. The writers may write public letters, but they are only public for the textual society. *Clarissa*, however, presents an alternate "story of the collection" which complicates the distinction between letter writers and editor and which overdetermines the reading of this collected text.

In the 537 letters of *Clarissa* there are many small acts of collection, any one of which might have served Rousseau or Laclos as a model. For instance, early in the novel Clarissa grants her mother access to her correspondence with Lovelace (*C* pt. 1, 17), but soon afterward Clarissa follows Anna's advice "to send out of [Clarissa's family's] reach all the letters and papers [she] would not have them see" (*C* pt. 2, 26). The advice is well taken, as a few days later "They made a strict search for [her papers]" (*C* pt. 2, 36). Like her family, Lovelace constantly tries to appropriate Clarissa's letters: "If I could find out that the dear creature carried any of her letters in her pockets, I can get her to a play or to a concert, and she may have the misfortune to lose her pockets" (*C* pt. 4, 13). Read symbolically, Lovelace's desire to appropriate Clarissa's letters is emblematic of his desire to appropriate her virginity. "Lose her pockets" in Lovelace's discourse is a metaphor for "lose her virginity"; his statement makes explicit a formal-thematic link between the letter and the hymen. As William Beatty Warner observes, "The course of events establishes an exact parallelism between Lovelace's violation of Clarissa's correspondence and his violation of her body."[20] Lovelace gives further credence to this symbolic reading when he places a description of Clarissa's ritualistic sealing and unsealing of her letters between two avowals of his desire to appropriate the letters:

> I shall never rest till I have discovered, in the first place, where the dear creature puts her letters; and in the next till I have got her to a play, to a concert, or to take an airing with me out of town for a day or two.
>
> I gave thee [Belford] just now some of *my* contrivances. Dorcas, who is ever attentive to all her lady's motions, has given me some instances of her *mistress's* precautions. She wafers her letters, it seems, in two places; pricks the wafers; and then seals upon them. No doubt but the same care is taken with regard to those brought to her, for she always examines the seals of the latter before she opens them.
>
> I must, I must come at them. This difficulty augments my curiosity. Strange, so much as she writes, and at all hours, that not one sleepy or forgetful moment has offered in our favour! (*C* pt. 4, 13)

Of course Lovelace does acquire many letters not intended for him; for example, the famous torn letter:

> ...this intended answer to my proposals: and how I adore her for it!
>
> But yet; another *yet*!—She has not given it or sent it to me.—It is not therefore *her* answer. It is not written *for* me, though to me.
>
> Nay, she has not *intended* to send it to me: she has even torn it, perhaps with indignation, as thinking it too *good* for me. By this action she absolutely retracts it. (*C* pt. 4, 41)

Moreover, Lovelace saves her traumatized post-rape fragments, which he describes as "so extravagant" (*C* pt. 5, 39).

These small acts of collection have their descendants in later epistolary novels, but the unique collection in *Clarissa* is the one Clarissa compiles to be published after her death. Because *Clarissa* is an epistolary novel of confidence, letters are almost always both written and copied, sent and collected. For this reason, the occasional lost letter goes against the logic of collection that obtains throughout the novel. And these smaller collections become essential to the narrative of *the collection's* transmission, wherein it is crucial that Anna's advice to Clarissa be carried out: "You are, it seems ... employed in writing. I hope it is in penning down the particulars of your tragical story. And my mother has put me in mind to press you to it, with a view that one day, if it might be published under feigned names, it would be of as much use as honour to the sex.... [S]he says, your noble conduct throughout your trials and calamities will afford not only a shining example to your sex, but at the same time ... a fearful warning to the inconsiderate young creatures of it" (*C* pt. 7, 26). As we discover in a later letter, Clarissa already "had begun the particulars" of her "tragical story," but she recognizes that she lacks information about "several of his machinations to ruin [her] ... so that some material parts of [her] sad story must be defective." Therefore, she decides that "the particulars of [her] story, and the base arts of this vile man" would "be best collected from those very letters of his." To this end, Clarissa proposes Belford as the executor of her will: "And if he accept the trust, and will communicate the materials [letters] in his power, these, joined with what you [Anna] can furnish, will answer the whole end" (*C* pt. 7, 33).

Clarissa's choice of Belford as executor, and in effect editor, is a masterstroke. By employing the two confidants as editors of the text, Clarissa shifts responsibility and authority for the final collection to others while preparing most of it herself. She shapes a text that will justify her claims of purity and innocence—despite the rape. Before the rape, Lovelace violates Clarissa's correspondence to gain an advantage that will lead to her surrender of her body; after the rape, Clarissa must appropriate Lovelace's letters to reconstruct the representation of her body as a scene of violation rather than volition. Lovelace's textualized plots, deceptions, and the rape itself countermark Clarissa's discourse of wronged innocence with a discourse of "base arts" that, more than her own discourse, reinterprets the fundamental virginity of her soul. In reading the novel, we actualize the text as the carefully crafted product of the main protagonist and her confidants. Although Anna suggests a work that will be an example and a warning, Clarissa must also construct a text that will save her soul.

Once Clarissa's plans are known, Lovelace demands his right to be executor of her will and his right to her papers (*C* pt. 7, 50); indeed, he writes (in his "delirious letter"): "I will take her papers. And as no one can do her memory justice equal to myself, and I will not spare myself, who can better show the world what she was, and what a villain he that could use her ill? And the world shall also see what implacable and unworthy parents she had. All shall be set forth in words at length. No mincing of the matter. Names undisguised as well as facts. For as I shall make the worst figure in it myself, and have a right to treat myself as nobody else shall, who will control me? who dare call me to account?" (*C* pt. 8, 45). Obviously, Lovelace's sincerity is open to question; and in a more candid moment he had revealed his basic editorial principles: "It is but the glossing over *one* part of a story and omitting *another*, that will make a bad cause a good one at any time" (*C* pt. 7, 97). Yet these two passages suggest a way of approaching "Clarissa's text." She includes Lovelace's letters to give him a fair hearing, knowing that the reader's sympathy with her plight will increase as a result. Yet despite its bulk and seeming comprehensiveness, there are seams in *Clarissa*'s narrative fabric—some letters are glossed over and others omitted. Belford, who will continue Clarissa's editorial legacy, recognizes her story's inherent literariness: "What a fine subject for tragedy, would the injuries of this lady, and her behaviour under them, both with regard to her implacable friends, and to her persecutor, make!" (*C* pt. 7, 67). But if she arranges her narrative as a tragedy, then she also appropriates the authority of the letter-exchange novel's editor.

The editor or collector in a letter-exchange novel, like an omniscient narrator, arranges the narrative discourse and creates meaningful juxtapositions between letters, although s/he is never an active correspondent.[21] Yet the editor is within the margin of the textual society, since s/he is also a fictional construct who may share the actual author's name but who functions within the text's *narrating instance* rather than its *literary instance*. Still, through his or her preface and footnotes, the editor directly engages the reader of the complete text, thereby linking the textual society with the general society of the reader. However, if we now examine the narrating instance rather than the literary instance, as Genette suggests,[22] we can isolate a letter-exchange novel's levels of narrative transmission.

There are three transmission levels in epistolary fiction: (1) the published text prepared by the editor/collector, (2) letters of confidence, and (3) dramatic letters and the events. These three levels correspond to Genette's categories of narrative level (outlined in chapter 1): (1) extradiegesis, (2) intradiegesis, and (3) metadiegesis. The relationship of the intradiegetic level (second-degree narration addressed only to members of the textual society) to the metadiegetic level (the story, as confided in intradiegetic narration) is clear, since most confidential letters in fiction are first-person accounts of events in which the narrator/letter writer participated. These two levels can be schematized as follows, with the arrows representing most letters' predominant temporal relationship to their content (proleptic confidences—"what I will do next"—would invert this relationship):

METADIEGETIC	INTRADIEGETIC
Event Narrated ⟶	Confidential Letter
Subject of Letter ⟶	Letter Writer
Hero ⟶	Narrator

However, as the blurring of confidential and dramatic epistolary aspects in the Valmont-Merteuil correspondence shows, letters can oscillate from a confidential to a dramatic mode, generating interpretive ambiguities. In confidential letters the hero must detach himself or herself from the event to become the narrator/letter writer, but the intradiegetic and the metadiegetic levels in epistolary fiction are logically connected through the image of the character. The third level obtains with the editor's role in arranging the text:

INTRADIEGETIC	EXTRADIEGETIC
Letter ⟶	Collection
Letter Writer ⟶	Editor/Collector
Narrator, Second Degree ⟶	Narrator, First Degree

As in *Clarissa*, certain characters simulate first-degree levels of narration and become *pseudo*-extradiegetic narrators or *characterized editors*. As opposed to the characterized reader already discussed, the characterized editor functions at the discourse level when the archive is made into a text. This activity prefigures the extradiegetic editor's task: s/he must also read and engage the intradiegetic and metadiegetic letters before arranging the published collection. And in arranging the letters to instruct the text's reader, the editor performs an active unintended characterized reading act at the level of narrative discourse. To a lesser degree at the metadiegetic level, Mme de Rosemonde, Danceny, Valmont and Mme de Merteuil serve as characterized editors in *Les liaisons dangereuses*. Having access to many letters, each enacts the editorial role by arranging and publishing parts of the collections. In *Julie* Wolmar becomes a characterized editor when he uses Saint-Preux's letters to secure his authority over the former lovers, and Saint-Preux's copybook could also be considered a pseudo-extradiegetic text, even though he is its only reader.

In addition to identifying the narrative transmission levels of a letter-exchange novel, we must consider Genette's two narrator relationships to the events narrated: "heterodiegesis," the absence of the narrator in the story, and "homodiegesis," the presence of the narrator.[23] By correlating transmission level and narrator relationship, we can now distinguish between the editor's and the confidential letter writer's relationship to the narration. The confidential letter writer's narrator status is intra-homodiegetic (often carried to the homodiegetic extreme of autodiegesis), while the editor's status is extra-heterodiegetic. Accordingly, narrator status can be aligned with reader status to describe more fully the letter-exchange novel's structure of narrative transmission. The characterized reader, in all manifestations, reads the letters intra-homodiegetically; the exception to this rule would be the embedded publication of a character's letters, which would create an intra-heterodiegetic reading public outside the homodiegetic society of the correspondence. An example of intra-heterodiegetic reading occurs in *Les liaisons dangereuses* when two of Mme de Merteuil's letters (81 and 85) are made public. In his or her preface and notes, the editor addresses an extra-heterodiegetic reading public, for whom the text is especially intended.[24]

BUT HOW are these letters and texts intra-homodiegetically and extra-heterodiegetically read with regard to the epistolary double narrative of transmission and transgression? To see this, we must thematize form and bring the narrative into dialogic relation with the culture text of its production. Since epistolary novels are secondary modeling systems derived from the primary modeling system of everyday letter writing, the study of narrative transmission leads to an interpretive perspective from which textual ideology and narrative technique can be seen as homologous with cultural ideology. Two previous studies, tracing different themes but through related formalist perspectives, have examined *Clarissa*, *Julie*, and *Les liaisons dangereuses* along these lines.

In *The Novel of Worldliness*, Peter Brooks sees these works as critiques of "worldliness."[25] Central to this concept are the individual and his or her place within the order of society. In the eighteenth century, however, "society" signified only the small, upper-class portion of the population—the educated reading public who were the predominant subjects of novels. The world of *Julie* opposes this closed society by turning its back on the Paris salons and the country retreats of the nobility. As noted earlier, Saint-Preux damns the loose morals of this society, and Julie opposes his attempts to understand through experience the moral corruption of Parisian society. The "world" is inconsequential to Julie (and Rousseau), and this novel of anti-worldliness offers the retirement of Clarens as an alternative. *Les liaisons dangereuses* directly attacks society's image of itself. The epistolary form lets the reader move behind the characters and see their motivations. Rather than mirroring Rousseau's alternative world, Laclos concentrates on the public world's private side, condemning the publicly sanctified hypocrites who feign virtue in the salon to hide the sordidness of their boudoirs. (Mme de Merteuil's incident with Prévan and its ultimate overturning is a perfect example.) Brooks recognizes, following Denis Diderot, that *Clarissa* is important to both Rousseau's and Laclos's attacks on worldliness. Richardson's fiction reoriented the eighteenth-century literary aesthetic away from detached, witty observation and toward immediate, participatory experience by the reader, who was forced by the epistolary form to confront a world through the eyes of one of its victims and one of its villains. Thus in its critique of worldliness *Clarissa* presents the conflict between the culture text of an essentially bourgeois private life, represented by Clarissa and her family, and Lovelace's more worldly culture text. This conflict of worlds results in a damning of both the worldly and the bourgeois in favor of Clarissa's spiritual devotion to the sanctity of soul.

Nancy K. Miller, in *The Heroine's Text*, reads all three novels within a "feminocentric" paradigm of seduction and betrayal.[26] For Miller, all three novels are overdetermined by the plot of the young woman's entry into the world, her seduction (rape) by an archetypal "rake" character, and either her ultimate triumph and assimilation into society (a "euphoric text") or, as in the novels before us, her ultimate betrayal and death (a "dysphoric text"). Following this paradigm, *Clarissa* is about a young woman who, because of her exceptional nature and reputation for virtue, is caught between conflicting codes of behavior: a repressive code of duty to family on the one hand, and on the other, a code of seduction, instituted by Lovelace and intended to test the genuineness of her reported virtue. This conflict puts Clarissa in a position of "exemplary vulnerability" to the dysphoric paradigm, which her rape brutally fulfills. However, with her self-isolation and subsequent self-willed death, Clarissa constructs a powerful anti-text to Lovelace's maxim: "That once subdued, is always subdued." *Julie* presents a program for redeeming virtue through repressing passion and instituting a different culture text—marriage, motherhood, and religion (with an added emphasis on God the *Father*)—which blocks a second transgression. Julie responds to her fate by rationally redirecting her conduct and rehabilitating her virtue, but even this cannot save her life. Miller examines Mme de Tourvel in *Les liaisons dangereuses*, who fits the paradigm perfectly although she is already married, and Mme de Merteuil, who represents a "negative heroine" striving to invert the paradigm through a masculine control (plotting) of her seductions; ultimately, however, she too is betrayed, abandoned, and left to a disfigured death-in-life. Although *Les liaisons dangereuses* leaves the feminocentric culture text intact, it presents the most serious challenge to it and condemnation of it so far.

The comparison of these novels by Brooks, Miller, and myself demonstrates an intertextual matrix of both form and theme linking these texts. Rousseau's novel rehearses Richardson's, but its characters are less extreme and its focus is on the consequences of seduction and transgression rather than on the act itself. It explores the process of redemption for both Julie and Saint-Preux. Essential to this exploration is letter 18, in part 3, in which Julie tells Saint-Preux of her marriage and transformation into a new woman. As stated earlier, this letter rereads the discourse of their letters and love, presenting, as Paul de Man observes, a "deconstructive narrative" of the metaphor that bound their two souls into one.[27] Significantly in this letter, Julie reflexively quotes, as the editor particularly notes, from one of Saint-Preux's early letters (pt. 1, 24) about her reading of Abelard and Héloïse's letters and his reading of their own teacher-student relationship through this anterior text.[28] Moreover, the editor's first note to Julie's letter presents the only direct mention of Richardson in the novel. The editor's marginal text thus reinscribes Julie's letter in a matrix of intertexts that extends the letter's horizon of meaning. According to Wolfgang Iser, "An allusion by the author himself certainly has a function for the context different from the one that is made in direct speech [or in a letter] by one of the characters. Thus extracts from reality and individual events are not contracted merely into allusions, but, through the different patterns of style, emerge in forms that endow them with a varied range of relevance."[29] Julie pinpoints her reply to Saint-Preux's first letter—required by epistolary etiquette—as the occasion, the "lettering," of her transgression: "You wrote. Instead of throwing your first letter into the fire or taking it to my mother, I dared open it. This was my crime and all the rest followed. I tried to force myself not to answer these nefarious letters which I could not prevent myself from reading."[30] Here we read palimpsestically Clarissa's identical crime (and Mme de Tourvel's, as we shall see).

Clarissa realizes that she "ought not to have corresponded" with Lovelace only after her abduction: "This last evil, although the *remote*, yet *sure* consequence of my first—my prohibited correspondence! by a father *early* prohibited" (*C* pt. 2, 52). Clarissa now understands that what Miller calls "a dialectics of desire"[31] was veiled behind the *"pragmatical motives* which induced me to correspond with him at first.... And what vexes me more is, that it is plain to me now, by all his behaviour, that he had as great a confidence in my weakness as I had in my own strength" (*C* pt. 2, 52). Thus Clarissa is trapped in a seductive discourse that paradoxically transgresses the patriarchal law of her father as it secretly attempts to make peace between her family and Lovelace. Julie first realizes the implications of epistolary transmission much later in her story, but Saint-Preux's—and the novel's—first letter contains the same logic of the "prohibited correspondence": "Show my letter to your parents; have your door denied to me; spurn me in whatever manner you please." Yet this warning not to read is buried at the letter's center, and the letter's suggestive closing—"If you have read this letter, you have done all that I would dare ask of you"—equates reading letters with fulfilling daring requests. And as Peggy Kamuf observes, by reading the letter, "Julie engages the mechanism of the double-bind, that is, the *written* imperative *not to read* (to show the letter to her mother) which in order to obey she must disobey. Once engaged, the double-bind will continue to proliferate the letters and thus widen the gap which separates Julie from her pretextual innocence and from the possibility of a return to the mother."[32] Because letters textualize the forbidden discourse of seduction, to answer a letter, even if only to discourage its author, is to enter into a seductive discourse and to engage the double narrative of transmission and transgression.[33]

Letters of seduction, with their particular discursive properties and semiotic codes, constitute a subgenre of written discourse. Similarly, letters of seduction constitute a subgenre in a larger semiotic system of seduction that includes enraptured gazes, blushes, hands held and withdrawn, and clandestine kisses in the drawing room. If this semiotic system of seduction operates within society's system of behavior, then it presupposes an openly acknowledged engagement, and the discourse of love entails marriage and assimilation into society. But if this semiotic system operates secretly in an intrigue between lovers, then the presuppositions and entailments change: societal constraints are circumvented, seduction becomes transgressive, the promise and celebration of marriage are made problematic, and society puts a higher price on assimilation. Transgression disrupts the transmission of social order, yet transgression requires transmission to write its disruptive text.

By "presuppositions" I mean the a priori context that defines a particular state of affairs in the culture text, and by "entailments" I mean the sequence of events generated from a particular presupposition. Presuppositions can occur in a text's relation to both the culture text and literary intertexts.[34] Accordingly, in the passage from Julie's letter quoted above (pt. 3, 18), her reading of Saint-Preux's letter presupposes a code of behavior within the semiotic system of seduction that requires intrigue. Since this secret act is a "crime" and against society's (her parents') code, it entails "all the rest" that follows. As the editor of Claude Prosper Jolyot de Crébillon's *Lettres de la Marquise* (1732) noted nearly thirty years earlier about that epistolary heroine: "The marquise was in love: this was the original calamity, and out of it all the rest was to some degree inevitable."[35]

Julie's retrospective analysis of her fall shows how presupposition and entailment affect a letter-exchange novel's narrative of transmission. In the eighteenth-century text, the semiotics of seduction becomes a descriptive system for reading the novel of seduction. Within this system, love letters are signs in a metonymic organization of seduction. In the epistolary novel, a narrative imperative overdetermines a letter's significance, and love letters exceed their metonymic function to become both metaphor and symbol. To the protagonists (except Mme de Merteuil), letters signify that they are loved (desired), but letters also symbolize their transgression of the social code (consider Clarissa's building of her book, Saint-Preux's copy book, or Mme de Tourvel's desire to reacquire her letters). Beyond this symbolization, which the characters perform themselves, letters of seduction become metaphors for the masculine plot of seduction: sexual contact and conquest.

The exchange of letters, which constitutes the narrative of transmission, is essential to the narrative of sexual transgression. The activity of exchange, and the phatic language it generates, is thus a metaphor for the sexual intercourse that fulfills the entailment presupposed in the granting of a correspondence. In all written communication systems the sender's *contact* with the receiver is the written text. In the novels examined, it is a presupposition of the descriptive system of epistolary seduction that this contact inevitably leads to sexual contact. As Miller argues, "In the epistolary novel of a feminine destiny, the exchange of letters concretizes a dialectics of desire already in place."[36]

Writing about the presupposition of adultery in *Madame Bovary*, Michael Riffaterre suggests a logic of entailment that also obtains in epistolary texts. Following the "voice of the sociolect," he argues that for the adulterous woman the first fatal step leads inevitably to the last fatal leap. These insepa-rable and complementary poles thus set the limits of the fictional space extending from an imaginary or metaphorical transgression (wicked thoughts nurtured by immoral and forbidden readings) to the most definitive of all actual or literal transgressions—the one that drags the heroine out of existence, and out of the text, simultaneously put-ting an end to what can be lived or to what can be told in words. The adulteress either commits suicide or sinks into prostitution.[37]

For Emma Bovary the metaphorical transgression comes through the reading of novels; for epistolary heroines, as *Clarissa* and *Julie* make explicit, it comes through the forbidden reading and exchange of unsanctioned letters. Laclos concretizes this process of transgres-sion when he has Valmont—ever confident of Mme de Tourvel's "inevitable fall" (*L* 96) because "her fate is sealed" (*L* 99)—express in exactly the same metaphor the voice of the sociolect that Riffaterre notes: "I like watching, contemplating this prudent woman as she takes, without knowing it, a path which allows of no return, which flings her willy-nilly in my wake down its steep and dangerous de-scent.... Care and skill can shorten the steps she takes: nothing can prevent their succeeding each other" (*L* 96). In his next letter to Mme de Merteuil, Valmont asks, "Once the first step is taken, are these strait-laced prudes ever able to stop?" (*L* 99). Six letters later Mme de Merteuil will pervert this formula when she advises Cécile, "You will soon learn that though a man takes the first step, we are nearly always obliged to take the second ourselves" (*L* 105).

Usually the epistolary heroine begins to write (the "second" step) to dissuade her seducer. She believes her virtue can overcome the entailments of her secret correspondence. Virtue, however, is not always rewarded, and her seducer often translates her arguments into his code of sexual discourse both to perpetuate the correspondence and to make virtue indeterminate. The heroine's submission is thus one code's submission to another in a semiotics of seduction. She falls because (1) she submits to an exchange of letters, and (2) she fails to deconstruct the epistolary activity's metaphoric organization.

Les liaisons dangereuses palpably demonstrates this failure to deconstruct, as the characters misread the metaphoric plot contained in their own letters and in the epistolary texts they read. To cite or quote another epistolary novel is to cite the descriptive system of the genre; therefore, characters inscribe in their letters intertexts that shape, for better or worse, their presuppositions. Mme de Merteuil reads *Julie* so she can imitate Julie's virtuous model of the redeemed transgressor. But she becomes trapped within her dissimulation, and in creating her own carefully plotted fiction she misreads Julie's text. Her autobiographical letter (*L* 81) parodically inverts Julie's confession (*J* pt. 3, 18). Rather than outlining, as Julie does, her plans for leading a virtuous life, Mme de Merteuil documents her crimes and writes a text that leads to her condemnation by society. Her letter is the private text made public: the deferred final move in her game of confidence with Valmont. For Mme de Tourvel, however, the intertext is *Clarissa*, and her private retribution is absolute.

Mme de Tourvel reads *Clarissa* during her attempt to escape from her feelings for Valmont (*L* 107). But because Valmont knows this, the events of her life become overdetermined by *Clarissa*. Like her English counterpart, Mme de Tourvel resists her rape until she is unconscious: "She did not return to herself until after she had submitted [*soumise*] and surrendered to her happy conqueror" (*L* 125). Valmont has indeed put her to sleep and made her "*une nouvelle Clarisse*," and he has effectively made her analogous to Émilie, the *fille soumise* upon whose back he wrote letter 48. But even though Mme de Tourvel reads *Clarissa* she fails to act like Clarissa, thus violating the intertextual link and sealing her fate as retribution. Instead of following Clarissa's example and disdaining Valmont, she willingly submits again. Consequently, she is ill-prepared for her betrayal and abandonment. Instead of writing an allegorical letter prefiguring her ascension into heaven (as does Clarissa), or rationally re-reading her "crime" (as does Julie), Mme de Tourvel can only dictate a raving letter (*L* 161), "s'adresser à trop de monde," that is transcribed by her ironically named maid, "Julie." Mme de Tourvel's raving letter has its precursor in Clarissa's fragments (*C* pt. 5, 39), but each responds to a different trauma: Clarissa to her rape, Mme de Tourvel to her abandonment by an adulterous lover.[38] Significantly, Mme de Tourvel is not given time to recover through rationalized counteractions, and the quickness of her death can be read symbolically as an inherent absence of the same fundamental innocence and virtue associated with Clarissa and Julie.

But heroines are not the only ones who misread intertexts; their seducers also fail to deconstruct the metaphoric plot overdetermining the events. Lovelace, as Miller contends, "makes a mistake of genre: he fails to perceive that Clarissa is not made for comedy."[39] Seduction plots prior to *Clarissa* largely turned on virtue's victory and the rake's reform. Even when transgressive sexual contact was made, the textual society reappropriated the transgressive couple through marriage. Inherent honor triumphed over base arts, restoring the transmission of the social code. Lovelace sees his actions in terms of this intertext of sentimental romance, and he regularly likens his own plotting to an elaborate stage play. Clarissa, however, does not yield to Lovelace's intertext; she sees her violation as a tragedy: submission to Lovelace's intertext would concede its validity. By overturning the intertext of sentimental romance, *Clarissa* redefines the entailments depicted in literary portrayals of seductive discourse and also the concept of "poetic justice," which many readers invoked in attempting to persuade Richardson to spare Clarissa's life.

Although Saint-Preux is clearly an anti-Lovelace, the crucial intertext for him is the historical correspondence between Abelard and Héloïse, which he discusses in letter 24 of part 1. Saint-Preux believes that he and Julie are fundamentally different from their two predecessors—that the oneness of their soul and the honor of their love exempts them from the consequences of transgression: "The most severe laws can impose upon them no other hardship than the natural consequence of their love. Their only punishment for their love is the obligation to love one another forever; and if there is some unhappy region in the world where a cruel authority may break these innocent bonds, it is punished, no doubt, by the crimes that this co-ercion engenders" (*J* pt. 1, 24). But the law of genre, codified by the intertext of Abelard and Héloïse, is inescapable. Five letters later, Julie writes to Claire: "It is impossible to recover my innocence" (*J* pt. 1, 29).

As for Valmont, who appears to understand so well the presup-positions in the epistolary activity, he remains blind to the conse-quences of his own epistolary activity despite Mme de Merteuil's early and cogent critique of his actions:

> Your real mistake is in allowing yourself to enter into a correspon-dence. I defy you now to foresee where this will lead you. Are you, by any chance, hoping to prove to this woman by logical demonstra-tion that she is bound to give herself to you? It seems to me that a truth such as this is better grasped by the feelings than by the under-standing; and that to persuade her of it you will have to appeal to her heart rather than to her head. But then what use is softening her heart if you are not there to take advantage of it? When your fine phrases have intoxicated her with love, do you suppose the intoxication will last long enough to be expressed before reflection supervenes? Con-sider how long it takes to write a letter, how long it takes getting it delivered, and tell me whether any woman, especially a woman of principle such as your Fair Devotee, could possibly sustain for that length of time an intention she struggles constantly to suppress. Such tactics might succeed with children who, when they write, "I love

you," do not know that they are saying, "I am yours." But it seems to me that Madame de Tourvel's disputatious virtue can better assess the value of words. Moreover, in spite of your having got the better of her in conversation, she is more than your match in letter-writing....

Another observation, which I am surprised you have not made for yourself: there is nothing more difficult in love than expressing in writing what one does not feel—I mean expressing it with conviction. It is not a question of using the right words: one does not arrange them in the right way. Or rather one does arrange them, and that is sufficiently damning. Read your letter again. It is so beautifully composed that every phrase betrays you. I should like to believe that your Présidente is innocent enough not to understand this, but what difference will that make when the effect is none the less missed? This is the great defect of all novels. Though the author whips himself into a passion the reader is left cold. Héloïse is the sole exception one might be tempted to make. Despite the author's talent, it is for this reason that I have always thought it true. (*L* 33)

I quote from this letter at length because it summarizes well the fusion of epistolary narratives of transmission and transgression present in all three novels. Significantly in the context of *Les liaisons dangereuses*, this letter serves as a challenge to Valmont's epistolary powers: by criticizing his writing, Mme de Merteuil is also criticizing Valmont's sexual power (as the echo of Héloïse suggests, the letter is an attempt to castrate Valmont's active epistolary pen). In this way she uses the letter to reveal how she carefully conducts her own correspondence with Valmont and how the lessons of Julie have not been lost on her. But just as Mme de Merteuil ultimately misreads *Julie*, Valmont misreads the novels from which he draws his tactics; he fails to realize that he has engaged one intertext against the other. As Cécile's sexual teacher he has become another Abelard or Saint-Preux, and as Mme de Tourvel's seducer he becomes another Lovelace. And although Mme de Tourvel fails to emulate Clarissa, Valmont fulfills a destiny similar to Lovelace's: he is killed in a duel, not by the Président de Tourvel, the husband of his *nouvelle Clarisse*, but by Danceny, the wronged lover of his *nouvelle Héloïse*.

Ultimately every separation, exile, or death at the end of these novels has been warranted, lettered by an epistolary activity that interpenetrates transmission and transgression in a double narrative of desire. Yet it is the deaths of the protagonists and of their transgressive desire that free the letters from one system of transmission so that they can be appropriated within the secondary system of the collected text. To this end, these novels fulfill their editors' directives to educate young readers in the dangers of secret correspondence. In comparing these three texts we find a complementary relationship between the letter and transgressive behavior that will recur in many epistolary and non-epistolary novels to come. The double narrative of transmission and transgression is a formal/thematic convention that marks the power of personal texts to disrupt and reorder one's existence and to threaten society's codes of transmission through legitimate marriages, births, and legacies. At its most traditional, the doubling of plots results in a death like Mme de Tourvel's. But as Clarissa and Julie demonstrate, death within the double narrative's logic of entailments can be transcendent, even to the point of reinterpreting the texts of their lives, the letters of their transgressions.

3 | Diary Narratives: Making Contact with the Self

> As I am not composing a novel for a benevolent reader,
> but am writing simply for my own satisfaction, there is
> no reason why I should resort to the usual stratagems of
> the littérateurs.
>
> —Turgenev, "The Diary of a Superfluous Man"

WHENEVER WE COME upon a diary—actual or fictional, published or unpublished, private or public—we tend to fashion a double response. First there is the feeling of the voyeur, peeping around pages as if they were curtains, searching out the secret thoughts and life recorded on the private page. But then comes a troubling response: Suppose this text is contrived and the writer is lying to the reader, writing a life as one would like it rather than as it is. With admitted fictional diaries this doubleness is compounded by our ideas of narrative logic and by an intolerance to the most mimetic of diary entries: the mundane entries of waking, eating, and returning to bed in the evening. It is not in spite of these problematics but rather because of them that diaries are so intriguing; moreover, the diary, like the confidential letter of pre-telephone culture, is a species of writing open to anyone literate (or illiterate, if we accept either tape-recorded oral diaries or videocassette diaries). Yet despite the democratic nature of the form, few actual diaries are published, and fictional diaries are more generally categorized as novels or short stories before they are subcategorized according to formal traits. Lorna Martens identifies such formal traits as first-person narration, written from day-to-day (often with dated entries), with an absence of a characterized reader.[1]

Diary texts include generic aspects of both autobiography and epistolary fiction. Diaries are almost invariably autobiographical (even when mainly intended as chronicles) and, indeed, are often the raw material for published autobiographies. Virginia Woolf, for instance, always intended for her now famous diary to be the quarry for a later memoir: "If Virginia Woolf at the age of 50, when she sits down to build her memoirs out of these books, is unable to make a phrase as it should be made, I can only condole with her and remind her of the existence of the fireplace, where she has my leave to burn these pages."[2] The choice Woolf gave her prefigured self is significant precisely because the diary, in its unshaped glory, remains, while the carefully phrased memoir was never written. Diaries evoke an immediacy that neither autobiographies nor memoir-novels can approach. A necessary gap may still obtain between the time of the experience and the time of the writing, but the diary text, unless it has been appropriated for counterfeit purposes, is never edited with the ending already known.[3]

Traditionally diary novels have been seen as descendants of both real diary writing and the epistolary novel, particularly epistolary monodies (single-writer epistolary narratives).[4] Both forms employ the immediacy of writing within the midst of the experience while the future is always somewhat uncertain, and they are also highly aware of the writing act and its place in constituting the text. This "reflexive drama," as H. Porter Abbott phrases it, is crucial to both diary and epistolary narrative strategies, since the narrative of textual transmission is often a significant event in itself.[5] As we saw in the preceding chapter, transmission is omnipresent in epistolary fiction; the narrative of transmission is organized into a logic of contact, with each act of transmission reaffirming the textual bonds of epistolary activity and the character's bonds with the inner society of the fiction. Moreover, the private transmission of letters becomes a paradigm for the public transmission of the text. Fundamentally this paradigm presupposes agency as a part of textual contact: addresser/addressee. These agents are present in the epistolary activity both on the private level of correspondence and on the public level of the editor and the audience addressed in a preface. But if the private reader is denied access to the private text, then we cease to have either a letter-exchange novel or an epistolary monody, such as *Die Leiden des jungen Werthers*, since even in single-sender epistolary texts certain phatic codes in the letters inscribe the image of a responding addressee.[6] Nonetheless, the epistolary monody, in its constrained narrative of transmission, connects the narrating instances of letter-exchange novels and diary narratives.

Diaries are private texts; indeed, they are usually secret, self-addressed texts. Therefore, diary narratives imply an absence of conventional contact between distinct addressers and addressees. The diarist will sometimes use a phatic discourse of contact to establish a narrating situation common to autodiegetic narration: the distinction Franz Stanzel has made between the "narrating self" and the "experiencing self" characterized within the narration.[7] For diary narratives, we must add to the narrating and experiencing selves the *reading self*, the addressed "I" of the diarist/reader in a solipsistic characterized act of reading the narrating self's text of the experiencing self's life story. Other characterized readers may be signified in diary narratives—diarists regularly leave their texts exposed for discovery by a reader, or they consider the time beyond death (diaristic closure) when the diary can no longer remain hidden from other readers—and such imagined acts of reading sometimes influence the text the diarist produces.

In some diary narratives, the distinction between different selves is made easy by large temporal gaps separating the events narrated and the narrating instance of the diary. But the diary form is often "written to the moment"—each day's events are recorded on that day, and the narrative develops a reflexive drama as both diarist and reader wait for the next day. This reflexive drama, however, is only a mimetic illusion, since the carefully shaped, literary, fictional diary follows patterns of entailment overdetermined by the narrative act's immanent literariness. For diaries that present underdetermined writing to the moment, we would have to turn to actual diaries; however, even here the pressures of narrative logic can affect the textual rendering of the diarist's life story. Since diary novels exhibit an obvious debt to actual diary writing, we should briefly consider the typology of diarists set out in Thomas Mallon's *A Book of One's Own*.[8] From this typology we can delineate representational models that influence fictional diaries and their narratives of transmission.

For the diarists he studies, Mallon creates the following categories: Chroniclers, Travelers, Pilgrims, Creators, Apologists, Confessors, and Prisoners. These are not rigid categories, however. One reason for this is the length of some of the diaries examined; Samuel Pepys's diary, clearly the most famous diary in English literature, spans ten years and contains over a million words. Because of his diary's length (and it is not the longest), Pepys shows he is more than just a chronicler: he is also a traveler, apologist, and confessor (this last especially, given his lusty approach to life). Yet the categories serve to highlight how the diarist's social conditions relate to the text produced; hence, the diaries of prisoners are radically different from those of travelers. Travelers usually look outward at new vistas of world discovery while prisoners look inward at the self trapped in a cage of steel and a cage of consciousness. But the question arises as to whether travelers or prisoners or the other types of diarists are genuinely honest with themselves—whether their texts truthfully recount events or imaginatively speculate on hopeful fictions. As readers we recognize that at times in diaries the border between the actual world and the fictional universe disappears. If anything, diaries lend themselves simultaneously to truth and fiction, to a not easily resolved problematic of utterances.

In *A Book of One's Own* Mallon momentarily confronts this issue in a chapter on "Confessors," in which he examines diaries that represent a "double life": "One can always have things as one wants them in a diary; it is easy to believe that one's own authorized version and the truth are the same thing."[9] The confessional diary is a text in which guilt that must be kept hidden from the world is allowed to speak. Psychoanalysis has long used the "talking cure," and diaries often function in such therapy as a site for inward scrutiny (an excellent fictional example of the therapeutic diary is John Updike's *A Month of Sundays*). But psychoanalysis assumes that the patient's true self will be revealed in the text once the self's unique system of codes can be deciphered. This assumption of authenticity is necessary for the therapy to work; but self-therapy is not held to the same rules, and confessional diaries embellish the events recorded: "The diary [is] a place where the *desire* to transgress is recorded. These are the diaries that contain kisses unstolen, the freight trains unjumped, the revenges untaken."[10]

Mallon suggests that only a handful of the diaries he examines are "probably a good deal less [than] authentic,"[11] but how much of any diary is fabrication? Fabrications are revealing for interpretation. Even though diary writing shrinks the temporal distance between experience and writing, the distance is never eliminated, and within that temporal hole, transformation can occur. Actual diaries tell us much about actual people, places and things, but actual diaries also use language to build textual universes that are charged with imagination. Not surprisingly, fictional diaries do much the same thing, and one cannot help reading Mallon's various examples without recalling diary novels that predate the actual diaries they resemble. The last diary Mallon considers is *The Journal of a Disappointed Man* (1919) by W. N. P. Barbellion (pseud. for Bruce Frederick Cummings); Mallon writes: "What disappointed him? The frustration of his literary ambitions by editors; the thwarting of his amatory ones by beautiful women; the years of waiting on the certain death that finally overtook him at thirty; mostly the knowledge that life would never love him as much as he loved himself" (285).[12] As we shall see, these are unmistakable traces of such nineteenth-century fictional diarists as Turgenev's superfluous man and Dostoevsky's underground man. Although the diary shows Barbellion as a voracious and eclectic reader, it may be impossible to determine whether such fictional characters influenced his perception of himself. Nevertheless, it is highly likely that, while fictional diaries evolved from the practice of real diaries, a reciprocity has now set in and each form borrows from the other.

Psychological anxiety, such as that indulged in by Barbellion, often affects most fictional diarists when they begin their texts. As Bertil Romberg observes, "the commonest type of diary narrator is the lonely, unhappy human being who cannot attain contact with others and turns inward upon himself."[13] This typical diarist must fulfill, Valerie Raoul asserts, "'basic prerequisites' for keeping a diary: the ability to write, time in which to do so, and personal motivation which makes the effort seem worthwhile."[14] The first prerequisite, that the diarist has a certain degree of literacy and intellect, is demonstrated by the text we read. The "intellectual hero" in the French fictional journal usually writes the text. The second prerequisite is demonstrated by the length and frequency of entries and becomes most obvious when time is limited or the writing must be done in secret to avoid disclosure. Both of these prerequisites have sociological implications as well. Diary narratives (and epistolary narratives) lend themselves readily, although not necessarily exclusively, to an educated fictional society with leisure time. Therefore, these subgenres contravene forms employed in narratives of the working classes. Characters without education or time usually require a different narrating situation. Similarly, the association of diaries (and letters) with women's writing stems from the large amount of time conventionally assumed to be available to middle- and upper-class women who had no out-of-house work options and who were excluded from other, more public, forms of writing.

"Motivation," Raoul's third prerequisite, has the most significant effect on a diary's narrative of transmission: "The narrator must be in a situation where he has something to say which he feels a pressing need to express, although he cannot immediately convey it to someone else."[15] This noncontact with a listener/reader occurs on two levels: (1) "physical isolation" and (2) "psychological alienation." We can read in these two conditions of absence the narrative of self-contact in diary fiction through both its structural sense and its thematized extension within the narrated world.

When we consider the dialogic interplay between structure and theme in diaries, we must read the narrative of transmission to expose the diary form's specific thematic functions in the text. The novel is a social document; its infrastructure depends on an interaction of characters within a society that shapes the textual universe.

To be cut off from the world is to be denied a normative interaction with other characters. Thrown back on the self, the isolated individual generates his or her diary out of a desire for communication, for contact—even solipsistic contact. Motivation for writing because of physical isolation was common to pre-novelistic nonfictional travel and adventure literature that employed homodiegetic narrating situations; strange environments induce writers to write.[16] The diary form allows the writer to record each new experience in a developing consciousness of the new world. In actual diaries such writing is usually episodic or anecdotal, indiscriminate in what it records, and lacking a narrative imperative for telling a particular story. Diary narratives that are so motivated can logically tell only tales of new lands and adventures, and we often read in such texts the colonial discourses of Western imperialism and the projection of Western systems of value onto the new land. Narration, therefore, becomes subordinate to description and the projection of ideology. Fictional diaries, on the other hand, are not constrained to actual yet trivial events; instead, they assert a narrative causality based on literary presuppositions and entailments.

Although physical isolation might be a primary motivation to write, novels often prefigure such isolation in an individual's personal alienation from or by society. The adventure tale develops this convention by having the protagonist "run away from home," but in other novels this separation from society marks a psychological rupture that the diary seeks to repair. Thus Raoul's two levels of motivation, physical isolation and psychological alienation, should not be read as a binary opposition. On the contrary, a spectrum of possibilities for motivation obtains, with the diarist's motivation measured by whether the narrating subject primarily represents the external course of events or the internal consciousness of the experiencing self in relation to the events. Travel diaries, with their emphasis on action and description, focus mainly on external events. But when the chosen structure of narrative transmission is a personal diary, then the events must be internalized, and a psychological element added to the motivation to write. And when the physical isolation of the diarist is not genre-determined (travel or adventure narratives), then the psychological motivation caused by a personal alienation from society begins to assert an even greater emphasis on the writing of the diary.

For instance, consider Pechorin, in Mikhail Lermontov's *A Hero of Our Time* (1841),[17] who has been banished to the Caucasus; he is physically isolated from the society he would prefer, but he is not absolutely isolated from society. His journal begins by focusing on external events in "Taman," but the two later sections, "Princess Mary" and "The Fatalist," definitely turn inward as Pechorin explores his alienation from society. Or consider Chulkaturin in Ivan Turgenev's "The Diary of a Superfluous Man" (1850),[18] who writes a diary/memoir while confined to a sickbed during the last thirteen days of his life; his subject is the moment when he realized he was "superfluous" to society. Or consider Victor Hugo's *Le dernier jour d'un condamné* (1829),[19] which presents the introspective writings of a condemned murderer awaiting execution, isolated in his prison cell, in contact only with his conscience.

These narratives present extreme cases, but in diary narratives as a whole the element of isolation is always inscribed in the text, since the act of writing is usually a solitary act and the diary a private document. To see diary motivation textually staged, we will turn to a significant early text in the history of diary narrative as a fictional genre: Samuel Richardson's *Pamela.* In it the full contact of the epistolary form is suddenly suspended and forced into a diaristic alternative.

PAMELA (1740)[20] offers a doubled transmission strategy. As an epistolary narrative, Pamela's letters are determined by their intended readers—Pamela's parents; as a "journal" narrative, Pamela's image of herself as reader comes to the fore. Moreover, although her journal maintains conventions of epistolary address, Richardson designs it to represent Pamela's solitary thoughts while she is both physically isolated (abducted and held against her will) and psychologically alienated (alien to the immediate society of Mr. B.'s Lincolnshire estate). Pamela's change in discourse system from letter to diary is analogous to her change from psychological ease (the supportive society of Mrs. Jervis) to psychological alienation (the repressive society of Mrs. Jewkes) and her change in geographic location from Bedfordshire to Lincolnshire. Many theorists describe the basic plot of all narrative as a movement from equilibrium to disequilibrium and then back to equilibrium, with the final equilibrium representing a transformation from the initial situation. This final equilibrium often marks either tragedy (e.g., death) or comedy (e.g., marriage). *Pamela* fits this transformative plot perfectly: virtue is rewarded with a socially advantageous marriage. This plot structure holds additional interest in *Pamela* because of its analogous structure of textualization (letters → diary → letters), its transformative narrative of transmission.

Pamela is characterized as "a mighty letter writer," who has "so much time upon [her] hands, that [she] must write on to employ [herself]" (188). She comments at one point on how her writing calms her: "I retired to my closet, and had recourse to my pen and ink, for my amusement, and to divert my anxiety of mind" (377). Throughout the text, Pamela exhibits moments of "anxiety of mind" and, therefore, is a natural candidate for diary writing. Her abduction necessitates the transformation from letters to journal, yet by the seventeenth day of her "bondage" she describes her text as "my oppressions, my *distresses*, my *fears*" (188). Later in the journal, after Mr. B. discovers her papers, she laments, "I know not what I shall do! For now he will see all my private thoughts of him, and all the secrets of my heart" (263). The difficulty of her situation is both physical and psychological, but even before her abduction, Pamela sees her letters as a text from which she can derive understanding and strength:

> As I may not have opportunity to send again soon, and yet as I know you keep my letters, and read them over and over,... and as it may be some little pleasure to me, perhaps, to read them myself, when I am come to you, to remind me what I have gone through, and how great God's goodness has been to me (which, I hope, will further strengthen my good resolutions, that I may not hereafter, from my bad conduct, have reason to condemn myself from my own hand, as it were): For all these reasons, I say, I will write as I have time, and as matters happen, and send the scribble to you as I have opportunity. (75–76)

Here Pamela is still writing in an epistolary mode, yet this passage marks both contact with the addressee and a future recontact with the addresser's reading self that will guide her future experiencing self. In addition, this passage inscribes the writer's great fear: that she will, by a transgression, be forced "to condemn [herself] from [her] own hand." Later in volume 2, after nearly resolving all her difficulties, Pamela echoes this conception of her accumulated text: "I am glad that I have fallen upon this method of making a journal of all that passes in these first stages of my happiness; because it will sink the impression [of Mr. B.'s domestic law] still deeper; and I shall have recourse to my papers for my better regulation, as often I shall mistrust my memory" (467). Her journal entries may be still literally addressed to her parents, but this passage reveals a true diaristic voice; and with the period of anxiety and alienation over, Pamela assumes a more defined identity—her journal continues out of habit.

Pamela undergoes severe trials, however; and her text reveals the psychological imperative behind her narrating act. Her two attempts to escape Lincolnshire fail, and the journal narration of each attempt depicts Pamela's extremely agitated mind. The first occurs on the eighteenth day of her "bondage" when Mrs. Jewkes uncharacteristically leaves Pamela alone while she visits the beaten and robbed Mr. Williams (who functions in the text both as a foil to Mr. B. and as a "contact character" between Pamela and her parents). The journal section depicting this attempted escape demonstrates effectively Richardson's technique of "writing to the moment." Pamela leaves and returns to her closet four times, each time writing of what happens at the garden door. Her journal not only records her reactions after each trip to the garden; it also gives Pamela a medium to argue with herself about her plans to escape.

The journal segment recounting the first attempt (191–93) opens with this inner debate: "I have strange temptations to get away in her absence.... 'Tis sad to have nobody to advise with! I know not what to do. But, alas for me! I have no money, if I should get away, to buy any body's civilities, or to pay for necessaries or lodging. But I will go into the garden, and resolve afterward." We see here how *contactless* Pamela is. Her desire to escape, to be free to reestablish contact with the world, is tempered by her lack of money and thus her inability to function in society's systems of economic contact and exchange. Moreover, even though she is a prisoner, the world outside her prison is more frightening—at least in her imagination. The first trip to the garden results in only a scouting of the door; all "looks well," and she writes, "I should never forgive myself for losing such an opportunity as this. Well, I will go down again, and see if all is clear, and how it looks out at the back-door in the pasture." Pamela's tentativeness is apparent; her resolve only goes as far as scouting the possibility of escape. Soon thereafter she tell herself, "here again I am at my pen."

The alternation of Pamela's trips to the garden and her writing has a multifaceted effect. Suspense builds with each trip, and the reader feels disappointment when Pamela ultimately fails—the expectations of both Pamela and the reader are frustrated. Even more significantly, each delay permits Pamela's imagination to overwhelm her sense of reality with numerous fears. On her second trip, Pamela opens the door and looks into the pasture; "but there," she writes, "stood that horrid bull, staring me full in the face, with fiery saucer eyes, as my antipathy to the creature made me think, and especially as the poor cook-maid's misfortune came strongly into my mind. So I got in again for fear he should come at me." In reacting to her experience, her imagination embellishes her fright with symbolic significance. But this does not end Pamela's inner debate:

> Do you think there are such things as witches and spirits? If there be, I believe in my heart, Mrs. Jewkes has got this bull on her side. But yet, what could I do without money or a friend? O this wicked woman, to trick me so! Then I know not one step of the way, nor how far to any house or cottage; or whether I could obtain protection if I got to a house: and now the robbers are abroad too, I may run into dangers as great as those I want to escape from; nay, much greater, if the present not unpromising appearances hold: and sure my master cannot be so black a creature, as that they should not! What can I do? I have a good mind to try for it once more; but then I may be pursued and taken; and it will be worse for me; and this wicked woman perhaps will again beat me, take my shoes away, and lock me up.

The opening address to her parents, "Do you think," is quickly overtaken by her present thoughts, and as Pamela's thoughts jump from subject to subject Richardson comes close to a "stream of consciousness" representation. Pamela decides to go down again and implores, "Direct me, O Thou who art the preserver of the innocent! direct me what to do!" Clearly, this address is not to her parents but to a higher authority.

"I went down resolved to get away, if possible." As soon as we read this we sense that Pamela has again failed, and she is again at her journal: "Fool that I was! could I not have thought of some errand to send [the gardener] out of the way? As I continue writing here, when I ought to act, that will shew you my strange irresolution, and how I am distressed between my hopes and my fears! But I will go down again." Pamela has correctly pegged her problem: instead of acting she writes. And we know this next trip to the garden is the last, or else the entire project will become a farce. Predictably, this last attempt also fails. Pamela is frightened by the "poor cows" that her fears transform into two "bulls." And she rationalizes after the fact: "Everything is so frightful to me, and as things have not so black an appearance as they had at first, I will not think of escaping: and indeed, if I were to attempt it, and were to have got at distance from this house, I should too probably be as much terrified at the first strange man that I met with." Her final excuses for inaction underscore the eighteenth-century woman's plight: her need of "money" and a "protective friend."

Significantly, when reporting this anxious moment, Pamela textualizes both her reactions and the reasoning process she uses in coming to her resolve. As with most diarists, Pamela's act of writing is detached from the written-about experience. As she writes of each trip to the garden, she textualizes both her experience and her imaginative projection of her fears. The alternation of her narrating moments with her experiencing moments lets Pamela think on paper, thus giving her arguments and perceptions palpable form. The text approaches a stream of consciousness at these moments, but the writing act necessitates a transformation from the deep structure of consciousness to the surface structure of grammatical form. Nonetheless, in the depiction of this first escape attempt, Pamela's consciousness is more closely tied to the moment than in the depiction of the second attempt.

The second escape attempt occurs almost ten days after the first and is marked by a steadfast resolve to escape. In this desperate attempt, Pamela brings herself to the brink of suicide. It is, she writes, "An enemy worse than any she ever met with; an enemy she never thought of before, and was hardly able to stand against: I mean the weakness and presumption, both in one, of her own mind! which, had not Divine Grace interposed, would have sunk her into everlasting perdition" (209). In this passage, the third-person pronoun shows Pamela's narrating self's displacement from her experiencing self, and the "Pamela" depicted in the journal becomes an object of close study for the writing Pamela. This escape attempt (209–16) is recounted retrospectively; therefore, the advantages of immediacy are lost, yet considering what happens, Pamela's journal would have been incoherent if it had been written to the moment.

Recounting her second try, Pamela begins by externally narrating her attempts to get out of the garden. After falling off the garden wall, Pamela contemplates an *escape from life*: "What to do, but to throw myself into the pond, and so put a period to all my terrors in this world!"[21] But "as I escaped this temptation," she writes, "I will tell you my conflicts on this dreadful occasion." Pamela's narrating focus now shifts from the external action to the internal "conflicts" she experienced at the edge of the pond. However, because Pamela reconstructs her consciousness at a moment of relative calm while recuperating from her experience, the reader must keep separate the narration and the experience.

The narrating codes deployed clearly signify a psychologically involved retrospective point of view. One code is Pamela's sudden dialogic use of a ritualized language to depict how she "reasoned with myself": "Pause here a little, Pamela, on what thou art about, before thou takest the dreadful leap; and consider whether there be no way yet left, no hope, if not to escape from this wicked house, yet from the mischiefs threatened thee in it!" The shift here is to the discourse pattern of a churchman who endeavors to save one of his flock, and as the scene continues, the "voice" becomes increasingly didactic as it refutes Pamela's arguments:

> But how do I know, thought I, on the other hand, that even *these bruises* and *maims* that I have got, while I pursued only the laudable escape I had meditated, may not have been the means of furnishing me with the kind opportunity I now have of surrendering up my life, spotless and unguilty, to that merciful Being who gave it!
>
> But then recollecting, Who gave thee, said I to myself, presumptuous as thou art, a power over thy life? Who authorized thee to put an end to it? Is it not the weakness of thy mind that suggests to thee that there is no way to preserve it with honour? How knowest thou what purposes God may have to serve, by the trials with which thou art now exercised? Art *thou* to put a bound to the Divine Will, and to say, *"Thus much I will bear, and no more?"* And wilt thou *dare* to say, That if the trial be augmented and continued, thou wilt sooner die than bear it? Was not Joseph's exaltation owing to his unjust imprisonment?
>
> If, despairing of deliverance, I destroy myself, do I not[,] in effect, question the power of the Almighty to deliver me? And shall I not, in that case, be guilty of a sin, which, as it admits not of repentance, cannot be hoped to be forgiven? And wilt thou, to shorten thy *transitory* griefs, *heavy* as they are, plunge both body and soul into *everlasting* misery! Hitherto, Pamela, thought I, thou art the innocent, the suffering Pamela; and wilt thou, to avoid thy sufferings, be the guilty aggressor?

The dialogue in Pamela's consciousness invokes other discourses and borrows more from moral tracts than from epistolary conventions. Generated by her psychological alienation, this second voice signifies the *contact* Pamela needs to save her life, the "[somebody] to advise with," the "Author" of her entire existence. The turn to a divine interlocutor through the contact of the meditative dialogue is a common feature of confessional literature—a literature often cast as a diary.

Pamela's confessional turn has literary antecedents. Cynthia Griffin Wolff, in *Samuel Richardson and the Eighteenth-Century Puritan Character*, has examined how many of Richardson's devices for developing character through writing technique relied on traditions of self-examination in Puritan literature. Of particular interest for *Pamela* are the extensive devotional literature aimed at teaching children virtue and the countless spiritual manuals that urged the Puritan to engage in hours of lonely self-examination. In practice,

Puritan self-examination could cause an identity crisis, so the self-examiner was instructed to keep a diary to discover sins and evil thoughts. As Wolff observes, "the potential sinner would be obsessed with asking whether an apparently harmless act had been tainted by hidden desires or by the indirect expression of sinful intentions."[22] Thus when Pamela examines in writing her near-suicide, she recasts her actual moment of self-examination at the edge of the pond into a written dialogue that allows her to confront her near-commission of a grievous sin. Moreover, in constructing this interlocutor for her inner debate, Pamela clearly mimics the style of the devotional literature of her childhood reading. By careful crafting, the dialogue detaches Pamela and the reader from the events: diegesis overwhelms mimesis.

Despite the power of the "authority" she invokes to save herself from suicide, another "authority," another interior voice, tempts Pamela to consider suicide. At one point she imagines the voice of Mr. B. as he stands over his drowned Pamela: "And my master, my angry master, will then forget his resentments, and say 'Alas!' and it may be, wring his hands. 'This is the unhappy Pamela! whom I have so causelessly persecuted and destroyed! Now do I see she preferred her honesty to her life. She, poor girl! was no hypocrite, no deceiver; but really was the innocent creature she pretended to be!'" The "stage direction" for Mr. B.'s hands suggests how thoroughly developed this death fantasy is, but this voice also signifies Pamela's desire for contact with Mr. B. on her terms—a "contact" she maybe presupposes in Mr. B. as a covert addressee of her entire text. Pamela must thus choose between two "authorial" texts for her life story: (1) a possibly sad but reformed Mr. B. in exchange for her perdition; or (2) life under the threat of rape, but with her afterlife assured. For Pamela, as for Clarissa, the second alternative carries more certainty and hope—divine authority transcends that of any earthly "master."

Her near-suicide makes Pamela's life story fully transmissible, and it will be Mr. B.'s reading of Pamela's journal, the textualization of his demands and her trials, that ultimately serves as the *peripetia* in *Pamela*'s feminocentric plot—reversing her fate from the "tragedy" of a supposed fallen woman to the "comedy" of a successful marriage. Yet we must remember that this textualized representation is first and foremost the objectification of Richardson's Puritan ideology of the ideal heroine—who is rewarded for the virtue of her resistance and who validates the Puritan patriarchy's codes of behavior. Thus, rather than representing a fully empowered woman's self-determination, Richardson's textual impersonation projects the father's (and by an especially Puritan metonymy the Father's) desire for the perfectly virtuous daughter and ultimately the husband's desire for a chaste and submissive wife. Pamela's transcription of Mr. B.'s rules for a wife is an ideological text displaying Richardson's hand guiding Pamela's pen.[23] Women's diary fiction that follows *Pamela* often tells a different story.

VALERY LARBAUD, writing about Edouard Dujardin's *Les lauriers sont coupés* (1887),[24] the work long credited as the first narrative to use interior monologue, commented that "One step beyond the 'personal diary' and the 'interior monologue' appears." Dorrit Cohn cites Larbaud's observation in *Transparent Minds*[25] when she briefly considers the presentation of consciousness in diary narrative. Dujardin's text marks this "step beyond" at its center (fifth) chapter by embedding in Daniel Prince's present thoughts his "documentary evidence"—letters and a fragmentary diary—of his affair with Leah. These documents juxtapose the earlier techniques for presenting consciousness with Dujardin's technique of "autonomous monologue" (Cohn's term).[26] Because of this juxtaposition the reader becomes hyperaware of how much closer to actual consciousness the autonomous monologue seems. And although autonomous monologue and its twentieth-century descendants are more products of narrative stylistics than of any sort of ideal mimesis, instances of consciousness in diary narrative are especially intriguing.

Cohn observes that "diarists ostensibly write, as monologists speak, only for themselves," but the temporal interval in the diaries between narrating and experiencing distinguishes the two narrative forms: "A diarist who managed to close the gaps between his entries (wrote as fast as he thought) would produce an autonomous monologue in written form."[27] Yet, automatic recording of every conscious moment would preclude any action away from the writing desk, since any other action would break the simultaneity of experience and narration. Such a text would exist on a fragile narrative logic that would delimit its narrative space to only the page and its narrative time to only an eternally present writing act.[28] To add even a fragment of past actions or to speculate on future events would transgress the narrative situation and free the mind from its enslavement to the narrating act. The diary's written imperative imposes on the narrative a textuality that delimits its potential for presenting consciousness: a pure diary of consciousness is unrealizable.

How then does a diary text present the diarist's mind? Fundamentally, the diarist can represent the thoughts of either the experiencing self or the narrating self. In the first case, the moments of interior view must be reconstructed, like dialogue, through the perfect-memory convention and are normally signaled by such phrases as: "I thought," "then I said to myself," or "I felt." The past tense indicates the experiencing self's consciousness, regardless of how nearly immediate the experience and its narration are.[29] The passages of consciousness following the signaling phrase are not, however, necessarily limited to the past tense. When the diarist writes what the experiencing self "thought" s/he can either attempt to recapture a "self-quoted interior monologue" in the present tense, or maintain a narrating distance, presenting a "self-narrated monologue" (Cohn's terms).[30]

For example, in Jean-Paul Sartre's *La nausée* (1938),[31] the following sentences are written in Roquentin's diary a few hours after the scene they describe: "Au bout d'un moment, il [l'Autodidacte] revint avec un livre illustré qu'il posa près de son paquet. Je pensai: 'Je le vois pour la dernière fois'" (226).[32] Here the signaling phrase, the tense shift from past to present, and the quotation marks clearly indicate the narration's movement from external observation to Roquentin's articulated thoughts *during* the experience. He could just as easily have written the second sentence as: "I knew I was seeing him for the last time," which would have represented equally well his consciousness at the moment.

However, the remainder of the passage makes clear why Roquentin shifts our sense of contact away from the narrating moment and to the experiencing moment:

> Je pensai: "Je le vois pour le dernière fois." Demain soir, après-demain soir, tous les soirs qui suivraient, il reviendrait lire à cette table en mangeant son pain et son chocolat, il poursuivrait avec patience ses grignotements de rat, il lirait les ouvrages de Nabaud, Naudeau, Nodier, Nys, en s'interrompant de temps à autre pour noter une maxime sur son petit carnet. Et moi, je marcherais dans Paris, dans les rues de Paris, je verrais des figures nouvelles. Qu'es-ce qui m'arriverait, pendant qu'il serait ici, que la lampe éclairerait son gros visage réfléchi? Je sentis juste à temps que j'allais me laisser reprendre au mirage de l'aventure. Je haussai les épaules et repris ma lecture.[33] (226)

The move to the conditional mood specifies a speculative moment of consciousness, which seemingly looks beyond the moment of Roquentin's self-quoted monologue toward the future actions of both Roquentin and l'Autodidacte. Although this speculation is ultimately indeterminate, it appears to move temporally beyond the writing moment. With the closed quotation marks of the first sentence, we might suppose that Roquentin is speculating during his narrating moment. Moreover, the shift back to a past tense at the passage's close returns the reader to a retrospective point of view with the narrating self. But those recalling l'Autodidacte's violent banishment from the library for homosexual advances to a school boy (the scene that ends this entry in the diary) recognize that these speculations could only belong to the experiencing self. The narrating self, from his temporal position of superior knowledge, knows that the speculations are ironic within the context of the completed narrative sequence; therefore, the narrating self tries to represent the experiencing self's moments of consciousness, regardless of the scene's eventual outcome.

The ambiguity surrounding Roquentin's speculations affects the reader's expectations about the scene's outcome. The reader must be alert to which "self," experiencing or narrating, is the subject of consciousness. A different contact with consciousness can be detected in the penultimate sentence of the passage: "Je sentis juste à temps qui j'allais ne laisser reprendre au mirage de l'aventure." Here consciousness is clearly retrospective, but we are not given a fully articulated thought. Instead, we get a "feeling," a subverbal representation of consciousness, resembling what Cohn calls "psychonarration" in heterodiegetic forms. At the experiencing moment Roquentin does not necessarily put into words his sense of almost succumbing to the "mirage de l'aventure," but in reconstructing the experience, he realizes his need to control his speculations.

Generally the narrating self's moments of consciousness are limited to contemplating the writing act itself—"Why did I write that?" or, "Why do I write?"—which are bound primarily to the present tense. Nevertheless, as the example from Sartre demonstrates, verb tenses are hardly reliable indicators of the narrative level represented. Moreover, both levels can share marks of interior monologue such as questions, exclamations, or prose fragments randomly strung together. In memoir narration, in which a significant temporal gap separates the experiencing and narrating selves, the distinction is fairly easy to perceive; but in diary narratives, often only a small temporal gap separates experiencing and narrating, and thus the reader expects more immediacy between action and narration, yet at the same time the potential increases for ambiguous indicators of character consciousness. Close attention to the context and narrative transmission signals of each utterance is necessary to avoid occasionally misreading passages of consciousness.

Such signals of consciousness are hard to overlook, since diary narratives and narratives purportedly presenting unmediated consciousness call overt attention to their transmission techniques. We can demonstrate this assertion by considering the verbal representation of consciousness from the standpoint of generative-transformational grammar. A fully mimetic representation of consciousness would have to present the deep structure of the subject's consciousness: the pure semantic content of each thought. But for the diary writer, the moment of writing always engages transformational processes that convert deep structure into surface structures of discourse. Even taking this view requires that we consider each thought in a verbalized form. Attempts to probe nonverbal moments of consciousness can only approximate what is actually thought, and the technique of psycho-narration, which according to Cohn permits a narrator to approach the unconscious, requires a powerful narrator. Self-contact in narrative is always a mediated discursive act that offers only an illusion of actually representing consciousness.

Nevertheless, this illusion of access to consciousness, combined with the illusion of reality generated by the diary narrative's formal mimetics, is regularly actualized by readers during the act of reading. Readers accept conventions of represented consciousness so they can interpret a character's truthfulness within the fictional world. This is particularly the case in autodiegetic narratives, especially diaries, in which the narrator is only granted access to his or her own mind.[34] Moreover, the reliability of the narrator's self-evaluation affects how the reader perceives the entire text. These statements assume, however, that a diary's contact-purpose is to certify the narrated world's authenticity. But occasionally the diarist is "mad," and instead of measuring the text against a reality context for the fictional world, the diary becomes a text of the imagination, a total product of an alienated mind.

Nikolai Gogol's short story "The Diary of a Madman" (1835)[35] is an exemplary case in which the reality context is overthrown. Poprishchin's diary begins conventionally—"An extraordinary incident occurred today"—but the incident is his overhearing and understanding a conversation between two dogs. Quickly the reader recognizes the absence in this diary of a reliable reality context—the madman's diary is a logomimetic text that encourages our disbelief. Gogol's story is not, however, completely devoid of a referential level; Leonard J. Kent observes, "In *Diary of a Madman*, Gogol is perhaps more directly involved with contemporary social reality than in any of the earlier tales.... It is full of references to contemporary society and Western politics."[36] But this referentiality is not generated or supported by the diary convention. In Poprishchin's narrating situation, these references recreate subconsciously an unusual world view; in Kent's words: "It is a detailed record of the subconscious because the world of madness is a dream, or rather, a nightmare."[37] Yet pardoxically, this text of the subconscious is extremely stylized by both diary conventions and the Russian narrative technique of *skaz* (the use of devices for a quasi-oral narration organized around a personal tone and open to the interjection of random thoughts and digressions). However, the verisimilitude that normally accompanies the diary form is strained to the breaking point by the madman's text, and rather than suspending disbelief, the reader must maintain disbelief to avoid also becoming mad.

In Gogol's story the mad diarist textualizes the psychological alienation of an individual in a world without hope. Yet Gogol's madman appears mad from the outset, thus simplifying the task of readerly detachment from his madness. In Charlotte Perkins Gilman's "The Yellow Wallpaper" (1892),[38] however, a different kind of mad experience is transmitted, an experience we have only recently learned to read. The mad diarist of Gilman's story is a woman apparently suffering from postpartum depression; she has been isolated by her doctor/husband in the attic room of a rented mansion for a "rest cure." This cure requires complete isolation from the world and the patient's absolute inaction—the diarist is supposed to neither read *nor write*, only rest. This diagnostic sentence, as Paula A. Treichler observes, is metaphorically a prison sentence as well, condemning the diarist to inhabit a room—with barred windows and a bolted down bed—that comes to resemble an actual asylum.[39] In a defiant gesture feminist critics have taught contemporary readers to recognize, the diarist violates the cure imposed upon her by her patriarchal husband and writes a diary that documents the onset of madness.

As a forbidden text, the diary becomes an essential, yet also problematic, element in her existence. From the outset the diarist recognizes that her writing offers her options of expression unavailable in her daily contact with John, her husband: "John is a physician, and *perhaps*—(I would not say it to a living soul, of course, but this is dead paper and a great relief to my mind)—*perhaps* that is one reason I do not get well faster" (9–10). But soon this writing which "is such a relief" becomes an "effort [that] is getting to be greater than the relief" (21). Although she continues to write, the diarist ceases to refer to her writing act—there are eleven references to the writing in the first two fifths of the story, none after that point. Instead, a different "dead paper" overwhelms her consciousness: the yellow wallpaper of her bedroom. The wallpaper, with its arabesque design that violates all principles of symmetry, becomes a text the diarist struggles to decipher; it becomes the text of her being as she discerns the image of a madwoman lurking behind the bars of the design. This other woman becomes an obsession to the diarist until a moment of transference occurs:

> As soon as it was moonlight and that poor thing began to crawl and shake the pattern, I got up and ran to help her.
>
> I pulled and she shook, and I shook and she pulled, and before morning we had peeled off yards of that paper. (32)

In a telling chiasmus, diarist and other become one, a merger that occurs on the last day of her "cure."

As a result, the diary suddenly shifts from the past tense of the above passage to an urgent present tense that is made further problematic by the diarist's self-bondage: "I am securely fastened now by my well-hidden rope.... I suppose I shall have to get back behind the pattern when it comes night, and that is hard!" (35). At this point it seems inconceivable that the diarist could be "writing to the moment"; the narrating and the narrated merge entirely in the last section of the text (although the final few paragraphs revert to the past tense). Yet we need to read beyond the literal problematics of how this powerful last scene gets written and to see how symbolically the woman's text and the textual woman (read and written by herself and others) subversively join with a potent, hidden other that patriarchal discourses such as John's diagnosis have sought to repress. Ironically, John's prediction that overstimulating her imagination would damage his wife's cure is confirmed; however, the necessary catharsis wrought by the talking cure of the diary reveals a feminist text that is profoundly different than the *Pamela* model, one that has long desired to be read.

BUT WHO "READS" within diary narratives? How is a complementary act of reading inscribed within the diaristic act of writing? As we have seen in the texts examined so far, the diarist's psychological motivation necessitates a turning inward on the self; the diary is a search for a better understanding of the diarist's essential being. To engage this search, the diarist must also read and reread the text to discover whatever truth the textualized image of the self might reveal. To read the text, however, is to interpret the text, rewrite, and transform the text. Thus, to actualize the narrative of transmission in diary texts we must consider the activity of the reading self in forming the final text.

Sartre's Roquentin, whom we saw in the last section, is an obvious descendant of Gogol's Poprishchin (along with other descendants such as Dostoevsky's underground man and Turgenev's superfluous man). Roquentin avoids madness, yet his diary is motivated by an almost pathological alienation from the society that surrounds him. Poprishchin's text and the diarist's in "The Yellow Wallpaper" merely come to the reader; no editorial apparatus proclaims authenticity or authority, and therefore the narrative of transmission forms itself. *La nausée*, on the other hand, is more problematic, since Roquentin's self-consciousness about his text and the editorial fiction of the text's discovery prepare the reader for one kind of text: a diary; but s/he receives another kind of text: a diary that has been partially novelized. The awareness of textuality in *La nausée*, and how the diary relates to the novel, postulates another transmission channel the reader must actualize.

According to Gerald Prince, "The origin of the diary, the circumstances of its publication, its physical shape, its dialectical relationship with the narrator: some of all these problems, as well as others related to them (what is the diarist's state of mind as he writes? how often does he reread his own entries? where does he keep his diary?), some or all of these problems are examined to a greater or lesser extent in every work considered to be a diary novel."[40] This extreme genre-consciousness in diary narration is largely a matter of conventions used to signal the genre-contact channel of the text. Another "problem," however, can be added to Prince's list: the diarist's concern to mark the text as *something other than a novel*, even though diarists often compare their own experiences to those of characters in "fictional" narratives. Conventions of intertextuality underwrite these playful comparisons: If a diary is to claim itself as "true," it must disassociate itself from the fictional, "false," genre—the novel. The old dichotomy between history and the novel is invoked, but these truth claims are always already ironic—characters making the claim never recognize that their own realization occurs on the pages of a novel. How could they?

Today, the postmodern novel would have little trouble fabulating a narrative situation that realizes its immanent novelness. If we consider Steven G. Kellman's concept of the "self-begetting novel," we see that already writers have approached the problem of immanent novelness from inside the text.[41] One of Kellman's central texts is Sartre's *La nausée*. Roquentin's diary ends with a quasi-decision to write his experiences as a novel, a second textualization of the experiencing self. This quasi-decision focuses the dichotomy of art and reality that troubles Roquentin: to put existence into form is to falsify it, to change it into something other. Yet cannot the composition of a diary, even at its most random, also be a falsification? Kellman states that "the question of whether *La nausée* is itself the novel that Roquentin will write is probably unresolvable."[42] But given the text we have, would the contact provided by either form, diary or novel, be more able to render truth? The text does not answer this question, but in some of its formal incongruities, it does offer the reader alternative modes of discourse.

Some scenes in *La nausée* seem to be contained in the diary only because of a chronological imperative of events and the editorial promise that the text was published "without alteration." The style in these scenes, however, suggests a completely different narrating situation. For example, when Roquentin visits Anny in Paris, the entire scene, from the opening of the door to its closing (191–216), is written in the historical present tense and is composed of dialogue combined with Roquentin's thoughts during the scene. Certainly Roquentin is not scribbling everything down during the meeting, and no direct reference is ever made to the narrating moment. There is, however, a moment late in the scene when Roquentin as narrator decides to accelerate his narrative of the meeting by skipping over some of his own speech:

> Je lui raconte mes aventures, je lui parle de l'existence—peut-être un peu trop longuement. Elle écoute avec application, les yeux grands ouverts, les sourcils levés.
> Quand j'ai fini, elle a l'air soulangée.[43] (211)

What he tells Anny is the substance of the pages in his diary prior to this scene, and to avoid redundancy or being caught in a conflicting narrative, he summarizes his story under the words "aventures" and "existence." The summary device has been common to narration since Homer embedded narrations of prior events into tales told within the epic universe. However, the summary device also exposes the narrating act, thereby deconstructing the illusion of immediacy suggested by the present tense. But is this revealed narrating act that of the diary, or is it a revised representation: the novelization of a diary entry that has been erased and replaced by a new text? If we actualize this palimpsest of the scene's narrative of transmission, then what has become absent in the transformation from diary to novel? Or, what has been added? What deep structure response to their meeting has been transformed by this new textualization? How has Roquentin recreated his self, his past, and his experience? The text recounts the events *as if* the narrating and experiencing selves are one. By then estranging the present-tense convention through narrative expediency (avoiding a digression that can flaw art but is commonplace in the transmission of everyday speech), Roquentin undercuts his hope of final self-acceptance, self-meaning, through literature.

Regardless of how we read this and similar scenes in *La nausée*, we must actualize the shifting contact channels through which the final text is transmitted. The reasons for these shifts can be attributed to the *reading self* structured within diary transmission. Since diarists write for themselves, they undoubtedly reread what they have written. According to Raoul, "The instances of self-reading [recorded within the journal itself] fall into three main categories: (1) reading of a few lines which have just been written, or of the last entry; (2) reading of a larger section of the journal from a greater distance, usually after a considerable gap and before resuming the journal activity; (3) reading of the whole journal before abandoning it."[44] Included in self-reading is the self-interpretation of the diary's textuality— the diarist establishes intertexts for evaluating the diary.

As we saw with epistolary narrative, the primary purpose of an intertext is to superimpose a system of presuppositions and entailments onto the logic of actions, thereby overdetermining what happens to the experiencing self. The intertext is thus a *mise en abyme* to the events of the narrated world. As Lucien Dällenbach defines this device, "*mise(s) en abyme* ... [are] one or more doublings which function as mirrors or microcosms of the text."[45] In diary narratives, the intertextual relationship at the level of the narrating self and the narrating act takes on an added importance in constituting the text's contact with the reader. Diaries often deny that their texts are anything other (meaning a "novel") than the truth. But by denying the novelistic, the diarist calls undue attention to the text, and the reader soon perceives the signals of novelistic transmission inscribed within the diary's discourse. These signals point to a powerful and essential form of intertextuality that has characterized the history of the novel: *parody*.

Fictional diary narratives, because of their incorporation of a semi-literary genre, always parody actual diaries. The conventions used to mark a diaristic contact also exaggerate any attention to the text found in real diaries: the real diarist has little need to recall so often the writing situation. Fictional diaries also parody memoirs, with which they share the autodiegetic narrating stance. Memoirs are distinguished from diaries by the extreme temporal detachment of narrating self and experiencing self, and by the illusion of "superior knowledge" created by a narrative recollected in tranquility. A diarist may often cross this formal delimitation of the narrating situation to include an *analepse externe* (a retrospective narrative further in the past than the opening temporal point of the diary), thus mixing the two autodiegetic forms. Yet memoirs are distinguished from diaries by the conception of the narratee: memoirs are public, diaries private. Turgenev's "The Diary of a Superfluous Man" (1850) mixes these two forms, parodying both, in creating a paradigmatic text for two later diary/memoir novels: Dostoevsky's *Notes from Underground* and John Updike's *A Month of Sundays*.

From the outset of the narrating situation, Chulkaturin, the self-proclaimed superfluous man, is physically isolated from society. He has only two weeks to live, and he seemingly is confined to his room. His only view outside comes from a window (thus many entries begin with a mention of the weather), and his only society is the maid Terentievna, whom he apostrophizes at one point: "O decrepit, yellow, toothless creature! So I am not a human being even to you?" (352). It is a question to which he dare not record an answer. Since his experiencing self is "forbidden to go out" (343), Chulkaturin decides to tell himself his own life, an action he believes "cannot offend anyone" (343). (The novel as a genre will have to wait a century until Samuel Beckett's present-tense narratives of experiencing selves who have no experiences.) But who is he thinking might be offended? If we accept the illusion of reality suggested by the diary, then "anyone" would signify other characters, particularly Liza, from whom he craves forgiveness and a recognition of his value. However, despite regular assurances that his diary is written only for his "own satisfaction" (348, 364, 379, 381), could Chulkaturin be concerned about offending *another* group of readers?

As observed in the discussion of consciousness in diary discourse, questions and exclamations often mark moments of consciousness during the narrating act that are inserted into the text automatically during the act of writing. And, as in *Pamela*, use of second-person addresses in a diary text can indicate a self-dialogue and not an address to a reader outside the text. But an interpretive problem arises when the diarist postulates an other as reader. Chulkaturin insists: "As I am not composing a novel for a benevolent reader, but am writing simply for my own satisfaction, there is no reason why I should resort to the usual stratagems of the littérateurs" (364). The sentence is a "stratagem" itself. By denying the text is a "novel," Chulkaturin creates suspicions about his narrative's reliability, and the "benevolent reader" is that extratextual addressee he at once despises and desires, the reader he wants both to offend and not to offend. A page later, however, a parenthetical remark directly addresses someone outside the diaristic narrating situation: "Do not laugh at me, whoever you may be whose eyes chance to fall on these lines" (365). Suddenly the diary ceases having only a singular contact with the same narrating and reading self; Chulkaturin expands his horizon of contact beyond his "own satisfaction."

But this public reader, who is warned (petitioned?) not to laugh, is a vital construct in this text's narrative of transmission, since Chulkaturin's statements now take on a clearly dialogic quality with respect to the addressee. Chulkaturin writes for himself, but also for a nameless other; therefore, every statement becomes doubly intended, as a secondary contact is inscribed upon the first. If the use of language is always an interpretive act, then here language becomes doubly interpreted within a dialogic play of significance. Yet can this other be identified? Clearly a "benevolent reader" would not consider laughing at Chulkaturin, and an offended reader would not be likely to laugh either. Chulkaturin desires but fears a reader. He desires a sympathetic reader who will understand his superfluousness, but he fears a reader such as Prince N., who would see through his superfluousness and scorn his weakness.[46] Chulkaturin is not a hero of our time like Lermontov's Pechorin (although he considers himself a "hero" once [373] and he cites Lermontov in his text [353]); instead, he resembles another literary character he compares himself to: Gogol's Poprishchin (379). This intertextuality of character further doubles the reader's sense of Chulkaturin's textual status and his status as a narrator, thus creating an indeterminate characterization of the narrator: Is this the diary of a superfluous narrator?

When Chulkaturin writes "do not laugh at me," he performs a radically indeterminate speech act because the images of both the addresser and addressee are unclear and ultimately dependent on frail literary assumptions. Whether this performative speech act is "commanding," "warning," "asking," or "pleading" is not signaled by the text and is ultimately unresolvable without an entire interpreted context, which is not immanent but must be imposed on the text. Fixing this moment of contact requires interpretation of the implicit performative in the speech act: "do not laugh at me." Any interpretation, however, is generated from presuppositions and establishes a logic of entailments for the reading and rereading of the text. As readers, we are always involved in this interpretive activity, and although the center of "The Diary of a Superfluous Man" uncovers the indeterminacy of contact and the superfluous nature of any fixed interpretation, the appended "Publisher's Note" suggests one reading that casts an interpretive shadow on the diary.

The publisher notes at the end of the manuscript, in a handwriting different from Chulkaturin's, that "someone has written the following words"

> *This Manuscript was read*
> *And Its Contents were not Approved*
> *by Piotr Zudoteshin*[47] (390)

How do we characterize this reader, who takes the role of a censor? Turgenev uses this censor—the figure of suppressed transmission—to suggest that either the reader has just read a forbidden work or Chulkaturin is too superfluous even to have his life approved for publication. Moreover, this appended gloss also raises interesting questions about the politics of interpretation at the level of the narrating instance. This censor, at least, is not the "benevolent reader," and we cannot be sure how he read the passage asking him not to laugh. Yet he fills the role of an "offended reader," possibly a petty official who cannot escape the reflection of his own superfluousness that appears in this text.

Dostoevsky's underground man resembles Chulkaturin, with the important differences that the underground man's position in the social hierarchy is much lower, his experiences are more alienating, and his isolation from society is psychologically induced. Chulkaturin begins to write once he is bedridden with a terminal illness; the underground man, on the other hand, begins to write once he has inherited six thousand roubles, which allow him to settle down in his corner and "talk about myself."[48] *Notes from Underground* (1864) contains many other parallels to its precursors. At one point, the underground man alludes to Gogol's madman (876), and throughout the notes he will question the state of his sanity. Like Turgenev's superfluous man, the underground man attempts to prove himself through insults and through contact with a woman. But the underground man is not given the romantic satisfaction of a duel (a common thematic and plot device in nineteenth-century Russian fiction), and his sexual contact comes with a naïve prostitute, parodically named Liza, over whom he exercises a ruthless power that, ultimately, only deepens his consciousness of his own degradation. This "disease of consciousness" prompts his decision to write:

> I got to the point of feeling a sort of secret abnormal, despicable enjoyment in returning home to my corner on some disgusting Petersburg night, acutely conscious that that day I had committed a loathsome action again, that what was done could never be undone,

and secretly, inwardly gnawing, gnawing at myself for it, tearing and consuming myself till at last the bitterness turned into a sort of shameful accursed sweetness, and at last—into positive real enjoyment! Yes into enjoyment, into enjoyment! I insist upon that. I have spoken of this because I keep wanting to know for a fact whether other people feel such enjoyment? I will explain; the enjoyment was just from the too intense consciousness of one's own degradation....

... But enough.... Ech, I have talked a lot of nonsense, but what have I explained? How is enjoyment in this to be explained? But I will explain it. I will get to the bottom of it! That is why I have taken up my pen. (849, 850)

Before examining some key passages in the narrative of transmission inscribed within these notes, I should justify including this work as a diary narrative. Technically, the signals of diary composition are absent from this text. Moreover, the second part of the text is strictly a memoir of events that occurred twenty years before the time of the writing: the dinner for Zverkov and the experience with Liza. Dostoevsky constructs a work that crosses traditional genre lines, thereby reinscribing in the text the literary heritage of which the underground man is so aware—such as when he speculates on Zverkov's dinner: "how paltry, unliterary, commonplace it would all be" (892). Nonetheless, *Notes from Underground* is clearly a work of confessional literature, and therefore its narrating situation stages the same reflexive drama as many diaries, factual and fictional. We can show this reflexiveness by examining the narrative of transmission at the center of the notes.

Notes from Underground is a bipartite text: part 1 attempts to explain the enjoyment of degradation and despair, and part 2 is a memoir that functions as evidence for the assertions made in part 1. The final section in part 1 (section 11) acts as a transition from the abstract theorizing of the first part to the example of the second. In making this transition, the underground man reveals his text's problematic transmission. The notes are prefigured and undone by an "Author's Note" that claims, "The author of the diary [elsewhere translated as "notes"] and the diary itself are, of course, imaginary" (846 n. 1). By deconstructing from the outset a reader's suspension of disbelief, Dostoevsky or an editorial persona makes the underground man a symbolic figure, "one of the characters of the recent past. He is one of the representatives of a generation still living" (846 n. 1). However, the underground man doubles the fictionality inhering in the narrative of his text's transmission by characterizing his audience and himself as fictions.

In section 11 of part 1, the underground man suddenly pulls back from a series of statements about his envy of the "normal man" and writes, "Oh, but even now I am lying" (870). He then extends this admission of lying to the entire text we have read so far: "I will tell you another thing that would be better, and that is, if I myself believed in anything of what I have just written. I swear to you, gentleman, there is not one thing, not one word of what I have written that I really believe. That is, I believe it, perhaps, but at the same time I feel and suspect that I am lying like a cobbler. 'Then why have you written all this?' you will say to me" (870).

This characterized reader is referred to throughout the text, but the underground man here recharacterizes this reader as himself, thus articulating his narrative transmission as an interior dialogue rather than contact with an external reader:

> Of course I have myself made up all the things you say. That, too, is from underground. I have been for forty years listening to you through a crack under the floor. I have invented them myself, there was nothing else I could invent. It was no wonder that I have learned it by heart and it has taken a literary form ...
>
> But can you really be so credulous as to think that I will print all this and give it to you to read too? And another problem: why do I call you "gentlemen," why do I address you as though you really were my readers? Such confessions as I intend to make are never printed nor given to other people to read. Anyway, I am not strong-minded enough for that, and I don't see why I should be. But you see a fancy has occurred to me and I want to realize it at all costs. Let me explain.
>
> Every man has reminiscences which he would not tell to every one, but only to his friends. He has other matters in his mind which he would not reveal even to his friends, but only to himself, and that in secret. But there are other things which a man is afraid to tell even to himself, and every decent man has a number of such things stored away in his mind.... [ellipsis added] Anyway, I have only lately determined to remember some of my early adventures. Till now I have always avoided them, even with a certain uneasiness. Now, when I am not only recalling them, but have actually decided to write an account of them, I want to try the experiment whether one can, even with oneself, be perfectly open and not take fright at the whole truth. I will observe, in parenthesis, that Heine says that a true autobiography is almost an impossibility, and that man is bound to lie about himself. He considers that Rousseau certainly told lies about himself in his *Confessions*, and even intentionally lied, out of vanity. I am convinced that Heine is right; I quite understand how sometimes

one may, out of sheer vanity, attribute regular crimes to oneself, and indeed I can very well conceive that kind of vanity. But Heine judged of people who made their confessions to the public. I write only for myself, and I wish to declare once and for all that if I write as though I were addressing readers, that is simply because it is easier for me to write in that form. It is a form, an empty form—I shall never have readers. I have made this plain already. (870–71)

To include such an image of the text within the text is to call into question the ontological status of the *Notes* we read. In other words, if the "diary" is, "of course,... imaginary," then we read the notes within a particular frame of fictionality. And if the "imaginary" underground man invents his addressee as himself and writes in "an empty form" with no intention of transmitting his text, and thus will "never have readers," then the frame of fictionality doubles or even multiplies into an infinite set of variable relationships. The text we read is ontologically undecidable: How can one declare never to have readers without already having readers? Or is the underground man once again lying? And if so, can we believe anything in the notes? In such an undecidable narrating situation, reading becomes an underground act; the readers, particularly the first readers of the *Notes*, lie to themselves about their own degradation revealed in the text. The narrative of diary transmission in *Notes from Underground* forces the reader into an uncomfortable proximity with the underground man. The narrative of transmission occurs at the center of the text, at a point when the phatic bond with the reader has been already forged. When the underground man fictionalizes his audience and himself, it is within the context of "lying." The assertion that the reader is a fiction turns on the ontological paradox of a confessed liar's truthful confession. The underground man degrades himself before a "loathing audience," but he also loathes his audience, and his notes are meant to degrade, in turn, his audience— which is always already himself.

Because a diary is private, the characterization of an audience other than the diarist takes on special significance. The underground man's problematic "gentlemen" and Chulkaturin's reader-avatars demonstrate different approaches to the reader. Chulkaturin fears and desires readers in an ironic hope to be understood; the underground man, on the other hand, dialogically dismisses his readers as stylistic conceptualizations of himself, but the extent of the dismissal only marks more clearly the actual reader's textualization within the discourse of the underground world. We must remember, nonetheless, that the physical isolation and psychological alienation motivating the diarist's inward turn also preclude any *simple* contact with an addressee. In spite of that, we can turn to a final example in which the diarist openly "courts" his addressee.

Culturally distant from the nineteenth-century Russian narratives just examined, John Updike's *A Month of Sundays* (1975)[49] is the month-long diary of Reverend Thomas Marshfield, who has been sent to a rehabilitation clinic for clergymen who have lost touch with their church-sanctioned duties and responsibilities. Marshfield is at the clinic because he has become "distracted," committing numerous adulteries with members of his congregation. His rehabilitation includes diary writing: "My keepers have set before me a sheaf of blank sheets—a month's worth, in their estimation. Sullying them is to be my sole therapy" (3). Like Dostoevsky's and Turgenev's diarists, Marshfield concentrates his diary upon the sexual existence from which he is now isolated and from which the clinic intends to alienate him psychologically through his scriptotherapy.[50] As he daily recalls a different stage in his distraction, Marshfield comes to understand how his actions were centered in ego gratification rather than in genuine concern for the woman who happened to be involved.

With this understanding comes something else: desire. Marshfield engages in a seeming auto-seduction of his diary's "Ideal Reader." He characterizes his ideal (sometimes "gentle") reader as Ms. Prynne, the manager of the clinic. (Updike's parodic play on Hawthorne's *The Scarlet Letter* extends to Marshfield's wife's maiden name: Chillingworth.) Consequently, he inscribes in the diary a narrative of transmission that tells of his longing to be "read":

> O, Ms. Prynne, she [Frankie Harlow, one of his former lovers] was fair and fine and spoiled and open-eyed, the web of time sat like the most delicate purdah upon her face, whereas you are dark and heavyset and militantly competent and uncivil in the hall, which vibrates with your patrolling step: forgive me for tormenting you with fond memories. If I knew what you wanted. If you would leave me a multiple-choice questionnaire as does the Ramada Inn. If you would grant me a sign, disturb the placement of these pages on the dresser top, invert the paper clip I cunningly sandwiched in a northeasterly direction between pages 89 and 90, anything. (111–12)

As he enters the third week of his stay, however, he detects an erased mark at the bottom of one page (167). A week later a penciled comment is made on the text (212), and Marshfield quickly seizes this contact channel and suggests that a sexual liaison between himself and Ms Prynne (since he is convinced she is his reader) is the "one rite, one grail [that] stands between [him] and a renewed reality" (213). And although no other comments appear, the last entry in the diary depicts Marshfield's sexual union with Ms. Prynne on the day of his departure from the clinic; the text closes: "What is it, this human contact, this blank-browed thing we do for one another? There was a moment, when I entered you, and was big, and you were already wet, when you could not have seen yourself, when your eyes were all for another, looking up into mine, with an expression without a name, of entry and alarm, and of salutation. I pray my own face, a stranger to me, saluted in turn" (228).

We might ask, of course, what kind of rehabilitation is it that concludes with another adultery, and that with the coordinator of the rehabilitation? But the intertext inscribed in Ms. Prynne's name suggests that this "adultery" carries within it a deeper significance for Thomas Marshfield, and the diary form of the text helps us interpret the closing paradox. As with spiritual diaries of the Puritans and the confessions of various churchmen, Marshfield's diary is an attempt to search the soul for the reasons behind his previous actions. The diary lets him put his actions in perspective; therefore, the ideal reader becomes a confidante. Confidantes, however, become lovers, and Marshfield sees this affair with Ms. Prynne as one between not simply a man and a woman, but between a narrating self who has learned to control his textual universe like a puppetmaster[51] and a reading other. The experience and the text fuse in a transmission of "human contact": the transcendence of the diary's inherent logic of isolation and alienation.

4 | Inserted Documents and Hybrid Narratives of Transmission

> Mlle. de La Mole appeared on the threshold of the library door, tossed him a letter, and fled. It looks as if this is going to be an epistolary novel, he said, as he picked up the missive.
>
> —Stendhal, *Le rouge et le noir*

> I announced, on beginning it, that this narrative would be a remarkable document. It has entirely answered my expectations. Receive these fervid lines—my last legacy to the country I leave for ever.
>
> —Collins, *The Woman in White*

WHEN A NOVEL is composed exclusively of either letters or a diary, we are aware immediately of its form, and, as I have sought to show in the preceding two chapters, we must also be aware of and attend to the narrative of transmission that accompanies those documents. Yet letters are certainly not limited to only these genres of prose fiction; indeed, most novels contain letters. In nearly all forms of narration, letters (or messages) serve as powerful plot devices—as Homer Obed Brown characterizes them, "the novelistic version of the *deus ex machina*."[1] A diary inserted in another narration occurs less frequently, but when it does, the diary becomes a window into the character, often revealing more than even the most omniscient of narrators.

Although these letters and diaries receive sufficient attention during reading, their narratives of transmission are often overlooked. I would argue, however, that these documents become even more significant in our reading because of their intertextual connection to established epistolary and diary narrative traditions—every letter or diary in fiction rehearses the genre that organized its logic within the literary universe. In this way, letters, diaries, and other documents that haunt prose fiction offer an alternative to the transmission processes of gossip that function in most novels. If there is an advantage to inserted documents over exclusively epistolary or diary fiction, it is because the narrator can modulate our distance from the document and can frame it within a commentary on its writing or reading. The reader may not experience the same imaginative pleasure s/he had with the other forms; but narrative economy improves as does the opportunity for creating conflict between the private transmission of letters (or the ultra-private transmissions of diaries) among individuals and the public transmission of gossip among the fictional community.

In the sections to follow I will examine the immanent narratives of transmission in inserted letters and inserted diaries in a few selected nineteenth- and twentieth-century prose fictions. The chapter's last section examines a species of prose fiction that I label "hybrid": texts that are patchworks of different documents that an extradiegetic narrator has pieced together to frame a coherent narrative. From Anne Brontë's letter/diary interplay in *The Tenant of Wildfell Hall*, to Wilkie Collins's suspense-generating complexity in *The Woman in White*, to Doris Lessing's postmodern masterpiece *The Golden Notebook*, these hybrid narratives exploit the processes of epistolary and diary transmission to their fullest.

IN CHAPTER 2 we examined three narratives of transmission and transgression in epistolary fiction, and it would be safe to say that many of the most interesting letters in fiction have to do at least with matters of the heart, if not actual transgression. We would not normally associate Jane Austen with plots of seduction and transgression, but her overriding concern with society's rituals of courtship and the fate of young women on the marriage market demonstrates her desensationalization of the common seduction plot. As her juvenilia shows, Austen took delight in parodying the sentimental romance plots of popular fiction. Early works, such as *Lady Susan*, "Love and Freindship [sic]," and "A Collection of Letters," let Austen burlesque the illogical elements in popular novels and begin to create models for some of her more eccentric secondary characters. In addition, many of these works mark Austen's early interest in writing her stories within an epistolary framework. Many commentators have observed the influence of Samuel Richardson and Fanny Burney on Austen's writing, but she abandoned the pure epistolary mode for her mature novels, breaking with a tradition that, as she probably recognized, had run its course.

Nevertheless, many letters find their way into Austen's novels, and the writing of letters (even if never printed in the text or used to facilitate plot) is a regular occupation of her characters. Austen clearly knew the literary value of a carefully selected letter as a device in her stories of courtship. In *Pride and Prejudice* (1813),[2] Austen arranges three letters of confidence as pivotal moments in the growth of Elizabeth Bennet's consciousness of her love for Darcy; the first is Darcy's famous letter of explanation following his rejected proposal of marriage.

Centering the novel, this letter is the previously missing anterior narrative—kept unavailable to gossip's system of transmission—that will explain everything. Darcy's confidential letter clarifies his and Elizabeth's relationship as that of confidants rather than that of lovers (although it is a strange role for both). Crucial to Darcy's letter is his faith in Elizabeth's ability to keep secret his sister's near-elopement with Wickham. By revealing this secret, Darcy inverts the seducer's stratagem of instituting a secret correspondence of seduction, setting in its place a single letter that *tells a secret* but invites no reply. Yet the extradiegetic narrator's account of Elizabeth's "mortifying perusal" (205) shows the advantage of the letter at just this moment in the narrative. The argument of Darcy's letter could not have been spoken effectively—the strained relationship between Elizabeth and Darcy would have precluded her sympathetic belief. By textualizing it, Darcy gives his position an air of permanence that demands rereading and contemplation; it offers a pact of confidence that forces Elizabeth to conclude, "Till this moment, I never knew myself" (208). As Brown observes generally about fictional letters, "the letter says what can't be *said* in any other way, can't be spoken. Instead of the endless round of speculation that is gossip [an extensive feature of Austen's texts], the letter gives answers (information); its emphasis is on *revelation*."[3]

By confiding his secret to Elizabeth, Darcy invites reciprocal trust when she receives Jane's confidential letter about Lydia's eloping with Wickham. There are many metonymic connections between the aborted elopement with Miss Darcy and the successful one with Lydia. Both are made known to the reader through letters of confidence, and the formal and thematic allusions to *Clarissa* are clearly expressed in the characters' fears. Moreover, Elizabeth laments the keeping of her bond of secrecy, blaming herself for not being able to warn her sister of Wickham's true nature. Lastly, the situation allows Darcy "readily [to assure] her of his secrecy" (278) and then secretly to act on her behalf. This secret action, guaranteeing Lydia and Wickham's marriage, is revealed in the third letter of confidence: Mrs. Gardiner's letter explaining the true circumstances of Lydia's wedding (321–25). All three letters involve events that Darcy or

Elizabeth prefer to keep secret and outside the system of gossip that organizes and validates community in Austen's novel, but in forming a pact of confidence, they develop a proper understanding of each other. For the novel, Austen uses the intradiegetic inserted letters as surrogate narrations, relieving the extradiegetic narrator of the awkward task of accounting for certain events; but more significantly, at crucial points the protagonists must come to know one another through reading (rather than gossiping about) the universe of discourse they inhabit.

Although confidential letters are still used in novels, dramatic letters are often more powerful devices for moving the plot forward and incorporating a narrative of transmission within the text. We can again turn to Austen for an example in *Persuasion* (1818).[4] In the penultimate chapter, Austen presents one of her famous drawing room scenes, in which conversation reveals so much about character. There is one main difference in this scene, however; while Anne Elliot discusses with Captain Harville the "nature of any woman who truly loved" (232), Captain Wentworth composes a letter. As Anne discovers, "While supposed to be writing only to Captain Benwick, he had been also addressing her!" (237). The epistolary activity thus invades the domain of conversation. The letter, which we read with Anne, is the long-awaited second proposal of marriage. Austen had originally written this chapter without the letter, but in her revision, she again shows her sense of scene and of the letter's narrative power to complete the reconciliation of the two former lovers.

In both novels, Austen is all seriousness with her letters (with the exceptions of pompous stylists such as Mr. Collins), but other novelists incorporate parody in their inserted letters or narratives of epistolary transmission. Stendhal, for instance, clearly has the epistolary tradition in mind when he depicts Julien Sorel's liaison with Mathilde de La Mole in *Le rouge et le noir* (1831).[5] Julien comes to the Hôtel de La Mole as a copyist of letters, specifically political letters; therefore, within the narrative he is always inscribed in an epistolary activity associated with power and the granting of favors within society's hierarchy. Mathilde, too, is inscribed within an epistolary activity:

> With grief do we say it, for we are fond of Mathilde, but she had received letters from several of [her admirers], and had on occasion written replies. We hasten to declare that this character is a complete exception to the general rules and customs of the age. As a rule, lack of prudence is not a charge that can be leveled against the pupils of the noble Convent of the Sacred Heart.

> One day the Marquis de Croisenois returned to Mathilde a moderately compromising letter she had written him the day before. He expected this token of supreme prudence would much advance his suit. But it was imprudence which Mathilde was aiming at in her letter writing. She loved to play with fire. (249)

The narrator's explication of this narrative of transmission shows that Mathilde's activity approximates that of her eighteenth-century predecessors, except that Mathilde shows little inherent virtue and innocence.

Not surprisingly, when she decides she "must be in love," she reviews "in her mind all the descriptions of passion she had read in *Manon Lescaut*, the *Nouvelle Héloïse*, the *Letters of a Portuguese Nun*, and so on" (250–51). Significantly, Mathilde does not reread these novels, and she does not review the warnings they contain. Instead, she initiates a liaison with Julien by sending him "quite simply, a declaration of love" (260). Julien recognizes the power her letters give him—"After this letter, I am [M. de La Mole's] equal" (262)—and he inscribes his reply within the established code of social caste that Mathilde transgresses: "Never imagine, Mlle. de La Mole, that I am going to forget my social position. I will make you understand and feel that it is for the son of a carpenter that you are betraying a descendant of the famous Guy de Croisenois, who accompanied St. Louis on his crusade" (262). By invoking the genealogical narrative of transmission Mathilde is about to transgress, Julien signifies the "monstrous" nature of the liaison—not only Mathilde's virginity but the metaphor of female purity that society insists upon to insure its economic and social perpetuation are at stake. Julien's use of seduction to effect his illegitimate rise in society presents a conjoining of narratives of transmission and transgression that we have seen figured in the process of epistolary transmission.

Mathilde is not unaware of the impropriety of this liaison with Julien and how it relates to her earlier epistolary actions:

> [In the past,] when she had written one of her letters, Mathilde could not sleep at night. But those letters were only answers.
>
> Now she had had the audacity to confess herself in love. She was writing, and writing *first* (what a terrible word!) to a man in the lowest ranks of society.
>
> This circumstance guaranteed, in case she were discovered, eternal disgrace. Which of the women who visited with her mother would have dared take her part? What polite formula could be handed to them which would soften the shock of society's fearful contempt?

And then talking was frightful, but writing was worse! *There are some things one doesn't put on paper....* And it was Julien himself who had told her of this expression, as if teaching her a lesson in advance.[6] (266)

By "writing *first*," a crime the narrator doubly marks in the text—and thus inverting the conventional narrative of epistolary contact and seduction—Mathilde places herself in a double bind of transgression: she does not have the option of no*t reading* Julien's first letter—she has submitted before he even sends it. With his reply, this dangerous liaison accelerates, and soon after sending his reply, Mathilde "appeared on the threshold of the library door, tossed him a letter, and fled. It looks as if this is going to be an epistolary novel, he said, as he picked up the missive. The enemy makes a false move; I reply with coolness and virtue" (268). Julien's observation marks the liaison within two analogical matrices: epistolary fiction and military action. Julien's devotion to Napoleon makes the military analogy second nature, but the military analogy for a campaign of seduction is also common to the seducer's confidential discourse in many epistolary novels, especially in Laclos. Julien again replies, but Mathilde's third letter that day demands action: he must visit her bedroom that night.

By using this whirlwind correspondence as a context, Stendhal lets his narrator narrate, and thereby make parodic, this epistolary narrative of transmission that has no time for the interminably slow seductions of earlier epistolary novels. But one parody was not enough. When Mathilde spurns Julien, he is advised of a strategy for regaining her attentions that includes the epistolary seduction of a "prude": Mme de Fervaques, the "leader of the party of virtue" (320). To carry out this strategy, Julien's advisor, Korasoff, supplies him with "a set [of letters] for the loftiest virtue" from his "six volumes of manuscript loveletters" (320). They are complete with transmission instructions, such as the following for the first letter: "*These letters are delivered by hand: on horseback, black necktie, blue greatcoat. Hand the letter to the porter with an air of contrition; deep melancholy in the gaze. If one catches sight of a chamber maid, wipe the eyes furtively. Say a few words to the maid*" (328). This mock seduction is meant to be a "comedy," and because it lacks seriousness, Julien copies the letters "line for line without giving a thought to the sense" (330)—at one point he even forgets to alter the geographic references in his model (333). Despite these blunders, the letters eventually elicit responses, which Julien receives but does not read. Mathilde's discovery of these unopened responses forces her to acknowledge Julien's power over her and to resume their liaison.

These two parodic correspondences, and the one that follows between Mathilde and her outraged father, are merely preparatory to the famous letter from Mme de Rênal, which reinscribes Julien in the conjunction of social and economic class, ambition for power, and the use of seduction for personal gain:

> Born poor and greedy, this man [Julien] has tried by means of the most consummate hypocrisy, and by the seduction of a weak and wretched woman, to find himself a position and rise in the world. It is part of my painful duty to add that I am forced to believe M. J____ has no religious principles. In all conscience I am obliged to think that his way to rise in a household is to try to seduce the woman who is most influential there. Cloaking himself under the guise of disinterestedness and phrases from novels, he makes it his great and only end to gain control over the master of the house and his fortune. (362)

This letter was "required of her by her present confessor" (364), and as a dictated text it inverts Mme de Rênal's amazing management of epistolary transmission in book 1, chapter 20: "Anonymous Letters."

In this earlier epistolary situation, an anonymous letter to her husband apparently accused Mme de Rênal of adultery with Julien (the actual text of this letter is suppressed by the narrator; therefore, we join with Julien and Mme de Rênal in speculating on its contents). Counteracting this letter, Mme de Rênal rashly sent Julien a letter— "written in haste, stained with tears, and full of misspellings" (95)— pinned inside a book. In addition to convincing Julien not to engage his pride by seeking out their accuser, she asked him to copy, out of words cut from a book (an epistolary novel?), an "anonymous" letter that she had herself composed, would receive and then, "with an incredulous look," would give to M. de Rênal.

Crucially, however, in both this "anonymous" letter and the dictated letter she sends M. de La Mole, the addressee has only minor narrative significance; it is the second reader (in the former intended; in the latter unintended) who acts in response to the letter. With the first letter, we see only a modification in the plot of intrigue Julien builds around his affair with Mme de Rênal; with the second letter, all plots, all the lines of successful social transmission Julien has appropriated for himself, are ruptured. Julien reads in the letter sent to M. de La Mole the betrayal of his first love. In a characterized reader's response, he attempts to kill the letter's author, which reinscribes the comedy of epistolary activity as a tragic document that echoes many previous epistolary betrayals.

Gustave Flaubert was also aware of the power contained in a letter of dismissal. In *Madame Bovary* (1857),[7] Flaubert presents three letters of dismissal, each with a fully delineated narrative of transmission that is more significant to the novel's readers than are the letters themselves. The first is Rodolphe's dismissal of Emma after he tires of their adultery. With this letter, Flaubert demonstrates an advantage of inserting a letter within an extra-heterodiegetic narration. Rather than showing the letter simultaneously with its reading, he presents the letter as Rodolphe *writes* it. By focusing on the act of writing, the narrator oscillates the perspective between the page and the writer, thus revealing Rodolphe's cold, calculating consciousness of his letter's ironic rhetoric. Each paragraph of the letter is framed by an interpolated reflection on its contents by Rodolphe's detached narrating self, which constructs in the letter a purely fictional experiencing self; the escape from the constraints of desire is achieved by a transference into language, into empty rhetoric. But empty rhetoric requires flawless textuality, and as a final touch, Rodolphe says to himself,

> "There ought to have been some tears on this; but I can't cry; it isn't my fault." Then, having emptied some water into a glass, Rodolphe dipped his finger into it, and let a big drop fall on the paper, making a pale stain on the ink. Then looking for a seal, he came upon the one "*Amor nel cor.*"
> "Hardly the right thing under the circumstances ... But who cares?"
> Whereupon he smoked three pipes and went to bed. (147)

Emma's reaction to this letter is predictable. She receives it hidden in a basket of apricots: "They used to correspond this way before" (147). By using a transmission method that had previously signified pleasure through the letters sent, Rodolphe's calculated, yet feeble, attempt to let Emma down easily comes undone. At first, Emma cannot find a room of her own in which to read the letter; ultimately, she goes to the attic to read her fate. Her initial response is to contemplate leaping from the attic window. But Charles calls her back to her senses only to drive her out of her senses again by making unknowingly tactless references to Rodolphe's journey and to the delicious apricots.

The second dismissal letter in *Madame Bovary* (part 3, chapter 1) is an inversion of Rodolphe's letter. Emma writes this second letter, intending not to end an affair she has tired of but to cancel a rendezvous with Léon. However, because Emma does not have his address, an obstacle is placed before her moral desire to avoid erotic desire; and because the logic of epistolary transmission requires delivery, she decides to hand-deliver her letter (172). What follows in the novel is the famous cathedral scene and the infamous shuttered coach ride through the streets of Rouen. These scenes are inscribed within both the narrative of the rendezvous and within the narrative of transmission of Emma's letter. The letter, however, is never delivered—"'Read this!' she said, holding out a piece of paper to him. 'Oh no!' And she abruptly withdrew her hand" (174). Emma's "interminable letter," focalized through Léon, is reduced to "a piece of paper" bearing no significance, and during the coach ride, the letter is reduced even further: "around noon,... a bare hand appeared under the yellow canvass curtain [of the coach], and threw out some scraps of paper that scattered in the wind" (177). Comparing these two letters clearly shows that within an epistolary seductive discourse the man has the power to cancel the relationship, but the woman is trapped in a dialectics of desire that denies her the power either to avoid or to cancel the affair. Emma only had to return to Yonville, thereby breaking the rendezvous and protecting her virtue, but by engaging in a plot of epistolary transmission her fate is sealed.

Chillingly, Flaubert leaves the final letter of dismissal until the end, when Emma pens her suicide note, indicating precisely its time of reading to "the hour" (230). But what Emma has tried spare Charles by her avowal, "Let no one be blamed" (231), comes undone when after her death Charles discovers, first, Rodolphe's letter of dismissal (250), and then, Emma's secret archive of love letters: "Out of respect, or because he took an almost sensuous pleasure in dragging out his investigations, Charles had not yet opened the secret drawer of Emma's rosewood desk. One day, however, he sat down before it, turned the key, and pressed the spring. All Léon's letters were there. There could be no doubt this time. He devoured them to the very last, ransacked every corner, all the furniture, all the drawers, behind the walls, sobbing and shouting in mad distress. He discovered a box and kicked it open. Rodolphe's portrait flew out at him, from among the pile of love-letters" (253–54). As so often happens in nineteenth-century narrative, death does not stop the flow of transmission; instead, death redirects letters and other documents to unintended addressees. These archives, enclosed in their secret crypts, suddenly reveal to Charles a completely different Emma from the one he thought he knew—we may pity the cuckold his belated awareness of Emma's transgressions.

Although almost every novel contains letters and narratives of transmission, I will only cite one more example, James Joyce's *Ulysses* (1922).[8] There are many letters in Joyce's long novel of a single Dublin day, but the most interesting vis-à-vis the other texts discussed in this chapter is the correspondence between Bloom (a.k.a. Henry Flower) and Martha Clifford. In this clandestine correspondence between total strangers (Martha answers an advertisement: "Wanted, smart lady typist to aid gentleman in literary work" [131]), Joyce perfectly parodies all other epistolary tales. In other epistolary works we have discussed, we sense the exceptionality of the epistolary characters—that their virtues or faults are larger than life. But Bloom, in his quintessential mundaneness, is by far the most comic manifestation of the epistolary "rake."

Bloom corresponds under the *nom de plume* of Henry Flower, and he receives his transgressive letters at the Westland Row Post Office. Indeed, as the letter pops in and out of Bloom's consciousness throughout the day, we see that Bloom derives pleasure from the furtiveness of the correspondence and the fantasies it generates, rather than from any overriding desire for *actual* sexual contact. In this correspondence, sexuality has been deliberately textualized as innuendo; and although we can never know why Martha engages in this vicarious activity, it appears to be a harmless correspondence, free from the logic of presupposition and entailments that delimit other epistolary seductive discourses. Although he does not tell his wife Molly of his "clandestine correspondence" (605), she has caught him "scribbling something in a letter ... to somebody who thinks she has a softy in him" (609), and she is suspicious of Bloom's possible adulteries.

Yet Bloom's comic correspondence is counterpointed by a more significant letter that arrives at 7 Eccles Street early on 16 June 1904: Blazes Boylan's letter of assignation. This letter arrives in chapter 4 with the morning mail: "Two letters and a card lay on the hallfloor. He stopped and gathered them. Mrs Marion Bloom. His quickened heart slowed at once. Bold hand. Mrs Marion" (50). By his usual action of picking up the mail, Bloom becomes an ironic accessory to Molly's adultery: he plays the role of the cuckold postman. Both he and Molly know the letter's contents even before it is opened, so upon delivery, Molly delays her reading and places the letter within a narrative of secrecy by "tuck[ing] it under her pillow" (50). When Bloom returns to the bedroom with Molly's breakfast,

> A strip of torn envelope peeped from under the dimpled pillow. In the act of going he stayed to straighten the bedspread.

—Who was the letter from? he asked.

Bold Hand. Marion.

—O, Boylan, she said, He's bringing the programme.

—What are you singing?

—*Là ci darem* with J. C. Doyle, she said, and *Love's Old Sweet Song.*
(52)

Back downstairs again, Bloom thinks of his wife: "Mrs Marion. Reading lying back now, counting the strands of her hair, smiling, braiding. A soft qualm, regret, flowed down his backbone, increasing. Will happen, yes. Prevent. Useless: can't move.... He felt the flowing qualm spread over him. Useless to move now" (55). The shift in name in each of the passages just quoted signifies that this epistolary stage of Molly's adultery with Boylan has detached her from her self. She becomes the "addressee," Mrs Marion; thus, Bloom displaces his conception of Molly from his conception of the events by substituting Boylan's formal cover name. And although he knows, he can do nothing; and his reply to Martha, written at the same time Boylan is calling on Molly during the Sirens episode, is a feeble counterthrust against the adultery that overshadows his day. Unlike Charles Bovary or M. de Rênal, Bloom is too aware of his wife's transgression and his own inability to prevent it.

Boylan provides Molly with much-needed sexual fulfillment, but his epistolary fulfillment, as she recalls in her soliloquy (ch. 18), was not as complete:

> I hope hell write me a longer letter the next time if its a thing he really likes me O thanks be to great God I got somebody to give me what I badly wanted to put some heart up into me youve no chances at all in this place like you used long ago I wish somebody would write me a loveletter his wasnt much and I told him he could write what he liked yours ever Hugh Boylan in Old Madrid stuff silly women believe love is sighing I am dying still if he wrote it I suppose thered be some truth in it true or no it fills up your whole day and life always something to think about every moment and see it all round you like a new world I could write the answer in bed to let him imagine me[.] (624)

Molly's desire for love letters leads her to recall Mulvey's letter, "making an appointment" (625), which she received on Gibraltar and led to her first sexual experience (if not her first intercourse). But we sense, along with Molly, that the letter itself has fallen in stature. Mulvey's letter of "appointment" and Boylan's seemingly terse

message of assignation both suggest a businesslike precision to seduction, and that the endless letters of persuasion and seductive argument that constituted the eighteenth-century epistolary novel are
no longer functional. Letters have certainly not disappeared from
novels, but they no longer serve as readily as the centerpiece for
arguments of seduction and transgression. Nonetheless, if we momentarily speculate on what shape these novels would have if they
were wholly epistolary, we see that the shift to the inserted letter
has expanded the narrator's ability to depict the narrative of contact
and transmission producing each letter.

As we saw in chapter 3, the evolution of letters into diaries in
fictional narrative permitted one of the first techniques of presenting consciousness. *Les lettres portugaises*, *Pamela*, and *Die Leiden
des jungen Werthers* have all been considered as texts working out
primitive means for presenting individual consciousness. Diary
fictions then took this technique further, until more subtle methods
of presenting a character's consciousness, such as Joyce's in
Ulysses, were developed. As I indicated in the preceding section,
such texts as *Ulysses* and its famous precursor, Edouard Dujardin's
Les lauriers sont coupés (1887),[9] openly demonstrate their debt to
these earlier forms. Dujardin's novel has at its center an alternat-
ing presentation of letters and diary passages Daniel Prince rereads
as he awaits the appointed hour of his assignation with Leah. This
textual homage to the earlier forms underscores Dujardin's break
with traditional narrational techniques. As readers we come to see
both the woeful incompleteness of this archive of precious texts and
the absence of passion in the cold, formal, businesslike prose of
Leah's letters and much of Daniel's journal of their affair. The
"documentary evidence," as Daniel describes it, should be enough
to prove the emptiness of their affair; but the mind overrules the
text, and the affair continues.

Ulysses's other famous precursor, Joyce's own *A Portrait of the
Artist as a Young Man* (1916),[10] also provides us with an inserted
diary. John Paul Riquelme has written that narrative devices such
as inserted diaries "that interrupt and disrupt the semblance of a con-
tinuous flow of narrative draw attention to the text's artifice, to its
status as art, and to themselves as relatively independent of the text
in which they are found."[11] Such is the case with the concluding diary
in *A Portrait*, coming as it does at the end of a text presented by a
highly focalized, yet uncharacterized, extradiegetic narrator. When
this diary is considered by Joyce critics, it is often shown as either

an inconclusive and nearly incomprehensible trailing off or, as Susan Lanser observes, a radical shift in the narrating point of view that demonstrates Stephen's still unborn artistic voice—a voice that has yet learned to fulfill its speaker's aesthetic theory.[12] More recently, Michael Levenson has shown through a close reading of the diary that this concluding text recapitulates in "a cipher that we must learn to read" the major epiphanies of Stephen's life and the pre-diary narrative.[13]

Riquelme takes the diary's role in the narration of *A Portrait* a step further, and in doing so revives and revises the reading of Joyce's text as autobiography. Riquelme focuses not on the split the diary produces between the two narrating voices but on the interpenetration of voices and literary genres as the narrator's and the character's discourse become one. Riquelme achieves this conjunction by a nifty bit of reading that includes within the diary (and the novel) the last lines printed in the text: "Dublin 1904/Trieste 1914" (253). According to Riquelme these dates mark the period from the closure of the diary to closure of the writing of the novel, a period during which Stephen discovers his voice as an artist and thus writes *A Portrait*. The result is a conjoining of character, narrator, and author in a textual transaction that forces the reader to revise his or her sense of the narrative's production. Within this reordered context, the diary precedes the rest of the narrative, which is the reconstructed and rewritten journal/autobiography of Stephen James Dedalus Joyce. Rather than show Stephen's incompleteness as an artist or his unconscious recapitulation of his past, the diary marks the beginning of his career as "the uncreated conscience of [his] race" (253).

Although less frequent a narrative device, inserted diaries certainly are more disruptive in a text's narrating situation than most inserted letters. Similar to *A Portrait* in this respect is Charlotte Brontë's *Shirley* (1849),[14] which presents two of its thirty-seven chapters (chs. 29 and 36) as excerpts from Louis Moore's diary about his relationship with his eventual wife, Shirley Keeldar. What is intriguing about this inserted diary is that it comes from one of the masculine characters instead of either Shirley or Caroline Helstone, the novel's two heroines. However, *Shirley* represents an odd text among Brontë's novels because it eschews the autodiegetic narrating stance that make *Jane Eyre* and later *Villette* such masterpieces of woman's self-discovery. Moreover, Brontë appears to have been uncomfortable with the heterodiegetic mode, because the narrating style shifts often during the novel. Yet the diary remains most remarkable, for by surrendering the narrative discourse to the masculine pen of Moore, the narration prefigures Shirley's ultimate surrendering of her status as an independent woman by marrying Moore. From a feminist standpoint, this ending presents a paradox. Shirley coopts her independent life story for the dependent story of a "willingly controlled" wife, yet simultaneously, Brontë appears to parody the conventional marriage ending of the Victorian novel—possibly looking ahead already to the single woman's story in *Villette*.

Disruptions may occur even from outside the fictional narrating situation. André Gide's *Les faux-monnayeurs* (1925)[15] is a notable example of an inserted-diary text. The novel is arranged so that the narration alternates between the story and Edouard's journal, in which he writes of his plans to write a novel entitled *Les faux-monnayeurs*. As the reader quickly realizes, the slippage between the narrative levels forces the reader into a constant negotiation between the discourses in an effort to find out which discourse is the counterfeit narration. To compound the interpretive problem, Gide also wrote a piece called "Journal des faux-monnayeurs" that is often published with the novel. This latter work inscribes itself within both the literary and the narrating instances of the text, becoming a *mise en abyme* of Edouard's journal. Like Joyce's *A Portrait*, Gide forces genres into a dialogic blurring of voices that calls into question the narrative's ability to present a negotiable story drawn from the complexities of modern life.

Possibly the most curious of all the inserted diaries are those that claim diary status at the same time they reveal they are not true diaries at all. Daniel Defoe's *Robinson Crusoe* (1719)[16] contains a diary from the island, but it is embedded in a memoir of Crusoe's adventures, which are recollected in tranquility after his return. Likewise, Edgar Allan Poe's two long tales, *The Journal of Julius Rodman* (1840) and *The Narrative of Arthur Gordon Pym* (1838),[17] are recollected narratives cast in diary form. The editor of *Rodman* tells us that Rodman "merely kept an outline diary of his tour, during the many difficulties of its progress; and that the MSS. with which we have been furnished were not written out in detail, from that diary, until many years afterward" (1188). He also tells us that Rodman has "imbued what he has written with a vast deal of romantic fervor, very different from the luke-warm and statistical air which pervades most records of the kind" (1187). Similarly, Pym writes that he "kept no journal during a greater portion of the time" (1007) he was on his voyage; his dates for events "are given principally with a view to perspicuity of narration, and as set down in [his] pencil memoranda" (1176; note). In the narrative strategies of both Defoe and Poe, physical isolation primarily motivates the protagonist to keep some sort of journal.[18] But the diaries that exist are scant shadows of the published narratives; why, then, not cast the entire tale in memoir form and dispense with the artifice of the diary, or vice versa?

For Defoe, the diary form clearly suggested the verisimilitude necessary for this fiction (just as he would again make use of the form in 1722 for *A Journal of the Plague Year*). The formal realism of the document gives his text a greater illusion of reality; it puts the reader seemingly in closer contact with Crusoe's experiences on the island. The diary was not a viable method for the complete work because of a technological problem Crusoe wisely recognized: "A little after this [the anniversary of the first of twenty-eight years on the island] my ink began to fail me, and so I contented my self to use it more sparingly, and to write down only the most remarkable events of my life, without continuing a daily memorandum of other things" (86). A little later in his narrative, Crusoe recalls the uselessness of money, and how he "would have given it all for sixpenny-worth of turnip and carrot seed out of England, or for a handful of pease and beans, and a bottle of ink" (106). The need to write is equated in Crusoe's lament with the need of sufficient provisions. If, however, we read closely the part of *Crusoe* meant to represent the "Journal" (59–86),[19] many of the entries contain later interpolations that allow Crusoe to move backward and forward in his narrative, relating an event with either its causes or its consequences. In the structure of *Crusoe*'s narrative of transmission, therefore, the diary is embedded in the memoir to imply the reality of the events (although it is hardly a complete record of those events).

Over a century later, Poe borrowed Defoe's model for the adventure story: the protagonist confronting an unknown world. But while Defoe imitated the journal technique of real explorers, Poe set about debunking the genre of adventure literature by concocting narratives that explored the fantastic. *The Journal of Julius Rodman* is a fairly straightforward account of an expedition that crossed the Rocky Mountains more than a decade before Lewis and Clarke. Since the text is incomplete (Poe broke it off after only six chapters), we can only speculate on whether Rodman was destined for fantastic adventures. It seems likely he was, because he writes that he "was anxious to *go on*—to get, if possible, beyond the extreme bounds of civilization" (1237). Yet despite this desire to "go on" during the journey, the delay between his return from the expedition and his writing of the journal is quite long. Rodman is described as having a "peculiar disposition," and he "never made his own journey a subject of conversation; seeming, rather, to avoid the topic" (1189). In this reluctance to textualize (or even verbalize) his experience,

Rodman stages the separation of the experiencing self from the narrating self: unspeakable experiences have silenced the narrating impulse. According to the fictitious editors, Rodman's "only object in re-touching his original Diary was to oblige M. Michau" (1189), who had requested it; but in a narrative of transmission that anticipates the next two chapters of this study, we are told

> The MS. when completed, however, never reached M. Michau, for whose inspection it had been drawn up; and was always supposed to have been lost on the road by the young man to whom it was entrusted for delivery at M. M.'s temporary residence, near Monticello. Scarcely any attempt was made to recover the papers.... [But] the Diary, *which had been given into the hands of the messenger for delivery to M. Michau*, was found about three months ago, in a secret drawer of a bureau which had belonged to Mr. Julius R. We do not learn by whom it was placed there ... but ... we cannot help thinking that the supposition of the narrator's having, by some means, reprocured the package from the messenger, and concealed it where it was discovered, is very reasonable, and not at all out of keeping with the character of that morbid sensibility which distinguished the individual. (1189)

Poe, the master of encrypted mysteries, again presents a purloined letter, and the play of the passive verbs even further complicates this text transmission for which no one claims responsibility. As is often the case in Poe, the narrative of transmission is designed to heighten our interest by presenting an arabesque of mystery around the truth value of the text.[20]

Despite its interesting narrative of transmission, *Rodman* was hardly a success and is rarely reprinted, yet it is an important work for the appreciation of its precursor, *The Narrative of Arthur Gordon Pym. Pym* is closer to *Crusoe* in spirit, as both tell of ocean adventures and shipwrecks, but *Pym* goes beyond the unknown into the realm of the fantastic. Crusoe needed to write to make contact with himself and to record his creation of civilization in the absolute isolation of his island; Rodman and Pym both move "beyond the extreme bounds of civilization," but they are never absolutely isolated. Hence, their diaries are not fully motivated forms. Rodman constructs his retrospective diary in the related form of the travel chronicle, and Pym constructs a hybrid memoir/pseudo-diary containing occasional encyclopedic interpolations on nautical matters—including quotations from the journals of other Antarctic explorers. As Pym tells us, he writes his *Narrative* ten years after the events, and only then after "Mr. Poe, lately editor of the Southern Literary

Messenger,... [drew] up, in his own words, a narrative of the earlier portion of my adventures, from facts afforded by myself, publishing it in the Southern Messenger *under the garb of fiction*" (1007–8). Pym's preface is an attempt to reclaim "this *ruse*" and to announce his text as "a *regular* [emphasis added] compilation and publication of the adventures in question" (1008), which he signifies as "duty" to present the "truth."

Of course this wonderfully elaborate truth claim, plus the title—*The Narrative of* rather than *The Adventures of*—should alert us to the narrativity of what is to follow. Pym is making contact with the reader's expectations of truth, but the pseudo-diary passages throw us back into the narrating act rather than substantiating our expectations. Pym's preface foregrounds the separation between narrating self and experiencing self, but the diary sections inserted in the "narrative" give the illusion of a closer proximity between the two than actually exists. And readers have been fooled into reading the reconstructed pseudo-diary as a text written to the moment. In S. Foster Damon's reading of the novel, for instance, Pym is "sucked ... down to his death at the South Pole."[21] If this were the case, the narrative becomes void of its producer: the "Pym" who signs the preface in July 1838 would not be the same Pym of the last entry, "March 22, [1828]." If we read carefully the preface and pseudo-diary signals (e.g., proleptic statements of the consequences of an action, Pym's note as to the "perspicuity" of dating for ordering the text), we know Pym survives the "cataract," and that the continuation of the narrative is bound to reveal a fantastic voyage. But we read instead a "Note," the opening paragraphs of which ambiguously recount Pym's fate:

> The circumstances connected with the late sudden and distressing death of Mr. Pym are already well known to the public through the medium of the daily press. It is feared that the few remaining chapters which were to have completed his narrative, and which were retained by him, while the above were in type, for the purpose of revision, have been irrecoverably lost through the accident by which he perished himself. This, however, may prove not to be the case, and the papers, if ultimately found, will be given to the public.
>
> No means have been left untried to remedy the deficiency. The gentleman [Poe] whose name is mentioned in the preface, and who, from the statement there made, might be supposed able to fill the vacuum, has declined the task—this for satisfactory reasons connected with the general inaccuracy of the details afforded him, and his disbelief in the entire truth of the latter portions of the narration. (1180)

The accident recounted in the "Note" can be easily confused with that of the last entry in the pseudo-diary, and the diary form makes that confusion all the more plausible. In an essay on *Pym* (and *Rodman*), Stephen Mainville insists on conjoining Pym's death with the end of his narrative: "in *Pym* the alleged editor claims that his [editor's? Pym's?] narrative ... is a fragment, that it lacks two or three final chapters, these having been lost in the accident which kills Pym." Later in his essay, Mainville repeats this conjunction: "Pym's narrative breaks off at the climactic moment, as Pym and Peters are being swept into the cataract; and *Pym* ends with the editor's Note stating that the final two or three chapters of Pym's narrative were lost at the time of Pym's death."[22] I quote these redundant passages because, despite a blindness that seems to repeat S. Foster Damon's misreading, there is an insight in Mainville's conjunction. Pym's narration and *Pym* are two different texts: the former ends inconclusively with the rush over the cataract; the latter contains the former and ends with a note that closes the former and makes it finally transmissible. (The inclusion of Rodman's death in the editorial preface of that work serves the same purpose, only proleptically.) Pym, indeed, dies at the end of *Pym*, but the ending of his pseudo-diary represents a pseudo-death. At the end of the narration it is the "experiencing Pym" who, in effect, "dies," and the Note reports the death of the "narrating Pym" and the "reading Pym." Significantly, the editor characterizes Pym as in the act of "revision": the conjunction of writing and reading the chapter beyond the edge. Moreover, Poe, the author of the first portion and the urger of the remainder, is not the "alleged editor,"[23] and he disbelieves "the entire truth of the latter portions of the narration." The intricacy of Poe's aesthetic distancing leaves him many options for a sequel had *Pym* been a success: it wasn't.

Unlike *Crusoe*, *Pym* has no sequel; the final chapters are never found. Possibly they are locked in some secret drawer, as Rodman's diary was, but as it stands, the text transforms itself from an adventure tale to a novel about narrative transmission. During the course of his adventures, Pym is stripped of all human contact, except for Peters. When he comes to compose his narrative, he chooses to put long parts of the narration into a pseudo-diary format. The choice of this format immediately entails the problematics of closure—one cannot write beyond one's own death, even though that very death ensures the transmissibility of *Pym*. As suggested above, *Pym* is a novel of multiple closures: the plunge over the cataract, the return from adventures, the extra-"narrative" accident. Therefore, the abrupt ending of chapter 25 should be read not as the closure of the "adventures" but as the closure of a text—*The Narrative of Arthur Gordon Pym*. And we would be correct to follow Jean Ricardou's clever reading of the plunge into the cataract as the "voyage au bout de la page": the narrator's confrontation with the limits of our belief and with the ultimate white margin closing the text.[24] Pym's voyage allegorizes the narrating act and the narrative of that act's transmission.

To ENGAGE A TEXT of hybrid narrative transmission is to engage a narrative matrix that connects different voices and different acts of writing within what appears to be a unified whole, yet such hybrid texts also enact a competition for priority among the linked, enclosed, or alternated narrations. In one sense, novels of this sort find their most immediate formal ancestor in the letter-exchange novel, but the shift from enchained letters to enchained diaries (and other texts) constitutes a significant alteration of the transmission logic. This is especially true in a text discussed in the next chapter, Aphra Behn's *Love Letters between a Nobleman and His Sister*, in which the letter-exchange format gives way to an extra-heterodiegetic narrator who by the end is only summarizing rather than representing the letters.

Hybrid narratives are pieced together after closure, sometimes with the necessary addition of texts written after the completion of the significant events. Because of this mode of textual production, the narratives actuate hierarchies of meaning as the novel's narrative of transmission plays out a drama of intratextuality. The relationship the reader has with these novels is constantly fluctuating as narrator perspectives and attitudes shift, and as the fictional documents interact with one another. In addition to formal complexity, the three novels I will discuss here—*The Tenant of Wildfell Hall*, *The Woman in White*, and *The Golden Notebook*—all have in common narratives that explore mysteries of identity. Whether the mystery is of a widow's past, a crime of fraud that has erased a woman's past, or the loss of self, it requires the special characteristics of the hybrid.

Anne Brontë's *The Tenant of Wildfell Hall* (1848)[25] has been criticized as structurally weak. E. P. Whipple, for instance, in the October 1848 issue of the *North American Review*, complains of "the excessive clumsiness with which the [novel's] plot is arranged"[26]— a comment Winifred Gérin echoes: "Its weakness lies in the structure, in the clumsy device of a plot within a plot. (Did not Emily Brontë use the same in *Wuthering Heights*?)."[27] This facile comparison is inappropriate, however; *Wuthering Heights* relies on the testimony of a witness and the transcription of an outsider to delimit its enclosed plot structure. *The Tenant of Wildfell Hall*, on the other hand, presents us with the key text of its protagonist—Helen Graham/Huntingdon—enclosed in a continuing letter her second husband—Gilbert Markham—writes to his brother-in-law long after the central events of the story have occurred. In a spatial description the plots are arranged similarly, but as I will show in chapter 8 for *Wuthering Heights* and here for *Wildfell Hall*, the arrangement is far from clumsy.[28]

Gérin tries to bolster her argument for clumsiness by citing George Moore's comments on the novel in his *Conversations in Ebury Street*. Gérin writes:

> He considered that the "weaving of the narrative in the first hundred fifty pages revealed a born story-teller," but deplored that half-way through the book Anne broke down[:] "Not from lack of genius but of experience. An accident would have saved her, *almost any man of letters would have laid his hand upon her arm and said*: You must not let your heroine give her diary to the young farmer ... Your heroine must tell the young farmer her story, and an entrancing scene you will make of the telling ... The presence of your heroine, her voice, her gestures, the questions that would arise and the answers that would be given ... would preserve the atmosphere of a passionate and original love story. The diary broke the story in halves ..." How right was Moore! By the device of the diary the drama that wrecked Helen's life is seen at one remove, not in the heat of action, in the palpitating moments of hurt and disillusion, at the height of anger and recrimination.[29]

Although both Moore and Gérin ultimately praise the novel, their reservation about its hybrid narrative transmission reveals a species of reading that tends to disparage complicated narrating situations in favor of a consistent narrating voice. But would they get the kind of narrative they imagine if the patronizing sexist advice, given by Moore, a patriarchal "man of letters," had been followed?

The part of the text Moore praises is the memoir letter written in 1847, nearly twenty years after the events it recounts—Gilbert Markham's meeting and falling in love with the supposed widow Helen Graham. In the narrative of transmission the reader is already at a remove, voyeuristically reading over the shoulder of Jack Halford, Markham's brother-in-law and addressee. The picture of Helen that Markham presents is of a strong woman with decided opinions; she is far from the caricature of the romantic widow through which he first attempts to define her and far from the scandalous caricature created by the gossips of the town, including Markham's own sister. This is a wiser and warier Helen, fresh from her trials with her husband, Arthur Huntingdon. The shift to the diary that Moore deplores is a crucial move in Brontë's feminist plot; it allows Helen's voice to come to the reader with only minimal mediation. Her devoted husband Markham would most likely preserve the integrity of her text (he shows care throughout his portions of the text in accounting for any document transcribed into his letter). However, Markham does admit to editing the diary for transcription (147), and he goes on to paratextually construct our reading of the diary by naming its opening chapter "The Warnings of Experience" (148). These editorial actions are significant for our overall reading of the text, since the significance of the mediation that does occur lies in the social nature of the narrative of transmission. We read the diary aware of whom Helen has become; thus, when we read in the diary the thoughts of the naïve and then rapidly matured woman, we must read through the context of the strong picture of her Markham has provided. Moreover, as Jan Gordon has observed, we read the diary as a countertext to the "gossip" of Linden-Car.[30]

Gossip is an exceedingly effective narrative device because it evokes incessant yet usually flawed transmission and it always raises questions as to its authority. As Gordon points out, the role of gossip in *Wildfell Hall* is to "devalue" Helen by either "'speculating'" or "'inflating'" her past and her present. This is clearly evident in Markham's mistaken belief in the gossip surrounding Helen's mysterious relationship with her landlord/brother Frederick.[31] Such a fraudulent discourse must be appropriated, melted down, and remade into legal tender—made into a text that fixes and contains the tale, therefore cutting it off from the counterfeiting action of gossip's speculation. This reminting of the tale is doubly important to the narrative of transmission because Halford has married, in Markham's sister, one of the gossips. The letter frame of *Wildfell Hall* makes clear at once that Markham tells his tale in exchange for "a very particular and interesting account of the most remarkable occurrences of [Halford's] early life" (33). The story Markham tells is hardly completely unknown to his brother-in-law, but Markham may fear that Rose's possibly still counterfeit account needs to be reminted.

Yet the narrative produces a paradoxical text. On the one hand we have a subversive text, Helen's diary, that tells the story of her extraordinary (for the time) flight from her drunken and debauched husband, from what N. M. Jacobs has called a "domestic hell."[32] This narrative of a woman's escape from the tyranny of marriage clearly articulates a feminist demand for fair treatment and for individual courage to overturn the status quo. But on the other hand, as Gordon makes clear, "the frame restores historicity" to "the gossip, diaries, partial letters, and other fragments of floating writing or speech" in the narrative.[33] By transcribing and enclosing the tale, Markham remints the tale within the conventions of the patriarchal, Victorian happy ending. The warning Markham intends is for women to choose carefully when entering matrimony, for the transmission of property—a crucial determinant in the history of sexual rights, since women rather than men traditionally have been responsible for the legitimacy of their children—depends on the fidelity of both the husband and the wife. In her novel, Brontë is striking out at the sexual double standard; but she also reinscribes her heroine within a transformed masculine life history. She thereby redeems Helen from the transgression of her earlier flight from her husband while still marking the revolutionary aspect of her text.

Jacobs, however, has found this reinscription particularly troubling in both *Wildfell Hall* and *Wuthering Heights*: "In both ... we approach a horrific private reality only after passing through and then discarding the perceptual structures of a narrator—significantly, a male narrator—who represents the public world that makes possible and tacitly approves the excesses behind the closed doors of these pre-Victorian homes."[34] Jacobs observes that the feminine texts embedded in the masculine narrations serve to "delegitimize" the patriarchal culture text that condones domestic abuse and to demythologize both Helen's and Gilbert's premarriage naïveté about romantic domestic bliss. Helen is transformed through her experience; Gilbert is transformed through his reading of Helen's diary—the textualization of the unspeakable conditions of the Huntingdon household. Significantly, Gilbert finds his own flirtatious plots to incite Helen's interest in him mirrored by Huntingdon's sadistic recounting to Helen tales of his amorous indiscretions in a narrative economy that devalues Helen to a point of self-bankruptcy (a bankruptcy that further mirrors the economic lack that defines Helen's subjection to a husband incapable of love). Upon reading the diary, Gilbert finds his conventional masculinity symbolically castrated, only to be eventually reclaimed when he follows Helen to Staningley Hall at the novel's close. As Jacobs concludes, "The effect on Gilbert of reading this document—of being admitted into the reality hidden within and behind the conventional consciousness in which he participates—is revolutionary, and absolutely instrumental to the partnership of equals their marriage will become."[35]

In a reprise of *Wildfell Hall*, Walter Hartright in Wilkie Collins's *The Woman in White* (1860)[36] also must reclaim his wife from the ashes of a disastrous marriage. Sir Percival Glyde descends from Arthur Huntingdon, just as Hartright and Markham represent the ideal reformed gentleman; however, the character of Helen is split in Collins's novel into Laura Fairlie (the wronged wife and the beautiful object of Hartright's love) and Marian Halcombe (Laura's plain half-sister). Marian has a more "masculine" intelligence, and, importantly, she writes the diary that is the central text of this hybrid narrative. Although the plots differ significantly, they share the basic contours of the female escape plot, and they both rely on a hybrid narrative transmission that is mirrored by concerns of genealogic and economic transmission within the plot.

Wildfell Hall opens with Markham's father's dying wish that Gilbert "transmit the paternal acres to [his] children" (35); and the tale ends with Gilbert's transference of this legacy to his brother because he will join Helen at Staningley, the large estate she has inherited from her uncle. Thus in addition to its narrative of textual transmission, *Wildfell Hall* also contains a narrative of genealogical transmission, "that maintenance of property from one generation to the next that made the Victorian will such an instrument of social control and order."[37] *The Woman in White*, likewise, turns on two questions of genealogical transmission: (1) Laura's inheritance, of which both Sir Percival and Count Fosco will defraud her; and (2) Sir Percival's forging of the church marriage record so that he can fraudulently claim the Glyde title and lands in the first place. Moreover, Laura is held by paternal law in her engagement to Sir Percival: as Marian Halcombe tells Hartright, "It is an engagement of honour, not of love—her father sanctioned it on his death-bed" (62). Although by 1860 contract marriages were on the wane in both life and the novel, this deathbed contract underwrites the complex matrix of transmission, identity, and legality that haunted the Victorian novel and fired Collins's sensation plot.

Borrowing from Gothic fiction the conventions of the asylum, the double, and abduction, Collins weaves a plot in which Laura is replaced in the eyes of the legal world by Anne Catherick, the lookalike companion of her youth. Anne dies a day too early for the plans of Sir Percival and Fosco, so the death certificate that fraudulently lists Laura's death instead of Anne's is officiously transmitted by the doctor attending in Fosco's absence. Laura, in turn, *two days after* her "officially recorded" death, replaces Anne as a prisoner in the asylum from which she had escaped at the opening of the novel. It is by this document (a descendant of the Gothic convention of the discovered document) and by the discrepancy of dates that the counterfeit plots are uncovered, Laura's identity restored, and her premature tombstone erased. But Collins inverts the novel's play of fraudulent texts by constructing the narrative from a sequential set of narrations produced by the participants in the events—some written in the midst of the events narrated, some written afterward at Hartright's request. Hartright intends the collective narrative to validate his wife's true identity and thus erase the forged text she has become through the fraudulent death certificate.

Certainly the most infamous narrator in the text is Fosco, a master in the tradition of Lovelace and Valmont of intercepting transmissions and controlling the power of the spoken and the written word. Fosco, often through the agency of his wife, overhears some of Marian and Laura's private conversations and intercepts nearly all of Marian's letters seeking aid or protection for the subjected Lady Glyde. During Marian's illness he takes this appropriation of Marian's discourse a step farther and reads her diary, penning at its conclusion an audacious letter praising Marian and her text: "Yes! these pages are amazing. The tact which I find here, the discretion, the rare courage, the wonderful power of memory, the accurate observation of character, the easy grace of style, the charming outbursts of womanly feeling, have all inexpressibly increased my admiration of this sublime creature, of this magnificent Marian" (308). As Peter Brooks observes, Fosco's reading marks "a remarkable moment of reversal in which our readerly intimacy with Marian is violated, our act of reading adulterated by profane eyes, made secondary to the villain's reading and indeed dependent on his permission."[38] Fosco's vanity and confidence in the fraudulent text he constructs for Sir Percival let him, like a father reading his daughter's diary, restore the text to its owner: "Finally, those sentiments dictate the lines—grateful, sympathetic, paternal lines—which appear in this place. I close the book. My strict sense of propriety restores it (by the hands of my wife) to its place on the writer's table. Events are hurrying me away. Circumstances are guiding me to serious issues. Vast perspectives of success unrol [sic] themselves before my eyes. I accomplish my destiny with a calmness which is terrible to myself" (308).

Fosco's cryptic references to "events," "eircumstances," "vast perspectives of success," and his "destiny" refer to the identity switch he is about to put into action, but the success that unrolls ultimately unravels, prompting Fosco's confession letter and the scene of its writing. This masterpiece within the novel's narrative of transmission relies on a complex semiotics of transmission and transgression. As it turns out, Fosco too has a secret life history, a history of political transgression in Italy. Hartright stumbles onto this clue to Fosco's other identity through his old friend and teacher Pesca's life story as a political exile. With this speculation and the knowledge of the codes of vengeance that define Pesca's duty concerning political transgressors, Hartright constructs an intricate epistolary plot—a sealed letter that would reveal Fosco, but which must remain sealed until dawn and be returned unopened if Hartright is successful—to force Fosco's hand to inscribe the confession of his guilt (which he denies to the last: "Is my conduct worthy of any serious blame? Most emphatically, No!" [571]) and the restoration of Laura's identity: "I might have taken Lady Glyde's life.... [I] took her identity, instead" (571). As Fosco concludes his confession with the bravado that marks his life, he also rehearses the theme of usurped inheritance that undergirds the text: "I announced, on beginning it, that this narrative would be a remarkable document. It has entirely answered my expectations. Receive these fervid lines—my last legacy to the country I leave forever" (571). Ironically, the confession of one crime only precedes the carrying out of Fosco's sentence to die for another. Fosco's text is indeed his last will and testament.

The novels of Anne Brontë and Wilkie Collins rely on suspense plots derived from Gothic conventions to resolve the mysteries of identity that prompt their narratives of transmission. Thus the narrative of transmission connecting and presenting the various documents inscribes each text's claims to reliability and truth, however much those claims might be contravened by the unbelievability of the narrative itself. In solving the mysteries of identity generating their plots, these nineteenth-century texts clearly mark in their documentary forms (letters, diaries, memoirs, marriage records, death certificates, wills, and tombstones) the power of texts to confer identity and a sense of self within nineteenth-century society; twentieth-century hybrid texts pose a different problem. Prose fiction had passed through a number of different conceptions by the time it reached the latter half of the twentieth century. Sentimentalism, romanticism, realism, naturalism, and modernism—to name a few— have all left significant marks on narrative conventions. But more significantly this evolution of narrative conventions and techniques left hybrids in a precarious position. The epistolary, diary, and memoir conventions of formal realism were hardly possible now except on either naïve or parodic levels. Nonetheless, the twentieth century's literary preoccupations with reflexivity and a distrust of language's pure referentiality (along with the advent of psychoanalysis) saved fictional letters, diaries, and memoirs, and allowed them to prosper in a changed literary context. This prospering, however, was often at the expense of precisely those qualities of genuineness, validation, expressiveness, and immediacy that had first marked the mimetic qualities of these narrative techniques. This fusion of twentieth-century concepts and a literary distrust of techniques of formal realism is exemplified in Doris Lessing's *The Golden Notebook*.

Although often cited as a "diary novel," *The Golden Notebook* (1962)[39] hardly resembles a conventional diary—either fictional or actual. The reader enters the novel's structure through a frame novella, entitled "The Free Women." This extra-heterodiegetic narration about a novel writer named Anna Wulf is divided into five parts, and between the parts are excerpts from Anna's notebooks. So far, there is nothing very strange about this arrangement; but the reader comes to realize that the notebooks and the novella do not correspond, and although "The Free Women" is written in a realist style, it fails to offer an authoritative text by which the reader may judge the notebooks. The notebooks themselves also break with diaristic convention in that Anna keeps four notebooks (in colored covers: black, red, yellow, and blue) simultaneously, and she divides her self into four parts to give each notebook a distinct perspective and theme. The notebooks identify *The Golden Notebook* as a diary novel, yet the convention of dated entries is maintained only sporadically. Therefore the juxtaposed sections from the notebooks produce only ambiguous conjunctions of events in Anna's life. Ultimately, Anna gives up her four notebooks for a "Golden Notebook" in which she records the final breakdown of her psyche. In this notebook we discover Anna's lover dictating the first line of Anna's next novel: "The two women were alone in the London flat." As readers of Lessing's novel know, this is precisely the sentence that opens "The Free Women" and, coincidentally, *The Golden Notebook*.

This moment of narrative inversion affects our reading of Lessing's novel because it undermines any stable point of reference, and it signifies this novel's formlessness—despite a nearly schematic arrangement of its various texts—compared to conventional realist practice. Yet in seeming contravention, this moment of narrative indeterminacy is the fully intended product of narrative form. Lorna Martens reminds us that Lessing described *The Golden Notebook* as "'an extremely carefully constructed book,' ... [whose] 'meaning is in the shape.'"[40] Yet the meaning Anna Wulf expresses over and over again in her notebooks is the breakdown of language's ability to order or "form" the world into any true or understandable shape. As this study has sought to make clear, diaries and letters were used in eighteenth- and nineteenth-century texts to at least maintain the fiction that a document was genuine, which served on one level to validate the text by providing a pseudo-referential record of the events written. Twentieth-century narratives, however, use diaries or letters to create a tension within the novelistic vision exploring the discontinuity, fragmentization, and open-endedness both of the text and of life itself.

Thus in reading *The Golden Notebook* as a twentieth-century example of diary fiction, H. Porter Abbott points to the reflexive drama of form (writing) and formlessness (existence) as they interact in Anna Wulf's attempts to write a text—novel or notebook—that will somehow tell the truth. Using Anna's psychoanalysis and mental breakdown as a focal point, Abbott shows how the hybrid of the notebooks and the novella can be used as a textual field in which the character can rediscover self—a metaphysical wholeness—in the midst of a historical fragmentization of the word and the world.[41] Martens comes to much the same conclusion, but from the direction of seeing the novel's dualistic presentation of fragmentization and wholeness in a theme of unity:

> Lessing's idea of splitting the diary into four allows her ... to make her point in several different ways. First, the four-fold diary mirrors Anna's split personality; second, the protagonist's problem stands for a universal condition of partial perception that is caused by social fragmentization and aggravated by the restrictive categories language imposes on our understanding. Third, the division into four also gives Lessing room to show the failure of language by example, by having Anna Wulf explore four different variations on a scale from fictional to factual writing and to fail in four different, exemplary ways. The contrasting Golden Notebook establishes the theme of unity. In it Anna experiences pure presence and attains transsubjectivity, which means a breakthrough out of mental illness. Presence is mediated through a cinematic form that is supposed to represent the dissolution of all artistic form. The Golden Notebook also, supposedly, effaces point of view (symbolized by the dual point of view) and therefore, in theory, achieves and symbolizes the ideal transsubjectivity.[42]

Crucial to Abbott's and Martens's readings is the play of the diary technique—a technique once seen as a stabilizing force—against a discontinuous world view that sees human beings distrusting language's ability to produce images of their existence, a distrust that consequentially cuts them off from any sense of complete presence in the written word. Ultimately, the diary (the letter, as well) symbolizes a myth of genuineness, an allegory of writing and reading the world. But to restrict *The Golden Notebook* to its diary aspects is avoid certain questions seated in its narrative of transmission. (Some of these questions I will address in the next chapter when I discuss the unnamed editor and arranger of the text.) Lessing has built a text that defies simple categorization by conventional genre indicators; instead, we read a collage of texts that intersect, overlap, and pull apart as we try to organize them into a narrative logic. The hybridization of discourses does not conjoin to solve a mystery; rather, it marks the complexity of the individual writer, and in so doing, it possibly represents more fully than earlier diary or epistolary texts the problematics of writing the self.

More than coincidentally, all three novels focus on problematics of female identity. Indeed some other works organized around hybrid transmission strategies—Caroline Norton's autobiographical account of her disastrous marriage, *English Laws for Women in the Nineteenth Century* (1854), Robert Browning's *The Ring and the Book* (1868–69),[43] and Bram Stoker's *Dracula* (1897), for instance—also have at their centers plots about female identity. In Norton's case it is the real life quest for a legal identity to present her claims against her tyrannical husband; in Browning's poetic novel it is Pompilia's fateful attempt to escape the repressive identity her husband imposed upon her ; and in *Dracula* it is the ultimate mythic tale of a horrific patriarch, the vampire, who not only sucks the blood of his victims but recreates them in his own image. These texts play out the search of women, especially women writers, for an adequate and individual form to tell the stories of their lives. Hybrid narratives of transmission figure in their narrative intricacy the difficulty conventional forms have in representing the woman's story—George Moore's paternalistic advice to Anne Brontë was, in the end, no advice at all.

5 | The Opening Frame of Narration

We think it our duty to warn the public that, in spite of the title of this work and of what the editor says about it in his preface, we cannot guarantee its authenticity as a collection of letters: we have in fact, very good reason to believe that it is only a novel.
—Laclos, "Publisher's Note," *Les liaisons dangereuses*

Vous pourriez lire ces envois comme la préface d'un livre que je n'ai pas écrit.
—Derrida, "Envois," *La carte postale*

FROM THE HOMERIC SINGERS to Cervantes in his preface to *Don Quixote*, authors have framed their tales with claims of either authority or nonauthority. The Homeric singer of tales always called on the Muses to inspire and authorize his epic song. Cervantes, on the other hand, denies authority by claiming not to "father" his text but to "stepfather" it, and as we saw in chapter 1, even this displacement of authority is compounded by the fiction of Cid Hamete Benengeli and the Arabic history of Don Quixote that must be translated. Amid its problematic play on authority, *Don Quixote* also articulates a second function of narrative framing: the authenticating or validation of the transmitted text. The rise of the novel since Cervantes has been marked by "editors," "publishers," and others who claim that the texts they pass on are historically authentic by elaborating, in Philip Stewart's phrase, "some fable about the origins of the manuscript."[1]

Critics have often denigrated these opening frames of narration as crude conventions that lost their effectiveness almost immediately. However, as modern-day literary hoaxes have proved, it sometimes takes quite a while to discover that both the frame and the tale are counterfeit. Still, despite the transparent nature of the convention, writers continue to use it for certain texts. To see clearly why such an obvious device can still have an effect, we must reconsider how we read such claims of authenticity and authority in the late twentieth century. In the wake of deconstructive and reader-response theories, reading is no longer characterized as a naïve or passive act motivated only by a text's plot of actions. Instead, reading has increasingly become a hermeneutic activity that actively engages the text in its own production of meaning and induces pleasure from constituting plots of questions and plots of transmission within the narrative. In this mode of reading, one interrogates the textual margins—the prefaces, notes, afterwords, etc.—that frame the fictions within an already interpreted context, frames that become in themselves objects of interpretation. In this *frame*work, conventional claims of textual authenticity and editorial authority metonymically engage themes of authenticity and authority ordering the framed tales. Before examining this relationship of framing narrative to framed narrative, we need to develop an operating procedure for analyzing the fictional editor's position in the narrative text.

Fictional editorial texts take the form of prefaces, notes, afterwords, and occasional textual intrusions; and, as in the epistolary novel discussed in chapter 2, they form an extradiegetic relationship to the document discovered. This narrating relationship is not always fully considered by readers, who often overlook these parts of the text. Gérard Genette, however, has devoted an entire study, *Seuils,* to the various "paratexts," as he terms them, that surround the fictional narrative (though one could extend Genette's categories of paratexts to all texts).[2] Genette is not only concerned with prefaces, afterwords, and notes in the structuration of narrative textuality; he is also interested in the textual features of title pages, epigraphs, tables of contents, dedications, and the name of the author. Moreover, there are extrafictional elements such as belated prefaces, interviews with the author, and biographical materials either provided by the author or uncovered by scholarship. Genette's point is that these paratextual elements function in a narrative's textuality by conditioning the reader in the direction of particular responses. Readers regularly ignore these directions, although the more authorial the directives the harder it is to ignore their effect on the texts that immediately follow them. Nevertheless, the paratextual elements must be part of interpretive reading if one seeks critical understanding of narrative texts. Paratexts are primary sites where we can locate narratives of transmission that are at times quite elaborate and as interesting as the texts they contain.

Significantly, the editor is *within the fiction* in many narrative texts; he or she is an extradiegetic narrator and *not* the author. As the arranger of the letters or discoverer of the diary, the editor handles the physical texts from the fictional world, even though his or her own story is usually temporally and spatially detached from the events related in the documents. Such editors, through their relationship with the intradiegetic texts they present, are part of the narrating instance of the text. Their power to include or exclude material significantly mediates the text presented. Editors not only assert the "authenticity" of the documents they present; they also claim authority over interpretation by conditioning the reader to a particular textual response. Readers may accept or dismiss such prefaced or appended interpretations, but to see editors as only a "bridge" or "intermediary," suggesting that they only passively transmit the text, is to read incompletely.

Nonrecognition of the editor's status in the fiction easily arises. All readers of narrative risk eliding narrating levels, and only careful reading can avoid misconstruing one level for another or excluding a level altogether. Susan Lanser has sensibly set forth the characteristics of "real readers" when confronted with an unidentified narrative voice: "In the absence of direct markings which separate the public narrator from the extrafictional voice, so long as it is possible to give meaning to the text within the equation author = narrator, readers will conventionally make this equation."[3] Nonetheless, as Bertil Romberg cautions, "The editor must be considered as a part of the fiction, whether the author makes of him an autonomous person equipped with fictitious civic rights and status and a fictitious past, or else himself appears in his person and lends him his name."[4] Of course the latter case raises interesting interpretive questions developing out of the signifying power of the proper name: we tend to accept more readily the speech acts we can identify with a historical speaker. As readers and interpreters, our hermeneutic desires lead us to seek an authorized voice whose speech acts we can believe. Because we construct "implied" or "postulated" authors and "extrafictional voices" to discuss the relation between textual meaning and the author, we must also construe this editor as a fictional and dialogic construct that might share the author's name but does not necessarily mark his or her presence, attitudes, or ideology. Similarly, the readers addressed in an editor's preface and notes should not be automatically construed as "you and I"; they too are a construct, although at some interpretive moments we might see ourselves through their eyes.

The problem of transmission at the extradiegetic level of narrating is in the contact formed by our mimetic expectations of the "Preface." Our desire for authenticity and authority posits that we read the fictional preface as demystifying the text. When we read diaries or collections of real letters by famous people, we might question an editor's motives concerning the text as these are revealed through a preface, but we rarely, if ever, question the authenticity of the editor or the reality of the editing act (questions of scholarly editing are another matter). Extradiegetic fictional prefaces often raise questions about the authority of the intradiegetic narration and the metadiegetic narrative of events, the truth of the text—and they are just as often intended this way.

Yet sometimes the actual authors either become the targets of unsympathetic critics or choose to reveal themselves and their texts' fictionality. The paratexts produced at this level of narration form what I will call an *historiodiegesis*: the actual author's belated discourse about the narrative. My term echoes the terminology of Genette, although in his own work on these elements he does not name their relation to the fictional narrations they frame. These paratexts belong to the literary instance of the work, but whether they are authorial prefaces, published advertisements, or some other public document, they can alter the text's horizon of reception, and thereby its interpretation. For my purposes here I exclude from historiodiegetic consideration any biographical materials (letters, diaries, interviews, or conversations, etc.) compiled and made available to the public by someone else. These latter materials have significant value to be sure, and may exert historiodiegetic pressure on the reader's production of textual meaning, but I am more interested here, and particularly in the next chapter, in authors' overt attempts to control the reading of their texts within the textual frames they devise.

Fictional prefaces are extradiegetic paratexts that suggest a reading of the narrative and an extradiegetic reader to complete that reading. As such, they frame and create an interpretive context within the text's fictional universe, which in turn affects our own interpretive acts. By contextualizing the narrative in certain ways, the extradiegetic frame makes interpretation possible by constituting a dialogue between the editorial voice of authority and the questioning voice of the reader. To study the narrative of transmission occurring at the extradiegetic level, we need to examine the narrating situation and the narrating subject of the extradiegetic narration. Therefore, the next two sections will examine the editorial narrations surrounding some epistolary and diary texts to see how the extradiegetic narrative of transmission affects our reading of the intradiegetic narration of the metadiegetic events. At the close of the chapter I will return briefly to how the question of historiodiegesis can affect the extradiegetic paratexts discussed.

EPISTOLARY FICTION does not always include an editor; however, built into the form is the presupposition that someone collects, edits, transcribes, and prepares the letters for publication. This editor usually addresses the readers with a preface, notes, or by intratextual interpolation. But as Valerie Raoul observes concerning fictional diaries, "the absence of an editorial frame is a sign of fiction in itself, since real journals [and real collections of letters] usually have one."[5] Other framing devices can be used; for example, Mary de la Rivière's epistolary tale "From a Lady to a Lady" (1711) intercalates an epistolary correspondence within a longer letter-memoir written long after the narrated events. Or in another case, John Littleton Costeker, in *The Constant Lovers* (1731), alternates a extra-heterodiegetic narration with the letters as they occur in the story.[6] These examples of extradiegesis, however, do not strenuously claim authenticity, and the epistolary sections of these narratives, like those examined in the preceding chapter, are subordinated to different narrating logics. In epistolary texts the letters should tell their own story, but the degree of authority exercised by an editor over the extradiegetic (and ultimately our own) reading of the arranged collection raises different interpretive questions; the narrative logic of the imitated documents themselves can be subsumed by an editor's didactic purposes.

Aphra Behn introduces her epistolary work *Love Letters between a Nobleman and His Sister* (1684–87)[7] with an "Argument" that foregrounds the textual correspondence that begins *in medias res*. At the end of the Argument is a paragraph narrating the fable of the collection's origin: "After their flight, these letters were found in their [Philander and Sylvia's] cabinets, at their house at St *Denis*, where they both liv'd together for the space of a year, and they are as exactly as possible placed in the order they were sent, and were those supposed to be written towards the latter end of their amours" (2). The editor invokes the "found text" convention, which, one imagines, was fairly fresh in 1684 and effective for establishing a believable narrative of transmission. Significantly for the many narratives of transmission to follow Behn's text, these letters have been left behind, orphaned within the world of discourse before they are "adopted" by the editor—the surrogate parent for the texts created by others. The editor also suggests the editorial function of arrangement and the re-presentation of only the "latter end" of the correspondence. The Argument, therefore, serves an important narrative purpose by establishing motivations for the dangerous liaison that will follow.

The editor occasionally comments within the text, usually to indicate where a letter was sent from or to describe a physical peculiarity in the letter: "*Writ in a pair of tablets*" (41), "*This letter was found torn in pieces*" (45), "*Written in a leaf of a table-book*" (94). At one significant point after Sylvia and Philander have fulfilled their erotic desire, the editor describes the reception of one of Philander's letters that is delivered outside the usual messenger system of the lovers' servants: "*That which was left in her hands by* Monsieur, *her father, in her cabinet*" (92). This last example, with the editorial frame all but giving way to the doubled authority of "Monsieur, *her father*," powerfully prefigures Clarissa's and Julie's clashes with patriarchal codes of behavior, and it underwrites the dangers of transmission. As the epistolary novel evolves, these devices will be reused and refined, but the editor's inclusion of these details about the transmission of the documents affects how we read the letters. In later novels the correspondence will internalize these devices, either reported by a third party or self-consciously marked in the letter itself. Behn also gives us an example of this internalization when Philander writes to Sylvia: "*I conjure you to burn this* [letter], *for writing in haste I have not counterfeited my hand*" (41). Significantly it is the letter writer and not the editor who recounts that the handwriting of the letters has been disguised—is this the clue the editor/detective might use to identify the correspondents?

Clearly, knowing that Sylvia's father has intercepted and read one of her letters is as important to our interpretation of this narrative of transgression as a similar interception and reading is for our interpretations of Pamela, Clarissa, Julie, Cécile, and Mme de Tourvel. However, Behn's text, for all its formal realism, derives more from the courtly love tradition of romance than from an emerging bourgeois ideology or a yet-to-emerge aesthetic of realism. Thus the Argument does not didactically suggest that the text might have a pragmatic, instructional value. Indeed, as we read the first volume of letters negotiating and then recounting the adultery and "incest" of the lovers (Sylvia is Philander's sister-in-law) we engage in the debate over "love and honor" that seems to honestly align two individuals whom Philander argues are "destined" for love despite societal prohibitions. By volume 2, however, the passion on Philander's part has begun to cool and the increased presence of the editor/narrator parallels Sylvia's complaint that he has abandoned a "lover's rhetoric" (177). As the reader already knows and Sylvia soon discovers, he has abandoned her in fact by pursuing the married Calista. Just as Sylvia prefigures such later heroines as Clarissa in her need to escape tyrannical parents and Julie or Cécile in her naïveté, Philander prefigures Lovelace and Valmont, and Calista prefigures Mme de Tourvel. Behn marks the physical and psychological distance among her characters by increasing the role of the editor/narrator to the point that by the end of the narrative she merely reports that letters were sent. This disappearance of the epistolary text figures the decline in love and the absolute loss of "honor."

Thus, although the initial volume's Argument avoids moralizing to overdetermine the libertine logic in the dialectics of desire inscribed in the letter exchange, the narrative progresses to uncover Philander's treachery and the social construction of Sylvia as an avenging prostitute. Significantly, the lovers receive no final punishment: Philander is ironically reclaimed by the Royal court and Sylvia is left to ply her trade. Nevertheless, *Love Letters between a Nobleman and His Sister*—its very title paratextually underwrites the theme of social transgression—marks the epistolary novel's concern, as a subgenre, with the entailments of transgressive desire, as I argued in chapter 2. Here, however, we see a result different from the recuperative marriage or punishing death. Sylvia learns, as Mme de Merteuil will a century later, to dissemble her texts (her last represented intrigue involves an elaborate cross-dressing and disguise) in ways that allow her to undo and ruin her lovers economically while her already "undone" and "ruined" body is satisfied physically. Behn's text transmits a social message eighteenth-century readers wished to silence, and her marginalization in literary history until recently suggests they almost succeeded.[8]

If, in contradistinction to Behn's subversive text, an epistolary novel is "published in order to cultivate the principles of virtue and religion in the minds of the youth of both sexes," as Samuel Richardson (the publisher) contends on the title page of *Pamela*,[9] then the editor (Richardson) has to ensure that the reader is led to the proper conclusions. Richardson is deeply committed to instructing his readers, and in his novels the tissue separating extradiegesis from historio-diegesis is very thin indeed. It can also be problematical—a fact he discovered when he tried to counter the publication by two rival booksellers of a sequel entitled *Pamela's Conduct in High Life* (1741). As Lennard Davis tells the story in *Factual Fictions*:

> Richardson responded to this literary ambush by advertising that Chandler and Kelly were writing "without any other knowledge of the story than what they are able to collect from the two volumes already printed: And that he [the "Author"] is actually continuing the work himself, from materials that, perhaps, but for such a notorious invasion of his plan, he should not have published."

Although Richardson calls himself an "author" here for the first time, he still perpetuates the necessary state of ambivalence by implying that he was editing "materials"—presumably some actual record or further letters—to which his rivals did not have access. However, Chandler and Kelly claimed in an advertisement in the *London Daily Post* that it was their book, not Richardson's sequel, that was published directly from Pamela's "original papers," and was "regularly digested by a gentleman more conversant in high life than the vain author of *Pamela*."[10]

Despite this troublesome undermining of his convention's textual authority, Richardson still did not sign his works; he preferred to hide behind the figure of an editor and to use the extradiegetic level of narration as a screen between himself and his characters.[11]

The editor's Preface to *Pamela* (book 1) makes clear the text's didactic purpose "to *instruct* and *improve*" and "engage the passions of every sensible reader" (31). Moreover, the text will do this "all without raising a *single idea* throughout the whole, that shall shock the exactest purity, even in the warmest of those instances where Purity would be most apprehensive." The editor identifies his purpose and reader, and he gives assurances that despite warm "instances" the text will not shock anyone. As with the additional paratextual frame of the subtitle, *Virtue Rewarded*, this editorial promise excludes an entire range of reader expectations: the narrative contract has been overdetermined by the editor's reading. The editor then valorizes his reading, on the grounds that "he can appeal from his *own* passions, (which have been uncommonly *moved* in perusing it) to the passions of *every one* who shall read it with attention." The reader is told to read "with attention" if s/he is to be moved by Pamela's letters. Thus the inattentive reader is denied any effect, but Richardson also seems to mean a special kind of Puritan attention that will allow the words of the text to signify powerfully and pragmatically. This delimitation of a reading public becomes a common editorial device; nevertheless, the reader described is an editorial ideal of an extradiegetic addressee who will only approximate real readers. The editor goes on to explain further his confidence in a "favorable reception," "because an *Editor* can judge with an impartiality which is rarely to be found in an *Author*" (31). This assertion is striking for two reasons: (1) because it seeks to establish firmly the editor/author split; and (2) because it is a self-deconstructing claim—the editor is always a construct of the author; hence, the editor's "impartiality" is modeled by the author's partiality.

Pamela is ultimately a patriarchal "comedy," and its lessons of sustained virtue are easily comprehended and just as easily forgotten

in a moment when reason succumbs to passion; to forestall forgetting, *Clarissa* was written.[12] The editor of *Clarissa* (the same as "of
Pamela," according to the title page) is again concerned with "youthful readers" (I: xli), and he specifically suggests that the text "will
probably be thought tedious to all such as *dip* into it, expecting a
light novel, or *transitory romance*"; instead, the editor sets as his
ideal "considerate readers," who "will not enter upon the perusal of
the Piece before them as if it were designed *only* to divert and amuse"
(I: xlii). Again the letters are foregrounded in a horizon of reception
that stresses the instructional quality of the message, which the editor describes as a warning:

> What will be found to be more particularly aimed at in the following
> work is—to warn the inconsiderate and thoughtless of the one sex,
> against the base arts and designs of specious contrivers of the
> other—to caution parents against the undue exercise of their natu-
> ral authority over their children in the great article of marriage—to
> warn children against preferring a man of pleasure to a man of pro-
> bity upon that dangerous but too commonly-received notion, *that a
> reformed rake makes the best husband*—but above all, to investigate
> the highest and most important doctrines not only of morality, but of
> Christianity, by showing them thrown into action in the conduct of
> the *worthy* characters; while the *unworthy*, who set those doctrines
> at defiance, are condignly, and, as may be said, consequentially
> punished. (I: xlii)

Notice, however, that the warning to extradiegetic readers—"the
inconsiderate and thoughtless of the one sex [female] ... parents ...
children [more specifically, girls]"—becomes fused with the inves-
tigative and allegorical aim of the text. The warning is invested with
an economy of the "*worthy*" based on the editor's particular hermeneutics for reading the letters as a "vehicle [for] instruction."
However, the parents' "natural authority over their children in the
great article of marriage" is repeated by the editor's textual authority over the collection of letters. As observed in chapter 2, Clarissa
shares *his* hermeneutics—indeed, it is partially quoted directly from
her letters—and her characterized act of editing the letters shapes
much of the text we read. But we can neither discount nor ignore
this extra-heterodiegetic editor, since he is Clarissa's strongest sup-
porter against all adversarial readers.[13]
　Because of Clarissa's tragic fate, her lessons are more difficult
for actual readers to accept. If Clarissa is genuinely "*worthy*," then
why is poetic justice overturned? Why does she die? Richardson,

with his Puritan beliefs, saw her death as a positive confirmation of her virtue rather than as a punishment. Lovelace's violent death could not be of the same order, however; and by using interpretive notes throughout the text, the editor attempts to ensure that Lovelace is not the object of reader sympathy. According to Glen M. Johnson, "Richardson felt free to invoke editorial privilege in order to support or contradict characters' statements, to praise Clarissa or damn Lovelace, and to castigate readers themselves for hasty judgments or inattentiveness.... At times, and particularly in notes added to editions after the first, Richardson uses the editor to direct interpretations. Instead of aiding the process of reading as an exercise in judgment, he comes close to taking that process over."[14] William Beatty Warner observes that with the changes in Richardson's attitudes toward the novel, and particularly toward misreadings of Lovelace's villainy, "the editor is no longer the benign and docile figure who invites the reader to judge and compare rival claims of the protagonists. Instead he enters the text with an army of footnotes and textual addenda designed to expose Lovelace's plot and tip the scales of justice in favor of his heroine, Clarissa."[15]

Richardson goes so far in correcting misreadings that in the postscript to *Clarissa* (which was greatly expanded for the third edition of the novel in 1751) he all but drops the guise of "authentic" letters and writes of the "author's" intentions for his work. The postscript is an attempt to respond to actual "letters to the editor" disputing the necessity of Clarissa's "catastrophe." In the postscript, the editor extends his textual position to figure the gap between the narrating instance of the letters and the now-exposed literary instance of the novel and authorial intention. The postscript opens by maintaining the author/editor split, the author being referred to in the third person. But just before quoting Joseph Addison's thoughts on "poetic justice," there is a pronoun shift to "we," the first first-person pronoun in the postscript. Even though the third person is reinvoked for establishing intentions, this "we" seemingly inscribes both the author and the editor, and it claims responsibility for the text. With *Clarissa* the editorial voice and function develop to a degree where extra-diegetic narrating informs the total text. "This is appropriate," according to Warner, "for the editor must select an account that will give the reader the fullest possible understanding of how and why events are unfolding the way they are."[16] The extra-heterodiegetic narrative of transmission is ultimately a *mise en abyme* for the text. The editor, like his two protagonists, must vie for control of the other, and for the editor the other is the extradiegetic reader and his or her acts of interpretation. "Perhaps," concludes Warner, "the role of the editor always concealed the dual possibilities of dispassionate judge and manipulative prosecutor."[17]

Because Richardson never lost his sense of his work's high seriousness, the boundary between extradiegesis and historiodiegesis is so slight that it seems to disappear. Parodies of Richardson's work made the most of his seriousness and took particular aim at the extradiegetic frame sanctioning overly moralistic readings of his novels. Henry Fielding's *Shamela* (1741),[18] for instance, encloses the intradiegetic correspondence in a letter sent between two moralists, Parsons Tickletext and Olivier. The three editorial notes (24, 28, 29) to the letters are not identified; presumably they belong to Olivier, who sends the collection of letters to Tickletext, assuring him that they "are authentick" (8). We later discover that Olivier has only assured the exactness of his "copies" (38). Tickletext is given permission to publish Shamela's letters, but his final postscript suggests how rooted the two parsons are in the fictional world: "P.S. Since I writ, I have a certain account, that Mr. Booby hath caught his wife in bed with Williams, hath turned her off, and is prosecuting him in the spiritual court" (38). This violation of closure, the deferral of the text's final signature, marks an excluded extratext, which we can only write in our imagination. The violation also involves the two parsons to such an extent that their narrating stance shifts from a heterodiegetic to a pseudo-homodiegetic relationship to the events. Fielding added another extradiegetic frame in the figure of "Conny Keyber," but this frame is deliberately transparent and serves no function with relation to the intradiegesis. However, Keyber's dedicatory letter and his selection of letters to the editor expose completely the artifice of extradiegesis. Despite such pointed parodies, extradiegetic and marginal texts continued as important parts of epistolary fiction. Only after the exposure of the device through parody (and Fielding was not the only one to do this) could editorial texts serve a more ironic purpose, and if we reexamine Rousseau's and Laclos's epistolary fictions, we will see further refinement and undercutting of the editor's role in the text.

The preface to the first edition of *Julie, ou la nouvelle Héloïse*[19] is a playful echo of the Richardsonian prefaces. Although the editor suggests the pragmatic value of the text, he cannot vouch for the authenticity of the letters. By denying full authority over the collection, the editor makes problematic the preface's primary convention: the fable of textual origin. The second preface (added to the novel's second edition)—or the dialogue between the editor and a man of letters—also confronts the problem of authenticity, but again reaches no acceptable answer. Both prefaces mark the editor's extreme self-consciousness about the validity of this *extradiegetic* paratext. At the end of the second preface, the man of letters suggests that the editor include the dialogue as a preface to the collection of letters, and this suggestion inscribes the fable of the preface's origin, while the origin of the letters yet remains unclear. Noting this difficulty surrounding textual authenticity and authority, Romberg asks, "If Rousseau is anxious to give his preface the illusion of reality, why then is he not equally anxious to use this preface for the purpose of bestowing the illusion of reality upon the letters following?"[20] Although we can speculate on possible answers to this question of intention, what is clear is Rousseau's desire to bestow an illusion of distance separating himself, his editor-persona, and the correspondence. This distance frees the extradiegesis and allows its system of narrative contact to act as a *mise en abyme* to the epistolary system in the novel's narrative of transmission.

An example of this narrative counterpoint occurs in the initial contacts made on both the extradiegetic and the intradiegetic levels. The editor writes in his first preface: "No chaste girl has ever read novels.... She who ... would dare to read a single page is lost, but that she not attribute her loss to this book, the harm has been signified in advance. Since she has begun, and will finish her reading, she no longer has anything to risk [my translation]." The contact established here with an extradiegetic "chaste girl [*la fille chaste*]" implies a transgressive narrative motivated by reading this novel in letters; the editor can only warn that if this chaste reader has read thus far, there is no stopping. The editor's warning echoes the contact warning Saint-Preux inscribes in his first letter: "Show my letter to your parents"—a warning that goes unheeded, as innocence is detoured into seduction. If the "chaste girl" has only novels to fear, then the extradiegetic mystification of the text in the first preface circumvents the inscribed warning: as long as the letters might be real, there is no danger. But as Paul de Man has observed: "The preface is the place in the text where the question of textual mastery and authority is being decided and where, in the instance of *Julie*, it is also found to be undecidable. With this threatening loss of control the possibility arises of the entirely gratuitous and irresponsible text."[21]

Clearly Rousseau did not intend his novel to be irresponsible; the didactic nature of the characters' utterances of Rousseau's beliefs suggests that the novel is an allegorical representation of concepts written about elsewhere. Nonetheless, de Man correctly sees the doubt cast by the prefaces on the authenticity of the letters and on the authority of the editor as a "loss of control" that forces our interpretation into a condition of undecidability. De Man shows that the dialogue in the second preface moves from a question of the referentiality of the letters (whether they are real or a fiction) to an argument for the ultimate undecidability of the letters. By making this argument, Rousseau displaces himself from the letters, leaving indeterminate his status as either author of a fiction or collector/editor of real letters. Thus the extradiegetic narrative of transmission becomes unreadable; it is caught between two conflicting logics of textual production.

De Man sees the second preface's undecidability as a *mise en abyme* for the allegory of reading that informs *Julie*. The epistolary system inscribes within itself its own acts of reading, but as Julie shows in the crucial letter telling Saint-Preux of her marriage (pt. 3, 18; discussed in chapter 2), she initially read their love incorrectly, and by rereading the letters she can now see only error where she had once read desire. The second preface does not take a conventional didactic stand and construct a believable narrative of transmission because the idea of simple substitutions, motivated by a logic of referential homology with the extratextual world, is unsustainable within a reading of the text. The reader must be cautioned against reading naïvely—the second preface is meant to correct errors in reading the first edition. This correction does not, however, substitute proper answers for the errors; instead, it casts the text into a hermeneutics of indeterminacy, making interpretation both difficult and rewarding.

Les liaisons dangereuses[22] also opens with a threatening loss of control as two warnings are given to the reader. The editor, echoing Richardson's editor, writes in his preface of "the usefulness of the work" "to reveal the methods employed by those who are wicked in corrupting those who are good," but says that "far from recommending this book to young people, it seems to [him] very important to keep it from them. The time at which it may cease to be dangerous and become useful" is to be determined by the daughter's mother. The editor now quotes a mother who read the correspondence in manuscript as saying she would "'consider it a true service to my daughter to give her the book on her wedding day.'" This pragmatic intent is supported by various claims to authenticity: the style is uneven, the published group is only part of the letters, and the names of the actual correspondents have been either suppressed or changed. For aesthetic reasons the editor had attempted to alter the style and to abridge lengthy letters, but "this course of action was not *approved*." "The final say *was not mine* and *I submitted* [emphasis added]" he says. Although we normally expect editors to make use of their privileges over the text, either the editor in *Les liaisons dangereuses* must answer to a higher arranger who remains unnamed, or he has constructed a second extradiegetic persona—a supereditor—to displace and disguise his own activities. Hence, the published collection contains "Letters Collected in One Section of Society and Published for the Edification of Others," but we are left to wonder what letters and edifications have been excluded by either the editor or by the judgmental supereditor.

Peggy Kamuf offers an interesting speculation on what texts have been editorially suppressed. According to Kamuf, "the editor is ... a backup system to insure nondelivery."[23] Apparently, Valmont has a secret that Mme de Merteuil knows and alludes to at the end of letter 81 and again in letter 152; moreover, the editor's note to letter 81 suggests that the editor also knows the secret. But letter 152, Kamuf observes, "more or less reveals what cannot be revealed about Valmont."[24] The letter intimates that his secret would oblige him to depart (from Paris? from France?). It says: "to leave, if, that is, they gave you enough time to get away.... On the whole, then, provided that the *French court* left you alone wherever you settled down, you would only be changing the scene of your triumphs."[25] The two qualifying phrases—"If ..." and "provided ..."—suggest the seriousness of Valmont's crime and the absolute need for discretion. Kamuf penetrates this veil of secrecy to offer a reading of this excluded text:

> The contract not to deliver Valmont's secret, moreover, is one to which the readers will no doubt agree once they have some idea of the kind of offence involved. Suffice it to say that, were it to become known, the Crown itself might not leave such a crime unpunished. Valmont's transgression, it is suggested, is no less than an act of lèse-majesté, an attack on the symbol of legitimate power in a monarchy. Readers will also therefore infer, from Valmont's typical mode of attack, that this act of lèse-majesté could—if revealed—challenge the legitimacy of inherited rule. It is this hereditary destination of power which is guaranteed a straight line of descent by the editor's pact of silence with the reader.[26]

Kamuf's imaginative filling of this spot of indeterminacy in the text is open to interpretive question, but it demonstrates an exploitation of the reading act with relation to contact and transmission. Valmont's crime underscores again the interplay of hereditary transmission and epistolary transmission within a logic of legitimacy and illegitimacy.

The contact bond made by the letters marks a unique body of knowledge between the correspondents: things can be alluded to, even unsaid, yet still be understood. The editorial text adds supplemental information for an extradiegetic reader, and, as Kamuf shows, information can also be repressed in this reader's interest and with his or her agreement.[27] Of course, the actual reader is not bound by the pact of silence at the extradiegetic level. The reader's role in narrative transmission is to enact a negotiation and actualization of textual indeterminacies so that reading produces an aesthetic experience of the literary text. The contact between the editor and the extradiegetic readers schematizes a fictional world that values highly what the letters reveal. The extradiegetic level of narrating and reading is organized on an economy of authenticity; therefore, the editor's assurances of authenticity are only aimed at his extradiegetic audience, and his suppression of secrets concerns only the extradiegetic society of the text. Of course, the parallels between the extradiegetic world and the extratextual world can be manifest, and those parallels serve whatever social and political functions a text might contain in addition to its aesthetic function. Perhaps there is a coded message about a royal transgression in Laclos's novel, but the text is valuable regardless.

Not everyone in the extradiegetic audience believes the editor, however. The convention of the editorial preface in epistolary fiction is designed to initiate contact with an audience, to profess the authenticity of the letters and the editor's authority over the collected text, and to direct the audience's reception, usually of the pragmatic lessons the text is supposed to show. We sense parody when the preface neglects or transgresses one of these conventions or is used for another purpose, but parody (as in *Shamela*) quickly loses its effect. Laclos recognizes this loss of effect and resists infusing his editor's preface with an overt satiric parody of other prefaces (although it can be read this way); instead, he decenters his preface's autonomy within the extradiegetic narrative of transmission by including a "Publisher's Note." Although the "publisher" (as a fictional construct) can be considered as a transmitter of the text, s/he is also the text's first (if not addressed) reader; therefore, his or her response to the text, when printed before the editor's preface, usurps the editorial convention of authority and subverts the extradiegetic reader's expectations: "We think it our duty to warn the public that, in spite of the title of this work and of what the editor says about it in his preface, we cannot guarantee its authenticity as a collection of letters: we have in fact, a very good reason to believe that it is only a novel." Thus even before the editor can begin to fulfill his function—

initiating contact, professing authenticity and authority, and direct-ing reception—his formal mimetics have been deconstructed by an authoritarian voice that seeks to displace the text it nonetheless does not suppress. Blinded by "the light of reason ... [that] has turned us all, as everyone knows, into honorable men and modest retiring women," the publisher warns "the over-credulous reader" against reading this text as a referential portrait of society. In what we can see as a parodic inversion of the frame correspondence in Fielding's *Shamela*—in which Olivier seeks to correct Tickletext's overcredulous reading of *Pamela*—*Les liaisons dangereuses* opens with an attempt to exclude the discourses of "persons of such vicious habits" by not granting them correlatives in "our age: this age of philosophy."

The extradiegetic readers are placed in a double bind. By heed-ing the publisher's warning, readers protect themselves from the text by construing everything as fiction, but if they instead form a pact of silence with the editor, they must assume that the letters are real and that Valmont's secret has some significance in their world. As in Rousseau's prefaces, the reader is in a condition of undecidability before the intradiegetic correspondence is even reached. The ironic stances of both note and preface enfold one another as the shifting contact between the publisher and editor creates an interpretive aporia for the reader.

Yet, at the end of *Les liaisons dangereuses*, the final note to the text is signed by the publisher, and it suggests a sequel that the pub-lisher is "compelled" not to present at this time. Again, as with *Shamela*, the final words violate any sense of closure; and signifi-cantly, the publisher no longer maintains the view that the text is only a fiction. If it was a fiction, why would there be any compel-ling reason not to publish the remaining adventures? The publisher's final word deconstructs his earlier warning, reinstating the formal mimetics of the editor and placing the total text in the economic system of the publishing world—a bourgeois move that signifies Laclos's final jab at conventional morality. The literary conventions of the transgressive text and the promised sequel are, as we know from Hollywood movies, not something unique to the novel, but in texts where transmission obtains through the imitation of other texts (diaries and private manuscripts as well as letters), this literary con-vention takes on a particular narrative force, delaying and displac-ing the ultimate closure of the text. Closure occurs through marriage, death, resolution of the epistolary conflict, or silence. Moreover, closure marks the moment at which the texts—the letters collected and transmitted to an editor—become transmissible. The extra-diegetic frame, however, can perpetuate a fable of continuation and a condition of indeterminacy about absolute ends, or about more letters yet to come, by leaving the text unsealed.

DIARY TEXTS sometimes employ an extradiegetic level to assure distance between the diarist and the novelist, and for all diary texts an editor can be postulated, even if there are no physical marks (prefaces or notes) of his or her presence in the narrating instance. This editorial paratext appears to be less common in diary novels than it is in epistolary texts, although an exhaustive critical inquiry and literary history of diary fiction would be needed to prove this point. There are several possible reasons for this lesser use of the extradiegetic editor. First, diary narratives as a literary form developed from a conjunction of memoir novels and epistolary monodies;[28] therefore, the convention of the editor had already lost much of its mystifying power for claiming authenticity. Furthermore, by the nineteenth century the novel had developed a greater variety in its narrating techniques and a certain respectability with the reading public—fictions no longer had to masquerade as fact. Still, suspending the reader's disbelief about a diary was an effect writers hoped their texts would be capable of maintaining or at least invoking, even though the reader would discard it during interpretation.

A second reason for the minimal use of marked editors could be the shift in the Western conception of the "self" brought about by the Enlightenment and by Romanticism in the late eighteenth and early nineteenth centuries. During this period, the conception of the "self" shifted from a belief that one was merely a thread in the finely woven fabric of nature—one had no free will and was subject to a determined destiny—to the idea that one was an individual, a feeling being, whose awareness of one's place in the world began with one's own knowledge and sensations. This individualizing of the self was reflected in literature by the expansion in the role of the hero, as exemplified by the popularity of Werther as a character model. The deepening interest in the hero called for a reduction of narrating filters. Diary texts give the appearance of being unmediated, but as shown in chapter 3, they also highlight the separation of the narrating self from the experiencing self. Narrative technique, therefore, had to develop new forms that appeared to remove all traces of the narrator, presenting what Henry James called "the illusion of life." Nevertheless, this new epistemology of the self did not eliminate entirely the convention of extradiegetic editors in diary novels.

As in most extradiegetic situations, the discourse's primary function is to initiate transmission and to narrate the circumstances that produced the diary to follow. Hence in Richardson's *Pamela*, when Pamela is forced into writing a journal instead of letters, the editor pointedly intervenes to explain what has happened and to present the scene between Mr. B. and Pamela's father. The editor, although still in an extradiegetic pose, alters his and his readers' relation to Pamela's subsequent journal by narrating information she could not know at the time. The editorial intrusion gives readers a greater understanding than Pamela has of her plight, and it makes them more sympathetic as well. Later epistolary novels that have recourse to partial diaries (e.g., *Evelina* by Fanny Burney) will date the letters as "In Continuation." A more standard example of the extradiegetic convention would be the short preface to *Robinson Crusoe*,[29] in which the editor assures the reader of the authenticity of the text to follow. But Defoe's conventional claim bears the distinction of having received possibly the first critical attack on such claims of authenticity. Lennard Davis finds it intriguing that Charles Gilden's attack in *An Epistle to Daniel Defoe* (1719) finally, and almost singlehandedly, raises the issue of "fictionality" in prose texts and finds that quality a transgression of the writer's responsibility to the reader: fictions are lies, and lies are damnable. In response, Defoe claims his texts contained an allegorical purpose that excused the occasional use he had to make of fictions; Gilden was not convinced.[30] And why should he have been? In a way, extradiegetic and historiodiegetic prefaces rewrite the old conundrum: "The next statement is a fiction. The previous statement is the truth." If the writer frames the text in such a paradox, then what is the reader to do?

Prefaces are not the only kind of extradiegetic text. As observed earlier in the cases of *The Narrative of Arthur Gordon Pym* and "The Diary of a Superfluous Man," the extradiegetic frame is not invoked until the end of the text. These short concluding notes, like the one in *Les liaisons dangereuses*, are highly problematic with relation to the intradiegesis. As the reader proceeds through the intradiegetic narrative, s/he may interpret as ironic the editorial judgments placed at the head of a text; moreover, since the editorial text is a marginal text, once it is shown to be ironic its control over the reading act changes from that of being a truth claim about the text to that of being an element in the textuality and the narrativity of the artistic literary work. However, an editorial judgment placed after the intradiegetic text has more potential for unsettling the reading experience. Instead of a reader working dialectically with the extradiegetic preface to process the intradiegetic text, a concluding note can authorize a radically different interpretation that forces a second reading and a revised experience of the text. Understanding and interpretation are thereby called into question, constructing a fable of the manuscript's *reception* rather than its origin, and the text meant for no other eyes than the diarist's becomes part of a hermeneutic circle of reading experiences.

The extradiegetic function is not limited, however, to just statements made at the beginning or end of an intradiegetic text. Diary texts usually do not require arrangement as epistolary collections do. Francis Stuart's *The High Consistory* (1981)[31] presents an interesting exception. In this novel the diarist's papers have been scattered by a plane crash. After collecting those fragments that could be found, the decision is made to publish the text in the order collected— no attempt is made to reconstitute the chronological sequence of the text's production. When more than one diary is involved, on the other hand, the texts are extradiegetically organized. Bram Stoker's *Dracula*[32] is prefaced by the statement: "How these papers have been placed in sequence will be made manifest in the reading of them." What follows are portions of different diaries (including a phonograph diary), a few letters, and even a newspaper clipping. Yet despite all this documentary evidence, a concluding note by Jonathan Harker calls into question the illusion of authenticity and authority: "We were talking of the old time.... I took the papers from the safe where they had been ever since our return so long ago. We were struck with the fact, that in all the masses of material of which the record is composed, there is hardly one authentic document; nothing but a mass of typewriting, except the later note-books of Mina and Seward and myself, and Van Helsing's memorandum. We could hardly ask any one, even did we wish to, to accept these as proofs of so wild a story" (400). With almost vampiric logic, the texts have been encrypted in a safe, but more significantly, the original documents have disappeared, leaving only the typewritten transcripts.

Wilkie Collins's *The Woman in White*,[33] like *Dracula*, does not set its "Preamble" at an extradiegetic distance:

> When the writer of these introductory lines (Walter Hartright, by name) happens to be more closely connected than others with the incidents to be recorded, he will describe them in his own person. When his experience fails, he will retire from the position of narrator; and his task will be continued, from the point at which he has left it off, by other persons who can speak to the circumstances under notice from their own knowledge, just as clearly and positively as he has spoken before them.
>
> Thus, the story here presented will be told by more than one pen, as the story of an offence against the laws is told in Court by more

than one witness—with the same object, in both cases, to present the truth always in its most direct and most intelligible aspect; and to trace the course of one complete series of events, by making the persons who have been most closely connected with them, at each successive stage, relate their own experience, word for word.[34] (1)

Despite establishing a fascinating narrative of transmission, in 1860 Collins presents the novel "to a new class of readers, in its complete form" (xxx), and he adds a historiodiegetic preface that undermines the illusion of reality the "witnesses" are meant to provide: "An experiment is attempted in this novel, which has not (so far as I know) been hitherto tried in fiction. The story of the book is told throughout by the characters of the book. They are all placed in different positions along the chain of events; and they all take the chain up in turn, and carry it on to the end" (xxix). Recalling Defoe's and Richardson's problems with the status of fictional discourse in the eighteenth century, we can see how far the acceptance of the novel and its conventions has come by the time Collins can forthrightly avow his text is a "novel."

A different form of arranging occurs in *The Private Papers of Henry Ryecroft* (1903)[35] by George Gissing. The editor, signed as G. G., tells the reader in his preface how, after Ryecroft's death, he has come "upon three manuscript books which at first glance seemed to be a diary" (xvi); however, the entries are fragmentary, only dated by month, and "assuredly ... not intended for the public" (xvii). Not wishing "to offer a mere incondite miscellany," the editor says he was struck upon "reading through the matter ... how often the aspects of nature were referred to, and how suitable many of the reflections were to the month with which they were dated." "So [he writes] I hit upon the thought of dividing the little book into four chapters, named after the seasons" (xviii-xix). The editorial activity constructs a coherent sequence, but it also transforms the fragments into a text; therefore, the transmission channel has been significantly modified by the extradiegetic paratext. A precursor to Gissing's work is Nathaniel Hawthorne's short story "Fragments from the Journal of a Solitary Man" (1837; never published in any of Hawthorne's collections).[36] Here the friend/editor, after burning all of Oberon's papers as requested in his dying words, is left with his "old disconnected journal" (Oberon dies on the verge, we assume, of instructing the editor what is to be done with this text). The editor writes that he cannot "resist an impulse to give some fragments of it to the public. To do this satisfactorily, I am obliged to twist this thread, so as to string together into a semblance of order my Oberon's 'random

pearls'" (487). What follows is an alternation between journal extracts and the friend/narrator/editor's extradiegetic "thread." Yet as
we have seen before, these texts only become transmissible after their
writers' deaths—the extradiegetic parenting of these now orphaned
texts reanimates the voice that had been reduced to silence.

Another example of extradiegetic arranging occurs in Doris
Lessing's *The Golden Notebook*. This complexly structured work
contains a five-chapter novel, "The Free Women" whose chapters
alternate with sections from its author's, Anna Wulf's, four notebooks (black, red, yellow, and blue). Between chapters 4 and 5,
Anna's "Golden Notebook" is presented. Like a scholarly edition,
the editorial comments interspersed in the text offer descriptive indicators of such oddities in the notebooks as pasted-in newspaper
clippings, different styles of handwriting, or passages that have been
crossed out. Yet notice how in introducing the notebooks, the
unnamed editor's objective description surreptitiously shifts to
speculation:

> [The four notebooks were identical, about eighteen inches square,
> with shiny covers, like the texture of a cheap watered silk. But the
> colours distinguished them—black, red, yellow and blue. When the
> covers were laid back, exposing the four first pages, it *seemed* that
> order had not immediately imposed itself. In each the first page or
> two showed broken scribblings and half sentences. Then a title ap-
> peared, *as if* Anna had, *almost automatically*, divided herself into
> four, and then, from the nature of what she had written, named these
> divisions. And this is what happened. The first book, the black note-
> book, began with doodlings, scattered musical symbols, treble signs
> shifted into the £ sign and back again; then a complicated design of
> interlocking circles, then words:]
> > black
> > > dark, it is so dark
> > > it is dark
> > > > there is a kind of darkness here
> [And then, in a changed *startled* writing:][37] (55–56)

How deep do the italicized speculations go? The editor appears to
be offering tentative observations on the apparent chaos of signs (not
reproduced in the text we read) that begins the black notebook, and
as editors of actual documents are well aware, such tentativeness is
an accepted scholarly convention and safety net; but the effect is
different with fictional documents, particularly when the editor is
about to enforce a reading through her arrangement of the texts. Thus,

even though the notebooks are written concurrently and construct a palimpsestic inscription of Anna's self in a fourfold tension among different notebooks, their extradiegetic arrangement imposes a regularized sequence that is additionally ordered by the alternation with the chapters from "The Free Women" (an autobiographic fiction, with an extra-heterodiegetic narrator, written possibly after the notebooks). This narrative of transmission and the contact system it articulates is bracketed to mark editorial distance. Despite the illusion of editorial control, the act of reading is realized in a condition of extreme indeterminacy.

Lessing's unnamed editor (could it be Anna in yet another persona?) avoids taking any stand by way of a preface or concluding note, but these forms of extradiegetic discourse still occur in other twentieth-century diary texts. Jean-Paul Sartre's *La nausée*[38] and Jeremy Leven's *Creator* (1980)[39] both begin with explanatory "editors." In Sartre's case, these editors are abrupt and descriptive: they present some brief biographical information about Roquentin, speculate on the time of the writing for some undated pages, and assert that the pages are being published without alteration. The very conventionality of this preface gives an ironic frame to the subversive writing that follows. From Leven's novel we learn more about the condition of the text (why certain pages are missing) and read a brief biography of the diarist, Dr. Harry Wolper. The editorial fiction is intended to frame the diary, but in *Creator* the intradiegetic text spills over the boundary set by the extradiegesis. According to the editors, Harry Wolper dies mysteriously "shortly before midnight, December 25, 1969"; therefore, closure of the diary is fixed by formal convention. The entry for 25 December is perfectly natural, since it marks the promised conclusion. Once we read beyond the date, however, we recognize another writer for this entry: "And so it came to pass that after years of torment, I finally rid myself of Harry Wolper. For the truth of it is, as I'm sure you've long ago come to realize, there never was a Harry Wolper. There never was a great Biologist and Author who propelled me through one unlikely adventure after another, but rather, it was I who concocted the preposterous Dr. Wolper, and now, as I had long ago promised, I had no choice but to kill him off" (489).

Wolper intercalates through his diary a novel, at times highly autobiographical, entitled "The Adventures of Boris Lafkin." During the writing, however, Boris violates the borderline of diegetic structure to discuss his destiny with Harry, his creator and author. The crux of their discussion is a reworking of the debate over poetic justice and the novelist's authority over the destiny of his characters. But rather than present the argument extradiegetically as

Richardson had done over two hundred years before, here it is placed inside between the intradiegetic and the metadiegetic levels. Boris's position comes down to the following: Since Harry determines who lives and dies in his novel, why can't he prevent the death of the woman Boris loves, particularly when Boris begs him to save her? Harry responds by denying authorial authority, insisting that it is out of his control; he cannot (or will not) influence the destiny of the characters in his novel. It should be observed here, that a main story line in the diary is Wolper's attempt to clone a new version of his own dead wife; therefore, Boris's fate may be sealed in the already-written autobiographical plot underlying Harry's novel. Diaries may be therapy writing or quarries for novelists, but a *mise en abyme* of this complexity portends, as it often does in Edgar Allan Poe's fiction, some sort of catastrophe.[40]

Boris's reversal of the text's narrating status at the end of the diary startlingly alters our contact with both the diary (is Boris the real creator?) and its editors' preface. If Boris concocts "the preposterous Dr. Wolper," then he has also concocted the authenticating editors. The fable of the manuscript's origin actually *is* a fable. The preface's illusion of reality and authority is doubled within a second illusion of its fictiveness by maintaining that "The following text is true; the preceding text is a fabrication." And to give one more turn of the screw to this narrative of transmission, a condition given in the preface for the publication of the diary is that "none of [Harry's] property was to be distributed until after his lifework was published." The ghost of the legacy haunts the narrative of transmission inscribed in this problematic "lifework."

An additional word needs to be said on the common confusion of extradiegesis and historiodiegesis in the editorial fictions that frame novels which represent other texts. The line that separates these two levels of narrative transmission is admittedly sometimes very thin. By a clever manipulation of text, Richardson made the line almost disappear so as to highlight the didactic scope of his fiction; Defoe, forced by the circumstances of Charles Gilden's attacks, had to claim his texts had an allegorical function that absolved their fictionality; and Wilkie Collins openly recast the claims of *The Woman in White*'s preamble before the reader's court of law, confessing to a narrative experiment. Lastly, there is the example of Victor Hugo's 1832 preface to *Le dernier jour d'un condamné* (1829)[41] which reconceptualizes the original one-paragraph preface that read:

> There are two ways of accounting for the existence of this work. Either there really has been found a bundle of yellow, ragged, papers on which were inscribed, exactly as they came, the last thoughts

of a wretched being; or else there has been a man, a dreamer, occupied observing nature for the advantage of art, a philosopher, a poet, who, having been seized with these forcible ideas, could not rest until he had given them the tangible form of a volume. Of these two explanations, the reader will choose that which he prefers. (5)

In 1832, Hugo frames this evocative paradox of transmission in a different key: "Three years ago, when this book first appeared, some people thought it was worth while to dispute the authorship" (7). Just whose authorship, he does not say. Moreover, although we cannot say with any certainty that this revised preface is not also fictional, its historical relationship to the text marks its concern with the text's literary instance as well as its narrating instance.

Under this condition, then, we can establish a principle of historiodiegetic transmission by recognizing its concern with the literary instance of the published text; however, the historiodiegesis authorizes a revised version of the reader's ontological conception of the fiction's speech acts. This distinction is necessary to delimit certain statements by the author about his or her text from autobiographical accounts of a particular work's publishing history (as interesting and significant as those might be). How much we accept or discard from these historiodiegetic paratexts will vary from text to text and from reading to reading.

The historiodiegetic author, when considered by interpretation, is a construct, as is his or her reader; but the historiodiegetic discourse situation is different from that of extradiegetic constructs. The chance for signifiers to shift among narrating levels is great, and even when historiodiegesis is clearly the product of an implied author's extrafictional voice, we must use interpretive caution. Otherwise, the contact channel can be misconstrued, affecting the reader's experience of the text. The next chapter explores some additional ways that the interplay between extradiegesis and historiodiegesis opens fissures in extradiegetic frames designed both to authenticate the text and to question its authority.

6 | *Framing Prefaces/ Framed Memoirs*

> An author may preface as elaborately as he will, the pub-
> lic will go on making precisely those demands which he
> has endeavored to avoid.
>
> —Goethe, *Autobiography*

IN DISCUSSING "frame" narratives, there is always an underlying assumption that the frame can be distinguished from the picture, to borrow a spatial metaphor from painting. Indeed, suggests John T. Matthews, "frames are meant to be forgotten";[1] yet framing in the spatial arts has evolved a perspectival function to enhance the dimensional quality of art, especially the illusion of depth in painting. But anyone familiar with the paintings of René Magritte (his series entitled *La Condition Humaine*, for example) will recognize that the border (margin) between the picture and what it represents can merge to the point of being indistinguishable. Magritte's paintings brilliantly evoke the mimetic undecidability inherent in art. *La Condition Humaine* asks us to see the inset painting as codeterminal with its landscape subject—which is always already a painting. As Magritte's title suggests, the questions of borders and truth (reality) signify our human condition, our epistemological and ontological "frameworks" for understanding the world.[2]

The more one studies frame narration—the literary analog to the painterly frame—the more one actualizes the competition between the framing narrative and the framed tale. The questions of borders that Magritte raises in his paintings are also challenged in narrative. In "Living On," Jacques Derrida questions framing under the name of "double invagination," which "has in itself the *structure of a narrative [récit] in deconstruction.*... Even before it 'concerns' a text in narrative form, double invagination constitutes the story of stories, the narrative of narrative."[3] In Derrida's figure of double invagination, the inside and outside enfold one another to mark each as always at the same time the other. The frame, borderline, boundary, or margin of a text is supposed to mark out (to plot) its field of being, but at every edge Derrida finds the frame problematic and always already invading and invaded by the framed.

Indeed, as Matthews observes, "The way painters use the term 'frame' might confirm our understanding of the literary frame, since frame refers both to the hidden understructure upon which the canvas is stretched and the highly visible but unnoticed outer ornament."[4] Matthews relates framing's double nature to Derrida's position, and he stresses the immanent interdependence of frame and framed in narration:

> Whatever specific effects any individual frame has for its core story or stories, we may generalize about its status by observing that the frame is always that which is first to be passed through or beyond. It is at once outside the reader's field of concentration and the determinant of that field, beneath one's notice yet the foundation of it. By indicating all that is not-the-story, the frame's marginality becomes indispensable to providing the ground which defines the figure of the narrative. Often, then, in both our reading experience and in our critical attentions, we neglect the frame, as in one respect we are meant to, because it has no place of its own. The literary frame exists as a function which enables a relation between differentiated realms (the reader and author, the world and the artwork, reality and imagination, and so on). So far as it is successful the frame must suppress its content, for otherwise it diminishes the enframed by exaggerating what is to be taken as preliminary ornamentation.[5]

Although Matthews's description is cogent, it begs the question of what can interpretation can make of the framing narrative. Matthews uses as his exemplary text Emily Brontë's *Wuthering Heights*, which, as we shall see in chapter 8, has an intricate and convoluted history of framing; but here I want to consider other equally problematic narrating instances of framing.

The structure of framing in literary transmission is analogous to our human condition; as Mikhail Bakhtin observes, "Discourse *lives*, as it were, on the boundary between its own context and another, alien context."[6] The framed tale, we often discover, is centered on questions of human contact and transmission: genealogies, inheritances, marriages, discourses. However, because such tales often organize their plots around disruptions or transgressions in their systems of transmission—illegitimate births, stolen legacies, illicit seductions, intercepted messages—we must look for similar transgressions in the framing structure. Throughout this study I have constructed and deployed levels of classification quite freely to uncover relationships among different narrating instances. It would be a mistake, however, to stratify rigidly a transmission system and its modes of contact that excludes or misconstrues those texts which merge transmission levels. In the diary-text examples from Gissing and Hawthorne discussed in chapter 5, the extradiegetic level is distinguished from the intradiegetic diary by the death of the diarist, an event that makes transmissible the intradiegetic text. In both examples, however, the extradiegetic "transmitter" is a close friend of the diarist and therefore highly familiar with the intradiegetic representations constructed in the diary. Extradiegetic figures are part of the textual world, but the degree of familiarity they have with the metadiegetic events and the textualization of those events in the intradiegetic narration will influence their extradiegetic texts: the frame not only delimits the picture, it merges with it.

How a transmissible text comes to be transmitted is always a narrative problem—one that sometimes requires the framing narrative and the framed tale to merge in interpretively significant ways. In this chapter I will examine texts in which the framing narrative marks a field of interference with the framed tale. This field of interference is exposed when reading focuses on extradiegetic narratives of transmission that employ a "contact character" who authenticates the document containing the intradiegetic narration. Moreover, I will now leave the largely epistolary and diary focus of the earlier chapters and focus on other document narratives that require a narrative of transmission to obtain contact with readers. In addition, this chapter will continue to inquire into the effects of historiodiegetic paratexts on the transmission of narrative discourse. The texts discussed here present an intradiegetic narrator who is also the writer of the main manuscript. The following two chapters will examine narratives in which the text is the product of an extradiegetic listener who transcribes the oral narration of a participant in the metadiegetic events.

In the texts examined in the previous chapter, contact between the intradiegetic and extradiegetic levels was obscured by the seemingly objective detachment of the editor, but even in prose narrative's early days it was possible for the intradiegetic "author" to contact his editor. Consider the opening of Jonathan Swift's *Gulliver's Travels* (1726).[7] In the first edition, the editor, Richard Sympson, accounts for the origin of the manuscript and his close relationship with the author, Mr. Lemuel Gulliver. As an example of an authenticating preface it is unremarkable, composed of the conventional truth claims and editorial explanations of any alterations that have taken place in the text. For a new edition in 1735, however, Swift appended—before the preface—a letter from Lemuel Gulliver (dated

2 April 1727), complaining of alterations that occurred in the process of publishing his travels. The letter functions paratextually as a second authenticating device, reappropriating authority and counteracting those who "are so bold as to think [his] book of travels a mere fiction out of [his] own brain" (viii). Yet at the same time the letter notes that "the original manuscript is all destroyed since the publication" of the first edition (vii). More significantly, by bringing certain issues out to the extradiegetic level, the letter conditions readers of the text by postulating a set of responses that the "author" perceives as misconstruals of his original document. This conditioning alters the contact channel through which the reader perceives Swift's satiric intentions and recognizes his targets. The corrective letter redelimits the intradiegesis by excluding a range of readings, thereby giving the text a more didactic rhetorical stance. But Swift's letter also signifies that within the fable of the manuscript's origin, the historiodiegetic author must disguise his commentary by forging an intradiegetic signature.

Usually, however, the writer of the manuscript does not or cannot step forward, and the transmitter/editor has to discover the text and be so moved by it that publication is the only resort. A book could be written on the fictions of found manuscripts that employ paratextual elements to lead the reader to revise his or her reading. Such a study could range from the overly contrived prefaces that save the text, as in Henry Mackenzie's *The Man of Feeling* (1771),[8] to the discovery of the text at closure, as in Charles Kingsley's *Alton Locke* (1850)[9] or Margaret Atwood's *The Handmaid's Tale* (1985).[10] In Mackenzie's novel, for instance, the manuscript has been left behind by its author, and has become gun wadding for its first discoverer. The editor exchanges another book (on logic) for this intriguing manuscript, and the large sections that are missing in its published form show the ravages of many a day's shooting. *Alton Locke*, on the other hand, appears to be a straightforward memoir, but the text ends with a letter informing the addressee that Alton died as the pages were finished, and that the text was probably written during his emigration to America. In Atwood's dystopian novel we receive a transcript of the tape-recorded memoir of Offred, a handmaid in the republic of Gilead. The novel closes with "Historical Notes," the partial proceedings of a scholarly conference (set many years after the close of Offred's narration) at which the text's (Offred's and maybe also Atwood's) referential basis is discussed.[11]

The highly conventional discovery process in Mackenzie's and Kingsley's novels exerts little thematic pressure on the tale found. But in Atwood's text, as in many dystopian fictions that use the device of the recovered text, the reflexive narrative of transmission both underwrites the historical prophecy recorded in the text and depicts a contact situation that reorients the reader to the intradiegetic manuscript, which the framing narrative authorizes. But what about such framing narratives in general? Although they serve as necessary access points to the intradiegetic narrations, what kinds of force do they exert on the reader's experience of the intradiegetic text and of the novel as a whole? The remainder of this chapter will explore four novels. They come from different countries and literary eras, yet they share an extradiegetic structure of narrative transmission that does exert thematic, phenomenological, and ontological pressure on the intradiegesis of the framed manuscript.

BENJAMIN CONSTANT'S short novel *Adolphe* (1816)[12] presents an interesting example of an extradiegetic narrative of transmission in which it appears that the two levels of narration come into contact. The "Note by the Publisher" that precedes Adolphe's manuscript,[13] which I quote here in full, tells the reader how the manuscript was discovered:

> Many years ago, when I was travelling in Italy, I was held up by the flooding of the Neto in the little Calabrian village of Cerenza, and had to stay at an inn. There was in the same inn a stranger who had been obliged to stay there for the same reason. He was very silent and looked sad. He showed no impatience. Now and again, as he was the only man in the place to whom I could talk, I grumbled to him about the delay of our journey. "I don't mind," he said, "whether I am here or anywhere else." According to our host, who had talked to a Neapolitan servant who looked after the stranger but did not know his name, he was not travelling out of curiosity, for he never went to see ruins, picturesque places, monuments or people. He read a good deal, but never continuously, he went for walks in the evening, always alone, and often spent whole days sitting motionless with his head in his hands.
>
> Just when the roads were reopened and we could have set off, the stranger fell seriously ill. I felt bound in ordinary human decency to stay on and look after him. There was only the one village doctor at Cerenza and I wanted to send to Cozenze for better qualified help. "It is not worth it," said the stranger, "this man is exactly what I need." He was right, and probably more right than he thought, for the man cured him. "I didn't think you were so clever," he told him almost peevishly as he dismissed him. He then thanked me for my care and set off.
>
> Some months later, at Naples, I received a letter from our host at

Cerenza, with a box found on the Strongoli road, the road that the stranger and I had taken, but separately. The innkeeper who had sent it to me felt sure that it belonged to one of us. The box contained a quantity of very old letters either unaddressed or on which the addresses and signatures were illegible, a woman's portrait and a notebook containing the anecdote or story you are about to read. The stranger to whom these things belonged had gone without leaving me any way of writing to him, and I kept them for ten years, not quite knowing what I ought to do with them, until I happened to mention them quite by chance while talking to some people in a German town, one of whom begged me to let him have the manuscript which was in my possession. A week later the manuscript was returned to me with a letter that I put at the end of this story because it would be meaningless if it were read before the story itself.

This letter persuaded me to publish now by telling me for certain that publication cannot offend or compromise anybody. I have not changed a single word of the original, and even the suppression of proper names is not of my doing; they were indicated in the manuscript, as they still are here, by initials only. (33–34)

Despite its conventionality, this is a curious narrative. First, it is a highly accelerated account that is fraught with marks of indeterminacy. The publisher, like the Neapolitan servant, seems unable to name "the stranger," yet he is certain that the box and the manuscript belong to the man he met at the inn. Ultimately the intradiegetic text's author is given a name—Adolphe—but verification comes from a second reader, who after borrowing the manuscript sends further letters of proof; however, these letters, along with some of the letters found with the manuscript, are withheld by the publisher. In writing this extradiegetic narrative of transmission, the publisher transforms his experience into a mystified narrative that overdetermines and, literally, estranges Adolphe. Everything is shrouded in a silence of suppressed true names and illegible signatures. As the subtitle to the novel makes clear, *Adolphe* is *An Anecdote Found among the Papers of an Unknown Person.*

Still, in his postnarrative letter, the publisher writes that he "shall publish it as a true story of the misery of the human heart" (124–25), trusting the second reader's avowal that he "knew most of the characters in this story, which is all too true" (123). But, again, the signatures, if not some of the letters, have been excluded. The second reader, the writer of the authenticating letter, is also a stranger, though by his own admission he is probably a character in the preceding pages. There are thus three texts here: Adolphe's intradiegetic narrative of his life and destructive love for Ellenore, the publisher's extradiegetic narrative of the manuscript's discovery, and the second reader's letter, which acts as a bridge between the two narratives and verifies the truth of the tale. Because the names are suppressed, complete suspension of disbelief is needed for this interlocking narrative of transmission to function as a chain of authority. The publisher, however, characterizes the text's readers as readily disbelieving the narrative: "Women who read it will all imagine they have met somebody better than Adolphe or that they themselves are better that Ellenore" (124). The publisher does not make this claim until the closing letter, and he expects the work to be instructive for society. However, by characterizing the extradiegetic reader after the reading experience, the publisher reorients the reading-effect he intends for the work. The postnarrative letters present two different readings of the intradiegetic narrative; thus, as at the intradiegetic level, no sufficient resolution appears possible.

Although it is not a degree-zero example, the extradiegetic narrative of transmission in *Adolphe* can be seen as a paradigm that obtains in many fables of manuscript origin. The degree-zero extradiegetic narrative would be the editor's discovery and later publication of the text without an interpretive preface. In this paradigm the levels of the narrating instance are clearly distinguished and the narrative contract with the reader depends only on the extradiegetic narrator's reliability, which is difficult to question or to establish without supporting documents or signatures. Significantly, conditions exist that can easily modify this situation: the discovery and publication could be made by a close friend, and therefore the extradiegetic text, as in the examples from Hawthorne and Gissing, would exceed the degree-zero conditions. More often the "discoverer" of the text is also the editor/publisher (by whatever name, the figure responsible for publication). In *Adolphe* we must recognize the intermediary function of the innkeeper, who ultimately is the discoverer and first transmitter of the lost manuscript. However, as the previous discussion implies, the innkeeper fulfills no *significant* function other than that of a relay.

If we postulate that an intermediary character is necessary to a fully developed extradiegetic narrative of transmission of this sort, then we must actualize the "second reader" as such a figure. Although he is neither discoverer nor editor of the text, he fulfills the function of *authenticator*. This authenticator is more significant than the discoverer, and his narrative function is sometimes more significant than the fleeting acquaintance (if it occurs) between intradiegetic and extradiegetic narrators. The authenticator must be a character at both levels; he must bridge the spatial-temporal gap separating the narrating instances, and therefore serve as a supplementary author/editor of the discovered text. Although it is tempting to build a new diegetic level for this figure, I will resist this move since authenticating characters rarely provide texts of their own. When they do, those texts clearly belong to an already existing level. In *Adolphe* this authenticator lends his voice to the extradiegetic discourse and also provides letters from the intradiegetic universe. Other narratives might only refer to his act of authentication without developing his character, and others might only imply his existence as the ultimate judge of the text's authenticity.

In many respects, the authenticator resembles on an extradiegetic level the "intermediary transmitter" and "confidant" of epistolary intradiegesis. In both cases we are dealing with a *contact character* whose primary function is to establish a realizable channel for secret, forbidden, or mysterious communications. By establishing this channel, the contact character also fixes a message's context and sometimes delimits the communication code, thereby overdetermining the social nature of its utterance, transmission, and reception. As I have been arguing, it is dangerous to dismiss extradiegetic fictions as mere conventions because the illusion of the text constructed therein is part of the narrative's textuality. Although retrospective in the substance of their extradiegetic function, contact characters prefigure a field of response that cannot be ignored. As with characterized readers (and many contact characters fulfill this role also), they foreground a perspective that affects even the most objective acts of reading. These theoretical observations should become clearer with a few more examples, which will also show variations on the schematized narrative situation of the contact character.

However, before moving on to these other examples, we must note that *Adolphe* also contains a historiodiegetic level. Twice Constant prefaced later editions of his novel. For the second edition (1816), Constant used the preface to discuss a potential pragmatic lesson that could be learned from his work. For the third edition (1824), Constant again stressed a didactic purpose for his text, and he disclaimed the pirated editions that added material to his work. But Constant's more significant purpose for both prefaces, particularly the first, was to counter claims that the novel was only thinly veiled autobiography (a reading, by the way, that has some validity); and he openly attacked such readers: "The rage to recognize in works of imagination the individuals whom one meets with in the world, is for these works a real plague. It degrades them, gives them a false direction, destroys their interest, annihilates their utility" (26). Both prefaces represent historiodiegetic attempts to shape a reading through statements of authorial intention. Although the actual effect of these prefaces is hard to estimate, they do represent clear examples of a paratextual narrating level beyond the fiction that can influence readers either rightly or wrongly.

IN 1840, Mikhail Lermontov compiled three previously published stories with two new stories to form the novel (if indeed it can be called that) *A Hero of Our Time*.[14] The stories are about Pechorin; of the three stories first published separately, two ("Taman" and "The Fatalist") are autodiegetic narrations from "Pechorin's Journal."[15] The third story, "Bela," as indicated by its original subtitle, "From the Notes of an Officer about the Caucasus," belongs to the genre of travel literature including interesting tales heard on the road. Thus the story about Pechorin told in "Bela" is told to the traveling "author" by Maksim Maksimich, a military comrade of Pechorin's. The traveling author never lets Maksim Maksimich completely take control of the narrating situation, and at one point the traveling author addresses his audience directly: "It is not a novella I am writing, but traveling notes" (31–32). Since, moreover, in the larger text "Bela" is the first story, Boris Eikenbaum is correct in saying that "*A Hero of Our Time* is not a tale, not a novel, but travel notes to which a portion of Pechorin's 'Journal' has been attached."[16] Of the remaining two stories, "Princess Mary" is told in Pechorin's diary (the only pure journal in the "Journal"), and "Maksim Maksimich" is told by the traveling author. This last story is most relevant to my study of extradiegetic narratives of transmission.[17]

"Bela" takes the form of a travel tale with a transcribed intercalated story that gives the tale its title. Formally, "Bela" presents an extradiegetic narrating situation in which the traveling author shifts from an autodiegetic presence, narrating his travels, to a pseudo-heterodiegetic absence, transcribing/reporting Maksim Maksimich's intradiegetic oral narration (this situation of shifting narration will be discussed more extensively in the next two chapters). These shifts are marked by genre-conscious references to travel literature and by the traveling author's prompting questions. The second story in the novel, "Maksim Maksimich," strictly functions as a transition from the travel notes to "Pechorin's Journal." As such, it is a *contact story* that signifies and establishes a second (now written) intradiegetic level. In this story, Maksimich again meets Pechorin, but he receives a cool reception from his one-time comrade, who is seen here for the first and only time by the traveling author. Because of Pechorin's disdain for their past friendship, Maksimich gives Pechorin's unwanted papers to the traveling author, throwing the notebooks onto "the ground with contempt" (61).

The meeting with Pechorin is significant for many reasons. As in *Adolphe*, the extradiegetic narrator is able to present his "portrait" of the journal's writer and hero. The traveling author first qualifies his portrait: "However, these are but my private notes based on my own observations, and by no means do I expect you to believe in them blindly" (56); but he then valorizes the portrait by referring to the reader's total dependence on him: "Perhaps all of these observations came to my mind only because I knew some details of his life, and perhaps upon someone else his looks might have produced an entirely different impression; but since you will hear of him from no one but me, you must needs be satisfied with this portrayal" (57). The *knowledge* the traveling author refers to comes from Maksimich's story in "Bela," but the sentence shifts in the third clause, and the reader addressed by the repetition of "you" is placed in a subordinate position of perception: the "you" is not the "someone else" who might have "an entirely different impression." Moreover, the traveling author again signifies his total appropriation, within the published text for which he claims responsibility, of Maksimich's oral narration and the parts of the journal yet to come. He later confesses his greedy acquisition of the text: "I seized the papers and hastened to carry them away, fearing lest the captain might repent" (61).

But the oral narrative and the written texts that have come into his possession have been discarded by their producers. We can speculate that "Bela" would be a much different story if told after the meeting with Pechorin, or it might even have been suppressed by the repulsed Maksimich. More significantly, Pechorin is completely uninterested in the fate of his papers: "'What shall I do with them?' [Maksimich asked]. 'Whatever you like,' answered Pechorin. 'Goodbye'" (59). This unconcern immediately transfers to Maksimich, who replies to the traveling author's reiterative question "And what are you going to do with them?" with, "What, indeed? I'll have them made into cartridges" (60). Possibly echoing the fiction of saving the text in *The Man of Feeling*, the traveling author asserts his right to the manuscript by playing on Maksimich's momentary resentment. Thus the text transmitted has been twice orphaned and twice framed by a discarding. Yet this contact story has a reasonably happy ending when the text, the story's true hero, is appropriated (adopted) by the traveling author, who seeks to exploit its literary potential.

The extradiegetic introduction to Pechorin's Journal, placed a third of the way into the novel, exposes this exploitation. Upon learning of Pechorin's death (the circumstances of which are never conveyed in writing, yet which makes the text finally transmissible), the traveling author wastes no time in publishing the journal along with the tale of its discovery: the travel notes. Yet just as Pechorin and Maksimich discard the journal, the traveling author discards his own experiences to present Pechorin's. In addition to presenting Pechorin's text, there is the promise (the sequel convention again) of yet another notebook: "There still remains in my possession a fat notebook wherein [Pechorin] narrates all his life. Some day it, too, will be presented to the judgment of the world, but for the present there are important reasons why I dare not assume such a responsibility" (64). The mystification caused by this statement (could it be similar to the mystery about Valmont that Peggy Kamuf discovered in *Les liaisons dangereuses*?) suggests how much undecidability obtains in this text—much of the story has been excluded. Indeed, we may speculate on this absence in the narrative and question whether the nature of Pechorin's exile to the Caucasus makes his life story politically dangerous to the transmission of power in imperial Russia, therefore, necessitating the suppression of (exiling of) the remainder of his text. Hence, within the context of the "exiled narrative," each narrator dispossesses his original narration, thereby undercutting the chain of authority that the narrative of transmission is supposed to signify. The truth of the story, which the conventions of transmission are supposed to affirm, is made problematic by the interference of one narrative with another. As a general rule, the more complex the extradiegetic narration is, the more problematic the intradiegetic narration becomes.

Lermontov ultimately extends this problematic further with a historiodiegetic preface added to a later edition. Like Constant before him, Lermontov had to respond to misreadings of the first edition of *A Hero of Our Time*. He writes, "In every book the preface is the first and also the last thing. It serves either to explain the purpose of the work or to justify it and answer criticism" (1). Then, like Constant, Lermontov goes on to question naïve readers who seek literal parallels in the characters, and he reveals Pechorin as a "portrait composed of all the vices of our generation in the fullness of their development" (2). Such statements are predictable, and they resemble other overdetermining statements by extradiegetic editors and narrators we have read. The significant difference in both Constant's and Lermontov's novels is that the historiodiegetic preface belatedly tries to undermine the illusion of reality that the extradiegetic narrative of transmission conventionally postulates. The text's reality lies in its generalized portrait of society, and the response of real readers to a perceived specific reality (a biographical fallacy) must be removed to the text's margin. The necessity for this action stems in part from the literary environment of the "romantic hero" in which both authors were writing. Yet neither author was ready to admit, as Oscar Wilde would decades later, that life imitates art. Instead, they used arabesque narratives of transmission and strategically placed paratexts to displace the referential codes echoing in their transmitted narrations.

NOVELISTS SOMETIMES take advantage of extradiegetic problematics and displacements, particularly if the story is about the supernatural or some other unsolvable mystery. A prime example of a text containing inherent problems is Henry James's *The Turn of the Screw* (1898, 1908).[18] Again we have the paradigm of an extradiegetic narrator who receives the text through a contact character. This contact character, Douglas, was a close friend of (maybe even in love with or loved by) the intradiegetic writer of the original manuscript— a woman who tells of her experiences as the governess of two children at an estate called Bly. This purposefully reductive account of the narrative's transmission places *The Turn of the Screw* within the paradigm I have used so far in this chapter. But whereas the first two texts contain relative ambiguities that the reader endeavors to reduce to meaning, James's tale is one of almost irreducible ambiguity.

At the narrative's most exterior point is the extradiegetic narrator, whose anecdote of the first public reading of the governess' manuscript introduces the story, initiating contact with a new circle of readers and clarifying the manuscript's fable of origin. However, this narrator, who remains unnamed, is inordinately evasive in accounting for his or her copy of the manuscript: "Let me say here distinctly, to have done with it, that this narrative, from an exact transcript of my own made much later, is what I shall presently give. Poor Douglas, before his death—when it was in sight—committed to me the manuscript that reached him on the third of these days [of the anecdote] and that, on the same spot [where he first mentioned the tale's existence], with immense effect, he began to read to our hushed little circle on the night of the fourth" (152). This address to the reader, a narrative chore "to have done with," dates the extradiegetic narrating act as "much later" than the scene of Douglas's public reading. The exactness of the transcription is a mere throwaway attempt at authentication and authority, while in other texts there is a distinctly articulated essential claim. Besides these two transmission acts (transcribing the text and then giving it to the public), the second sentence fuses, in a reordering of the linear course of transmission, three more transmission acts: Douglas (on his deathbed?) *commits* the manuscript (as a legacy?) to the narrator, Douglas *receives* the manuscript (whose reading was deferred) from the town where it was stored (encrypted?) in a locked drawer, and Douglas *reads* the manuscript with "immense effect."

If we examine the five transmission acts occurring in the passage, we observe that each one involves a mechanical handling of the text. Only the parenthetical qualification of Douglas's reading as having an "immense effect" suggests a full narrative transmission including reception and response. To describe reception as an "immense effect," however, is to be particularly, and in James characteristically, vague. The extradiegetic narrative introduction stages the reading and listening, but the aftermath, the "effect," is missing. The extradiegetic narrator never returns to tell us how the "hushed little circle" broke its silence and responded to the reading of the governess' text. Response is transferred, instead, to the reader of the novel; thus, James breaks with many earlier extradiegetic situations by not using a posterior narrating position to reorient reader response and thereby diminish or increase the problematics inherent in the novel's narrative of transmission. What James achieves in the extradiegetic narrative is the illusion of the first reading and the effect of terror he intends.

Instead of the introduction foregrounding a reader's response to the intradiegesis, the extradiegesis replaces the unwritten prologue to the governess' narrative. Therefore, rather than being an interpretive document, the introduction records the *pretext* for the manuscript and the horizon of expectations preceding its first public reception. The prologue is Douglas's sole original narrating act, although his account of the pretext for the manuscript apparently transforms a verbal transmission he had previously from the governess.[19] Added to this temporal gap between tellings is the extradiegetic narrator's after-the-fact transcription of the *mise en scène* of the prologue. Although still an essential text in critical interpretations of the governess and the events at Bly, the prologue, which is supposed to establish a meaningful context for the manuscript, is lost in a regress of transmissions and transformations. Moreover, the distancing effects of both the extradiegetic narrative of transmission and the prologue displace even further the narrating act of the governess' text.

Crucial to understanding the narrative in *The Turn of the Screw* is the recognition of the indeterminacy that inheres in all the narrating situations. The complexity of the extradiegetic narration is a *mise en abyme* for the complexity of the intradiegetic narration. The extradiegetic narrator's narrating situation mirrors the governess'. A temporal gap separates the writing of the introduction and the occasion of Douglas's prologue and reading; similarly, a temporal gap separates the governess' writing of her manuscript and the events recorded. The narrating situation marks a distance between narrating self and experiencing self that produces an act of narrative reconstruction. Unlike most of James's novels, where a sense of immediacy is created by the figural narrative techniques that allow the reader minimally mediated access to the central character's consciousness, the autodiegetic narrating situation posits a clearly mediated and retrospective narrative.

The manuscript opens with "I remember," and twice more in the first paragraph the governess refers to her remembering of how things were. In the second paragraph, she "recollects," and in the third paragraph the retrospective view is linked with a foreshadowing of a different state of affairs: "But these fancies [hearing things in the morning] were not marked enough not to be thrown off, and it is only in the light, or the gloom, I should rather say, of *other and subsequent* [emphasis added] matters that they now come back to me" (160). A few pages later, as the governess recalls her first tour of Bly with Flora, we read:

> I have not seen Bly since the day I left it, and I dare say that to my *present older and more informed eyes* [emphasis added] it would show a very reduced importance. But as my little conductress, with her hair of gold and her frock of blue, danced before me round corners and pattered down passages, I had the view of a castle of romance inhabited by a rosy sprite, such a place as would somehow, for diversion of the young idea, take all colour out of story-books and fairy-tales. Was n't [sic] it just a story-book over which I had fallen a-doze and a-dream? No; it was a big ugly antique but convenient house, embodying a few features of a building still older, half-displaced and half-utilised. (163)

This passage marks a triple displacement: (1) the perspective from the time of the narration recontextualizes the time of the narrated events; (2) Flora becomes a "rosy sprite" dancing in a "castle of romance" out of a "story-book"—one that the governess, like Alice in Wonderland, imagines she might have fallen "a-dream" over; (3) when the projected metaphoric fantasy of the "castle" gives way to the reality of the "antique but convenient" house, the house itself frames "a building still older, half-displaced and half-utilised." In a text so aware of architecture and storymaking, the governess conflates these latter two displacements when she signifies the Gothic code of her narrative: "Was there a 'secret' at Bly—a mystery of Udolpho or an insane, an unmentionable relative kept in unsuspected confinement?" (179). Not only is this a reference to Ann Radcliffe's *The Mysteries of Udolpho* (a novel full of framing and transmission devices), but it echoes the "secret" buried alive at Thornfield in Charlotte Brontë's *Jane Eyre*—clearly a governess novel James is returning in *The Turn of the Screw*. All these passages are emblematic of the shifting, already-written, and ever-enclosing perspective the governess brings to bear on her tale recollected in tranquility.

Indeed, throughout the manuscript, the governess marks her belated scene of narrating, wondering whether the text will be able to "retrace to-day the strange steps of my obsession" (244). Her tale of her experience, however, reconstructs both events and her impressions (mental constructs) of those events. Often there are gross contradictions between what the governess remembers of the event and what she remembers "reading" into the event at the time: "I only sat there on my tomb and read into what [Miles] had said to me the fulness of its meaning" (254). Yet even with a perfect memory of her contradictory feelings at the time, the governess marks the transformational effect of her narrative distance: "I suppose I now read into our situation a clearness it could n't [sic] have had at the time, for I seem to see our poor eyes already lighted with some spark of a *prevision* [emphasis added] of the anguish that was to come" (302). With her "present older and more informed eyes," the governess reads into her reconstruction of the final scene with Miles a "prevision," or rather a *construct* that overdetermines the final scene as one of "anguish." The governess is trying to represent how the events affected her consciousness, but writes "I scarce know *how to put my story into words* that shall be a *credible picture* of my state of mind" (198). Earlier she had written, "As I recall the way it went reminds me of all *the art I now need* to make it *a little distinct*" so that "To me at least, making my statement here with *a deliberation* with which I have never made it, the whole feeling of the moment returns" (172, 176; emphasis added).

The questions that arise from these passages concern the governess' reasons for writing at all. Why does she reexperience her terror by writing about it? For whom does she write her text? Moreover, given the version of the experience she commits to paper, could this experience be recollected in tranquility with any degree of objectivity? These questions of the governess' motivation and intention in narrating her tale imply a writing scene in which the narrating self reconstructs the experiencing self in words as a means of trying to understand the experience, which was fraught with uncertainty when it occurred. The governess must make certain for herself what was then so uncertain. In modern psychoanalytic terms, the manuscript resembles a "talking cure," a means of voicing what desires to remain unvoiced, a means of relieving guilt for the outcome of the events. The experience at Bly has contaminated the governess' consciousness with a memory she now wants to textualize to effect her own cure: her writing will relieve her of the presence of memory by giving the events a substance in language that can be read as definitively past.[20]

We see the psychic drama of her narrating act at a moment in the text when the governess voices her anxiety over her task, and we learn that the writing forces her to suffer again the trauma of the events: "I find that I really hang back; but I must take my horrid plunge. In going on with the record of what was hideous at Bly I not only challenge the most liberal faith—for which I little care; but (and this is another matter) I renew what I myself suffered, I again push my dreadful way through it to the end. There came suddenly an hour after which, as I look back, the business seems to me to have been all pure suffering; but I have at least reached the heart of it, and the straightest road out is doubtless to advance" (220). To "renew" by suffering through the displaced medium of writing, however, is to renew by transformation. The suffering must be made manageable through textualization; then, and only then, can the events be invested with an illusion of reality that allows the governess to "fix" Peter Quint: "I saw him as I see the letters I form on this page" (177). Indeed, this activity of "fixing" the other is given spatial and metaphoric force when Quint is described by the governess with painterly references to a "frame": "The man who looked at me over the battlements was as definite as a picture in a frame" (176–77). Indeed, he usually appears at windows, framed from the waist up as in a portrait, and when the governess recalls her first telling Mrs. Grose about her experience, she remembers "seeing in her face that she already, in this, with a deeper dismay, found a touch of picture," the governess writes, "I quickly added stroke to stroke" (190). Whether Peter Quint is a ghost or the product of an hallucination, he becomes in the text a *sign* in a private universe of signs where the governess can exert some authority and thereby cure herself of her contaminated memory.

In challenging "the most liberal faith"—a highly ambiguous phrase—and then disdaining it, the governess deconstructs her reader's suspension of disbelief and marks her text as a personal document, composed for a personal catharsis. But the audience for the manuscript expands: first to Douglas, then to the circle of listeners around the fire, then to the extradiegetic narrator's readers, and lastly to us. And the narrative of transmission becomes a narrative of a reading that overlooks the effect of textuality. As its title metaphorically implies, to turn the screw of narrative transmission is a special effect, and each turn (transmission or reading) only displaces the point further from the surface of what happened at Bly. In many respects all narratives of transmission turn a screw of narration and fabulate a figure already displaced and undecidable; thus, the object of interpretation is the textualized scene of writing and not the written scene. In other words, the act of narrating, which produces the text of the narrated events, must be interpreted before the narrated events can be interpreted.

The scene of writing becomes multiple as "the chain transmission of the story" establishes a system of repetition. Shoshana Felman calls this "a chain of readings[:] Readings which re-read, and re-write, other readings." She observes, "Each narrator, to relay the story, must first be a *receiver* of the story, a *reader* who at once records it and *interprets* it, simultaneously trying to make sense of it and *undergoing* it, as a lived experience, an 'impression,' a *reading-effect*."[21] Even though the *"reading-effect"* informs the functions of narrative levels and can affect the relayed text through editorial interference, it has a decidedly secondary position on the extradiegetic level. However, the reading activities at the extradiegetic level are meant to teach us how to read by negative example. Most extradiegetic narrators fail to question the status of the text, concerning themselves instead with the interpretation of the written scene. The scene of writing is marked only as the physical production of a text, the reading of which transforms textuality into an actualized illusion of lived experience. But what is the limit of this illusion's power? Can a text's scene of writing be so radical that suspension of disbelief becomes impossible?

Of course, historiodiegetic prefaces are notorious for dismantling any naïve notion of suspended disbelief, but here as well James offers a difference. As we have seen in this chapter and the one preceding, the difficulty in transmission at the extradiegetic level of narrating rests in the contact generated by our mimetic expectations of the "Preface." Our desire for authenticity and authority posits that we read the fictional preface as a demystification of the text. In reading Henry James's prefaces to the New York edition of his works, for instance, we would hardly consider that a fictional editor is addressing us. Yet if Richard Poirier is correct about the "theatricality" of James's "performing self" in his notebooks,[22] then we should indeed consider carefully the persona inscribing James's public prefaces. The opening paragraph of the New York edition's preface to *The Turn of the Screw* shows James's recollection of "the private source" of the story, but the anecdote is so carefully ambiguous that its summary hints about the source story take on a particular significance with relation to the fictional text:

> Thus it was, I remember, that amid our lament for a beautiful lost form [the really effective heart-shaking ghost-story], our distinguished host expressed the wish that he might but have recovered for us one of the scantest of fragments of this form at its best. He had never forgotten the impression made on him as a young man by the withheld glimpse, as it were, of a dreadful matter that had been reported years before, and with as few particulars, to a lady with whom he had youthfully talked. The story would have been thrilling could she have but found herself in better possession of it, dealing as it did with a couple of small children in an out-of-the-way place, to whom the spirits of certain "bad" servants, dead in the employ of the house, were believed to have appeared with the design of "getting hold" of them. This was all, but there had been more, which my friend's old converser had lost the thread of: she could only assure him of the wonder of the allegations as she had anciently heard them made. He himself could give us but this shadow of a shadow—my own appreciation of which, I need scarcely say, was exactly wrapped up in that thinness. (xv)

Instead of demystifying his tale, James remystifies it by a decayed system of narrative transmission that implies through its "thinness" that the original story was possibly true. When James reworks his *donnée* for his tale, he saves the text in a document, constructing a narrative of transmission that alleges the truth value of the governess' manuscript. Reading James's New York preface, we neither assume it narrates a fictional event nor expect it to disavow a biographical origin of the story; its characters are presumably identifiable with real people, given more information.[23] James gives us instead in his New York prefaces, a carefully crafted portrait of the artist that complements the fiction by subtly appearing to let us into secrets while it simultaneously remodels the house of fiction to create new portals of discovery.

In *The Turn of the Screw*, Henry James exhausts the paradigm of the extradiegetic narrative by creating an irreducible tension of ambiguity between belief and disbelief. It could even be argued that James's narrative of transmission is designed to confirm our disbelief and thus save our sanity from a complementary madness. According to John Barth, literary forms go through periods of exhausted possibility and periods of replenishment.[24] For example, Pierre Choderlos de Laclos's *Les liaisons dangereuses* is acknowledged by many as the culmination of the first era of epistolary fiction; it fulfills nearly the entire range of formal possibilities for its genre. Formal exhaustion is not, however, formal extinction, and although many second-rate authors will adopt a form without contributing any innovations (formal or thematic), an exhausted form can be replenished by a genre-conscious recognition of the changed context within which the form is to function. Barth's *Letters* and Jacques Derrida's "Envois" replenish epistolary formal thematics by shifting thematic emphasis to different aspects of the epistolary narrative act, especially the difficulties of transmission, that address the contemporary state of narrative fiction and of Western philosophical epistemologies. Similarly, after James's exhaustion of possibility for the extradiegetic narrative of transmission that has concerned us here, we perceive a period in literary history in which no effective use of the paradigm is made. To replenish the convention, a changed prestructure must come into existence.

If we reexamine the texts discussed here we can see a fairly consistent prestructure: despite the problematics of displacement in the transmission system, the intradiegetic text is always the product of human agency and, moreover, of literary sensibility. John Barth, in *Giles Goat-Boy* (1966),[25] questions the role of the narrating agent responsible for the intradiegetic text in order to replenish (among other things) the extradiegetic narrative-of-transmission paradigm within a postmodern prestructure. Barth describes his novel as one of those "novels which imitate the form of the Novel, by an author who imitates the role of Author"; he further points out that "this sort of thing" is "about where the genre began, with *Quixote* imitating *Amadis of Gaul*, Cervantes pretending to be the Cid Hamete Benengeli (and Alonso Quijano pretending to be Don Quixote), or Fielding parodying Richardson."[26] Within the present context, we can extend Barth's comparison to include, to some degree, Constant, Lermontov, and James. But to write today a novel with nineteenth-century conventions, or even a convention-ridden narrative of transmission, is to be out-of-date with many of modernism's and postmodernism's contributions to narrative technique. To replenish the older technique, the novelist must revise its presuppositions, thereby altering its intertextual relationship with earlier versions of the same

narrative device. The deep structure paradigm holds, but with a revised surface structure.

Giles Goat-Boy presents a postmodern example of the extradiegetic
narrative of transmission I have been discussing; it also presents an
extradiegetic paratext borrowed from Laclos (among, no doubt, others): the publisher's disclaimer. The novel opens with this disclaimer,
which sets out immediately to put the reader on guard: "The reader
must begin this book with an act of faith and end it with an act of
charity. We ask him to believe in the sincerity and authenticity of
this preface, affirming in return his prerogative to be skeptical of all
that follows it" (ix). Such a statement leads the contemporary reader,
who is well aware that this disclaimer is a fiction, into creating an
ironic horizon of expectations for all that follows. The claims of truth
and fiction become indistinguishable as the editor-in-chief goes on
to summarize the text's narrative of transmission:

> The professor and quondam novelist whose name appears on the title-
> page (*our* title-page, not the one following his prefatory letter) de-
> nies that the work is his, but "suspects" it to be fictional—a suspi-
> cion that two pages should confirm for the average reader. His own
> candidate for its authorship is one Stoker Giles or Giles Stoker—
> whereabouts unknown, existence questionable—who appears to have
> claimed in turn 1) that he too was but a dedicated editor, the text
> proper having been written by a certain automatic computer, and 2)
> that excepting a few "necessary basic artifices"* the book is neither
> fable nor fictionalized history, but literal truth. And the computer,
> the mighty "WESCAC"—does it not too disclaim authorship? It does.
>
> *The computer's assumption of first-person narrative viewpoint,
> we are told, is one such "basic artifice." The reader will add others,
> perhaps challenging their "necessity" as well. (ix)

The one transmission step missing here is George Giles's act of
entering the story of his life into the computer, like one would
enter items into a journal. The editor-in-chief further includes in
the Publisher's Disclaimer the readers' reports of four different con-
sulting readers, whose "replies anticipate ... what will be the range
of public and critical reaction to the book" (x). By their contradictions, these readers' reports trivialize the extradiegetic convention
of overdetermining response. Instead of giving the reader direction,
the elaborate, even byzantine, paratextual apparatus overwhelms
and displaces the reader's sense of fictionality and the status of the
text. In this extravagant parody of the extradiegetic narrative of

transmission, Barth not only makes the status of the intradiegetic scene of writing indeterminate, but he makes himself and the entire literary instance indeterminate.

While in most cases narrative analysis must guard against confusing the narrating instance with the literary instance, Barth makes this confusion a functioning part of his fiction. An example of the confusion occurs in the paratextual play of title pages, which is laid bare by the editor-in-chief's strict distinction between the two. The fictional title page for novels that imitate other texts is a convention of the narrating instance, whereas the title page that signifies the economics of literary production is a part of the literary instance. In the history of the novel, the two title-page forms often overlap in a palimpsest; the reader separates the instances as s/he chooses. Some transmission distortion occurs today when previously anonymous or pseudonymous published texts are published with the author's name and gender identified.[27] Barth, however, exposes the double nature of such a title page that signifies both the reality of the book and the fictionality of its contents.

This playful questioning and doubling goes on throughout Barth's text, but the indeterminacy that results from the reader's nonsatisfaction focuses attention on the problematic of postmodern replenishment of exhausted form. Tony Tanner articulates the problem facing the reader by speculating that "if a writer chooses a form which undermines the status of all forms, a fiction which questions the validity of all literary genres and modes, then that writer has excluded the possibility that any particular section of his rhetoric can be taken seriously."[28] Tanner's assessment is, of course, extreme, and it is delimited by a conception of literature as rhetoric, a notion that presupposes a reading strategy. That strategy might be inappropriate for postmodern texts, might be out-of-date, might be exhausted with relation to the present state of fiction.

But as if enough isn't enough, Barth replays the questions of truth and fiction at the conclusion of *Giles Goat-Boy* when the "Postscript to the Posttape" by "J. B." (the extradiegetic narrator) calls into question the "Posttape," considering "internal evidence against its authenticity" (709), and noting lastly that "even the type of those flunkèd pages is different" (710). This statement is followed by a "Footnote to the Postscript to the Posttape," which informs the reader that "the type of the typescript pages entitled 'Postscript to the Posttape' is not the same as that of the 'Cover-Letter to the Editors and Publishers'" (710). So round and round we go.

Postmodern writing, and Barth's work especially, has often staged a heightened genre-consciousness and parody of literary forms, and this reflexive consciousness alters and renews the reading of conventions. As in the eighteenth century, when Fielding's *Shamela* parodied the conventions of the early epistolary novel, the extradiegetic narrative of transmission in *Giles Goat-Boy* parodies the paradigm discussed in this chapter. And Barth's subversive thematics of narrative convention also suggest the potential for a subversive reading of the extradiegetic narrative of transmission in premodernist texts. This new subversive reading would revise the reader's affective stylistics for interpreting the extradiegetic narrative of transmission. Therefore, the reader would process the text under a changed set of interpretive strategies, which would produce in turn a changed construct of the narrating instance. Undoubtedly, there would be some insight in these new readings, but when seen with relation to the full structure of narrative transmission, the reader would become completely responsible for creating his or her own meaning out of the text. Consequently, the original story is displaced by an added filter in the transmission system, and the object of interpretation moves from the scene of writing to the scene of reading, with reading itself becoming a self-conscious activity and yet another transmission open to critical scrutiny. Nevertheless, all practical literary criticism produces stories of a reading, and such stories could be said to create yet another frame for the literary text.

Barth has yet to place a preface of his own at the head of *Giles Goat-Boy*; however, his essay "The Literature of Exhaustion" (1967)[29] is an important historiodiegetic paratext for this novel should Barth decide to sanction it as such. The difficulty in such a move comes from the prestructure by which this novel is processed by contemporary readers. Barth has plotted for himself a literary territory filled with narrative experiments and critical essays on the efficacy of the experiments. Readers trained in the "traditional" novel may have trouble following Barth's experiments or understanding his fictions, but as an author Barth probably would find the historiodiegetic problems of a Constant or a Lermontov interesting but of little note for his fictional universe. And if Barth is ever given a chance to write a New York (or rather, Baltimore) preface to his works, one imagines it would be an occasion for a more elaborate fabulation than James ever would have considered. Barth still has time to add a historiodiegetic preface to *Giles Goat-Boy*, but within the detached-from-reality context of postmodern literature, such a preface may never need to be written.

7 | *Frame Transmission and the Narrative Contract*

> At this point I must make it clear that I wrote down his
> story almost immediately after hearing it; consequently
> this narrative is perfectly accurate and faithful.
> —Prévost, *Manon Lescaut*

S O FAR THIS INQUIRY has concentrated on prose fictions that are
constituted by documents (letters, diaries, private manuscripts)
written by characters in the fictional universe. In following the narratives of transmission that bring these documents from their inner
societies to the larger society of the reading public, we have observed how the scene of writing can be as important as the written
scene. Any complete reading of a narrative depends, in part, on an
understanding of the distinctions that mark the narration's relationship to the narrated events. These distinctions have been identified
in the previous chapters as the differences in textualization that
occur in an epistolary system of discourses, as the separation of the
narrating self and the experiencing self in diary writing, and as the
distance between the intradiegetic world of letters, diaries, or private
manuscripts and the extradiegetic world of editors, uncharacterized
narrators, and text discoverers. Yet even in this last case, the main
texts are generated by the participants in the events; each character
has been motivated to write, to textualize experience. In addition
to examining these acts of writing, we have also been concerned
with analogous acts of reading that occur in these prose fictions. In
nearly every narrative of transmission examined, characterized
readers—either real or imagined, intended or unintended—have
either influenced or determined what narrators commit to paper, to
permanence as a document. Thus these narratives of transmission
mark consciously willed processes of communication and social
interaction; both narrators and readers are motivated in their acts
of writing and reading.

There is, however, yet another kind of textualization that occurs
in prose fiction: the transcription of an oral narration by someone

outside of, or on the margin of, the universe of the oral narrative. An example of such a textualization was mentioned last chapter in the discussion of the "Bela" section of Lermontov's *A Hero of Our Time*.[1] In "Bela" the traveling author meets Maksim Maksimich, who tells him the story of Pechorin's adventure with Bela. In this tale we have an extradiegetic narrating situation in which the traveling author shifts from an autodiegetic presence, narrating his own travels, to a pseudo-heterodiegetic absence, transcribing/reporting Maksimich's intra-homodiegetic oral narration. "Bela" is important to Lermontov's novel because it introduces Pechorin from a distance, thereby making the shift to his journal gradual and heightening the reader's interest in this asocial character. "Bela" is important for my purposes here because it can serve as a model of the narrative paradigm considered in this chapter and the next: the transcribed oral narration. Before examining some theoretical issues that obtain in transcribed oral narration, I will examine two cases in which the narrative of transmission merges with both a narrative of transaction (a narrative contract) and a narrative of transference (a psychoanalytical exchange of narrative personalities): George Sand's *Leone Leoni* and its formal/thematic precursor, Abbé Prévost's *Manon Lescaut*.[2]

IN *S/Z*, his classic study of Honoré de Balzac's novella *Sarrasine*, Roland Barthes describes narrative transaction, the storytelling act that marks a contract between storyteller and listener. In certain fictions, Barthes observes, "one narrates in order to obtain by exchanging; and it is this exchange that is represented in the narrative itself: narrative is both product and production, merchandise and commerce."[3] In Balzac's *Sarrasine*, the story is to be exchanged for a night of love with the listener ("a contract of prostitution"). Yet as Peter Brooks suggests, "'contract' is too simple a term, and too static; something more active, dynamic, shifting, and trans-formatory is involved in the exchange."[4] For Brooks, narrative plotting plays out an allegory of "desire" for self or for sexual fulfillment, for a return to (or cure of) a repressed past, even a desire for death. Desire thus motivates both narrative and narration, particularly in narrating situations staging the negotiations between narrator and narratee. But desire is never innocent or static; instead, it is a dynamic process that Brooks likens to Freudian analysis, which by its very practice seeks to build a coherent narrative from repressed material in the unconscious. George Sand's novel *Leone Leoni* (1834)[5] exemplifies an erotic narrating situation requiring a narrative contract to negotiate its fund of desire.

In the 1853 introduction to a new edition of *Leone Leoni*, George Sand wrote that in 1834 she was in Venice, experiencing "the painful contrast which results from inward suffering, alone amid the wild excitement of a population of strangers." Her relationship with Alfred de Musset was dissolving; indeed, he had all but broken with her because she returned the attentions of his doctor. She found herself "on Mardi Gras, in the heart of the classic carnival city, in a frame of mind ... painfully meditative." She says, "I began at hazard a novel which opened with a description of the locality, of the festival out-of-doors and of the solemn apartment in which I was writing. The last book I had read before leaving Paris was *Manon Lescaut*.... And I had said to myself that to make Manon Lescaut a man and Desgrieux [sic] a woman would be worth trying, and would present many tragic opportunities, vice being often very near crime in man, and enthusiasm closely akin to despair in woman" (179) As these references indicate, to understand the narrative structure of *Leone Leoni*'s dialectic of desire, we must first examine Sand's narrative model: *Manon Lescaut*.

As Sand did, today we read *Manon Lescaut* (1731; 1753)[6] as a novel in its own right; however, it was first published as a digressive tale appended to Abbé Prévost's six volume work, *Les mémoires et aventures d'un homme de qualité qui s'est retiré du monde*. Prévost called his text *L'histoire du Chevalier des Grieux et de Manon Lescaut*, but as with the longer work to which this story had been appended, readers soon ignored the first part of the title, leaving only *Manon Lescaut*. This brief history of the novel's literary instance is instructive for two related reasons. First, the literary instance marks Prévost's original placement of the novel within the frame of a larger work, including that work's prestructure (the presentational context formed by the reading public familiar with *Les mémoires*). This prestructure is transformed as the text emerges as its own entity. Secondly, with the transformed frame and prestructure of the literary instance, the presuppositions of the narrating instance are also transformed. Still, such framing requires a narrative contract: why does Des Grieux tell his tale to the man of quality?

In fact, it is a narrative bought in advance, for during the short meeting at Pacy presented at the opening of the novel, the man of quality gives Des Grieux enough money to continue his attendance on Manon. Two years later, when Des Grieux and the man of quality meet again, the former needs little persuading to tell his tale of misfortune. It is crucial to see the structural relationship of the narratives. Des Grieux's narrative is intercalated in *Les mémoires*, but his act of narrating and his narration are embedded in the man of quality's narrative. The narrative frames significantly influence how we read Des Grieux's tale because the narrative contract marked by the outer frame calls for a "moral tale" suitable for the man of quality's memoirs. Hence, we find that throughout the narration Des Grieux sees the events of his life as subordinate to a higher order: "There is something uncanny about the way in which Providence links one event to another" (107), and when he and Manon are in America and are contemplating marriage, he tells her: "Let us leave our fate in God's hands" (177). An important part of the philosophical system undergirding *Les mémoires* is the concept of a divinely ordered universe in which the individual is punished for transgressing his or her social duties—personal tragedy follows each transgression. This divine order is mirrored in the tightly structured narrative order, as Des Grieux's narrative discourse foreshadows each tragedy, and places the transgressive acts he and Manon commit within an economy of predestined retribution that undercuts the tendency of his narrative to become a romance about likable rogues.

An example of this foreshadowed (proleptic) undercutting occurs at the beginning of chapter 9, just before the episode with young G. M. Des Grieux says, "I have noticed all through my life that Heaven has always chosen the time when my happiness seemed most firmly established for aiming its cruellest blows at me. I thought I was so happy with Manon's love and the friendship of M. de T. that it would have been impossible to convince me that I had any new disaster to fear. But even then a new one was being prepared so terrible that it reduced me to the state you saw me in at Pacy, and by degrees to such deplorable straits that you will scarcely be able to believe that my story is true" (122). Des Grieux can only rationalize the severity of the events by citing Heaven's will and an unnamed determiner who "prepared" the "new disaster" about to befall him and Manon. By articulating this prolepsis within the context of a deterministic world view, Des Grieux ascribes the justness of his punishment to a higher authority. The prolepsis also functions in the narration to prescribe a closure to the events about to be narrated; by warning his audience that the events will end disastrously, Des Grieux lets the audience step back from the sequence of the events to examine their substance. Lastly, the final plea for audience belief in the truth of the tale underwrites the prestructure that the narrative of Des Grieux's narration hopes to establish for the entire text.

In the end, *Manon Lescaut* is a moral apologue for the readers of *Les mémoires*, as the man of quality's preface makes clear: "The whole work is a moral treatise entertainingly put into practice" (23). This treatise charts the innocent Des Grieux's movement from a state of equilibrium in adolescence, through the disequilibrium of his passionate obsession with Manon, to his eventual return to the sanctioned equilibrium of society and family. However, this novel is not as easy to pin down as the last sentence would suggest. Manon, who has died in the wilderness of America, is absent from the narrating situation and cannot speak for herself, and her only appearance in the frame narrative is marked by an appropriation of her voice by the man of quality: "Before going out I had a word or two with the girl, and she sounded so charming and modest that I found myself making many a reflection on the inscrutable nature [*le caractère incompréhensible*] of woman" (29). "The inscrutable nature of woman"—this inscrutable phrase marks the man of quality's orientation to the events and his incomprehension of Manon. He is drawn to Manon by her beauty and the seeming incongruity of her being chained to a group of soon-to-be deported prostitutes. He discovers something more about her by his meeting with Des Grieux, but he does not record her own words. Instead, he describes how she "sounded so charming and modest," and this leads to reflections "on the inscrutable nature of woman."

Manon Lescaut is an erotic narrative of transgressive desires fulfilled and punished, but its narrative contract between Des Grieux and the man of quality, the text's transcriber, is far from erotic. Instead it marks a patriarchal covenant for a moral apologue articulating family obedience and sexual restraint. The novel's narrative of transmission reveals its contractual nature: the masculine narrators' impersonation of Manon paradoxically marks the feminocentric narrative within the patriarchal narration—the story of a woman bought, sold, and talked about by men. In *The Heroine's Text* Nancy K. Miller discusses the feminocentric paradigm at work in *Manon Lescaut*:

> The pattern of events [in *Manon Lescaut*] conforms to the narrative cliché referred to ... as "illicit love punished." The sequence, which [is] repeated [four] times in the course of the novel, constitutes the matrix of *Manon Lescaut*: fleeting happiness, followed by Manon's betrayal, in turn followed by retribution from paternal authority. The inevitability of the sequence is built into the social and psychological structure of the couple's relation.... Manon, by definition, cannot be faithful to Des Grieux within *his* economy. While his desire is susceptible to fulfillment by Manon alone, her desire for him (at least until they enter the New World) requires *supplementation*.[7]

In this reading, *Manon Lescaut* fulfills the dysphoric paradigm of feminocentric narrative and presents "a double ending: the death of the heroine and the 'reform' of the hero."[8]

The paradoxical nature of this narrative transaction is embodied in Manon's presence and absence. As the narrative comes to us, it is a story about Manon, but the narrating frames always keep her at a distance, always filter her discourse through a series of masculine impersonations and interpretations. Although Des Grieux claims he loves her, and the man of quality himself was once smitten by her beauty, the transcribed text does not justify the ways of Manon to man. The man of quality transcribes "her" story "almost immediately after hearing it [and] consequently this narrative is perfectly accurate and faithful" (30). The "almost" in this short account of the transcription marks a fold in the narrative transmission that hides Manon from our eyes. "His" text presents an "inscrutable," incomprehensible woman, an enigma, a linguistic sign, "Manon"—exploited to the end by men of quality.

Manon Lescaut rehearses the conventional moralism of the fallen woman punished and the young-man-led-astray returned to virtue and familial control. And this narrative precisely fulfills the man of quality's contract. But how much of this moral narrative results from masculine control over the text? Would the outcome be different if the roles were reversed and the woman given a voice? Such a text exists in George Sand's *Leone Leoni*. Leoni, the male Manon, and Juliette, the female Des Grieux, come from a long line of rogues and devoted mistresses, and as such they are hardly more interesting than their stereotypical counterparts in second-rate fiction. Yet Sand's novel, with its overblown rhetoric of passion and insatiable desire, is clearly a parody of Prévost's text. The gender inversion Sand uses significantly rereads Prévost's tale, especially the narrating instance it dramatizes, and the novel presents a more powerful narrative of transmission and transaction. Ultimately it rewrites its model. For the more significant narrative in *Leone Leoni* occurs not, I would assert, in its core story, but in the frame that recounts Juliette's telling of her tale—in the erotic narrative contract negotiated between the teller and her listener.

Leone Leoni clearly imitates Prévost's narrating strategy, but the narrating situation contains essential differences. Juliette fills Des Grieux's narrating position, and she tells her current "lover," Aleo Bustamente, of her obsessive love for Leoni. Bustamente, in turn, impersonates the man of quality by listening to the oral narration and then transcribing it as reported speech in a text. Crucially, Sand's novel and Prévost's differ in the narrator/transcriber's relationship to the narrated events, and in the transaction that occurs between the frame narrative and the framed story.

The man of quality only fleetingly meets Manon; Bustamente, in contrast, is obsessed with Leoni, his absent rival. So is Juliette. In chapter 1 Bustamente makes Leoni's power over Juliette manifest when, falsely accusing Juliette of reluctance to leave Venice, he invokes the heretofore prohibited name of "Leoni"; to which Juliette responds "in a sort of frenzy," "as if she had received an electric shock." She cries, "repeat what you said; repeat his name, let me at least hear his name once more!" before she "almost [loses] consciousness" (186). By naming Leoni, Bustamente names the object of Juliette's repressed desire, and the object of the reader's desire—the titular character. Yet a desire to leave the city in which Juliette and Leoni once lived motivates Bustamente. He has sought to keep Juliette from any place containing a memory of her earlier love; however, she has deceptively lured Bustamente to Venice by keeping silent about her past:

> "O Venice! how changed thou art! how beautiful thou once wert in my eyes, and how desolate and deserted thou dost seem to-day!"
>
> "What do you say, Juliette?" I cried in my turn; "have you been in Venice before? Why have you never told me?"
>
> "I saw that you wanted to see this beautiful city, and I knew that a word would have prevented you from coming here. Why should I have made you change your plan?"
>
> "Yes, I would have changed it," I replied, stamping my foot. "Even if we had been at the very gate of this infernal city, I would have caused the boat to steer for some shore unstained by that memory; I would have taken you there, I would have swum with you in my arms, if I had had to choose between such a journey and this house, where perhaps you will find at every step a burning trace of his passage!" (185–86)

Similarly, he has prohibited Juliette's speaking of Leoni, but she finds it "beyond [her] strength always to avoid speaking of him" (185). Bustamente will rescind the pact of silence that has been the operating agreement of their relationship in an effort to "cure" Juliette of the repressed past contaminating her present.

Bustamente opens the narrative frame by recounting his marriage proposal to Juliette, but this master contract contains conditions prompted by Juliette's past with Leoni:

> "I am branded in society with an ineffaceable designation, that of a kept mistress."

"We will efface it, Juliette; my name will purify yours."

…"Do you really mean that you will marry me, Bustamente? O my God! my God! what comparisons you force me to make!" (183)

In negotiating this marriage contract, Juliette has only her body to offer in exchange for a new "name," a return to society, and economic security. In Leoni's marriage contract she had also been offered a "name" and place in society, but his economic credentials were absent. Moreover, this comparison that prompts Juliette's remembrance of Leoni also calls up her "dread [of] that species of servitude consecrated by all laws and all prejudices; it is honorable, but it is indissoluble" (189). Yet Bustamente overcomes this objection and seemingly gains her consent to leave Venice the next day. She tells him, "With all my heart. What do I care for Venice and all the rest? In heaven's name, don't believe me when I express regret for the past; it is irritation or madness that makes me speak so! The past! merciful heaven! Do you not know how many reasons I have for hating it? See how it has shattered me! How could I have the strength to grasp it again if it were given back to me?" (189). As it turns out, by their not leaving Venice immediately, a deeper contract of the heart will abrogate this concession.

In these two passages of their negotiation, Juliette addresses some of her responses not to Bustamente but to "God" or "heaven," suggesting a more significant conflict occurring in her consciousness. "God" in this context is something other than the providential punisher invoked in *Manon Lescaut*; instead, "God" signifies the absent but idolized Leoni—her "husband" and thereby lord of her soul. Bustamente senses that Leoni's image separates them, and he imagines a desolate world in which Juliette seems "like a corpse wrapped in its shroud" and every gondola suggests "the idea of a drowning man struggling with the waves of death" (190). Bustamente cannot allow this state of affairs to continue, but the course of action he now proposes reveals a fundamental blindness about Juliette's melancholy disposition. He first admits to himself that "Juliette's cure was progressing very slowly," and he then blames the "powerlessness of [his] affection" to replace Leoni in her heart (190). Then, revising his diagnosis of her melancholy, he tells her,

I have just imagined a new cause for your unhappiness. I have repressed it too much, you have forced it back into your heart too much, I have dreaded like a coward to see that sore, the sight of which tears my heart; and you, through generosity, have concealed it from me. Your wound, thus neglected and abandoned, has become more inflamed every day, whereas I should have dressed it and poured balm upon it. I have done wrong, Juliette. You must show me your sorrow, you must pour it out in my bosom, you must talk to me about your past sufferings, tell me your life from moment to moment, name my enemy to me. Yes, you must. Just now you said something to me that I shall not forget; you implored me to let you hear his name at least. Very well! let us pronounce it together, that accursed name that burns your tongue and your heart. Let us talk of Leoni. (191–92)

This uncanny moment of psychoanalytic insight states the essential article of the as yet unsigned marriage contract—in fact, the enabling condition on which all the rest relies. Juliette must tell her tale, relive her past, to heal her "wound," to cure her self-proclaimed "'madness'" and "frenzy." But by naming himself as her analyst, Bustamente has blinded himself to what he risks as narratee of this tale. In coming to his conclusion, Bustamente reveals his attempts to duplicate Leoni's practice of rootless movement, thus doubly perpetuating Juliette's detachment from "society" and her designation as a "kept mistress." His seemingly noble marriage offer veils a desire to usurp Leoni's place in Juliette's memory. Because of Juliette, Bustamente's sense of self has been equally contaminated by the disease of Leoni. In urging her to tell her tale he makes this contamination clear: "Tell me all, Juliette; tell me by what means this Leoni succeeded in making you love him so dearly; tell me what charm, what secret he possessed; for I am weary of seeking in vain the impracticable road to your heart" (192). By making his "bosom" a vessel for Juliette's sorrows, he fails to see his own psychic wound, his own lack of wholeness. More is at stake in this contract than Bustamente realizes; he implies that, like most framing narrators, he is safe from incorporation within the framed story he solicits, but the analyst is always potentially subject to the disease.

And how does Juliette respond to this invitation to speak the forbidden words she has rehearsed silently in her consciousness for two years?

"Yes," she said with a serious air, "I believe that you are right. You see, my breast is often filled with sobs; the fear of distressing you keeps me from giving them vent, and I pile up treasures of grief in my bosom. If I dared display my feelings before you, I believe that I should suffer less. My sorrow is like a perfume that is kept always confined in a tightly closed box; open the box and it soon escapes. If I could talk constantly about Leoni and tell of the most trivial incidents of our love, I should bring under my eyes at the same moment

> all the good and all the harm he did me; whereas your aversion often seems to me unjust, and in the secret depths of my heart I make excuses for injuries which, if told by another, would be revolting to me." (192)

Juliette's acceptance articulates more than she or Bustamente recognizes. In unpacking the tightly closed box of this passage, we see that Juliette's "sufferings"—described by Bustamente as a "sore" or inflamed "wound"—now become her "treasures of grief." With this metaphoric substitution, Juliette marks her narrative's high value and her grief's origin—she and Leoni eloped wearing costumes made of the "treasures" of her father's jewelry business. Her second substitution, "My sorrow is like a perfume that is kept always confined in a tightly closed box; open the box and it soon escapes," is emblematic of the process of repression in which she has been engaged, but it also prefigures the "box" in which Leoni hides the stolen treasures until he can exchange them for cash. Furthermore, this "box" represents the narrating structure of the novel itself: the technique of "Chinese box" narration. Embedded in Juliette's narration is the story of Leoni's earlier rival—Henryet—a narrative that finally reveals the crime to which Leoni forced her unwittingly to be an accomplice. Lastly, Juliette marks the private narrative activity she has engaged in "the secret depths of [her] heart," where she makes "excuses for injuries which, if told by another, would be revolting."

Such passages in the first two chapters of *Leone Leoni* demonstrate Peter Brooks's concept of "narrative transaction and transference." Brooks observes in *Reading for the Plot*:

> Those texts that dramatize narrative situation, contract, and transaction may most patently demonstrate the value of a transferential model. This is particularly the case when "framing" is an issue, for the frame of the framed tale comes to represent Freud's "real life," that outer margin that makes the life within narratable, figures it as the "artificial illness" treated for what it has to say about the story written by unconscious desire.... The narratee is brought into the position of analyst—becomes the present surrogate for the past desire—who tries to cure his patient by working through the dynamics of transference to the point where the story told can be reabsorbed and transcended in the outer frame of reality.[9]

The Freudian practice of analysis, as Brooks describes it, mirrors the narrating situation in *Leone Leoni*, but significantly Bustamente cannot manage the transference that occurs during this narrative transaction.

As we have seen, Juliette values the "treasures" of her grief, but devalues her self. She measures her self-value in terms of Leoni— in his presence she is always "wealthy"; and it is only when Leoni erases that presence by scheming to pander her sexual favors that Juliette seeks to erase her own presence by attempting suicide. But this act, which seemingly separates Leoni and Juliette forever, reinscribes Leoni's presence in Juliette's unconscious. He becomes an obsession, interrupting the progress of her life's story in the present. To reinstate her life's story and self-value, Bustamente establishes a medium of exchange for her "cure"—marriage and social respectability will reclaim the self she has "unworthily" lost to Leoni. Again, Brooks's description of transference best explains this transaction: "In the nature of the transference, in the psychoanalytic sense, [the narrative transaction] intends to make an obsessive story from the past present and to assure its negotiability within the framework of 'real life'—the outer narrative frame—and thus to work the patient's 'cure.'"[10] By rescinding his prohibition on talking of Leoni, Bustamente wants to cure Juliette by bringing her past into her present. Bustamente's motives, however, are less purely objective than a clinical analyst's; his outer narrative frame marks another obsessive story. Bustamente desires Juliette's "present"—her body and soul—and therefore must effect the transfer of her repressed desire for the absent Leoni into an expressed desire for the spatially and temporally present Bustamente.

Transference is both vital to Juliette's cure and a metonymic trope in the narrative frame. Brooks observes that "there is in the dynamics of the transference at once the drive to make the story of the past present—to actualize the past desire—and the countervailing pressure to make the history of this past definitively past: to make an end to its reproductive insistence in the present, to lead the analysand to understanding that the past is indeed past, and then to incorporate this past, as past, within his present, so that the life's story can once again progress."[11] From Juliette's comments at the end of her narration, it appears that the transference has succeeded; but Bustamente "frames" her announcement of being cured within his own "insatiable" desires:

> "I long to be loved as Leoni was.... Juliette! when will you love me as you are capable of loving?"
>
> "Now and forever," she replied. "You saved me, you cured me, and you love me. I was mad, I see it now, to love such a man. All this that I have told you has brought before my eyes anew a multitude of vile things. Now I feel nothing but horror for the past, and I do not

mean to recur to it again. You have done well to let me tell it all to you. I am calm now, and I feel that I can never again love his memory. You are my friend; you are my savior, my brother and my lover."

"Say your husband too, Juliette, I implore you!"

"My husband, if you will," she said. (329)

The ambivalence of Juliette's "if you will" signifies a troublesome surrender to the terms of their contract. It also signifies the dialogic nature of "husband," an alien word in Sand's authorial discourse for the text, and here forcibly dislocated in the subject/object play of utterances in this exchange that encodes Bustamente's desired plot.

Leone Leoni, however, startlingly tropes this triumph of transference by not only having brought the past narrative into the present by Juliette's narration, but also into the present of Bustamente's life story. The geography of the narrating situation is a Venice hotel room during the carnival season. This setting is emblematic of two important themes in the novel: alienation and disguise. In this room Juliette is detached from the world, but as her narrative of Leoni shows, isolation with him was precisely what she desired—to Juliette the corrupting influences of society trapped Leoni in an endless cycle of crime and deception. The text symbolizes this deception by the Venetian carnival, which mirrors the masked ball in Brussels from which Leoni convinced Juliette to flee. There are thus the enclosed room, where the heart may be revealed, and the outside world of the carnival, where identities are hidden and the sorrows of the heart masked.

This narrative geography becomes significant as Sand modifies Prévost's frame structure. Des Grieux narrates his relationship with Manon from a distance beyond closure; Manon's death completed that narrative sequence, making her story fully transmissible. Juliette narrates her relationship with Leoni from an indeterminate position; Leoni disappeared after her attempted suicide, leaving his story available to reproduction. This difference distinguishes the two texts on the question of narrative justice. Manon is condemned in a patriarchal treatise inscribed upon the narrative of her life and death. Leoni has not been finally punished, and Juliette does not tell her tale in terms of an absolute catastrophe from which she has learned a lesson in life. As the narrative transaction and transference in *Leone Leoni* show, Juliette is still obsessed with Leoni, still aware that he is more sexually significant to her than Bustamente ever can be.

Sand, however, does not leave her novel incomplete. She first uses Henryet's embedded narration (an act of telling that costs him his life) to provide Juliette with Leoni's past and his "secret." If Manon's story lacks a clear beginning but has a definite end, then Leoni's story has a clear beginning but an indefinite end. And within this logic of the indefinite, Sand brilliantly tropes the narrative of transference to bring Leoni into Bustamente's life story. The day after Juliette completes her narration, the plans to leave Venice are forgotten, and they emerge from their room for a canal ride to enjoy the carnival. But once on the canal the narrative geography and narrative logic merge to bring Bustamente and Juliette near a gayly decorated gondola carrying one masker who stands above the rest, and whom Bustamente points out to a distracted Juliette. This unique masker, drawn to them by forces of water and narrative, is suddenly revealed as the narrated Leoni now made flesh:

> He called her name in an undertone, and she started as if she had received an electric shock.
> "Juliette!" he repeated in a louder voice.
> "Leoni!" she cried, frantic with joy.
> It is still like a dream to me. A mist passed before my eyes; I lost the sense of sight for a second, I believe. Juliette rushed forward, impulsively and with energy. Suddenly I saw her transported as if by magic to the other boat, into Leoni's arms; their lips met in a delirious kiss. The blood rushed to my brain, roared in my ears, covered my eyes with a thicker veil. I do not know what happened. I came to myself as I was entering the hotel. I was alone; Juliette had gone with Leoni. (332)

Like many of the scenes mentioned above, this scene is stylistically extravagant, and its parodic send-up of the archetypal reunion scene reveals an exact narrative logic of repetition and transference. The themes of alienation and disguise merge when Leoni reappears in Juliette's life story and appears in Bustamente's. Juliette feels the same electricity the mere mention of his name produced in chapter 1, and "as if by magic" she is "transported" (physically transferred) into both Leoni's gondola and *his narrative*. Having been confronted and bested by his "enemy," Bustamente loses control of his senses, only to regain them when he has returned to the site of Juliette's narration—the only part of her he now possesses—where he again flies "into a frenzy of passion, and for three hours [he raves] like an epileptic" (332) until a dismissal letter from Juliette restores his sanity and completes Leoni's story.

In addition to parodying Prévost's text and its many reunion and separation scenes, the parody here undermines Bustamente's narrating. Although Sand gives the woman voice in this text, Bustamente is still the transcriber/narrator—an act of writing possibly required to "cure" his epileptic flights "into a frenzy of passion." Even though he seems able to quote her verbatim, Bustamente, as the transcriber, possibly works transformations on Juliette's discourse; therefore, two discourses of desire overlap, although each marks a different conception of desire. Bustamente's verbal-ideological-conceptual horizon points toward conventional marriage and a sentimental dialectic of reclamation for the "fallen" Juliette. Juliette's horizon points toward recovery of the past and a romantic dialectic of desire she has had to repress. The interaction (and incorporation) of these two voices—Juliette's oral narration and Bustamente's transcription—dialogically marks the text as a tension between differing belief systems. Only now, after Juliette and Leoni have left and Bustamente is alone, do we see the true inadequacy of his monologic text and plot—and the extent of Sand's satiric parody of his absurd attempts at passion and desire.

Although Bustamente tries to regain Juliette, his obsessive plot to lure Leoni into a transgression fails. In fact, his bungled revenge plot ironically completes Juliette's cure. Juliette, through Henryet's embedded tale, articulates her desire to somehow separate Leoni from the Marquis Lorenzo de _____, who instigated many of Leoni's evil actions such as Henryet's murder. When Bustamente kills the Marquis by mistake, he does not invoke Juliette's name: "'You die by my hand as Henryet died by yours'" (341). Unwittingly, Bustamente has avenged his true counterpart in Juliette's narrative: Henryet, the devoted yet spurned lover. In the end, this action designed to regain Juliette may ensure Leoni's reform and Juliette's future happiness. Sand is often criticized for such romantic, happy endings. As Miller observes, "Georges Sand's heroines in their multiple guises ... protest against standard female destiny, but ... their heroine-ism, for the most part, is subsumed by Romantic paradigms."[12] Yet in breaking both the patriarchal model of *Manon Lescaut* and the erotic narrative contract of Juliette's narrating act, this ending clearly fulfills the logic of desire in Juliette's narrative and the logic of transference in Bustamente's. Moreover, without pushing a final biographical interpretation too far, we can see how the romantic model determining the ending of *Leone Leoni* metonymically marks Sand's desire for a reconciliation with Musset. He, however, returned to Paris without her.[13]

Narratives of Transmission, as I have already shown, often parallel narratives of sexual transgression, and in *Leone Leoni* this is marked by the erotic narrative contract between Juliette and Bustamente. Although *Manon Lescaut* is also about sexual transgression, the narrative of transmission occurs at the textual margin where sexuality can be repressed by the man of quality.[14] As the next chapter will show with Mary Shelley's *Frankenstein* and Emily Brontë's *Wuthering Heights*, the transgressive behavior narrated within the frame only briefly engages the extradiegesis (although contracts will be invoked in these texts as well). But before we turn to these texts in the English tradition of the transcribed tale, we should consider the formal elements at work in transcribed narrations and some of the theoretical questions raised by this narrating situation.

Oral narration is by no means limited to texts in which the act of transcription is innately part of the narrative transmission. Homer offers us an early example of oral narration within oral narration when Odysseus tells his own tale to the Phaiakians in books 9–12 of *The Odyssey*.[15] Odysseus's telling, however, is at the same time embedded in the narrating act of the epic narrator's performance; in other words, the epic narrator reports Odysseus's narration by quoting Odysseus's speech. Not all embedded narratives are transmitted as reported speech; at the same dinner (book 8), before Odysseus tells his tale, Demodokos has been summoned to entertain the guests:

> But when they had put away their desire for eating and drinking,
> the Muse stirred the singer to sing the famous actions
> of men on that venture, whose fame goes up into the wide heaven,
> the quarrel between Odysseus and Peleus' son, Achilles,
> how these once contended, at the gods' generous festival,
> with words of violence, so that the lord of men, Agamemnon,
> was happy in his heart that the best of the Achaians were quarreling;
> for so in prophecy Phoibos Apollo had spoken to him
> in sacred Pytho, when he had stepped across the stone doorstep
> to consult; for now the beginning of evil rolled on, descending
> on Trojans, and on Danaans, through the designs of great Zeus.
> These things the famous singer sang for them, but Odysseus,
> taking in his ponderous hands the great mantle dyed in
> sea-purple, drew it over his head and veiled his fine features,
> shamed for tears running down his face before the Phaiakians;
> and every time the divine singer would pause in his singing,
> he would take the mantle away from his head, and wipe the tears off,
> and taking up a two-handled goblet would pour a libation
> to the gods, but every time he began again, and the greatest
> of the Phaiakians would urge him to sing, since they joyed in his stories,
> Odysseus would cover his head again, and make lamentation.
>
> (bk. 8, 72–92)

Demodokos is singing of the Trojan War, and Odysseus, by listening to the song, is forced to relive all that he suffered during the twenty-year siege. Thus the narrative of this song's reception marks a double audience: the Phaiakians, who "joyed" to hear of the conflict, and Odysseus, whose "lamentation" will ultimately reveal his identity and prompt the Phaiakians to "urge [him] to sing." Demodokos's song is not presented as reported speech as Odysseus's will be; we "hear" none of the quarrel between Odysseus and Achilles; instead, it is narrated by the epic narrator (whom Demodokos and other singers double within the epic), who identifies only the salient points of the narrative. The epic narrator expects his audience to be aware of Odysseus's role in the Trojan War. The significance of this scene is its staging of two conceptual frameworks in the extra-heterodiegetic audience's response: joy or lamentation.[16]

We can draw some important formal distinctions from these two narrating situations embedded in *The Odyssey*. Following Plato, we see that Demodokos's song has been compressed by the diegesis so that only its recognizable contours remain. Odysseus's narrating act, on the other hand, fills in missing information about events on the voyage home from Troy and is presented mimetically by the epic narrator. The listener to *The Odyssey* is thereby given what seems to be a first-hand account of the various adventures. In both cases, however, Homer has embedded diegetic narrations of previous events; the mimetic reporting of Odysseus's speech act does not shorten the diegetic distance between the narrative and the events narrated; instead, it increases the distance. We must actualize in books 9–12 the structural relations within the discourse-event of the epic. Odysseus's narration is, according to Meir Sternberg's terminology, "an *inset* within the surrounding *frame*" of *The Odyssey*.[17] The discourse-event of Odysseus's narrating is the dinner held in his honor, but this discourse-event is enclosed by another discourse-event: the epic narrator's telling of *The Odyssey*. Sternberg observes that "however accurate the wording of the quotation and however pure the quoter's motives, tearing a piece of discourse from its original habitat and recontextualizing it within a new network of relations cannot but interfere with its effect.... To quote is to mediate and to mediate is to interfere," and "interference in transmission has necessary consequences."[18]

This mediation highlights a second formal distinction of the embedded narrating situation. Embedded narrations are always analeptic (retrospective) in nature: the teller relates events that have already been completed by the time the narration takes place. For instance in *Manon Lescaut*, despite the brief meeting of narrators and characters at Pacy, Des Grieux's narrative is contained within *Les mémoires*, and his act of narrating and his narration are embedded in the man of quality's narrative. Des Grieux tells his tale approximately two years after the meeting at Pacy that opens the text. Therefore, Des Grieux narrates an analeptic narrative that is first external and then internal, embedding within the metadiegesis the opening of the extradiegetic narrative. Also embedded in Des Grieux's narrative are many metadiegetic narrations. Frequently Des Grieux and Manon are separated; with each reunion Manon's history must be recounted. Also, Des Grieux's friend Tiberge regularly serves an internal analeptic function: recounting missing parts of Manon's story or telling his own story to Des Grieux. The coexistence of these two analeptic spaces—Manon's and Tiberge's—that must be filled is emblematic of the adversarial relationship Manon and Tiberge have in Des Grieux's life. Manon's story is always one of vice, inconstancy, and selfish pleasure, whereas Tiberge's story offers the alternatives of virtue, constancy, and self-sacrifice. (Henryet repeats Tiberge's character in *Leone Leoni*.) Des Grieux's narrative traces the conflict he undergoes when faced with these two programs for his life, and despite his devotion to Manon, clearly his passion follows the life program set forth by Tiberge.

Sometimes, as we saw in *Leone Leoni* and shall see in the next chapter with *Frankenstein* and *Wuthering Heights*, the embedded narration and narrative invades the frame narration and narrative, involving the extradiegetic narrator in the continuation of the intradiegetic narrative. This transgression of the textual order is doubly significant as an authenticating device and as a feature of subversive plotting. There is nothing unusual in these temporal displacements caused by the multiplication of transmission lines; in *The Poetics of Prose* Tzvetan Todorov observes that in all narratives "every new character signifies a new plot.... The appearance of a new character invariably involves the interruption of the preceding story, so that a new story, the one which explains the 'now I am here' of the new character, may be told to us."[19] Yet in *Manon Lescaut*, a narrator who tells us his or her story, having complete knowledge of the full narrative sequence, can signal proleptically (foreshadow) the outcome of any sequence of events. Thus the embedded narration could be an external analepsis (retrospection to a time before the opening time of the extradiegetic narrative) or an internal analepsis (retrospection to a time after the opening time of the extradiegetic narrative). Moreover, internal analepsis and external analepsis can occur whenever the intradiegetic narrator introduces a new character or incorporates a written text or another narrative to his or her narration.

Embedding can become extreme. In *The Poetics of Prose*, Todorov includes a chapter entitled "Narrative-Men," in which he outlines some extreme cases of tales-within-tales. For example, *The Thousand and One Nights* contains many examples of embedding:

> The record seems to be held by the narrative which offers us the story of the bloody chest. Here
> > Scheherazade tells that
> > > Jaafer tells that
> > > > the tailor tells that
> > > > > the barber tells that
> > > > > > his brother (and he has six brothers) tells that ...
> The last story is a story to the fifth degree; but it is true that the two first degrees are entirely forgotten and no longer have any role to play.[20]

John Barth, as we saw with *Giles Goat-Boy*, is also fascinated by narrative framing, and in "Tales Within Tales Within Tales" he cites Plato's *Symposium* as a particularly complex example:

> When we sort it all out, we discover that:
> > 1) Apollodorus is telling an unnamed friend
> > 2) the story of Apollodorus telling Glaucon
> > 3) the story of Aristodemus telling Apollodorus
> > 4) the story of Socrates telling Agathon's company
> > 5) the story of Diotima telling Socrates
> > 6) the story of the Topmost Rung on the Ladder of Love.
> That is, we are about as many removes from Diotima's story as there are rungs on the Ladder of Love itself, even before we add the next frame out—Plato telling all this to the reader—and the next frame out from there: me reminding you what Plato tells the reader.[21]

And by embedding Barth's discussion in my own study, I have added yet another "frame out"; it remains to be seen whether this proliferation of transmissions will continue.

A theoretical distinction must be drawn, however, between an *embedded* narrative or narration and an *intercalated* narrative or narration. According to A. J. Greimas and J. Courtés: "In narrative semiotics, the term embedding is sometimes used in order to designate the insertion of a narrative into a larger narrative, yet without specifying the nature or precise function of the micro-narrative. This is a metaphoric use of the term embedding, which alludes more to its common meaning (insertion of one element into another) than to its meaning in generative grammar. Thus it is better to use the term *intercalation*."[22] If, however, the inset narrative is a sequentially displaced part of its frame (fundamental) narrative (as when Odysseus tells of the events up to his departure from Calypso), then the inset narrative is within the same narrative sentence.[23] The generative trajectory of the narrative structure contains a "syntactic component" that on the deep level is the fundamental (linear historical) order of events, and on the surface level is the articulated narrative order (plot), in which events may be reordered in a narrative logic of suspense or hidden secrets. An example from drama would be *Oedipus Rex*, in which there are many embedded narrations, each one revealing something about Oedipus's past. When all these embedded narratives have been told, Oedipus knows his full history, the "syntactic component" of his existence, and he blinds himself as a result. Significantly, Sophocles's tragedy is a drama of narrative transmissions that precipitate the action on stage.

Intercalated narratives, on the other hand, are inset narratives that are not part of the fundamental narrative sentence (they could be called parenthetical narratives). For example, the play within the play in *Hamlet* is an intercalated rather than embedded second drama. In the novel, we can see examples in many different works such as "The Tale of Foolish Curiosity" or "The Captive's Tale" in *Don Quixote* and "The Town Ho's Story" in *Moby Dick*. Herman Melville's Ishmael must shift from his homodiegetic relationship with his own story to a heterodiegetic relationship to the intercalated story. In *Don Quixote*, the intercalated tales are told by characters in the fictional universe of the fundamental narrative; therefore, the narrating of intercalated tales marks a shift in the diegetic level of narration. Texts such as Geoffrey Chaucer's *The Canterbury Tales* and Giovanni Boccaccio's *Decameron* are composed of a linked set of embedded narrations of intercalated narratives. Some critics claim intercalated narratives are digressive disruptions of the core narrative plot. For a narrator like Scheherazade, however, each digressive tale defers the fulfillment of the caliph's promised narrative of her life: her death.

Merging of these distinctions can occur, however, as in Thomas Pynchon's *V.* (1963).[24] In chapter 9 of *V.*, Herbert Stencil retells with much "stencilization" (Pynchon's ironic term for how Stencil recasts for his own purposes the stories he has been told) the story of Kurt Mondaugen's experiences in South-West Africa. On the one hand, Stencil makes no effort to repeat verbatim Mondaugen's words, and on the other hand, the center of this multiply inset narrative is a return of a repressed European collective un-conscious. While in Africa, Mondaugen apparently dreamed of earlier colonial atrocities carried out by a chatracter that can only be identified as "Firelily's rider." Using seamless transitions to move between the diegetic levels of experience and of dream, Stencil's narration collapses an elaborate structure of narrative in-sets that would normally provide the reader with some aesthetic distance. The result in *V.* is to make the horror of this particular heart of darkness in human history uncomfortably immediate. This problematic inset transmission is a symbolically loaded narrative of history's strategies for transmitting its dirty secrets about the colonization of Africa. It explodes the mythology of bringing civi-lization and progress to the "savages"—a discursive category in the narratives of colonization that always allowed the colonizers distance from the Africans. As this example shows, much more can be at stake in the use of inset narratives, and we denigrate them as mere digressions at our peril.[25]

Particular digressive tales called "apologues" are also inserted in narratives to present moral lessons. An apologue is a moral fable that should teach its listeners or readers inside and outside of the text a particular lesson about life. Henry Fielding's work presents especially cogent examples of what Sheldon Sacks calls "digressive apologues." When apologues are intercalated in a novel, the main character is usually the listener, and this is the case in *Tom Jones* when Tom meets the man of Mazzard Hill. According to Sacks, the tale told by the man of Mazzard Hill is a "semi-independent apologue," which means it could be detached from the novel and still be meaningful. However, "the deft manipulation of the relation-ship between the digressive narrator and the major character who hears his tale is at once a means by which the semi-independent apologue of which the tale consists is attached to the novel and by which it is evaluated."[26] Even though an intercalated apologue is digressive, suspending the main storyline, it nonetheless provides insight into the major character's behavior. Not all intercalated nar-ratives are apologues (some are merely weak digressions), and not all apologues are intercalated. An apologue could be embedded if the narrator used him/herself as a positive or negative moral example (Mme de Merteuil's autobiographical letter 81 in *Les liaisons dangereuses*, for instance).

Another distinction that obtains in frame narratives of transmis-sion occurs in the social nature of the utterance as it moves through the transmitting narrations. Mikhail Bakhtin sees this overt mixing and impersonating of "other" discourses as a way the novel incorporates and organizes "heteroglossia" by use of "personified and concretely posited author[s] (written speech) or teller[s] (oral speech)." Bakhtin's concept of heteroglossia is particularly relevant here because the narrative of transmission in texts such as those examined in this chapter and the next is contained in a single text that palimpsestically layers narrating acts. Importantly, Bakhtin asserts, "The posited author and teller assume a completely differ-ent significance where they are incorporated as carriers of a par-ticular verbal-ideological linguistic belief system, with a particular point of view on the world and its events, with particular value judgments and intonations."[27]

Clearly we can see how the both the man of quality and Bustamente fit this role, and Bakhtin goes on to cite Ivan Petrovich Belkin of Alexander Pushkin's *The Tales of Belkin* (a collection of stories told to and transcribed by Belkin, posthumously published by an editor) as an example of a posited author whose "'unpoetic' point of view" results in his "failure to understand poetic pathos." Similarly, Bakhtin asserts that posited tellers "recommend them-selves as specific and limited verbal ideological points of view, be-lief systems, opposed to the literary expectations and points of view that constitute the background needed to perceive them; but these narrators are productive precisely because of this very limitedness and specificity."[28] Failure to distinguish the limitedness of such posited authors and tellers, Bakhtin contends, leads to a failure in reading the author's intentions and in understanding the text. By using the posited author/teller and the frame narrative situation, the author can distance him/herself from the narrative discourse. This distancing intensifies the dialogic play of discourses and of the horizon of responses occurring in both the narrating instance and the literary instance.

In transcribed narrations the transcriber is always first a listener; therefore, the oral narrator's "orientation toward the listener," Bakhtin states,

> is an orientation toward a specific conceptual horizon, toward the specific world of the listener; it introduces totally new elements into his discourse.... The speaker strives to get a reading on his own word, and on his own conceptual system that determines this word, within the alien conceptual system of the understanding receiver; he enters into dialogical relationships with certain aspects of this system. The speaker breaks through the alien conceptual horizon of the listener, constructs his own utterance on alien territory, against his, the listener's, apperceptive background.[29]

The speaker's breakthrough, however, might only be short-lived, for as the listener transforms into a teller (transcriber) the "alien conceptual horizon" may reassert itself. But it never reasserts itself totally—in the dialogic play of narrations the final transcribed text cannot avoid infection from the discourse and conceptual horizon of its first speaker. What remains for us now to determine is the extent of the last narrator's transformation of the original story.

A final formal distinction of transcribed narrations that underscores the effect of distancing which Bakhtin describes is the temporal relationship of the time of the narration to the time of the transcription. As Jean Ricardou has cogently shown in his essay "Time of the Narration, Time of the Fiction," all narrative texts articulate a dual relationship between the time of the fiction (the narrated events) and the time of the narration.[30] In the texts examined in this chapter and the next, a third temporal plane crucial to the narrative of transmission has to be considered: the time of the transcription. When an extradiegetic narrator reports an oral narration, he never transcribes, as a court reporter might, the narration as he hears it. There is always a temporal gap between the spoken narration and its transcription. Although occasionally a transcriber will edit the oral narration, most will, amazingly enough, retain the phatic signals of oral communicative contact made by the intradiegetic narrator to his listener during the narrating act. These signals of the oral narrating channel remind us of the narrating situation. In much the same way heterodiegetic narrators will address the "gentle reader," oral narrators will pause in their narrations to address their listeners. Although these interruptions might seem extraneous, they are significant markers in delimiting the narrative of transmission in transcribed texts. As Brooks suggests, "Framed narratives ... that incorporate the listener in the discourse of the speaker illustrate most explicitly a condition of all narrative: shape and meaning are the product of the listening as of the telling."[31]

Moreover, Bakhtin suggests that the transmission of speech in prose narrative leads to hybrid constructions in which language takes on a radically dialogic quality:

> The same hybridization, mixing of accents and erasing of boundaries between authorial speech and the speech of others is also present in other forms for transmitting characters' speech. With only three templates for speech transcription (direct speech, indirect speech, and quasi-direct speech) a great diversity is nevertheless made possible in the treatment of character speech—i.e., the way

characters overlap and infect each other—the main thing being how the authorial context succeeds in exploiting the various means for replicating frames and re-stratifying them.[32]

Bakhtin's description forcefully accounts both for micro-speech events in texts (simple dialogue) and for an oral narration's transcription by a posited author. In *Leone Leoni*, Juliette's speech infects Bustamente's discourse with the highly dialogized sign of Leoni, yet Sand's use of Prévost's frame structure restratifies the voices and allows us to read the narrative of transmission inscribed within their dialogue.

As we will see in the next chapter, the tension that develops between dialogic slippage and stratified frames leads the reader to consider the social nature of the oral narrating situation. With *Leone Leoni* and *Manon Lescaut*, the character of the listener/transcriber is a crucial determinant of the narrative told—the listener in the text exerts tremendous pressure on narrative production. The listener contracts for a specific tale in an economy of exchange that will end either fully valued or bankrupt. *Manon Lescaut* presents a narrating situation overdetermined by the man of quality's innate moralism; *Leone Leoni* presents a narrating situation overdetermined by Bustamente's obsessive passion. In *Frankenstein* and *Wuthering Heights* we will again see the operation of narrative contracts, but more significantly we will see the transcriber cut off from society and forced to live imaginatively and ultimately incompletely within the alien stories of strangers.

8 | Tales Told and Transcribed

> I have now heard all my neighbor's history, at different sittings, as the housekeeper could spare time from more important occupations. I'll continue it in her own words, only a little condensed.
>
> —Brontë, *Wuthering Heights*

> I made notes concerning his history: he asked to see them, and then himself corrected and augmented them in many places.
>
> —Shelley, *Frankenstein*

As WE HAVE SEEN, a main current in the French tradition of the transcribed oral narration flows through tales of strong passion and desire. The one desired—whether Manon or Leoni—embodies an almost indescribable uniqueness that requires a framed structure of narration to be told. In the English novel, this narrative of transmission is repeated in Emily Brontë's *Wuthering Heights* (1847)[1] in which an indescribable passion must also be rendered into words; however, in this case, as we will come to see, the reader is distanced even further from the events by the narrating strategies of Lockwood and Nelly Dean. Besides the tale of passion in *Wuthering Heights*, there is also an indescribable mystery or horror concentrated in the figure of Heathcliff and the bleakness of the Heights. This quality in Brontë's novel stems from another tradition in transcribed tales: the Gothic.

Enough examples exist of Gothic novels with narratives of transmission to fill a study of this subgenre of the novel. Earlier chapters discussed *Dracula*, *The Woman in White*, and *The Turn of the Screw*, for instance; and I also could have included such Gothic texts as *The Castle of Otranto* (1764) by Hugh Walpole, which is transmitted by an editor of a discovered manuscript of the tale; *The Old English Baron* (1771) by Clara Reeve, a structural clone of *Otranto*, but with a historiodiegetic move in the second edition to suppress the claim made in the first edition's preface that "the tale is from an ancient manuscript written in Old English";[2] *Dr. Jekyll and Mr. Hyde* (1886) by Robert Louis Stevenson, which is transmitted by a cumulation of documents; *The Italian* (1797) by Ann Radcliffe, which is transmitted by a handed-down manuscript; *The Private Memoirs and Confessions of a Justified Sinner* (1824) by James Hogg, which contains both the memoir and an editor's account of the events, which in turn is based largely on the testimony of an old woman whose account of the events has been preserved in "tradition" (the kind of oral histories Walter Scott relied on so often for transmission). Yet two works I will examine presently deserve special attention: Charles Maturin's *Melmoth the Wanderer* and Mary Shelley's *Frankenstein*.[3]

Elizabeth MacAndrew, in studying the Gothic tradition in fiction, observes that in Gothic novels "the narrative method is always used to make the world of the novel strange."[4] To create a fantastic landscape where the horrific events of Gothic tales can occur, the novelist often resorts to a transmission strategy that distinguishs between the world of the telling and the world of the tale. MacAndrew writes:

> Special means are needed to produce such unusual weather along the rugged mountains, tranquil plains, seas alternately calm and stormy, and buildings that are prisons or fortresses or havens, all of them expressive of character. They necessitate a structure that makes a closed-off region within an outer world. To create both these worlds, the outer and the closed, within the novel, a special narrative method is used. When, for instance, a narrator returns to tell his hearers about people and events they know nothing of, this narrative method places the reader in the same relation to the world described as the listeners to the tale. Imagery, characterization, and action are made an interpretable whole through the spatial and temporal relations among the narrator, his account, and his audience, which includes the reader.[5]

MacAndrew does not delineate the fine distinctions of transmission levels I have been trying to articulate throughout the foregoing pages, but her conception of another world bordered and enclosed by the telling of the tale to a group of hearers is a significant correlative to the narrative framing that interests me here.

But the mere strangeness of the setting, characters, or events is not necessarily enough to prompt this narrative of transmission. Aligned with this strangeness are two themes identified by Eve Kosofsky Sedgwick in *The Coherence of Gothic Conventions*: the "unspeakable" and the "live burial." The first of these conventions marks both the indescribable nature of the dreadful horrors that we are told the characters experience and "a play ... in the narrative structure itself of a novel that ostensibly comprises transcriptions of manuscripts that are always illegible at revelatory moments." In *Melmoth*, the logic of the "unspeakable" extends to "narrators who fall into convulsions at the word 'Melmoth.'"[6] Like the governess in Henry James's *The Turn of the Screw*, narrators of the "unspeakable" must relive through their narrations moments of high emotional anxiety, but when the narration is oral that anxiety must ride closer to the surface, and the smooth narrative we read is the product of the detached transcriber who retells the tale. The second of these conventions, the "live burial," can be seen as a metaphoric description of the inner world MacAndrew describes, but Sedgwick sees this common punishment in Gothic fictions as emblematic of a psychoanalytic "repression of libido ..., especially since it is sexual activity that literal live burial most often punishes." Moreover, she is tempted "to use 'live burial' as a structural name for the Gothic salience of 'within'—as an explanation, for instance, of the deep satisfaction readers get from describing *Melmoth the Wanderer* as a story within a story within a story within a story."[7]

Charles Maturin's *Melmoth the Wanderer* (1820)[8] is an exemplary text in Gothic fiction. It contains many scenes of horror within a monastery of the Inquisition and many characters pushed to the limits of human endurance by corrupt forces in the world. Moreover, it contains the marvelous character of Melmoth. He is a wanderer who has sold his soul in exchange for everlasting life, and in the novel's moral theme we see Melmoth seeking release by trying to entice others to take up his burden. In the telling of these various tales of enticement, *Melmoth* represents an overwrought example of enclosed narration.

The extra-heterodiegetic frame narration in *Melmoth* tells the tale of young John Melmoth, who at the opening of the novel comes into his family inheritance (the mode of transmission that most haunts the nineteenth-century English novel) and learns of an ancestor hundreds of years old. The first enclosure occurs with the reading of Stanton's journal, which recounts the first tale of Melmoth the Wanderer. At the same level with Stanton's journal but later in the diegesis is the long oral narration of Alonzo Moncada which extends essentially to the end of the novel. Alonzo's narration includes the reading of a manuscript that recounts the story of Imalee/Isadora, whom Melmoth tempts into marriage. Within this narrative there are two further tales of Melmoth's diabolical exploits: "The Tale of Guzeman's Family" (an orally read manuscript) and "The Lover's Tale" (orally narrated by Melmoth). This latter tale contains an enclosed narration by a clergyman about yet another encounter with Melmoth.

These various overlapping narratives fix in the reader's mind Melmoth's timelessness and pervasiveness of purpose. The elaborate encasing of the narrations serves to heighten the mystery and uncertainty surrounding Melmoth's existence; in this way Maturin avoids creating a Gothic picaresque novel that episodically recounts Melmoth's many adventures. Yet Maturin comes to the verge of burying alive his narrative within its own complexity, and with undue narrational acceleration he brings the reader through four narrative levels to the climactic scene of Melmoth's tormented death. In making this move, Alonzo's tale, which has occupied nearly a third of the novel, is interrupted and abandoned rather than closed in this text. Significantly, there is no reason Maturin should have fallen into this trap. He could have seen a perfect example of a precisely enclosed narrative of transmission if he had looked to Mary Shelley's *Frankenstein*, published two years before.

THE READER of Mary Shelley's *Frankenstein* (1818; 1831)[9] confronts letters, journals, literary intertexts, oral narrations within oral and written narrations, and summary narratives. This complex structure of different narrations is the medium for a story of fantastic creation; in Victor Frankenstein's words: "It is indeed a tale so strange, that I should fear you would not credit it" (199).[10] The story of the creation of the Creature is well-known, although the film versions have disseminated an often drastically reworked account. In nearly every twentieth-century reworking of the novel, the elaborate frames of narration have been eliminated. Since each narration is interrupted by other narrations, causing the temporal relationship between narrative and narration to be continuously displaced, a film retaining the narrating frames would be awkward and digressive.[11] But literary narratives are not hemmed in by the constraints of cinematic logic, and any attempt to understand *Frankenstein* must examine the novel's intricate narrative of transmission.

Frankenstein opens with a series of four letters; three are sent and the fourth becomes a journal in which the remaining narrative is transcribed. The letters are addressed by Robert Walton to his sister, Mrs. Margaret Saville. The first two letters tell of Walton's plans and preparations for an exploration voyage to the North Pole. The third letter is written during the voyage and is sent "by a merchantman now on its homeward voyage" (22). These letters home foreground particular themes that will continue throughout the novel.

First, Walton outlines the direction of his intellectual development by describing his study of the literature of the sea and Romantic poetry. Second, he emphasizes his "ardent curiosity" (16) coupled with his desire for fame and glory. And lastly, he laments the absence of a *friend*: "But I have one want which I have never yet been able to satisfy; and the absence of the object of which I now feel as a most severe evil. I have no friend, Margaret: when I am glowing with the enthusiasm of success, there will be none to participate [in] my joy; if I am assailed by disappointment, no one will endeavour to sustain me in dejection. I shall commit my thoughts to paper, it is true; but that is a poor medium for the communication of feeling. I desire the company of a man who could sympathise with me; whose eyes would reply to mine" (19). Although both Victor and the Creature are shaped by their reading and both exhibit unbounded curiosity, the theme of friendship (and its inverse: alienation), in its sexual and nonsexual manifestations, is the most significant thematic correlative to the narrative of transmission in *Frankenstein*. Walton's passage marks the motivation for his writing: in the absence of friendship, one must write.

Although in *Frankenstein* we do not have a conventional novel of sexual seduction and transgression, epistolary contact, as we saw in chapter 2, marks an absence of physical contact. Walton, thousands of miles from England, attempts to establish contact with his sister as a means of making up for the physical absence of a friend. In his second letter Walton identifies one potential friend, "a mariner ... noted for his kindliness of heart," and intercalates "his story":

I heard of him first in a rather romantic manner, from a lady who owes to him the happiness of her life. This, briefly, is his story. Some years ago, he loved a young Russian lady, of moderate fortune; and having amassed a considerable sum in prize-money, the father of the girl consented to the match. He saw his mistress once before the destined ceremony; but she was bathed in tears, and, throwing herself at his feet, entreated him to spare her, confessing at the same time that she loved another, but that he was poor, and that her father would never consent to the union. My generous friend reassured the suppliant, and on being informed of the name of her lover, instantly abandoned his pursuit. He had already bought a farm with his money, on which he had designed to pass the remainder of his life; but he bestowed the whole on his rival, together with the remains of his prize-money to purchase stock, and then himself solicited the young woman's father to consent to her marriage with her lover. But the old man decidedly refused, thinking himself bound in honour to my friend; who, when he found the father inexorable, quitted his country, nor returned until he heard that his former mistress was married according to her inclinations. "What a noble fellow!" you will exclaim. He is so; but then he is wholly uneducated: he is as silent as a Turk, and a kind of ignorant carelessness attends him, which, while it renders his conduct the more astonishing, detracts from the interest and sympathy which otherwise he would command. (20–21)

I quote this short tale in full because it contains elements that are repeated throughout the ensuing narrative. The story is one of contact and *contract*: marriage contact occurs through a marriage contract. The young mariner breaks the convention of this economic system of exchange by an act of "noble" self-sacrifice that ultimately involves self-exile. More significant is Walton's reaction to this "astonishing" individual; instead of seeing and sympathizing with the inner virtue displayed by the mariner's actions, Walton makes a superficial judgment of his character: "he is as silent as a Turk, and a kind of ignorant carelessness attends him." Significantly, this reaction prefigures the response of Victor and Felix De Lacey to the Creature's physical presence and reveals the Romantic contract between physical and psychical "Beauty."

Various contracts will be made and broken throughout *Frankenstein*, and paralleling the contracts between characters are the contracts between narrators and narratees. According to Roland Barthes, narratives can become "legal tender, subject to contract"; the narrative is given in exchange for something else (the most obvious paradigm is authors and their publishers). Barthes shows how in Honoré de Balzac's *Sarrasine* "the narrative is exchanged for a body (a contract of prostitution); elsewhere it can purchase life itself (in *The Thousand and One Nights*, one story of Scheherazade equals one day of continued life)."[12] In *Frankenstein*, the Creature will use his story to bargain with Victor for a mate, and Victor will use the sympathetic bond he forms with Walton to contract completion of his quest to destroy the Creature. Both contracts, however, will be broken.

His fourth letter is untransmittable because of his ship's isolation amid the ice of the Arctic Ocean, and Walton shifts to a journal form. But rather than composing a solipsistic tale of his adventures (the explorer's diary was a common literary genre when Shelley was writing), Walton begins to write about "the stranger" (Victor) he rescues from a floating fragment of ice. Walton thus moves from an autodiegetic to a homodiegetic relationship to his text: "I shall continue my journal concerning the stranger at intervals, should I have any fresh incidents to record" (27). Soon after this statement he records Victor's offer to tell Walton his tale: "'I do not know that the relation of my disasters will be useful to you; yet, when I reflect that you are pursuing the same course, exposing yourself to the same dangers which have rendered me what I am, I imagine that you may deduce an apt moral from my tale; one that may direct you if you succeed in your undertaking, and console you in case of failure'" (30). Walton, in turn, resolves "every night ... to record, as nearly as possible in his own words, what he has related during the day" (30), thereby shifting again his relationship to the text, now from an autodiegetic to a pseudo-heterodiegetic one.

For the next seven days Walton listens to and transcribes Victor's tale, but before we turn to Victor's narration, we must consider the prestructure he gives it. He prefaces his tale by cautioning Walton: "Prepare to hear of occurrences which are usually deemed marvellous. Were we among the tamer scenes of nature, I might fear to encounter your unbelief, perhaps your ridicule; but many things will appear possible in these wild and mysterious regions, which would provoke the laughter of those unacquainted with the ever-varied powers of nature:—nor can I doubt but that my tale conveys in its series internal evidence of the truth of the events of which it is composed" (30). Victor perceives that the context for presenting his tale— Walton's state of mind and the circumstances of their meeting—will allow for the necessary suspension of disbelief needed to give his tale a fair hearing. During his tale, Victor will refer to moments when he maintained his silence (significantly, after his brother's murder [77, 80] or when his "tale [is taken] as the effects of delirium" [201]). Some stories require particular narratees; a special sympathy must obtain before the story can be told. Victor finds in Walton a sympathetic narratee. Also, Walton has discovered a "friend"; therefore, he can suspend his own story and substitute Victor's. Victor's narrative, however, is a parable not of nobility, like that of the mariner, but of a perversion of nature that leads to a series of losses. His narration spans twenty-four chapters, but embedded within his narrative is the Creature's narration (chs. 11–16) and some shorter narratives. Therefore, we will consider Victor's narrative in three parts: (1) before his meeting with the Creature on the glacier, (2) the meeting with the Creature and the Creature's tale, and (3) after his meeting with the Creature.[13]

Even though Victor tells a narrative of misfortune, he does not succumb, as Des Grieux did in *Manon Lescaut*, to the great tendency toward proleptic announcements of impending disaster; the narrative logic thus builds suspense rather than undercutting the events with moral reflection. The first part of Victor's narrative can be divided into three sections: (1) the period before the creature has life (chs. 1–4), (2) Victor's illness after creating the Creature (chs. 5–6), and (3) the murder of William and the trial of Justine (chs. 7–8). The story of Victor's development repeats Walton's development. There is the love of books (alchemy and natural philosophy this time), the unchecked curiosity and desire for glory, and the establishment of essential friendships. But there is also the tragedy of his mother's death, which precipitates her deathbed contract for the marriage of Victor and Elizabeth—a sanctified contract whose fulfillment is disastrous. In creating the Creature, Victor isolates himself from his friends; he is in contact only with his work. The horrific product of this work nearly robs him of his sanity, but the devoted friendship of Clerval brings him back to life.

Victor's return to health is a mixed blessing. In telling this sequence of his story to Walton, Victor embeds two letters and two summary narrations. The first letter is from Elizabeth (63–67), and it arrives at the end of his convalescence. Although this letter is largely "gossip," it has embedded in it the history of Justine Moritz (64–66). This history is necessary to establish her character in the story. Ironically, Elizabeth juxtaposes Justine's history with news of William, telling of his "two little *wives*." The next letter, from Victor's father (71–73), tells the story of William's death from the perspective of the family. The first summary narration is Ernest's narration of the evidence the implicates Justine in William's murder (79), and the second is Justine's testimony at her trial (83–84).[14]

Each of these four embedded narratives is from a different member of the family and is about loss (as is Victor's narration to Walton at this point), but we must consider the silenced voices. Obviously William cannot tell his tale; he has been strangled into silence (see 142–43). Likewise, the voice of William's dead mother is also absent, though her presence is iconographically marked by the miniature William was wearing (an object that becomes the deciding piece of circumstantial evidence against Justine). Most significant is Victor's silence:

> My first thought was to discover what I knew of the murderer, and cause instant pursuit to be made. But I paused when I reflected on the story that I had to tell. A being whom I myself had formed, and endued with life, had met me before midnight among the precipices of an inaccessible mountain. I remembered also the nervous fever with which I had been seized just at the time that I dated my creation, and which would give an air of delirium to a tale otherwise so utterly improbable. I well knew that if any other had communicated

such a relation to me, I should have looked upon it as the ravings of insanity. Besides, the strange nature of the animal would elude all pursuit, even if I were so far credited as to persuade my relatives to commence it. And then of what use would be pursuit? Who could arrest a creature capable of scaling the overhanging sides of Mont Salêve? These reflections determined me, and I resolved to remain silent. (77)

Although Victor knows the truth, it is an unspeakable truth that cannot be voiced because no adequate prestructure exists for it to be "credited" as truth rather than "delirium." The devalued discourse of the mad during the nineteenth century has been well-documented of late, and Victor understands the status his narration would be given. However, the text contains another retelling of the circumstances of William's murder.

J. Hillis Miller has written that "any novel is a complex tissue of repetitions and of repetitions within repetitions, or of repetitions linked in chain fashion to other repetitions."[15] When the Creature tells Victor his tale (part 2 of Victor's narration), the narrating instance of the text shifts again as Victor moves from an autodiegetic narrating stance to a pseudo-heterodiegetic relationship to the Creature's meta-autodiegetic narration. What the Creature tells Victor takes much the same shape as Walton's and Victor's narratives (even the location of the telling is similar, since the Creature tells his tale amid the ice of a mountain glacier). The Creature tells the story of his intellectual development: how he learned to survive, how he learned language, how he learned to read, and what he read. His tale dramatizes a fierce curiosity about life and existence, and the months he spends observing the De Lacey family attest to his desire for knowledge.

But when we come to the theme of friendship, the Creature's tale marks an absolute absence. He discovers that he lacks even the most fundamental friendship: a family. What he discovers instead is Victor's journal of his creation (cf. Walton's journalizing of Victor), of his "accursed origin" (130), and he realizes that his creator has abandoned him. The Creature contrasts his situation to that of the De Lacey family—a model of complete devotion by all family members. The history of the family he constructs (with documentary evidence: Safie's letters, which will eventually reach Walton but not appear in the transcript) and embeds in his own narration shows how the family stayed together despite adversity and exile (ch. 16).[16] Yet even with these people he knows so well, he cannot make contact; his attempt is favorably received by the blind father (the Creature's eloquence is indeed remarkable), but he is driven off by Felix, the son, who reacts violently against what he perceives to be a monster.

Recognizing this lack of contact with another being as the origin of his evil, the Creature seeks to make a contract with Victor for a mate. He demands that Victor respond to his request that Victor create for him a mate:

> How is this? I must not be trifled with: and I demand an answer. If I have no ties and no affections, hatred and vice must be my portion; the love of another will destroy the cause of my crimes, and I shall become a thing, of whose existence every one will be ignorant. My vices are the children of a forced solitude that I abhor; and my virtues will necessarily arise when I live in communion with an equal. I shall feel the affections of a sensitive being, and become linked to a chain of existence and events, from which I am now excluded. (147)

As Peter Brooks observes, the Creature's tale is a rhetorical argument, designed to persuade Victor of his duties as a creator to his creation.[17] Since the Creature's innate goodness can only be nurtured through companionship, and since his creator's race refuses him basic friendship, he entreats Victor to show him one sign of compassion, that sign being the "authorship" of a female Creature.

Interestingly, the Creature's plea for a mate echoes the views of Mary Wollstonecraft, Mary Shelley's mother, on the ideal relationship of the sexes regarding the transfer of virtue and sensibility between husband and wife. Yet the Creature represents a double disenfranchisement from the common views of the social order of his time: he is male—and thus imbued with natural virtue by his sex—yet in the sociobiological hierarchy his status is even less than that of the lowest woman. Moreover, the Creature makes literal the notion of "monstrosity" often used to label characters whose actions place them outside conventional morality. Manon, for instance, marks the monstrosity of excessive sexuality, and Leoni the monstrosity of criminal behavior, but with the Creature we are forced to confront both figurative and literal monstrosity—a doubling of the outsidedness inherent in the monstrous.

In his narrative/argument the Creature damages his cause by honestly recounting his murder of William and his planting of the miniature on Justine. Now, the unspeakable tale of madness that Victor refused to tell is voiced, but as a tale of monstrosity—a metonymic parricide, a metaphorically oedipal drama in which William is characterized by the Creature as a substitute for Victor, the Creature's "father." The metonymic chain of signification is prompted by William's utterance of his father's name: "Hideous monster! let me go. My papa ... is M. Frankenstein—he will punish you" (142). At the same time, the reaction of the Creature upon hearing the name of the "father" the disruption of the metonymic chain of generation and naming signified by the unnamed, unchristened, Creature. Moreover, the Creature inverts the chain of generation by gloating over his victim: "I, too, can create desolation" (143). This doubly monstrous creation and metonymic overthrow of the patriarch marks in Shelley's text her inheritance of her mother's feminist ideas. This part of the Creature's tale, however, puts Victor in a double bind: he recognizes the validity of the Creature's argument, but the Creature is also the murderer of two members of his family. In this double bind, the narrative contract is always indeterminate, and the part of Victor's narration told after his meeting with the Creature tells of the breaking of that contract and the violent reassertion of the oedipal tension between "father" and "son."

Victor does begin creating another being, but to complete his task he must isolate himself—as long as Victor is among friends he cannot elude the image of his murdered brother. Yet as soon as Victor is cut off from the confines of friends and family, the universal horror of his task is revealed to him and he destroys this second creation (166). Victor's rationale for his action is a proleptic narrative of his creation's potentiality. He imagines a sequence of events in which the Creatures do not live in peace as promised; instead, his creations will "incestuously" procreate their own kind, giving birth to a race of monsters bent on destroying the human race. Of course, Victor's scenario of this monstrous sexual transgression is all conjecture, but the Creature's response reinscribes Victor's proleptic scenario: "*I will be with you on your wedding-night*" (168). This narrative threat ominously recalls the Creature's earlier exultation after strangling William: "I, too, can create desolation; my enemy is not invulnerable; this death will carry despair to him, and a thousand other miseries shall torment and destroy him" (143).

Victor fails, however, to interpret correctly the Creature's threat, thinking that *he* will be the target of the Creature's revenge. From a narrating standpoint, Victor does not reveal to Walton his hermeneutic blindness until the fulfillment of the threat is imminent: "As if possessed of magic powers, the monster had blinded me to his real intentions; and when I thought I had prepared only my own death, I hastened that of a far dearer victim" (191). Brooks observes that the Creature "does not strike directly at his creator—at the sacred name that is the signified of all signifiers—but, by displacement, by metonymy, at closely related elements in Frank-enstein's own chain of existence and events: at his friend Clerval, at Elizabeth when she becomes Frankenstein's bride."[18] Elizabeth's death fulfills the narrative logic of the double bind and of the oedipal plot. Her marriage to Victor had been contracted by his mother's dying wish, but the marriage also fulfills the narrative logic of the Creature's threat, set in motion by Victor's act of de-creation. As Victor's wife, Elizabeth becomes metonymically the Creature's "stepmother" and thus her murder marks a double violation of the ritual marriage bed.

In this, as in other instances, we clearly see that every act in *Frankenstein* is repeated, and Victor and the Creature (and Walton to a marginal degree) are aligned and made equal, each becoming a victim of the other's vengeance. Victor completes his tale by recounting his pursuit of the Creature and the events leading up to his rescue by Walton. He ends, however, by invoking a narrative contract with Walton: "If I [die], swear to me, Walton, that he shall not escape; that you will seek him, and satisfy my vengeance in his death" (208). Although he will ultimately retract this pact, Walton's narrative contract has been negotiated with payment—the telling of the tale—in advance.

Robert Walton continues his journal, returning us to the extra-diegetic frame, but the narrative we receive is that of Victor's oral transmission, of the documentary proofs, and of Victor's correction of the transcript:

> You have read this strange and terrific story, Margaret; and do you not feel your blood congeal with horror, like that which even now curdles mine? Sometimes, seized with a sudden agony, [Victor] could not continue his tale; at others, his voice broken, yet piercing, uttered with difficulty the words so replete with anguish. His fine and lovely eyes were now lighted up with imagination, now subdued to downcast sorrow, and quenched in infinite wretchedness. Sometimes he commanded his countenance and tones, and related the most horrible incidents with a tranquil voice, suppressing every mark of agitation; then, like a volcano bursting forth, his face would suddenly change to an expression of the wildest rage, as he shrieked out imprecations on his persecutor.
>
> His tale is connected, and told with an appearance of the simplest truth: yet I own to you that the letters of Felix and Safie, which he showed me, and the apparition of the monster seen from our ship, brought to me a greater conviction of the truth of his narrative than his asseverations, however earnest and connected. Such a monster

has then really existence! I cannot doubt it; yet I am lost in surprise and admiration. Sometimes I endeavoured to gain from Frankenstein the particulars of his creature's formation: but on this point he was impenetrable.

"Are you mad, my friend?" said he; "or whither does your sense-less curiosity lead you? Would you also create for yourself and the world a demoniacal enemy? Peace, peace! learn my miseries, and do not seek to increase your own."

Frankenstein discovered that I made notes concerning his history: he asked to see them, and then himself corrected and augmented them in many places; but principally in giving the life and spirit to the conversations he held with his enemy. "Since you have preserved my narration," said he, "I would not that a mutilated one should go down to posterity." (209–10)

These paragraphs force us to reconsider our reading experience of the text. Walton describes here a narrator tortured by his own passionate narration. In its translation into a text, the drama of the telling is temporarily displaced from the reader's view. But it appears from the last paragraph that Victor himself has contributed to the textualization of his narration by rewriting portions of Walton's transcript. (He is, to my knowledge, the only intradiegetic narrator ever to do this.) In describing this revisionary act, Walton recounts metonymically Victor's original sin as he "[gives] the life and spirit to the conversations he held with his enemy," and Victor himself acknowledges his desire to avoid "a mutilated" text. Victor's act inscribes a parallel between his act of creation and his act of narration: the novelist is forever like Frankenstein, a creator piecing together bits of narrative to create a live, organic text free of mutilation.

Robert Walton, at the urging of his crew, abandons his exploration, and soon after turning his ship around, Victor dies. In the confluence of Walton's and Victor's narratives, the closure of one (by the reversal of the ship) marks the end of generation for the other, yet Victor's death confers the right of transmissibility to Walton's text. Walton's journal finally reverts to a diary of the self, but his act of writing is once again interrupted:

I am interrupted. What do these sounds portend? It is midnight; the breeze blows fairly, and the watch on deck scarcely stir. Again, there is a sound as of a human voice, but hoarser; it comes from the cabin where the remains of Frankenstein still lie. I must arise and examine. Good night, my sister.

> Great God! what a scene has just taken place! I am yet dizzy with
> the remembrance of it. I hardly know whether I shall have the power
> to detail it; yet the tale which I have recorded would be incomplete
> without this final and wonderful catastrophe. (218)

Walton then fills the temporal/spatial gap between the two paragraphs, telling of the Creature's visit to Frankenstein's death chamber. As we have seen before, the appearance of a character from one
narration in another narration changes our perspective of the character. The Creature's appearance changes Walton's perspective too:
"My first impulses, which had suggested to me the duty of obeying
the dying request of my friend, in destroying his enemy, were now
suspended in a mixture of curiosity and compassion" (219). Victor's
contract with Walton is thus broken, and a new narrative pact—to
hear the Creature's last words and spare his life—is formed. With
Victor's death, the Creature becomes the heir to his "father" and to
the "curiosity and compassion" of his "father's" friend.

The Creature does not wreak havoc on the ship; instead, he con-
firms and calls into question Victor's narrative: "You, who call Frankenstein your friend, seem to have a knowledge of my crimes and
his misfortunes. But, in the detail which he gave you them, he could
not sum up the hours and months of misery which I endured, wast-
ing in impotent passions" (221). The Creature is undoubtedly correct in his assessment, but would he have been a better narrator?
Would anyone have transcribed his tale? Would anyone publish it?
The narrating act requires a contact that is also a contract with a
narratee. For the being who is contactless and forever on the margin, as in this allegory of the always already excluded other, the
storytelling contract goes unsigned and the full narrative of his or
her life goes untransmitted.

"STORYTELLING," J. Hillis Miller observes, "is always after the fact,
and it is always constructed over a loss. What is lost in the case of
Wuthering Heights is the 'origin' which would explain everything."[19]
In all narrative transmission, each retelling of the history of events
transforms that history into a new construct, displacing it further from
its lost origin. Interpretations claiming to solve the mystery at
the center of Emily Brontë's *Wuthering Heights* often display a
hermeneutic blindness concerning the storytelling act comprising the
text we read. In *Wuthering Heights*, as in *Frankenstein*, one text must
mark two or more retellings of the narrative events. In *Wuthering
Heights*, however, the storytelling act signifies an even further

remove; here the narrating situation is defined by the distinction between Nelly Dean and Lockwood: between witness and intruder, experience and ignorance, speaking and writing, telling and retelling. But what logic motivates these narrating acts? How is the original history lost and revealed in these outsiders' dialogic play of narrative transmission? In attempting to answer these questions, we must examine the dialogic narrative of transmission structured between Catherine and Heathcliff's life stories and the reader's reading of *Wuthering Heights*.

Of course, critics have not neglected the narrators and narrative structure of *Wuthering Heights*. Nearly every commentator on the novel either disparages or praises the narrators and their narrations. Usually this commentary focuses on the narrator's *character*, postulating narrative reliability as a character trait rather than a function of narrative discourse. Lockwood has been characterized as a "'heartless' listener"[20] with an "incapacity for insight,"[21] who is utterly "incompetent"[22] and whose narrative is "uncomprehending."[23] But he has also been seen as "normal,"[24] an "innocent,"[25] the image of the reader, and "fully equal to the duty allotted him."[26] In Carl Woodring's words, "If he seems inane, he suffers from the inanity his author attributes to the average London reader"—he "shares the reader's wonder at the characters and events."[27]

Many critics find Nelly Dean a "platform of sensible understanding,"[28] taking their cue from Charlotte Brontë's assessment: "For a specimen of true benevolence and homely fidelity, look at the character of Nelly Dean."[29] However, she is also characterized as "an admirable woman whose point of view ... the reader must reject,"[30] and in James Hafley's even more extreme view she is the "Villain in *Wuthering Heights*." He calls the fact that she tells the story to Lockwood "her crowning act of villainy."[31] Lately, feminist critics have offered a revisionary view of Nelly, depicting her as simultaneously the voice of traditional patriarchal values—"Nelly Dean is patriarchy's paradigmatic housekeeper"—and "a nurse, a nurturer, a foster-mother."[32] Despite both of these problematic narrators, most critics agree that "we are allowed to unlock the novel's inner core only through Nelly's guarded account,"[33] that "both [narrators] fade into impersonality, and the story thus gains in objectivity,"[34] and that their narrative acts "[encase] the truths of fantasy and myth" surrounding Heathcliff and Catherine.[35]

Since 1981, when I began work on transmission and on *Wuthering Heights* in particular, many more studies of the novel have been published, and two focus directly on issues of frame narration that concern me here. The first, N. M. Jacobs's "Gender and Layered

Narrative in *Wuthering Heights* and *The Tenant of Wildfell Hall*," I referred to in chapter 4. Jacobs sees *Wuthering Heights* as following a "process of approaching a pervasively violent private reality through a narrator who embodies an ideology that justifies the violence." Because of his masculine perspective, Lockwood demonstrates narratorial blindness as he witnesses the violence of the Heights during his visits and as he hears of more through Nelly's narration. In the first case he tries to "interrupt the violence" but he is incapable of any more positive action or of any indignation when he comes to record the scenes in his journal. In the second case, we can speculate whether he derives a vicarious thrill from Nelly's accounts of Heathcliff's and Hindley's brutalities. Nelly "serves as the recorder or uncoverer of a hidden reality of the novel," writes Jacobs, but "her story is also one of impotence and suppression."[36] Nelly's is the framing feminine voice, but her narrating situation is as a servant to Heathcliff, as a now powerless adjunct to the world of the Heights.

The second study is John T. Matthews's meticulous examination, "Framing in *Wuthering Heights*." In examining the novel's "rhetoric of framing," Matthews shows how "Brontë brings into play a subtle and widespread terminology of framing that sounds almost all of its senses: to frame is to set off, to encompass, to edge, but also to invent, to lie, even—in the idiomatic 'frame-off'—to cease, to leave off, to escape. Likewise, a frame may be a border, but also one's state of mind, skeletal build, or bodily condition. Brontë invites us to entertain agreements between these kinds of framing as she considers how establishing a ground for the story's figure is indistinguishable from inventing the story 'itself.'" Within this thoroughgoing inquiry into the function of framing at various levels of narrative and narrating, Matthews asserts that the text's narrative of transmission "goes beyond the view that the narrators' personalities simply color the story they relate; rather, in this novel so absorbed by the instabilities of identity, *story becomes the only mode of being*."[37] Matthews then shows how Lockwood and Nelly move both inside and outside the narrative and their narrations. They are forced to see themselves mirrored in the inside/outside relationship of Catherine and Heathcliff—a relationship for which their narration is supposed to provide a context, but which inversely also provides a context for the narrators' sense of self in the act of narration. The frame and the enframed are interpenetrated to a point where any "ground" is always already figured.

Ample textual evidence supports these characterizations and others, but we must judge Lockwood and Nelly as they judge themselves through their narrative discourse. Moreover, even though Nelly and Lockwood fail in many ways to perceive accurately the events surrounding them, their narrations are also confessional, meticulously including every error in judgment. Do their confessions prove their narrating reliability, thereby making the remainder of their narrations more credible? Answering yes to this question does not affirm that the true story has been staring us in the face all these years. A narrator's self-credibility signifies neither full understanding nor sound interpretation of the events. Furthermore, each narrator is limited either by his or her self-presence at the event or by a constructed self-presence through the narration of another. But even now gaps in the narrative begin to appear, and the reader must still frame a reading of *Wuthering Heights*—a text inscribing the absence of a narrative center. Before such a reading can be constructed, the difficulties inhering in the text's narrative of transmission need to be uncovered.

We can identify Lockwood as an extra-autodiegetic narrator who shifts to a pseudo-heterodiegetic stance when he transcribes Nelly's narration, which is an intra-homodiegetic narrating act. As we have seen before, these levels mark the embedding of one narration within another in the text's main linear narrative, the relationship of the narrator as a character in the narrative, and the temporal rearrangement of events for plotting and narration. Nevertheless, this essentially static spatial description begins to come undone in *Wuthering Heights* when Lockwood's marginal involvement in the events blurs this embedding structure. As this and the previous chapter have shown, most narratives that use a similarly intricate narrating instance either detach the different levels of the narrating instance— the extradiegetic narrator plays little or no part in the intradiegetic narrative universe—or the frame narrative invades the framed tale in interpretively significant ways. Lockwood, following the latter paradigm, insinuates himself into the midst of the history, thereby making the threshold separating the levels extremely narrow and making it impossible for readers to believe that his transcription is totally objective and reliable.

Miller has suggested an even more exterior narrating frame than Lockwood's journal within the fiction of *Wuthering Heights*, and if this frame could be substantiated it would significantly alter the structural description so far presented. Miller suggests that Emily Brontë's pseudonym Ellis Bell "is also the name of a character in the book: someone who has survived Lockwood, an 'editor' into whose hands Lockwood's diary has fallen and who presents it to the public."[38] Miller's playful construction of another narrating act clearly establishes a detached extra-heterodiegetic narrating frame inscribed at the farthest textual margin. Such an additional frame is in many respects consistent with Brontë's documented marginalizing of her self with relation to the world. As Charlotte Brontë wrote in an 1849 letter to W. S. Williams, "Emily would never go into any sort of society herself, and whenever I went I could on my return communicate to her a pleasure that suited her, by giving the distinct faithful impression of each scene I had witnessed. When pressed to go, she would sometimes say, 'What is the use? Charlotte will bring it home to me.' And indeed I delighted to please her thus."[39]

Whether Brontë learned the technique of embedding from her sister's habitual narratives of the world outside the parsonage; or from listening to the country tales of the Brontës' servant Tabby; or from her reading of Walter Scott, another practitioner of narrative embedding; or from French fictions she might have read in Belgium; or from such Gothic examples as Maturin's *Melmoth the Wanderer* or Shelley's *Frankenstein*; or from her experience with her sister Anne in creating the Gondal legend—she learned her craft down to the unit of the sentence. As Mieke Bal has demonstrated, Brontë's sentences provide many examples of the embedding technique Bal calls "focalization." Bal finds that even in such simple sentences as "He evidently wished no repetition of my intrusion" (17), "Lockwood relates that Lockwood sees ("evidently") that Heathcliff sees ("wished")." This example of "complex embedding with mixed focalization" demonstrates the subtle levels of perspective and framing Brontë deploys in the narrative act.[40]

Establishing a structural account of narrative levels and focalizations only provides an account of the reader's structuration of the text's *frame*work, signifying the process of transmission, retransmission, and re-retransmission that constitutes the dialogic single *text* we read and for which Lockwood ultimately claims responsibility within the fiction of the document: his journal. Actualization of the different levels does, however, uncover hybrid constructions (in which dialogic discourses speak through a single utterance) and violated narrating conventions such as Joseph's dialect, as we shall momentarily see. For this reason, a more appropriate theoretical model for the narrative of transmission in *Wuthering Heights* is Mikhail Bakhtin's concept of "dialogism." Structural narratology in some of its applications tends to fix the narrative structure in too limited a model; the frames and discourse become too stratified and seemingly unproblematic. Bakhtin, in contrast, stresses the full communication process at work in every utterance; therefore, it is not just the narrator's relationship to the events or his or her attitudes about the events that define the transmission process. In addition it is the narrator's relationships to a listener, a language, and a literature that exert dialogic pressure on the text. Both its audience and its intertextual relationship to other discourses produce the text.

When Bakhtin's ideas are applied to *Wuthering Heights*, they suggest a useful set of considerations for understanding the narrative of transmission in the novel. Lockwood (and Nelly) would be seen as a "posited author and teller," a carrier "of a particular verbal-ideological linguistic belief system, with a particular point of view on the world and its events, with particular value judgments and intonations," who is "productive precisely *because* of this very limitedness and specificity."[41] The teller's limitations are made clear when we consider the narrative of transmission in *Wuthering Heights*. Lockwood's transcription of Nelly's discourse is always double-voiced: a hybrid narrative discourse which is spoken/interpreted/transcribed. This means that we need to be aware of more than one voice speaking (writing) the narrative. As readers we conventionally forget the frame and suspend our awareness of narrative transmission to grant presence to whoever speaks in the text (thereby forgetting that it is a "text"), and we forget that Catherine or Heathcliff or Isabella tells Nelly, Nelly tells Lockwood, and Lockwood tells the eventual reader of his journal (either himself or someone else). The text represents this triple process (which at times is even more extensive) by what appears at its surface to be a single discourse.

Following Bakhtin's ideas, we would need to account for the social nature of the utterance *each time it occurs in either speech or writing*. For instance, we must consider what motivates Catherine to tell her deepest and hardest-to-articulate feelings to Nelly, what motivates Nelly to repeat them to Lockwood, and what motivates Lockwood to transcribe Nelly's reiteration of Catherine's secrets. By seeing the text of *Wuthering Heights* as a dialogically hybrid discourse, we come to recognize the significant place the narrative of transmission must have in any interpretive reading of the novel.

Moreover, Bakhtin's notion of dialogism is instructive for our reading of thematic narratives of transmission that are also underway in *Wuthering Heights*. Jacobs observes the dialogic significance of the gender layering within the narrative transmission of the story of Heathcliff's violent domestic abuse, and Edgar's pale repetition of that abuse in his benign neglect of first Isabella, then his wife, and then his own daughter. Lockwood's narration, generated ultimately from a deep-seated incorporation of patriarchal discourse and conventional moralisms, becomes a "covering" narration intended to hide patriarchal abuses; as Jacobs asserts, "Notwithstanding

Heathcliff's ghoulish fancies, the evil hidden at the center of [this] pseudo-gothic [narrative] is not supernatural or even particularly diabolical; it is mundane, vulgar, and grounded in the legal and economic structures of the time and the effects of those structures on the consciousness of both those in power (the 'covering' narrators) and those without power (the 'covered' narrators)."[42]

Significantly in Jacobs's reading of a second logic organizing the narration, we sense the active role of Heathcliff as master plotter— the builder of plots to destroy the conventional lines of genealogical and economic transmission. By operating within (but at the boundary of) legal constraints, Heathcliff appropriates all lines of transmission to himself until even his energy can no longer force the systems of transmission toward his desired destination. Paradoxically, Heathcliff's marginalization in the social order of Wuthering Heights places him in a symbolically "feminine" position, and his rage to destroy can be read metaphorically as a feminist desire to tear down the patriarchal constraints on the passionate soul. Lockwood, an agent of the patriarchy who first felt a sympathetic bond with Heathcliff, unwittingly becomes the agent of his narrative's transmission. Lockwood's textualization paradoxically represses the feminine narratives (the "covered" narrators) that Heathcliff has silenced (largely because they echoed patriarchal cant), yet also provides a channel for their speaking (through Nelly) and for their revolutionary force to affect the reader.

Ultimately, the reader constructs the text by actualizing the many different narrating acts—covered and covering—voiced through the writing of Lockwood's journal. As we saw at the end of the previous chapter, Bakhtin's ideas can be extended as a general principle for novels structured in the same manner as *Wuthering Heights*, since the texts in these novels must mark both the oral narration, with its play of narrative and narrating voices, and its transcription. The space between the narrating acts raises the issue of narrative integrity: with each transmission transformation occurs. In quoting Heathcliff, Catherine and others, Nelly recontextualizes what she often has been told in confidence; and Lockwood, by transcribing Nelly's narration and by narrating his own tale, also recontextualizes the narratives he hears and reads, placing these narratives within a frame of reference that has its origins in the conventional moralism of pre-Victorian England. Moreover, as Bakhtin has postulated, the social nature of the narrative utterance requires consideration of the role of the listener, reader, or other in forming the context of the discourse. Thus Nelly and Lockwood are *particular audiences* who influence— by their position in the discourse process—the tales they are told.

In addition to actualizing their influence as listeners, "the reader must," as Margaret Homans observes, "maintain a constant skepticism about the alterations Nelly must have made in the remembered speeches of her characters and also about the alterations Lockwood may have made in his transmission of Nelly's report and in his own remembrances of conversations he himself heard."[43] However true such a literal conception of actual transmission is, we can only imagine what has been lost through alteration. This is why the narrative of transmission holds such interest: the drama most present in *Wuthering Heights* is its telling. For instance, the transmission of Catherine's diary, scribbled in the margins of her books, is extremely problematic. The diary is, according to Homans, "the only unmediated record of the veritable voice and attitudes of one of the central characters."[44] But is the diary "unmediated"?

The narrating situation of a diary always marks a gap between the narrating self and the experiencing self. In addition, Catherine's diary engages her interior other, a second self she addresses in the diary. The doubleness of a diary's discourse process undermines the credibility of this "veritable voice" just as Lockwood's voice comes to undermine the authority of his account of Heathcliff, Catherine, and the others. Yet even if the diary could represent an unmediated utterance, the diary fragment comes to the text through Lockwood's transcription and intercalation within the context of his own story, apparently written before he knows the value of Catherine's document. Moreover, can we assume that, after Lockwood's transgression of sleeping in Catherine's bed, Heathcliff would permit that sacred text to leave Wuthering Heights with such an interloper? The last we hear of the diary occurs when Lockwood reconsiders his excuse to Heathcliff for being in Catherine's room: "'The truth is, sir, I passed the first part of the night in—' here, I stopped afresh— I was about to say 'perusing those old volumes;' then it would have revealed my knowledge of their written, as well as their printed contents; so correcting myself, I went on—" (32). And even if he had purloined the diary, wouldn't he have quoted it again, possibly to correct, extend, or check Nelly's narration? Put another way, if he had purloined the diary, why does he quote so little of it? What subversive feminine message might be written within the margins of the religious tracts that he decides to suppress it?

Catherine's "marginal" diary can also be read as both an emblematic paradigm of Brontë's writing for publication and an archetypal feminocentric text. Catherine writes her diary in the margins of a religious (logocentric) tract, and clearly, from the brief sample Lockwood presents, masculine suppression by either Hindley or

Joseph prompts her writing. The narrative of transmission compounds this archetype by dramatizing Lockwood's usurpation and probable transformation of Catherine's text. This usurpation occurs with all women's texts in *Wuthering Heights*, and it is played out in the literary instance as well when the conventions of the time contributed to Emily Brontë signing herself Ellis Bell. Moreover, the usurper Lockwood's latent misogyny is clearly revealed in the dream he has of Catherine's ghost trying to enter through the window near her encrypted bed, which Lockwood has unknowingly appropriated. The ghost is produced in Lockwood's dream from the traces of Catherine's marginal diary, but his violent response to the dream image—scraping the image's wrist along the broken glass of the window, the figure of a transparent but untransmissible border that recurs throughout the narrative—signifies an attempt to silence the ghost's pleas for entrance and symbolically marks the resistance of patriarchal culture to the cries of tormented and repressed female sexuality.[45]

We would have to suspend the same disbelief to accept the fragment of Catherine's diary as "unmediated" as to accept the remainder of the text under the convention of perfect memory. A slightly more likely case for unmediated transmission could be made for Isabella's letter, which Nelly still retains and reads to Lockwood (115–23), and which he could copy verbatim into his text (although there is no evidence in the text that he does so). Putting aside momentarily this letter's length, we see that the letter's style is far more narrative than epistolary (even if we allow Samuel Richardson's texts as models); but more significantly regarding mediation, the letter reports Joseph's speech in dialect. Although dialect is a staple convention of mimetic fictions, here it paradoxically stretches these conventions to assume that each narrator (other than Lockwood) who reports Joseph's speech mimics his dialect.

Writing about the incorporation of dialect in literary language, Bakhtin observes that dialects, "on entering the literary language and preserving within it their own dialectological elasticity, their other-languagedness, have the effect of deforming the literary language."[46] Although Joseph is seemingly the most native speaker in *Wuthering Heights*'s narrative universe, his alien voice disrupts and deforms the narrating act; therefore, its inclusion must be specifically motivated. By containing Joseph's dialect, an aspect of the novel Charlotte Brontë tried to revise when she edited the 1850 second edition, the text signals to the reader the questionable nature of the transmission process framing and composing the narrative text. *Wuthering Heights* is a novel fascinated with the problems of language and the troubled expressions of identity and desire, but it is equally a narrative of transcriptions and ventriloquisms meant to signify its own thematic heteroglossia.

For instance, if we reexamine Isabella's narrating acts, we must see that transcribing dialect is a special skill that Isabella could hardly have practiced as a child. Recall Isabella's language-conscious (monologic) mother's remark on first hearing Heathcliff: "'Did you notice his language, Linton? I'm shocked that my children should have heard it'" (49), and in the later Christmas scene at the Heights "Mrs. Linton begged that her darlings might be kept carefully apart from that 'naughty swearing boy'" (52). Lastly, although dialect is a convention of "literary mimesis," a transmission unself-conscious of any need to claim authenticity or authority would probably transform the dialect into its own idiom or use indirect speech and summary. When Isabella first encounters Hareton on her return to the Heights after eloping with Heathcliff, he speaks "in a jargon [she] did not comprehend" (116); but before the letter closes, she draws attention to Joseph's speech when he shows her to her "rahm" (121). Later in the text, after Isabella escapes from the Heights, her oral narration to Nelly reveals another brief moment of self-reflexiveness about Joseph's dialect. Quoting Heathcliff, she says, "'"Isabella, let me in, or I'll make you repent!" he "girned," as Joseph calls it'" (146). Isabella shows she has learned the dialect by this time, yet this highly self-reflexive comment is not only significant in her own narration. The transmission of this phrase through Nelly and then Lockwood suggests a metanarrational need to account for the textual discourse, for the replication of voices. The narrative logic, therefore, dictates that although Joseph's dialect might be representing and evoking the immediacy of his speech, its alien presence in so many diverse narrations signals a transforming diegesis appropriating and reconstructing the voices in the text.

From this perspective of narrative transmission, the view of storytelling as being constructed over a lost "'origin' which would explain everything" becomes quite persuasive. However, we must extend this view to include the reader's actualization of the novel and to recognize what Wolfgang Iser would call *Wuthering Heights*'s "virtuality."[47] According to Iser's principle of virtuality in the literary text, the complexity and pervasiveness of the novel's narrative discourse marks its many moments of *silence*. Iser sees a text as both a sequence of words arranged by an author and an actualization of those words by the reader during the act of reading. The "virtuality" of the literary text is a dynamic process containing the text's potential actualizations; however, this dynamic process can never be identified solely with either the sequence of words or any single actualization by a reader. There is no ready-made message apprehensible by all readers. The virtual text is the text read by the reader's creative imagination, which is conditioned by his or her particular verbal-ideological linguistic belief system. This virtual text contains the continually transmitted and untransmitted narrative: an always shifting history of the events that is always in the process of composition.

Reading *Wuthering Heights*, we perceive gaps or ellipses in the story of the events. In these extended moments of indeterminacy the reader responds to the text, concretizing in the imagination an account of what has remained untransmitted. Both Lockwood and Nelly have limited perspectives on the events they narrate, and most of the embedded narrations—even those attributed to the protagonists—are also questionable because of the often extreme unrest underlying the narrating moment and the narrated events. The reader replaces what is lost in the story through imagination and interpretation, thereby constructing a reading despite the many moments of narrative absence throughout the text. Yet as if these moments of nontransmission were not enough, Nelly wants to skip "three years" at one point in her narration (58), and Lockwood, once he has heard Nelly's tale up to his own entrance into it, will "continue it in her own words, *only a little condensed* [emphasis added]" (130). In many respects, this first attempt to withhold and the later admission of having withheld some of the tale are the most significant moments in the narrative of transmission, and they mark each narrator's different motivation for narrating.

In all novels employing a narrative transmission structure similar to *Wuthering Heights*, a clear gap separates the time of the narrated events and the time of the intradiegetic narration. In overcoming this gap readers often invoke the convention of perfect memory. But a second temporal gap separates the oral intradiegetic narration and the extradiegetic transcription. Readers regularly overlook this second gap, not actualizing the inevitable role of the composing process. Albert Lord, writing of the oral tradition in epic, observes that "for the oral poet the moment of composition is the performance. In the case of a literary poem there is a gap in time between composition and reading or performance; in the case of the oral poem this gap does not exist, because composition and performance are two aspects of the same moment.... An oral poem is not composed *for* but *in* performance."[48] Could this also describe the oral narrators in novels? Are their narrations, like gossip, part of an evolving and transformatory series of tellings? But then what of the transcriptions?

Lord also observes that when an oral tale is transcribed, it is taken out of performance, out of circulation, out of a dynamic process of composition, and is therefore utterly different: a text. But Lord is referring to attempts at perfect transcription and transmission; framed novels certainly present profoundly problematic conditions for transcription. The indeterminate temporal gap separating the telling and the transcribing raises the question of a second composition of the narrative, and hence about the authority of the transcribed text. Lockwood transcribes in his journal the narrations that comprise *Wuthering Heights* in stages during his stay at the Grange. The writing of the journal can be divided into transcription units (periods when Lockwood transcribes after hearing or acting in the history of events) by chapter: chs. 1, 2–3, 4–9 (at 7, Nelly pauses in her narration), 10–14, 15–30, 31, 32–34. Why, then, does Lockwood condense some material in the second half of the text? In answering this question we must consider both the narrating act of transcription and the narrator's motivation for narrating.

Lockwood's condensations, whatever they are, might result from either narrative expediency or gender attitudes about the narrative; most of Nelly's narration, after he admits to condensing it, is about the second Catherine—her "beloved young mistress." (Chapter 18 is a likely spot of compression, since it opens with Lockwood jumping ahead twelve years in the story.) Considering Nelly's pronounced preference for the daughter over the mother, we can safely assume that her narrative would be more expansive and digressive about her *absent* mistress, and Lockwood is possibly showing some good literary sense in editing Nelly's "gossip." However, not knowing what he edits out allows us to speculate on the missing portions of Nelly's narrative, on the possible elements of the feminocentric plot that have been silenced. It is ultimately an undecidable interpretive question, but one that must be asked, nonetheless. What is also intriguing about Lockwood's admission of condensing Nelly's narration is its placement in the text and the gap it marks in her narration.

The resumption of her tale, after the fourth week of Lockwood's illness (ch. 10), is interrupted short of its climax (Heathcliff and Catherine's last meeting) by the arrival of Dr. Kenneth at the end of chapter 14. In the literary instance of *Wuthering Heights*, this interruption ends volume 1 of the first edition. Although the conventions of nineteenth-century multi-volume publishing might have influenced the placement of this interruption, this cliff-hanging transitional device is significant to the narrating instance of *Wuthering Heights*. A week after Dr. Kenneth's visit, Lockwood has heard the entire tale and he decides to condense it. His admission of withholding some of the narrative, however, comes immediately before he transcribes Nelly's report of Heathcliff and Catherine's final meeting. In telling the story of a desire that defies reduction into mere language, Lockwood chooses this central moment, in a sentence that signifies both a narrating economy and a narrating inevitability, to lay bare his text's incompleteness or its *différance*. As Matthews observes, "condensation is a form of composition."[49] The writing of a text *differs* from the oral narration and by extension the true history of events and thus *defers* that history from ever being told. Additionally, to condense a text is to deplete it, and every retelling is a transformation that threatens to deplete or revise the transmission of the narrated events even further.[50]

Nelly's attempt to articulate the life stories of her employers is emotionally difficult because she must continually relive her own not insignificant part in the tragedy of events. Nelly's voicing of her desire to suppress three years of her narrative (58) is thus doubly significant. Her metanarrational statement (which Lockwood dialogically engages through quotation and response: he forbids her suppression) once again exposes the narrating act's potential for incompleteness, but more significantly, it marks Nelly's attempt to repress the scene for which she feels most guilt. According to C. P. Sanger's chronology of events, Nelly would be repressing the part of her narrative that comprises chapters 8 and 9.[51] This portion of the narrative includes Catherine's "degrading" of Heathcliff and later revelation: "Nelly, I *am* Heathcliff" (74). This utterance at first glance appears to be as close as the reader can come to the lost "'origin' which would explain everything." In its directness and simplicity, this utterance would withstand alteration, regardless of the number of retellings.

We can see how this scene and its moment of discourse are focused for the reader by applying Mary Ann Caws's concept of "reading frames."[52] Brontë has set Catherine's tête-à-tête with Nelly within the double frame of the fireplace and the kitchen doorway. These spatial frames focus the reader's attention on the scene, heightening its effect on the reading. Significantly, just as he has always been outside the family definition of the Heights, Heathcliff is outside these focusing frames which intensify Catherine's statements (even for Heathcliff as a listener). Nelly, on the other hand, recognizes the framing of her conversation with Catherine by her awareness of Heathcliff's presence at the frame's margins (a position she—and Lockwood—can identify with), but she fails to comprehend the significance of this arrangement on the reception of Catherine's discourse. We can read the spatial framing of this scene as a metonymy for the narrating frames I have been discussing. Narrative transmission requires an understanding of the contextual frame surrounding any discourse event, but the frames that mark different transmission acts also serve to distance the reader or listener from any original meaning, from the truth of the utterance.

Recognizing the power of this scene and its potential for linguistic transmission uncovers only part of its dialogic power within the text. Catherine chooses Nelly as a confidante for her "secrets," but the true social nature of the utterance is dramatically more extensive. Heathcliff, an unintended audience, overheard Catherine, as Nelly tells Lockwood, "till he heard Catherine say it would degrade her to marry him, and then he stayed to hear no farther" (73). Nelly's narration, however, is self-condemning because it marks her silence when her tongue should have been most active. The shift in the social nature of the utterance caused by Heathcliff's departure is then made ironic by Catherine's later expression of the depth of her passion for Heathcliff. Nelly, unfortunately, is not the proper audience to understand Catherine's assertions as she intends them (only Heathcliff, presumably, is capable of such understanding). Nelly reveals her failure to comprehend Catherine when she cuts their dialogue short: "If I can make any sense of your nonsense, Miss,... it only goes to convince me that you are ignorant of the duties you undertake in marrying; or else that you are a wicked, unprincipled girl. But trouble me with no more secrets. I'll not promise to keep them" (74).

Nelly's incomprehension signals a key moment in the reader's understanding of the problematics of transmission. Nelly cites "duty" in a conventional coding of marriage that contravenes Catherine's "wicked, unprincipled" conception of an all-but-bigamous relationship with Heathcliff and Edgar. But the focus of the problem is Catherine's attempt at self-definition, her attempt to frame her identity in terms of an other whose presence is always already marked by absence: "Nelly, I *am* Heathcliff." This utterance is so syntactically simple it almost defies explanation, but if we consider what it signifies and attempts to signify, then we see it as indicative of the text's undecidable discourse. The utterance apostrophizes its hearer, "Nelly," phatically marking and checking its channel before its content is voiced. Its subject is the archetypal "I"—the original subject of all speech acts, the original voice of authority and confession.[53] Its predicate emphasizes the subject's ontological oneness with the object of the discourse (and of desire) in a dialogic move of redefinition. Lastly, we have the object—"Heathcliff"—the object of Lockwood's original request for Nelly's narration (in which, we must always remember, Catherine's utterance is embedded). But with "Heathcliff" our effort at reading this utterance breaks down, the utterance becomes suddenly untransmissible, deconstructively reversible. As a signifier, "Heathcliff" signifies what Bakhtin calls an "alien word"—a word that contaminates its framing discourse at every layer with the disease of "otherness." Thus we read the utterance backward to discover "am," "I," and "Nelly" as a matrix of frames that simultaneously marks an inexpressible void similar to Heathcliff's version of this utterance: Catherine's ghost.

Like Manon, Leoni, Melmoth, and the Creature,[54] "Heathcliff" ultimately resides in the transcribed text as a sign within the discourses of others. As Bakhtin observes,

> any concrete discourse (utterance) finds the object at which it is directed already as it were overlain with qualifications, open to dispute, charged with value, already enveloped in an obscuring mist—or, on the contrary, by the "light" of alien words that have already been spoken about it. It is entangled, shot through with shared thoughts, points of view, alien value judgments and accents. The word, directed toward its object, enters a dialogically agitated and tension-filled environment of alien words, value judgments and accents, weaves in and out of complex interrelationships, merges with some, recoils from others, intersects with yet a third group: and all this may crucially shape discourse, may leave a trace in all its semantic layers, may complicate its expression and influence its entire stylistic profile.[55]

Applying this conception, we must see the "internal dialogism" constituting the signifier "Heathcliff"—a signifier lacking a determinate signified. The gypsy boy who is first brought to the Heights is unnamed, a signified with no signifier—a condition marked by Nelly's initial signifier of "it" as she places Heathcliff "on the landing of the stairs, hoping it might be gone on the morrow" (39). In the symbolic act of naming, Heathcliff is given "the name of a son who died in childhood" (39).

But which son was this? Neither Sanger's nor A. Stuart Daley's chronologies shed any light on this question so crucial to the internal dialogism of Heathcliff's name.[56] For if the "dead son" was the firstborn, then by the act of naming, Heathcliff "inherits" the firstborn status Mr. Earnshaw lavishes upon him and which motivates Hindley's later brutal treatment and Heathcliff's consequent revenge. Moreover, we note that Heathcliff's name inscribes the locales of his greatest happiness with Catherine—the moors (Heath) and Penistone Crags (cliff)—and the geographical boundaries of his vengeful usurping of Hindley's inheritance. His methods of disrupting these lines of transmission are dark and mysterious, his money as untraceable as is his original parentage. But it is in this lost origin that the process of framing and transmission are marked in Heathcliff's psyche by Nelly's speculations: "You're fit for a prince in disguise. Who knows but your father was Emperor of China, and your mother an Indian queen.... Were I in your place, I would frame high notions of my birth" (54–55). The tales of Scheherazade and of Gondal echo in this fantasy of noble birth, a narrative of royal transmission disrupted by kidnappers. However, to "frame" such notions of one's birth is to introduce yet another alien plot and discourse, what Freud has termed the "family romance," to the linguistic matrix of the narrative.

As listener to this tale of origin, this attempt to affix a signified to the floating signifier of his being, Heathcliff mirrors the efforts of all listeners/readers to negotiate between the conceptual system of the speaker and that of the listener. Nelly, however, makes doubly alien Heathcliff's conceptual system by citing a fantasy that has only momentary effectiveness at the Christmas Day scene and will be ultimately replaced by Catherine's fiction of marriage to Heathcliff as "degrading." Thus foregrounded, we must perceive the utterance—"Nelly, I *am* Heathcliff"—within another of Bakhtin's formulations: "The living utterance, having taken meaning and shape at a particular historical moment in a socially specific environment, cannot fail to brush up against thousands of living dialogic threads, woven by socio-dialogical consciousness around the given object of an utterance; it cannot fail to become an active participant in social dialogue."[57] At the margin of the "social dialogue" is Lockwood, the transcriber who finally fixes the words on the pages of his journal but cannot fix their dialogic play within the ongoing process of transmission—Catherine's assertions echo in the narrative of transmission that marks the two lovers' fatal separation and absence.

Nelly, on the other hand, can only fill their absence with the narrative of her guilt. This is not the guilt of a villainess, as Hafley contends, but the guilt resulting from her part in a sequence of events that has excluded the young Cathy from her maternal presence. Nelly sees herself as a surrogate mother to Cathy, Hareton, and even Heathcliff, but the latter has banished her from their presence. Her double narration *expresses* her guilt by representing her naïve perspective during the events and *purges* her guilt through her experienced recognition of what she has lost. Her narrating act, motivated by a desire that Lockwood will fall in love with and save her "beloved young mistress," reincorporates her in a history and a society from which she has been excluded.

Until Lockwood's arrival, Nelly can only repeat, in the silent voice of conscience, her story to herself. Lockwood provides her with a social context for her narrating and provides an other different from herself and the universe of Wuthering Heights. Her mind has evidently long been on the Heights, since her first question to Lockwood is for news of Cathy (37); and after telling her tale, Nelly entreats him "to bear a little note from her to her young lady" (236). When Heathcliff summoned her to the Heights after Lockwood's departure from the Grange, she "obeyed joyfully, for Catherine's sake" (245). As for Nelly's sequel, told upon Lockwood's unplanned return, the narrative is of recovery—not of the lost origin that torments Heathcliff and Catherine, but of a hereditary imperative, a righting of the genealogical and economic narratives of transmission that Heathcliff had appropriated. This reconstructed line of transmission permits the beginning of a new generation—and of Nelly's regained social context for her discourse in the narrative universe.[58]

Early in the text Lockwood also unwittingly tries to incorporate himself into the history of events, but the dream of Catherine's ghost forces him to retract his overture, if not his curiosity. His journal and transcription of Nelly's narration are an attempt to lose himself safely in a fantastic world, far removed from London society. From the first, Lockwood seeks to fill the absence left by his loss of conventional society. The world he finds, however, stages a violent assault on the ideology of domestic harmony that permeated nineteenth-century notions of the relations between men and women. Despite his claims of misanthropy, Lockwood's early excursions to the Heights show his deep-seated needs for a polite, well-mannered society—and the "polite" blunders he makes on his first visits convince us of his inappropriateness as the transcriber of the tale his text contains. Tellingly, however, his paradoxical desire for society (first with Heathcliff, who rejects him, and then with Nelly) is tempered by the anecdote of his vague attempt at seducing a "most fascinating creature" at the seacoast (15).[59] His inability to communicate in such a center of English social discourse suggests the elements that most intrigue him about Nelly's narration: how Heathcliff became "master" of the area, and how desire expresses itself. Therefore, when Nelly tries to suppress part of her tale, he cannot permit it—he needs all her gossipy society to replace the romantic discourse now absent from his life. But the narrative he transcribes reveals the brutal subtext of romantic discourse—the voice of the patriarchy proclaiming its rights within the boundary of the law, rights that are paradoxically alien to the dialectics of passion and desire symbolized by Catherine and Heathcliff. Once Nelly has finished narrating, however, the act of transcribing becomes a process of condensing the narrative. Lockwood's narrative is rushed because of his desire to quit the Yorkshire moors for the drawing rooms of London. He makes this clear when he responds to Heathcliff's question of what brought him to Yorkshire: "'An idle whim, I fear, sir,' was my answer, 'or else an idle whim is going to spirit me away. I shall set out for London next week ...'" (240). We wonder whether he has learned anything from Nelly's tale.

Lockwood and Nelly compose and transmit their narratives to replace what they have lost in their lives. Yet the story they tell together of Heathcliff and Catherine is also one of loss. The narrative of transmission in *Wuthering Heights* is a palimpsest for the story of Heathcliff and Catherine, marking through its many transmissions of their life histories the double bind of the narrating act and the original history's loss in the dialogic play of narrative transmission. Unlike other novels employing a similar structure for their narratives of transmission, *Wuthering Heights* uses the embedding of multiple voices in a structure of frame narration to encrypt a story of passion and revenge that cannot speak for itself. Neither Catherine nor Heathcliff could ever have told their tale—consider the barely containable passion in their few narrational efforts filtered through Nelly's narration and Lockwood's text. Yet the story we receive, as incomplete as it might be, captures our imagination, letting us actualize through its narrative of transmission a more fantastic tale out of the alien words of its dialogic discourse.

Notes

INTRODUCTION

1. Erich Auerbach, *Mimesis: The Representation of Reality in Western Literature,* trans. Willard R. Trask (Princeton University Press, 1953), 4-5.

2. Homer, *"The Odyssey" of Homer,* trans. Richmond Lattimore (New York: Harper and Row, 1967). Subsequent citations are noted parenthetically in the text by line numbers.

3. Calder, "Introduction," *Old Mortality,* by Sir Walter Scott (Harmondsworth: Penguin Books, 1975), 9.

4. Joseph A. Kestner, "Linguistic Transmission in Scott: *Waverley, Old Mortality,* and *Redgauntlet," The Wordsworth Circle* 8 (1977): 341.

5. M. M. Bakhtin, "Discourse in the Novel," *The Dialogic Imagination,* ed. Michael Holquist, trans. Caryl Emerson and Michael Holquist (Austin: University of Texas Press, 1981), 341.

6. Ibid., 284.

7. Roland Barthes, "Textual Analysis of a Tale by Poe," trans. Matthew Wald and Richard Howard, in *On Signs,* ed. Marshall Blonsky (Baltimore: Johns Hopkins University Press, 1985), 84.

8. Ian Watt, *The Rise of the Novel: Studies in Defoe, Richardson, and Fielding* (Berkeley and Los Angeles: University of California Press, 1957).

9. John T. Matthews, "Framing in *Wuthering Heights," Texas Studies in Literature and Language* 27 (1985): 56-57.

10. Tzvetan Todorov, "The Categories of Literary Narrative," trans. Joseph Kestner, *Papers on Language and Literature* 16 (1980).

CHAPTER 1 | TOWARD A TRANSMISSION THEORY OF NARRATIVE

1. Miguel de Cervantes, *The Ingenious Gentleman Don Quixote de la Mancha,* trans. Samuel Putnam (New York: Viking, 1949). Translation slightly altered. Subsequent citations are noted parenthetically in the text.

2. Ralph Flores, *The Rhetoric of Doubtful Authority: Deconstructive Readings of Self-Questioning Narratives, St. Augustine to Faulkner* (Ithaca: Cornell University Press, 1984), 95. Flores's work was published at a significant time for the shaping of this study; for an extended account of Flores's readings of narrator authority, see Bernard Duyfhuizen, "Questions of Authority and (Dis)Belief in Literary Theory," *New Orleans Review* 12, no. 3 (1985): 67–74.

3. Ibid., 99.

4. Robert Alter, *Partial Magic: The Novel as a Self-Conscious Genre* (Berkeley and Los Angeles: University of California Press, 1975), 6.

5. Jorge Luis Borges, "Partial Enchantments of the Quixote," *Borges: A Reader*, ed. Emir Rodriguez Monegal and Alastair Reid (New York: E. P. Dutton, 1981), 234–35. Borges himself has written a "disquieting" story using *Don Quixote* as a pre-text: "Pierre Menard, Author of the *Quixote*." The story is written in the discourse of a critical essay, and it recounts Menard's brave attempt to write *Don Quixote* in the twentieth century. Menard's failure to complete his task signifies the uniqueness of any narrative, but the few passages in which he succeeds are masterpieces because of the different literary prestructures—the presentational context that surrounds a book and thereby determines a reader's specific expectations about the text—that make the rewriting of *Don Quixote* an impossible quest.

6. Franz K. Stanzel, *Narrative Situations in the Novel*, trans. James P. Pusack (Bloomington: Indiana University Press, 1971). See also Stanzel's "Second Thoughts on *Narrative Situations in the Novel*: Towards a Grammar of Fiction," *Novel* 11 (1978): 247–68.

7. Seymour Chatman, "The Structure of Narrative Transmission," in *Style and Structure in Literature: Essays in the New Stylistics*, ed. Roger Fowler (Ithaca: Cornell University Press, 1975): 215. See *Story and Discourse: Narrative Structure in Fiction and Film* (Ithaca: Cornell University Press, 1978); and Chatman's more recent study, *Coming to Terms: The Rhetoric of Narrative in Fiction and Film* (Ithaca: Cornell University Press, 1990), 3, where he apparently backs away from the term "transmission," but he doesn't explain why.

8. Franz K. Stanzel, *A Theory of Narrative*, trans. Charlotte Goedsche (Cambridge: Cambridge University Press, 1984), 53.

9. Ibid., 4.

10. Ibid., 20.

11. Ibid., 17. Emphasis added.

12. Ibid., 20.

13. Gérard Genette, *Narrative Discourse: An Essay on Method*, trans. Jane E. Lewin (Ithaca: Cornell University Press, 1980), 229.

14. Stanzel, *A Theory*, 20.

15. Genette, *Narrative Discourse*, 228–29. The asterisk marks where Genette offers the following note to explain his terminology: "These terms have already been put forth in my *Figures II*, p. 202. The prefix *meta-* obviously connotes here, as in 'metalanguage,' the transition to the second degree: the *metanarrative* is a narrative within the narrative, the *metadiegesis* is the universe of this second narrative, as the *diegesis* (according to a now widespread usage) designates the universe of the first narrative. We must admit, however, that this term functions in a way opposite to that of its model in logic and linguistics: metalanguage is a language in which one speaks of another language, so metanarrative should be the first narrative, within which one would tell a second narrative. But it seemed to me that it was better to keep the simplest and most common designation for the first degree, and thus to reverse the direction of interlocking. Naturally, the eventual third degree will be a meta-metanarrative, with its meta-metadiegesis, etc." Genette's term "metadiegetic" has been disputed by some narratologists; for accounts of this dispute see Mieke Bal, "Notes on Narrative Embedding," trans. Eve Tavor, *Poetics Today* 2, no. 2 (1981): 53–59; Shlomith Rimmon-Kenan, *Narrative Fiction: Contemporary Poetics* (London: Methuen, 1983), ch. 7; and Genette's response, *Nouveau discours du récit* (Paris: Seuil, 1983), ch. 14.

16. Robyn R. Warhol, "Toward a Theory of the Engaging Narrator: Earnest Interventions in Gaskell, Stowe, and Eliot," *PMLA* 101 (1986): 811–18.

17. Genette, *Narrative Discourse*, 244–45.

18. Gérard Genette, *Seuils* (Paris: Éditions du Seuil, 1987), 10.

19. Susan Lanser, *The Narrative Act: Point of View in Prose Fiction* (Princeton: Princeton University Press, 1981).

20. Ibid., 157–61.

21. An interesting reversal of this hypothesis about the levels of textually encoded transmission channels and contacts is the second-person narrative such as Italo Calvino's *If on a Winter's Night a Traveler*, trans. William Weaver (New York: Harcourt Brace, 1981). In this text, the reader becomes the protagonist, and the action centers on acts of reading different "texts" in an effort to read beyond the first chapters of various intercalated novels within the novel. Yet, even here the transmission/contact ratio returns to the norm at the level of the literary instance. For a reading of the play of textuality in Calvino's novel, see Steven Cohan and Linda M. Shires, *Telling Stories: A Theoretical Analysis of Narrative Fiction* (New York: Routledge, 1988), 149–53.

22. Jonathan Culler, *Structuralist Poetics: Structuralism, Linguistics and the Study of Literature* (Ithaca: Cornell University Press, 1975), 203.

23. Roland Barthes, "Textual Analysis of a Tale by Poe," trans. Matthew Wald and Richard Howard, in *On Signs*, ed. Marshall Blonsky (Baltimore: Johns Hopkins University Press, 1985), 94.

24. Ibid., 96.

25. Ibid., 93.

26. Roman Jakobson, "Closing Statement: Linguistics and Poetics," in *Style in Language*, ed. Thomas A. Sebeok (Cambridge: MIT University Press, 1960), 350–77.

27. Ibid., 353.

28. Raman Selden, *A Reader's Guide to Contemporary Literary Theory* (Lexington: University Press of Kentucky, 1985), 3–4.

29. Wallace Martin, *Recent Theories of Narrative* (Ithaca: Cornell University Press, 1986), 155.

30. Robert Scholes, *Semiotics and Interpretation* (New Haven: Yale University Press, 1982), 21.

31. Lanser, *Narrative Act*, 92.

32. Ibid., 91–92.

33. Ibid., 174–84.

34. Lanser's discussion always assumes the identifiable presence of a narrator behind the narrative voice. Tzvetan Todorov suggests an opposite description of the "I" narrator: "The true narrator, the subject of the speech-act of the text in which a character says 'I,' is only the more disguised thereby. A narrative in the first person does not make the image of its narrator explicit, but on the contrary renders it still more implicit. And every effort at such explication can lead only to a more nearly perfect dissimulation of the subject of the speech-act; this discourse that acknowledges itself to be discourse merely conceals its property as discourse" (*Introduction to Poetics*, trans. Richard Howard [Minneapolis: University of Minneapolis Press, 1981], 39). Todorov is suggesting that when the narrator is also a character or the protagonist, the narrator and the actor do not form one composite and identifiable subject; instead, the distinction between the narrating subject and the narrated object is made absolute by a third image that is embedded between the two textual images but is absent from the text—both the narrating self and the experiencing self are projections of a self that undergoes transformation during the process of transmission.

35. Tzvetan Todorov, *Mikhail Bakhtin: The Dialogical Principle*, trans. Wald Godzich (Minneapolis: University of Minnesota Press, 1984), 55. Emphasis added.

36. M. M. Bakhtin, "Discourse in the Novel," *The Dialogic Imagination*, ed.

Michael Holquist, trans. Caryl Emerson and Michael Holquist (Austin: University of Texas Press, 1981), 263.

37. Ibid., 338.

38. Ibid., 332.

39. Bakhtin describes this process of transformation as follows:

> Everyday speech is not concerned with forms of representation, but only with means of *transmission*. These means, conceived both as a way to formulate verbally and stylistically another's speech and as a way to provide an interpretive frame, a tool for re-conceptualization and re-accenting—from direct verbatim quotation in a verbal transmission to malicious and deliberate parodic distortion of another's word, slander—are highly varied. The following must be kept in mind: that the speech of another, once enclosed in a context, is—no matter how accurately transmitted—always subject to certain semantic changes.... For this reason we cannot, when studying the various forms for transmitting another's speech, treat any of these forms in isolation from the means for its contextualized (dialogizing) framing—the one is indissolubly linked with the other. The formulation of another's speech as well as its framing (and the context can begin preparing for the introduction of another's speech far back in the text) both expresses the unitary act of dialogic interaction with that speech, a relation determining the entire nature of its transmission and all the changes in meaning and accent that take place in it during transmission. ("Discourse in the Novel," 339–40)

40. Ibid., 353.

41. Peter Brooks, *Reading for the Plot: Design and Intention in Narrative* (New York: Alfred Knopf, 1984), 27–28.

42. Ibid., 34.

43. Ibid., 311.

CHAPTER 2 | EPISTOLARY NARRATIVES OF TRANSMISSION AND TRANSGRESSION

1. For further elaboration of this typology of epistolary fiction see Bertil Romberg, *Studies in the Narrative Technique of the First-Person Novel*, trans. Michael Taylor and Harold H. Borland (Stockholm: Almqvist and Wiksell, 1962), 46–55; for other standard works on epistolary fiction see Godfrey Frank Singer, *The Epistolary Novel: Its Origin, Development, Decline, and Residuary Influence* (1933; New York: Russell and Russell, 1963); Frank Gees Black, *The Epistolary Novel in the Late Eighteenth Century: A Descriptive Bibliographic Study* (1940; Folcroft, Pa.: Folcroft, 1969); François Jost, "Le roman épistolaire et la technique au XVIIIe siècle," *Comparative Literature Studies* 3 (1966): 397–427; Robert Adams Day, *Told in Letters: Epistolary Fiction before Richardson* (Ann Arbor: University of Michigan Press, 1966); and Janet Gurkin Altman, *Epistolarity: Approaches to a Form* (Columbus: Ohio State University Press, 1982).

2. Samuel Richardson, *The History of Clarissa Harlowe*, 8 vols. (1902; New York: AMS Press, 1970). Subsequent citations are to part and letter and are noted parenthetically in the text with the abbreviation *C*.

3. Jean-Jacques Rousseau, *Julie, ou la nouvelle Héloïse*, in *Oeuvres complètes*, vol. 2, eds. Bernard Gagnebin and Marcel Raymond (Paris: Gallimard, 1961); *La nouvelle Héloïse*, trans. Judith H. McDowell (University Park: Pennsylvania State

University Press, 1968). Subsequent citations, to the translated edition unless otherwise noted, are to part and letter, and are noted parenthetically in the text with the abbreviation *J*.

4. Pierre Choderlos de Laclos, *Les liaisons dangereuses*, in *Oeuvres complètes*, ed. Maurice Allem (Paris: Gallimard, 1951); *Les liaisons dangereuses*, trans. P. W. K. Stone (Harmondsworth: Penguin Books, 1961). Subsequent citations, to the translated edition unless otherwise noted, are to the particular letter and are noted parenthetically in the text with the abbreviation *L*.

5. Joseph Kestner, *Spatiality of the Novel* (Detroit: Wayne State University Press, 1978), 34. Kestner sees the epistolary novel's spatial isolation of its characters as exemplifying the "novel of point," in which multiple perspectives, in this case those of the correspondents, are arrayed, like points on a plane, in a geographic and a narrative relationship (33–35).

6. Jacques Derrida, "The Law of Genre," trans. Avital Ronell, *Critical Inquiry* 7 (1980): 55–81. Interestingly, Derrida has also written an epistolary text, "Envois," in *La carte postale de Socrate à Freud et au-delà* (Paris: Flammarion, 1980); for a probing reading of the epistolarity of Derrida's text, see Shari Benstock, "From Letters to Literature: *La Carte Postale* in the Epistolary Genre," *Genre* 18 (1985): 257–95.

7. Alan D. McKillop, "Epistolary Technique in Richardson's Novels," in *Samuel Richardson: A Collection of Critical Essays*, ed. John Carroll (Englewood Cliffs, NJ: Prentice-Hall, 1969), 139.

8. Tzvetan Todorov, *Introduction to Poetics*, trans. Richard Howard (Minneapolis: University of Minnesota Press, 1981), 31–32. In one of the earliest letter-exchange novels, Aphra Behn's *Love Letters between a Nobleman and His Sister* (1684–87), Behn uses the double-reading device to great effect in developing the plot of Sylvia's discovery of and reaction to her lover Philander's betrayal of her; see chapter 5 for a further discussion of this epistolary novel.

9. W. Daniel Wilson, "Readers in Texts," *PMLA* 96 (1981): 848–63.

10. For an incisive reading of Clarissa's allegorical letter, see Jonathan Loesberg, "Allegory and Narrative in *Clarissa*," *Novel* 15 (1981): 39–59.

11. Altman, *Epistolarity*, ch. 2.

12. Jost, "Le roman épistolaire," 406.

13. Tzvetan Todorov has shown that the characters in *Les liaisons dangereuses* change confidants as their relationships with other characters change ("The Categories of Literary Narrative," trans. Joseph Kestner, *Papers on Language and Literature* 16 (1980): 16–18); also, see Todorov's extended study of Laclos's novel: *Littérature et signification* (Paris: Larousse, 1967).

14. Altman, *Epistolarity*, 75–81.

15. Altman, *Epistolarity*, 53.

16. My translation. Although not far off, the Stone translation reads: "confidante of all my inmost secrets"; however, the original French is: "dépositaire de tous les secrets de mon coeur." "*Dépositaire*" could idiomatically, and within the context of the novel, signify "confidante," yet it also signifies "trustee" or "depositary" (which in turn signifies repository or archive), suggesting both the collection of candid sentiments from the heart and the assumed safekeeping of the letter collection's confidentiality. Though the phrase has the ring of cliché, Valmont might be ironically quoting Rousseau's text and the crucial opening of letter 18 in part 3: "Vous êtes depuis si longtems le dépositaire de tous les secrets de mon coeur."

17. See the editor's note to letter 169 that mentions "Certain letters entrusted, also to Mme de Rosemonde, by Madame de Volanges." Included here could be Cécile's other letters.

18. Those letters of Mme de Merteuil that are seemingly unavailable to the editor are: from Cécile, letters 12, 27, 28, 97, 109; from Danceny, 118, 148, 150; and from Mme de Volanges, 98. Todorov briefly discusses the collecting of the collections, but he overlooks the problematics of collecting every letter (*Littérature et signification*, 47).

19. Gérard Genette, *Narrative Discourse: An Essay in Method*, trans. Jane E. Lewin (Ithaca: Cornell University Press, 1980), 218.

20. William Beatty Warner, *Reading "Clarissa": The Struggles of Interpretation* (New Haven: Yale University Press, 1979), 100.

21. An exception would be John Barth's *Letters*, in which Barth extends the epistolary genre's boundaries by characterizing himself as a participant in an epistolary novel that brings together characters from his other novels, or rather their "real"-life counterparts. An intriguing reading of the various transmission strategies used in Barth's text has been provided by Patrick O'Donnell, *Passionate Doubts: Designs of Interpretation in Contemporary American Fiction* (Iowa City: University of Iowa Press, 1986), ch. 3.

22. Genette, *Narrative Discourse*, 229.

23. Ibid., 243–48.

24. The extradiegetic discourse of the editor is discussed in chapter 5.

25. Peter Brooks, *The Novel of Worldliness: Crébillon, Marivaux, Laclos, Stendhal* (Princeton: Princeton University Press, 1969). Brooks defines worldliness as "an ethos and personal manner which indicate that one attaches primary or even exclusive importance to ordered social existence, to life within a public system of values and gestures, to the social techniques that further this life and one's position in it, and hence to knowledge about society and its forms of comportment. The 'literature of worldliness' is then a literature directed to man's self-conscious social existence—to know, assess, celebrate, master and give meaning to man's words and gestures as they are formed by his consciousness of society. The 'novel of worldliness,' finally, is a fictional exploitation of the drama inherent in man's social existence, the encounters of personal styles within the framework and code provided by society" (4).

26. Nancy K. Miller, *The Heroine's Text: Readings in the French and English Novel, 1722–1782* (New York: Columbia University Press, 1980).

27. Paul de Man, *Allegories of Reading: Figural Language in Rousseau, Nietzsche, Rilke, and Proust* (New Haven: Yale University Press, 1979), 205.

28. For significant readings of the literary descendants of Abelard and Héloïse, see Peggy Kamuf, *Fictions of Feminine Desire: The Disclosures of Héloïse* (Lincoln: University of Nebraska Press, 1982) and Linda S. Kauffman, *Discourses of Desire: Gender, Genre, and Epistolary Fiction* (Ithaca: Cornell University Press, 1986).

29. Wolfgang Iser, "Indeterminacy and the Reader's Response in Prose Fiction," in *Aspects of Narrative*, ed. J. Hilles Miller (New York: Columbia University Press, 1971), 35.

30. De Man's translation, *Allegories of Reading*, 194.

31. Miller, *Heroine's Text*, 85.

32. Kamuf, *Fictions of Feminine Desire*, 125.

33. Aphra Behn in *Love Letters between a Nobleman and His Sister* (New York: Penguin-Virago, 1987) had coded this maxim of epistolary seduction in 1685 when her editor/narrator observes, "for [Octavio] knew well those that argue will yield, and only she that sends him back his own letters without reading them can give despair" (155).

34. For fuller accounts of presuppositions and intertextuality, see Jonathan Culler, *The Pursuit of Signs: Semiotics, Literature, Deconstruction* (Ithaca: Cornell University Press, 1981), 100–19, and Michael Riffaterre, "Flaubert's Presuppositions," *Diacritics* 11, no. 4 (1981): 2–11.

35. Quoted in H. Porter Abbott, *Diary Fiction: Writing as Action* (Ithaca: Cornell University Press, 1984), 55–56. The translation is by Abbott.

36. Miller, *Heroine's Text*, 85.

37. Riffaterre. "Flaubert's Presuppositions," 6.

38. Mme de Tourvel's raving letter and Clarissa's fragments mark what Altman calls the "eclipse of the confidant" (*Epistolarity*, 57–59), when the letter writer, because of high emotional stress, can lose all sense of an addressee.

39. Miller, *Heroine's Text*, 89.

CHAPTER 3 | DIARY NARRATIVES: MAKING CONTACT WITH THE SELF

1. Lorna Martens, *The Diary Novel* (Cambridge: Cambridge University Press, 1985), 4.

2. Virginia Woolf, *A Writer's Diary*, ed. Leonard Woolf (New York: Harcourt Brace, 1953), 7. The entry is dated 20 January 1919.

3. Undoubtedly exceptions to this rule exist (Turgenev's "The Diary of a Superfluous Man," for instance), but the self-discovery that accompanies diary writing is uniquely worked into the form from its inception.

4. For a discussion of the epistolary monody, see Jean Rousset, *Narcisse romancier: Essai sur al première personne dans la roman* (Paris: Corti, 1973).

5. H. Porter Abbott, *Diary Fiction: Writing as Action* (Ithaca: Cornell University Press, 1984).

6. Abbott (ibid.), however, inverts this conventional distinction between diary and epistolary fictions; he argues that single-writer epistolary texts such as *Les lettres portugaises, Die Leiden des jungen Werthers*, and *Pamela* (vols. 1 & 2 only) should be considered as a subcategory of "diary fiction," a term that Abbott does not intend as a formally derived genre designation: "Diary fiction, as I use the term, includes single-writer epistolary fiction, and since (as the Underground Man would point out) letters are not the same thing as diaries, I should defend my conjoining of them before the reader gets under way" (9). This defense centers on the absence of a *participating addressee* in the texts Abbott wishes to consider—once the addressee responds we have a correspondence narrative (e.g., *Clarissa*). For Abbott, single-writer epistolary fiction dramatizes a diary impulse to record one's life story expressively without any expectation of a response. However, if the letters in a single-writer epistolary fiction simply go unanswered or the answers are not included in the novel's narrative of transmission, is this a sufficient ground for terming such expressive and reflexive texts diaries? The question is significant because Abbott insists on focusing his attention on "a presentational strategy rather than [on] a repeatable constellation of literary elements or [on] a single necessary function or buried speech act" (17). This "diary strategy" contains the "diary novel" but goes beyond it to consider as possible diaries a variety of texts that use "the strategy of casting one's fiction as a nonretrospective document authored by a single fictive agent" (17).

The problem here centers on the term "diary." Culturally coded, diary signifies a text kept daily that records events soon after they happen and foreshadows events in the near future (e.g., appointments); it may certainly be expressive, reflexive, and nonretrospective. Moreover, diaries are conventionally assumed to be private texts written only for the writer's eyes, although this last condition is violated as often in real life as it is in fiction. But Abbott seemingly wants to overlook, or at least qualify, some of these characteristics to discuss a wider variety of texts; hence, we must recognize his use of "diary" as a metaphor for a species of writing not strictly diaristic.

On the other hand, Lorna Martens in *The Diary Novel* seeks a more precisely defined understanding of diary fiction, and specifically the diary novel as a unique subgenre of first-person narration. Martens is alert to the gray areas surrounding this genre and to the traps into which many commentators on literary genres fall. Martens first establishes a formal definition of the diary novel: "It is a fictional prose narrative written from day to day by a single first-person narrator who does not address himself to a fictive addressee or recipient" (4). Based on this definition, she marks distinctions between two related first-person forms: the memoir novel and the epistolary novel. Abbott likewise distinguishes the former because of its retrospective orientation; however, Martens insists on distinguishing the latter precisely because of the intended fictive reader(s) in the text. Thus Martens recognizes that "the borderline between the diary novel and the epistolary novel is fluid" (7), and she cites *Les lettres portugaises* and *Werther* as examples. Nevertheless, Martens refuses to overlook formal distinctions and literary history to include *Werther* in the genre of the diary novel. As the difference of opinion between Abbott and Martens shows, the diary is far from an agreed-upon form that can be easily dismissed as a formal convention.

7. Franz K. Stanzel, *Narrative Situations in the Novel*, trans. James Pusack (Bloomington: Indiana University Press, 1971).

8. Thomas Mallon, *A Book of One's Own: People and Their Diaries* (New York: Ticknor and Fields, 1984).

9. Ibid., 209.

10. Ibid., 247.

11. Ibid., 226.

12. Ibid., 285.

13. Bertil Romberg, *Studies in the Technique of the First-Person Novel*, trans. Michael Taylor and Harold H. Borland (Stockholm: Almqvist and Wiksell, 1962), 44.

14. Valerie Raoul, *The French Fictional Journal: Fictional Narcissism/Narcissistic Fiction* (Toronto: University of Toronto Press, 1980), 27.

15. Ibid., 29.

16. Michal Glowinski observes, however, that "at the earliest stage of the development of prose fiction, the first-person story was often not a matter of choice but—unlike in the epic—rather a matter of necessity, since the other forms had not yet been developed. In certain cases, the first-person narration appears even in the adventure novel, the main element of which is an exuberant plot and which, in the process of historic development, became the domain of a different type of narration" ("On the First-Person Novel," trans. Rochelle Stone, *New Literary History* 9 [1977], 111).

17. Mikhail Lermontov, *A Hero of Our Time*, trans. Vladimir Nabokov and Dimitri Nabokov (Garden City, N.Y.: Doubleday, 1958).

18. Ivan Turgenev, "The Diary of a Superfluous Man," trans. Harry Stevens, in *The Vintage Turgenev*, vol. 2 (New York: Vintage, 1960). Subsequent citations are noted parenthetically in the text.

19. Victor Hugo, *Le dernier jour d'un condamné*, trans. as *Last Day of a Condemned*, by Eugenia de B. (1894; New York: Howard Fertig, 1977).

20. Samuel Richardson, *Pamela, or, Virtue Rewarded*, ed. Peter Sabor (Harmondsworth, Penguin Books, 1980). Subsequent citations are noted parenthetically in the text.

21. In a narrative so conscious of its textuality, the use of "period" to signify "death" can appear overindulgent. However, texts that stage narratives of transmission often deploy linguistic, writerly, and textual matricies of analogy, thus inscribing the code of transmission in the code of the story. As we saw in the previous chapter, the letter in epistolary fiction can be both a literal document and a symbolic feminine page about to be violated by the masculine pen.

22. Cynthia Griffin Wolff, *Samuel Richardson and the Eighteenth-Century Puritan Character* (Hamdon, Conn.: Archon Books, 1972), 18.

23. For an account of Pamela's changed views on domestic life in the later volumes of *Pamela*, see Tassie Gwilliam, "*Pamela* and the Duplicitous Body of Feminity," *Representations* 34 (1991): 128.

24. Edouard Dujardin, *Les lauriers sont coupés*. Translated as *We'll to the Woods No More* by Stuart Gilbert (New York: New Directions, 1938). Subsequent citations are noted parenthetically in the text.

25. Dorrit Cohn, *Transparent Minds: Narrative Modes for Presenting Consciousness in Fiction* (Princeton: Princeton University Press, 1978), 208.

26. By introducing the term "autonomous" Cohn delimits the narrative technique for presenting the direct expression of a character's thought (e.g., Dujardin's novel or Joyce's Penelope section in *Ulysses*). She posits this term to distinguish between it and other forms of presenting consciousness that come under the heading of "interior monologue." To see how Cohn relates diary narrative to the special type of "autonomous monologue," see ibid., 208–16.

27. Ibid., 208, 212.

28. Cohn presents Wilhelm Raabe's *The Chronicle of Sperling Street* (1857) as an example of a text experimenting with the idea that the diarist can "record everything he sees and hears within an hour's time, dating his running record by the minute" (ibid., 212).

29. The exception to this "rule" of the past tense would be texts using an artificial present tense, as in E. M. Delafield's *Diary of a Provincial Lady* (1931; Chicago: Academy Chicago, 1982); a brief example will make clear this exception: "Ethel returns, ten minutes late, and says Shall she light fire in spare room? I say No, it is not cold enough—but really mean that Cissie is no longer, in my opinion, deserving of luxuries. Subsequently feel this to be unworthy attitude, and light fire myself. It smokes. Robert calls up to know What is that Smoke? I call down that It is Nothing. Robert comes up and opens the window and shuts the door and says It will Go all right Now. Do not like to point out that the open window will make the room cold" (14–15). The time of the writing is so indeterminate in this passage and its syntax and punctuation so unconventional (yet clearly modernist) that the reader begins to write the text during the act of reading.

30. By "self-quoted interior monologue" Cohn means the presentation of thoughts with signaling phrases and/or quotation marks, as in: "Andrew had been shot, and I thought, 'Better him than me'"; whereas, by "self-narrated monologue" Cohn means the presentation of thoughts without any signaling other than a shift in tense, as in: "Andrew had been shot; better him than me"—the character thinks "better him than me," but the narration of that thought becomes more problematic because we cannot clearly assign it to either the narrating self or the experiencing self.

31. Jean-Paul Sartre, *La nausée* (Paris: Gallimard, 1938). Subsequent citations are noted parenthetically in the text.

32. "After a moment, he returned with an illustrated book which he placed near his package. I thought: 'I am seeing him for the last time'" [my translation].

33. "I thought: 'I am seeing him for the last time.' Tomorrow evening, the evening after tomorrow, and all the following evenings, he would return to read at this table, eating his bread and chocolate, he would patiently continue his rat's nibbling, he would read the works of Nabaud, Naudeau, Nodier, Nys, occasionally interrupting himself to note a maxim in his small notebook. And I would be walking in Paris, in Paris streets, I would be seeing new faces. What could happen to me, while he would still be here, with the lamp illuminating his large face? Just in time I felt myself drifting back to the mirage of adventure. I shrugged my shoulders and resumed reading" [my translation].

34. In recounting an event the diarist/narrator may "focalize" thoughts through other characters; for example: "I saw a puzzled look on her face. She seemed to be thinking of many different answers before she responded to my question." In this example, the homodiegetic narrator has no way of knowing for sure that the other person was "thinking of many different answers," but in attempting to portray the moment, the narrator "reads" the other and offers the most likely explanation for the temporal gap between question and answer by having the narration focalize the other's consciousness.

35. Nikolai Gogol, "The Diary of a Madman," in *Dostoevsky and Gogol: Texts and Criticism*, ed. and trans. Priscilla Meyer and Stephen Rudy (Ann Arbor: Ardis, 1979), 3–20.

36. Leonard J. Kent, *The Subconscious in Gogol and Dostoevsky and Its Antecedents* (The Hague: Mouton, 1969), 77.

37. Ibid., 78.

38. Charlotte Perkins Gilman, *The Yellow Wallpaper* (Old Westbury, N.Y.: Feminist Press, 1973). Subsequent citations are noted parenthetically in the text.

39. Paula A. Treichler, "Escaping the Sentence: Diagnosis and Discourse in 'The Yellow Wallpaper,'" *Tulsa Studies in Women's Literature* 3 (1984).

40. Gerald Prince, "The Diary Novel: Notes for the Definition of a Sub-Genre," *Neophilologus* 59 (1975): 480.

41. Steven G. Kellman, *The Self-Begetting Novel* (New York: Columbia University Press, 1980).

42. Ibid., 48.

43. "I tell her my adventures, I speak to her about existence—perhaps at too great a length. She listens carefully, her eyes open wide, her eyebrow raised.
"When I have finished, she looks soothed" [my translation].

44. Raoul, *French Fictional Journal*, 42.

45. Lucien Dällenbach, "Reflexivity and Reading," trans. Annette Tomarken, *New Literary History* 11 (1980): 435. For further discussion of the *mise en abyme* in narrative, see Jean Ricardou, "L'histoire dans l'histoire," *Problèmes du nouveau roman* (Paris: Seuil, 1967), 161–70, translated as "The Story within the Story" by Joseph Kestner, *James Joyce Quarterly* 18 (1981): 323–38; and Dällenbach, *Le récit spéculaire: Essai sur la mise en abyme* (Paris: Seuil, 1977).

46. There is a second intertextual line of transmission in Turgenev's story: the "superfluous man" in Russian literature. Behind Chulkaturin is the literary legacy of Pushkin, Gogol, and Lermontov. In these precursors there are many protagonists who are somehow at odds with the society in which they live.

47. My reading hinges on the nonapproval of Chulkaturin's text; however, two of the four translations I have located (Isabel F. Hapgood, trans. *"The Diary of a Superfluous Man" and Other Stories* [New York: Charles Scribner's, 1923], 91 and David Patterson, trans. *Diary of a Superfluous Man* [New York: Norton, 1984],

78) translate this passage in the positive; wherein the Stevens translation cited in the text and that of Richard Freeborn ("The Diary of a Superfluous Man," in *"First Love" and Other Stories* [Oxford: Oxford University Press, 1989], 72) follow the original Russian more closely:

Сѣю рукопись. Читалъ
И Содѣржаніе Онной Нѣ Одобрилъ
Пѣтръ Зудотѣшинъ

In this text, the "Нѣ" indicates the negation; from I. S. Turgenev, *Polnoye sobranye i pisem*, vol. 5 (Moskva-Leningrad, 1963), 232; my thanks to my colleague Blagoy Trenev for help with this text. Needless to say, the problems of translation make up another whole area of transmission studies.

48. Fyodor Dostoevsky, *Notes from Underground*, trans. Constance Garnett, in *The Norton Anthology of World Masterpieces: Continental Edition*, vol. 2, ed. Maynard Mack et al., 4th ed. (New York: Norton, 1980), 848. Subsequent citations are noted parenthetically in the text.

49. John Updike, *A Month of Sundays* (New York: Alfred Knopf, 1975). Subsequent citations are noted parenthetically in the text.

50. One might contrast this diagnosis "to write" with the absolute prohibition of writing that Gilman figures in "The Yellow Wallpaper."

51. At one point in the journal Marshfield writes: "It occurs to me that at least three times before in these enforced confessions have I discovered myself above, exalted, *raptus*, looking down as at the golf ball ere smiting it so triumphantly into the heart of the eighteenth green. Once, when returning from a nocturnal mission of mercy to find Ned and Jane fumbling in boozy friendliness beside my fire. Twice, when serving communion to a kneeling recent fellatrice from the height of my priestly role. Thrice looking down *in my overarching embodiment as author* [emphasis added], through the lifted roof at the Harlows' domestic bliss, their house and its inhabitants reduced by reminiscence to a *doll-sized* [emphasis added] seizability" (188–89).

CHAPTER 4 | INSERTED DOCUMENTS AND HYBRID NARRATIVES OF TRANSMISSION

1. Homer Obed Brown, "The Errant Letter and the Whispering Gallery," *Genre* 10 (1977): 589.

2. Jane Austen, *Pride and Prejudice*, vol. 2 of *The Novels of Jane Austen* (Oxford, 1933). Subsequent citations are noted parenthetically in the text.

3. Brown, "Errant Letter," 581.

4. Jane Austen, *Persuasion*, vol. 5 of *The Novels of Jane Austen* (Oxford, 1933). Subsequent citations are noted parenthetically in the text.

5. Stendhal, *Le rouge et le noir* (Paris: Gallimard, 1972); translated as *Red and Black* by Robert M. Adams (New York: Norton, 1969). Subsequent citations, to the translated edition, are noted parenthetically in the text.

6. By characterizing Julien as her teacher, Mathilde echoes the relationship of Abelard and Héloïse; and when Julien speculates on a series of plots against him that may be behind Mathilde's request that he come to her bedroom, he reminds himself, "Beware the fate of Abelard, master secretary" (271).

7. Gustave Flaubert, *Madame Bovary* (Paris: Garnier-Flammarion, 1979);

trans. by Paul de Man (New York: Norton, 1965). Subsequent citations, to the translated edition, are noted parenthetically in the text.

8. James Joyce, *Ulysses*, ed. Hans Walter Gabler (New York: Random House, 1986). Subsequent citations are noted parenthetically in the text. For a full discussion of the letters in *Ulysses*, see Shari Benstock, "The Printed Letters in *Ulysses*," *James Joyce Quarterly* 19 (1982): 415–27.

9. Edouard Dujardin, *Les lauriers sont coupés*. Translated as *We'll to the Woods No More* by Stuart Gilbert (New York: New Directions, 1938).

10. James Joyce, *A Portrait of the Artist as a Young Man* (New York: Viking, 1982). Subsequent citations are noted parenthetically in the text.

11. John Paul Riquelme, "Pretexts for Reading and for Writing: Title, Epigraph, and Journal in *A Portrait of the Artist as a Young Man*," *James Joyce Quarterly* 18 (1981): 301.

12. Susan Lanser, "Stephen's Diary: The Hero Unveiled," *James Joyce Quarterly* 16 (1979): 417–23.

13. Michael Levenson, "Stephen's Diary in Joyce's *Portrait*—The Shape of Life," *ELH* 52 (1985): 1024. The diary form, Levenson suggests, traps Stephen's pre-flight discourse within a dialectic of personal history and an intertextual matrix with Turgenev's "The Diary of a Superfluous Man"—a text Levenson asserts was a model for Joyce's diaristic technique (1022–24).

14. Charlotte Brontë, *Shirley* (Harmondsworth: Penguin Books, 1979).

15. André Gide, *Les faux-monnayeurs* (Paris: Gallimard, 1925); translated as *The Counterfeiters with the Journal of "The Counterfeiters"* by Dorothy Bussy and Justin O'Brien (New York: Modern Library, 1927).

16. Daniel Defoe, *Robinson Crusoe and Other Writings*, ed. James Sutherland (1968; New York: New York University Press, 1977). Subsequent citations are noted parenthetically in the text.

17. Edgar Allan Poe, *Poetry and Tales*, ed. Patrick F. Quinn (New York: Library of America, 1984). Subsequent citations are noted parenthetically in the text.

18. Although these pseudo-diaries represent physical isolation from "regular" society, the diarists all begin on a similar note of personal alienation from the familiar society of their preadventure life. In the first paragraph of Crusoe we read, "I was called *Robinson Kreutznaer*; but by the usual corruption of words in England, we are now called, nay, we call ourselves, and write our name *Crusoe*" (5). As the story progresses, we see that Crusoe's adventures stem from his rebellion against his father's middle-class program for life; and upon his return, there is no family remaining to which he can return. Rodman also begins his chronicle cut off from family and home: "After the death of my father, and both sisters, I took no farther interest in our plantation" (1196). Pym does not begin his own narrative; this is the portion he tells us "Mr. Poe" wrote, but its opening claim to identity, "My name is Arthur Gordon Pym" (1009), gives way to a character who rebels against the family, and whose narrative, in its unrelenting linearity forward, seems little concerned with the family left at home. (Is the narrative the long-delayed letter home?) And, of course, the next great novel of sea adventure will begin just as rootlessly: "Call me Ishmael."

19. The latter page number is an approximation based on when Crusoe mentions the depletion of his ink supply—how much of the remaining text we are to assume was first recorded in the diary is a mystery.

20. Poe's classic short story, "The Purloined Letter" (1844), can also be considered as a tale that dramatizes a narrative of transmission. The key element in that tale of a letter appropriated, used by its mere presence as a political weapon and ultimately redirected to its rightful addressee, is the absence of the letter's

contents from the narration. Rather than a part of the substance of the story or a generating element in the plot relations of two characters, the letter becomes an object and the story a marginal gloss on its transmission. Within a larger narrative context the reader might have been given access to the letter (as we are to Mme de Merteuil's compromising letter in *Les liaisons dangereuses*), but as Poe so often does, the absence of the letter (its doubled purloining) leaves a void in the text that foils any attempt at complete understanding.

21. Quoted in Sidney Kaplan, "An Introduction to *Pym*," in *Poe: A Collection of Critical Essays*, ed. Robert Regan (Englewood Cliffs, N.J.: Prentice Hall, 1967), 153.

22. Stephen Mainville, "Language and the Void: Gothic Landscapes and Frontiers in Edgar Allan Poe," *Genre* 14 (1981): 349, 355.

23. In considering *Pym* we must remember that we are talking of constructs, either intrafictional or extrafictional. However, on the level of criticism that concerns the literary instance of the novel, the conjunction of Poe/Pym/editor suggests an interesting relationship between the real author and his text.

24. Jean Ricardou, "Le caractère singulier de cette eau," in *Problèmes du nouveau roman* (Paris: Seuil, 1967), 202. Ricardou's reading also applies to *Pym*'s precursor, "MS. Found in a Bottle" (1833), which is more purely a diary of "physical isolation." Like *Pym*, the story turns on a shipwreck, but the narrator is unintentionally saved by the ghost ship that destroyed his first vessel. On the ghost ship the text is written: "It was no long while ago that I ventured into the captain's own private cabin, and took thence the materials with which I write, and have written. I shall from time to time continue this journal. It is true I may not find an opportunity of transmitting it to the world, but I shall not fail to make the endeavor. At the last moment I will enclose the MS. in a bottle, and cast it within the sea" (Poe, *Poetry and Tales*, 195). This MS. is not a pseudo-diary; the technological problem of writing materials has been solved; and even the means of its transmission, as fantastic as it is, has already been inscribed within the text. Also like *Pym*, "the ship proves to be in a current ... which ... thunders on to the southward with a velocity like the headlong dashing of a cataract" (198), and the final words the narrator can write, before launching his bottle are, "the ship is quivering—oh God! and——going down!" (199). In "MS." Poe masterfully conjoins suspense with the narrative of transmission. The medium of transmission—a bottle—might be open to disbelief, but it is not ambiguous in this "voyage au bout de la page."

25. Anne Brontë, *The Tenant of Wildfell Hall* (Harmondsworth: Penguin Books, 1979). Subsequent citations are noted parenthetically in the text.

26. E. P. Whipple, "*The Tenant of Wildfell Hall* by Acton Bell," *North American Review* (October 1848); rpt. in *The Scribner Companion to the Brontës*, ed. Barbara Evens and Gareth Lloyd (New York: Scribner's, 1982), 382.

27. Winifred Gérin, "Introduction," *The Tenant of Wildfell Hall*, by Anne Brontë, 13. See note 25.

28. For insightful readings of the relationship between *Wuthering Heights* and *Wildfell Hall*, see Jan B. Gordon, "Gossip, Diary, Letter, Text: Anne Brontë's Narrative *Tenant* and the Problematic of the Gothic Sequel," *ELH* 51 (1984): 735–42; and N. M. Jacobs, "Gender and Layered Narrative in *Wuthering Heights* and *The Tenant of Wildfell Hall*," *The Journal of Narrative Technique* 16 (1986): 204–19.

29. Gérin, "Introduction," 14. Ellipses are in the original. Emphasis added.

30. Gordon, "Gossip, Diary."

31. Ibid., 724–25. For a thorough account of gossip, see Patricia Meyer Spacks, *Gossip* (New York: Alfred Knopf, 1985).

32. Jacobs, "Layered Narrative," 210.

33. Gordon, "Gossip, Diary," 739.

34. Jacobs, "Layered Narrative," 204.

35. Ibid., 213.

36. Wilkie Collins, *The Woman in White* (Oxford: Oxford University Press, 1980). Subsequent citations are noted parenthetically in the text.

37. Gordon, "Gossip, Diary," 721.

38. Peter Brooks, *Reading for the Plot: Design and Intention in Narrative* (New York: Knopf, 1984), 169.

39. Doris Lessing, *The Golden Notebook* (New York: Bantam Books, 1973). Subsequent citations are noted parenthetically in the text.

40. Lorna Martens, *The Diary Novel* (Cambridge: Cambridge University Press, 1985), 234.

41. H. Porter Abbott, *Diary Fiction: Writing as Action* (Ithaca: Cornell University Press, 1984).

42. Martens, *Diary Novel*, 244.

43. Henry James, in 1912, recalled his youthful response to Browning's text, saying he felt "the sense, almost the pang, of the novel [it] might have constituted." In the same address, which James delivered before the Academic Committee of the Royal Society of Literature in Commemoration of the Centenary of Robert Browning, James also praised the transmission frame Browning employed: "No page of his long story is more vivid and splendid than that of his find of the Book in the litter of a market-stall in Florence and the swoop of practiced perception with which he caught up in it a treasure" (*Literary Criticism: Essays on Literature, American Writers, English Writers*, ed. Leon Edel with Marc Wilson [New York: Library of America, 1984], 792–93). This famous story of Browning's actual discovery rehearses the fictional narratives of discovery that Cervantes inscribed in *Don Quixote* (see chapter 1).

CHAPTER 5 | THE OPENING FRAME OF NARRATION

1. Philip Stewart, *Imitation and Illusion in the French Memoir-Novel, 1700–1750: The Act of Make-Believe* (New Haven: Yale University Press, 1969), 64.

2. Gérard Genette, *Seuils* (Paris: Éditions du Seuil, 1987).

3. Susan Lanser, *The Narrative Act: Point of View in Prose Fiction* (Princeton: Princeton University Press, 1981), 151.

4. Bertil Romberg, *Studies in the Narrative Technique of the First-Person Novel*, trans. Michael Taylor and Harold H. Borland (Stockholm: Almqvist and Wiksell, 1962), 76–77.

5. Valerie Raoul, *The French Fiction Journal: Fictional Narcissism/Narcissistic Fiction* (Toronto: Toronto University Press, 1980), 18.

6. Mary de la Rivière, "From a Lady to a Lady," and John Littleton Costeker, *The Constant Lovers*, in *The Novel in Letters: Epistolary Fiction in the Early English Novel, 1678–1740*, ed. Natascha Würzbach (Coral Gables: University of Miami Press, 1969).

7. Aphra Behn, *Love Letters between a Nobleman and His Sister* (New York: Penguin-Virago, 1987). Subsequent citations are noted parenthetically in the text.

8. Robert Adams Day, in *Told in Letters: Epistolary Fiction before Richardson* (Ann Arbor: University of Michigan Press, 1966), 159–64, was one of the few literary historians to recognize Behn's achievement in *Love Letters*. For more on Behn's fate in literary history, see Judith Kegan Gardiner, "The First English

Novel: Aphra Behn's *Love Letters*, the Canon, and Women's Tastes," *Tulsa Studies in Women's Literature* 8 (1989): 201–22.

9. Samuel Richardson, *Pamela; or, Virtue Rewarded*, ed. Peter Sabor (Harmondsworth: Penguin Books, 1980). Subsequent citations are noted parenthetically in the text.

10. Lennard J. Davis, *Factual Fictions: The Origins of the English Novel* (New York: Columbia University Press, 1983), 180–81, my interpolation. I have reinstated some parts of the quotation from the advertisement that Davis had excluded. For another account of this incident in the story of *Pamela*'s publication, see Alan D. McKillop, *Samuel Richardson: Printer and Novelist* (Hamden, Conn.: Shoe String Press, 1960), 54.

11. In a letter to Aaron Hill, concerning the composition of *Pamela*, Richardson described his preface as "assuming and very impudent" since he had taken "the umbrage of the editor's character to screen myself behind"; *Selected Letters of Samuel Richardson*, ed. John Carroll (Oxford: Clarendon Press, 1964), 42.

12. Samuel Richardson, *The History of Clarissa Harlowe*, 8 vols. (1902; New York: AMS Press, 1970). Subsequent citations are noted parenthetically in the text.

13. For a survey of Richardson's editorial responses to his readers, which became increasingly aggressive and expansive with each edition, see William Beatty Warner, *Reading "Clarissa": The Struggles of Interpretation* (New Haven, Yale University Press, 1979), chs. 5–6.

14. Glen M. Johnson, "Richardson's 'Editor' in *Clarissa*," *The Journal of Narrative Technique* 10 (1980): 99, 107.

15. Warner, *Reading "Clarissa*," 130. For discussions of the authorial use of notes in novels other than epistolary ones, see Genette, *Seuils*, 293–315; and Shari Benstock, "At the Margin of Discourse: Footnotes in the Fictional Text," *PMLA* 98 (1983): 204–25.

16. Warner, *Reading "Clarissa*," 128.

17. Ibid., 130.

18. Henry Fielding, *"Joseph Andrews" and "Shamela*," ed. A. R. Humphreys (New York: Dutton-Everyman, 1973). Subsequent citations are noted parenthetically in the text.

19. Jean Jacques Rousseau, *Julie, ou la nouvelle Héloïse*, in *Oeuvres Complètes*, vol. 2, eds. Bernard Gagnebin and Marcel Raymond (Paris: Gallimard, 1969). Subsequent citations are to part and letter and are noted parenthetically in the text.

20. Romberg, *First-Person Novel*, 73.

21. Paul de Man, *Allegories of Reading: Figural Language in Rousseau, Nietzsche, Rilke, and Proust* (New Haven: Yale University Press, 1979), 296.

22. Pierre Choderlos de Laclos, *Les liaisons dangereuses*, in *Oeuvres complètes*, ed. Maurice Allem (Paris: Gallimard, 1951); *Les liaisons dangereuses*, trans. P. W. K. Stone (Harmondsworth: Penguin Books, 1961). Subsequent citations, to the translated edition, are noted parenthetically in the text.

23. Peggy Kamuf, *Fictions of Feminine Desire: The Disclosures of Héloïse* (Ithaca: Cornell University Press, 1986), 141.

24. Ibid., 140.

25. Ibid. Kamuf's translation of letter 152. Emphasis added.

26. Ibid., 140–41.

27. Kamuf confuses her point by suggesting that "the pact [between editor and reader] recognizes a danger to an order exterior to the novel" (141). This move can only be made if disbelief is fully suspended and the actual reader identifies with the extradiegetic reader addressed by the editor. Such a suspension

of disbelief is not impossible, but it is itself a paratextual structuration, an illusion that could have only a momentary political effect.

28. H. Porter Abbott (*Diary Fiction: Writing as Action* [Ithaca: Cornell University Press, 1984]), for example, dates the first "pure" diary fiction's appearance in 1777; Lorna Martens (*The Diary Novel* [Cambridge: Cambridge University Press, 1985]) lists only ten diary texts predating 1777.

29. Daniel Defoe, *"Robinson Crusoe" and Other Writings*, ed. James Sutherland (1968; New York: New York University Press, 1977). Subsequent citations are noted parenthetically in the text.

30. Davis, *Factual Fictions*, 156–57.

31. Francis Stuart, *The High Consistory* (London: Martin Brian and O'Keefe, 1981).

32. Bram Stoker, *Dracula* (Toronto: Bantam, 1981). Subsequent citations are noted parenthetically in the text.

33. Wilkie Collins, *The Woman in White* (Oxford: Oxford University Press, 1980). Subsequent citations are noted parenthetically in the text.

34. The same principles for compiling a multiple narration were applied by Walter Scott in *Redgauntlet* (the other novels in the Waverly series are equally interesting for transmission effects), Robert Browning for his multi-transmission poetic masterpiece *The Ring and the Book*, and Caroline Norton for her multi-transmission autobiography *English Laws for Women in the Nineteenth Century*.

35. George Gissing, *The Private Papers of Henry Ryecroft* (New York: Modern Library, n.d.). Subsequent citations are noted parenthetically in the text.

36. Nathaniel Hawthorne, "Fragments from the Journal of a Solitary Man," *Tales and Sketches* (New York: Library of America, 1982), 487–500. Subsequent citations are noted parenthetically in the text.

37. Doris Lessing, *The Golden Notebook* (New York: Bantam, 1973). Subsequent citations are noted parenthetically in the text. In the passage quoted, brackets are Lessing's; emphasis added.

38. Jean-Paul Sartre, *La nausée* (Paris: Gallimard, 1938.

39. Jeremy Leven, *Creator* (New York: Coward, McCann, 1980). Subsequent citations are noted parenthetically in the text.

40. Edgar Allan Poe's "The Fall of the House of Usher" offers a good model for the *mise en abyme* of the intercalated narrative used in *Creator* and other novels that rely on structures of repetition using either intratextuality or intertextuality.

41. Victor Hugo, *Le dernier jour d'un condamné*, trans. *Last Day of a Condemned*, by Eugenia de B. (1894; New York: Howard Fertig, 1977). Subsequent citations are noted parenthetically in the text.

CHAPTER 6 | FRAMING PREFACES/ FRAMED MEMOIRS

1. John T. Matthews, "Framing in *Wuthering Heights*," *Texas Studies in Literature and Language* 27 (1985): 25.

2. Mary Ann Caws's *Reading Frames in Modern Fiction* (Princeton: Princeton University Press, 1985) presents a different conception of framing in fiction. Her important work strikes off in different directions from my own. In addition to narrational frames, Caws discusses scene painting focusing on door and window frames, works of art as examples of a *mise en abyme* device, and verbal frames produced through repetition of key words. These frames focus the reader's attention and produce moments of illumination during reading. Thus Caws's conception represents

a spatial matrix produced in reading, whereas I am more concerned with the narrative of transmission that leads readers across different narrational borders.

3. Jacques Derrida, "Living On," trans. James Hilbert, in *Deconstruction and Criticism*, ed. Harold Bloom et al. (New York: Seabury, 1979), 100. Hilbert inserts the interpolation "[*récit*]."

4. Matthews, "Framing in *Wuthering Heights*," 27.

5. Ibid., 26.

6. M. M. Bakhtin, "Discourse in the Novel," *The Dialogic Imagination*, ed. Michael Holquist, trans. Caryl Emerson and Michael Holquist (Austin: University of Texas Press, 1981), 284. Emphasis added.

7. Jonathan Swift, *Gulliver's Travels* (New York: New American Library, 1960). Subsequent citations are noted parenthetically in the text.

8. Henry Mackenzie, *The Man of Feeling* (New York: Norton, 1958).

9. Charles Kingsley, *Alton Locke, Tailor and Poet: An Autobiography* (Oxford: Oxford University Press, 1983).

10. Margaret Atwood, *The Handmaid's Tale* (Boston: Houghton Mifflin, 1986).

11. Offred herself speculates about the transmissibility of her narration: "If I'm ever able to set this down, in any form, even in the form of one voice to another, it will be a reconstruction then too, at yet another remove. It's impossible to say a thing exactly the way it was, because what you say can never be exact, you always have to leave something out, there are too many parts, sides, crosscurrents, nuances; too many gestures, which could mean this or that, too many shapes which can never be fully described, too many flavors, in the air or on the tongue, half-colors, too many" (ibid., 134). For a reading of *The Handmaid's Tale* as epistolary fiction, see Linda Kauffman, "Special Delivery: Twenty-first-Century Epistolarity in *The Handmaid's Tale*," in *Writing the Female Voice: Essays on Epistolary Literature*, ed. Elizabeth C. Goldsmith (Boston: Northeastern University Press, 1989), 221–44.

12. Benjamin Constant, *Adolphe; Le cahier rouge; Cécile* (Paris: Gallimard, 1951); translation of *Adolphe*, by Leonard Tancock (Harmondsworth: Penguin Books, 1964). Subsequent citations, to the translated edition, are noted parenthetically in the text.

13. Two historiodiegetic prefaces precede the "Note," but I will defer discussing them until the end of this section.

14. Mikhail Lermontov, *A Hero of Our Time*, trans. Vladimir Nabokov and Dimitri Nabokov (Garden City, N.Y.: Doubleday Anchor, 1958). Subsequent citations are noted parenthetically in the text.

15. Although the device of Pechorin's journal is motivated by the narrative situation of the full text, John Mersereau notes that "the manuscript of ['The Fatalist'] is headed 'Notebook III' [indicating] that at the time of writing it Lermontov already planned it as the third of the stories from *Pechorin's Journal*" (*Mikhail Lermontov* [Carbondale: Southern Illinois University Press, 1962], 134–35).

16. B. M. Eikenbaum, *Lermontov: A Study in Literary-Historical Evaluation*, trans. Ray Parrott and Harry Weber (Ann Arbor: Ardis, 1981), 165.

17. The order of the stories and the date of first publication can be listed as follows:

"Bela"	1839
"Maksim Maksimich"*	1840
"Taman"	1840
"Princess Mary"*	1840
"The Fatalist"	1839

(*first published in the separate edition of the novel, 1840)

Added to these two orders in the text's literary instance is the internal structure of the tales. According to Boris Eikenbaum, Lermontov "dropped the idea of constructing a unitary story, [and he] thereby rid himself of the need to introduce a biography of his characters into the novel.... Breaking up the novel ('the composition,' as Lermontov called it) into tales, he made his hero a static figure. In place of the customary chronology, in which the hero's life is set forth, we have another kind of sequence connected not with the hero but with the author: from his encounter with Maksim Maksimych to the tale about Pechorin, from the tale to the accidental meeting with him, from the meeting to his 'journal.' The secondary sequence (the story of the author's acquaintance with the hero) plays a structural role, and the basic sequence (the hero's life) is so displaced that even after reading the entire novel it is difficult to arrange the reported events in chronological order" (ibid., 164).

18. Henry James, *The Turn of the Screw*, vol. 12 of *The Novels and Tales of Henry James: New York Edition* (New York: Charles Scribner's, 1908). Subsequent citations are noted parenthetically in the text.

19. Douglas's relationship with the governess has been the subject of much discussion. The most interesting, and also radical, account of the relationship is Louis Rubin's in "One More Turn of the Screw," in *A Casebook on Henry James's "The Turn of the Screw,"* 2nd ed., ed. Gerald Willen (New York: Crowell, 1969), 350–66. Rubin contends that enough textual evidence exists to identify Douglas with the young Miles of the governess' narrative.

20. I am sidestepping here the long history of controversy surrounding the Freudian interpretations of *The Turn of the Screw*. Nonetheless, any psychoanalytic interpretive approach to this novel must clearly mark as an object of its inquiry not just the experiences themselves but the textualized reconstruction of those experiences.

21. Shoshana Felman, "Turning the Screw of Interpretation," in *Literature and Psychoanalysis: The Question of Reading: Otherwise*, ed. Shoshana Felman (Baltimore: Johns Hopkins University Press, 1982), 124.

22. Richard Poirier, *The Performing Self: Compositions and Decompositions in the Languages of Everyday Life* (New York: Oxford University Press, 1971), 107–11.

23. More information about both the occasion of James's hearing the anecdote and its substance is given in the version James recorded in his notebooks. In that version, it is clear that James saw from an early date the potential for a "story to be told ... by an outside spectator, observer" (*The Notebooks of Henry James*, ed. F. O. Matthiessen and Kenneth Murdock [New York: Oxford University Press, 1947], 178–79).

24. Barth sets forth his ideas in two essays written over a decade apart: "The Literature of Exhaustion," reprinted in *Surfiction: Fiction Now ... and Tomorrow*, ed. Raymond Federman (1967; Chicago: Swallow, 1975), 19–33; and "The Literature of Replenishment: Postmodernist Fiction," *Atlantic Monthly* Jan. 1980: 65–71.

25. John Barth, *Giles Goat-Boy, or, The Revised New Syllabus* (Garden City, N.Y.: Doubleday, 1966). Subsequent citations are noted parenthetically in the text.

26. Barth, "Literature of Exhaustion," 28.

27. Tony Tanner incisively comments on the indeterminacy of Barth's text: "The recession of frames to [*Giles Goat-Boy*] seems like a bid by Barth to liberate himself from any of the available modes of authorship and narration, to create a fictional space into which anything may be admitted and anything done with it, without the author (whoever or whatever he is) being held responsible. In

this way the relationship of the author to his material is never clear, and since all these devices for stressing the equivocal status and origin of the fiction only serve to make us more aware of Barth's own constant presence, we become aware of a writer going to perverse lengths (710 pages) not only to demonstrate what he can invent—and that is prodigious—but to demonstrate how he can equivocate about, trivialize and undermine his own inventions" (*City of Words: American Fiction 1950–1970* [New York: Harper and Row, 1971], 246–47).

28. For an extended examination of the paratextual function of both the title page in literature and the "name of the author," see Gérard Genette, *Seuils* (Paris: Éditions du Seuil, 1987), 38–97.

29. Tanner, *City of Words*, 252.

30. See note 24, above.

CHAPTER 7 | FRAME TRANSMISSION AND THE NARRATIVE CONTRACT

1. Mikhail Lermontov, *A Hero of Our Time*, trans. Vladimir Nabokov and Dimitri Nabokov (Garden City, N.Y.: Doubleday Anchor, 1958.

2. In 1987, I published much of the first section of this chapter in *The Texas Review*; that same year Kathryn J. Crecelius, in her study of Sand's early novels, made the same comparison and drew some similar conclusions, although our readings also diverged on many points and pursued different goals. For more, in particular, on *Leoni Leone*'s place in Sand's career, see Crecelius's *Family Romances: George Sand's Early Novels* (Bloomington: Indiana University Press, 1987).

3. Roland Barthes, *S/Z*, trans. Richard Howard (New York: Hill and Wang, 1974), 89.

4. Peter Brooks, *Reading for the Plot: Design and Intention in Narrative* (New York: Alfred Knopf, 1984), 216.

5. George Sand, *Leoni Leone*, trans. George Burnham Ives (1900; Chicago: Academy, 1978). Subsequent citations are noted parenthetically in the text.

6. Abbé Prévost, *Manon Lescaut* (Paris: Gallimard, 1972); trans. by L. W. Tancock (Baltimore: Penguin Books, 1949). Subsequent citations are noted parenthetically in the text.

7. Nancy K. Miller, *The Heroine's Text: Readings in the French and English Novel, 1722–1782* (New York: Columbia University Press, 1980), 71–72.

8. Ibid., 82.

9. Brooks, *Reading for the Plot*, 235.

10. Ibid., 225–26.

11. Ibid., 227–28.

12. Miller, *Heroine's Text*, 156.

13. It is easy to infer that George Sand's life influenced directly the writing of *Leone Leoni*; however, details of this period in her life are sketchy at best. In Sand's *L' histoire de ma vie* (translated as *My Life* by Dan Hofstadter [New York: Harper and Row, 1979]), only a few pages are devoted to her 1834 trip with Musset to Venice, but Sand says nothing of her novel or of the break that occurred with Musset at that time. Ruth Jordan tells us some more: "By that time [after Musset had recovered from typhus] George and Musset had moved into two separate rooms in a modest hotel.... Hardly removed from the emotional scene of the past few weeks, she was already able to use some of its elements in a new novel. In February she wrote *Leone Leoni* in fourteen days and sent it off ... for publication" (*George Sand: A Biographical Portrait* [New York: Taplinger, 1976], 109). Curtis

Cate clears up the connections by aligning Leoni with Musset and Bustamente with Pietro Pagello, Musset's doctor and the third member of Sand's fragile Venetian love triangle (*George Sand: A Biography* [Boston: Houghton Mifflin, 1975], 301). Still, it would be a mistake to read this novel too biographically, since its intertext is clear; but we can infer that the text may have served as a "talking cure" for Sand herself, an outlet for a passion or desire she constantly had to repress.

14. Another descendant of *Manon Lescaut* and *Leone Leoni* is Eugène Fromentin's *Dominique* (1862), which is dedicated to Sand. *Dominique* borrows its narrating situation and much of its basic plot from these earlier novels, but there are some essential thematic differences. Fromentin's novel does not tell the story of well-bred illicit lovers who live sordid lives of criminal intrigue. The characters in this novel are well-bred, but the novel is set in the demure salons of Paris or in the parks of country estates, rather than in bedrooms, gambling houses, and prisons. Moreover, the transgressive love affair in this novel is never fulfilled; when Madeleine finally tells Dominique, "I love you," she speaks "the forbidden word" that irretrievably parts them (trans. Edward Marsh [London: The Crescent Press, 1948], 239). When Dominique tells his tale, Madeleine is presumably still alive— both have seemingly conquered the obsessive passion that was inescapable for their literary ancestors. The frames of narration also mark an interesting formal change. The text opens in a confusion of narrating moments, as the extradiegetic narrator begins his written text with the last words of Dominique's intradiegetic narration. For this reason, the narrative of transmission is subordinated at the outset to an image of closure that marks the inherent incompleteness of Dominique's narrative of transgression.

15. Homer, *"The Odyssey" of Homer*, trans. Richmond Lattimore (New York: Harper and Row, 1967). Subsequent citations are noted parenthetically in the text by book and line numbers.

16. By having the epic singer present at Odysseus's narrating act, Homer clearly marks the means by which future transmission could be assured: Demodokos listens, learns, and will later sing *The Odyssey*. Moreover, from a purely economic perspective of epic's literary instance, the narrative summary of Demodokos's song would suggest to the audience that the epic singer had more tales to tell; hence, the epic singer could receive a further commission to sing. As we have seen elsewhere, the lure of the promised sequel is inherent in many narratives of transmission. Ironically, the textual transmission of Homer's epics has become a major scholarly enterprise as professional "readers" rather than "singers" seek an authoritative *text*—the *song* itself having been long lost.

17. Meir Sternberg, "Proteus in Quotation Land: Mimesis and the Forms of Reported Discourse," *Poetics Today* 3, no. 2 (1982): 108.

18. Ibid.

19. Tzvetan Todorov, *The Poetics of Prose*, trans. Richard Howard (Ithaca: Cornell University Press, 1977), 70.

20. Ibid., 71. Of course, embedding such as Todorov describes it can occur in epistolary, diary, or memoir fictions as well; for instance, Todorov observes that in *Les liaisons dangereuses* such stories as "the adventures of Valmont at the Countess's chateau or with Émilie; those of Prévan with the 'inseparables'; that of the Marquise with Prévan or Belleroche" are "less integrated to the ensemble of the narrative than the principal stories, and we perceive them as embedded" ("The Categories of Literary Narrative," trans. Joseph Kestner, *Papers on Language and Literature* 16 [1980]: 22–23).

21. John Barth, "Tales Within Tales Within Tales," *Antaeus* 43 (1981): 53. Barth has written many tales within tales. Possibly his most complex and

playful exercise with the form is the "Menelaiad," which contains embeddings to at least the seventh degree and which plays relentlessly with the punctuation conventions of quotation marks-within-quotation marks-within-quotation marks.

22. A. J. Greimas and J. Courtés, *Semiotics and Language: An Analytical Dictionary*, trans. Larry Crist and David Patte, and others (Bloomington: Indiana University Press, 1982), 99.

23. The concept of the narrative sentence informs much of Todorov's and Roland Barthes's early narrative theories. For example, Barthes writes, in his landmark essay "Introduction to the Structural Analysis of Narratives," "Structurally, narrative shares the characteristics of the sentence without ever being reducible to the simple sum of its sentences: a narrative is a long sentence, just as every constative sentence is in a way a rough outline of a short narrative" (*Image-Music-Text*, trans. Stephen Heath [New York: Hill and Wang, 1977], 84); and with relation to embedding, Todorov writes, "The formal structure of embedding coincides (nor is such a coincidence an accident) with that of a syntactic form, a particular form of subordination, which in fact modern linguistics calls *embedding*.... The narrative of embedding has precisely the same structure [as certain sentences], the role of the noun being played by the character" (*Poetics of Prose*, 70–71). See also Todorov's discussion "Narrative Syntax" in *Introduction to Poetics*, trans. Richard Howard [Minneapolis: University of Minnesota Press, 1981], 48–53.

24. Thomas Pynchon, *V.* (1963; New York: Harper and Row, 1986).

25. For more on transmission in *V.*, see Bernard Duyfhuizen, "GeStencilde transmissies: Geschiedenis vertellen in *V.*," trans. Annick Cuynen and Luc Herman, *Yang* 28 (1992): forthcoming.

26. Sheldon Sacks, *Fiction and the Shape of Belief: A Study of Henry Fielding, with Glances at Swift, Johnson, and Richardson* (Chicago: University of Chicago Press, 1964), 200.

27. M. M. Bakhtin, "Discourse in the Novel," *The Dialogic Imagination*, ed. Michael Holquist, trans. Caryl Emerson and Michael Holquist (Austin: University of Texas Press, 1981), 312.

28. Ibid., 313.

29. Ibid., 282.

30. Jean Ricardou, "The Story within the Story," trans. Joseph Kestner, *James Joyce Quarterly* 18 (1981): 323–38. For an application of Ricardou's concept of the dual temporal relationship, see Bernard Duyfhuizen, "On the Writing of Future-History: Beginning the Ending in Doris Lessing's *The Memoirs of a Survivor*," *Modern Fiction Studies* 26 (1980): 147–56.

31. Brooks, *Reading for the Plot*, 236.

32. Bakhtin, "Discourse in the Novel," 320.

CHAPTER 8 | TALES TOLD AND TRANSCRIBED

1. Emily Brontë, *Wuthering Heights*, ed. William M. Sale, 2d ed. (New York: W. W. Norton, 1972). Subsequent citations are noted parenthetically in the text.

2. Elizabeth MacAndrew, *The Gothic Tradition in Fiction* (New York: Columbia University Press, 1979), 127.

3. Although they are not Gothic narratives in the fullest sense, one certainly sees a continuation of these various transmission devices in the Sherlock Holmes stories of Arthur Conan Doyle and in many narratives by Joseph Conrad and William Faulkner.

4. MacAndrew, *Gothic Tradition*, 111.

5. Ibid., 110.

6. Eve Kosofsky Sedgwick, *The Coherence of Gothic Conventions*, revised ed. (New York: Arno, 1980), 3, 21.

7. Ibid., 3–4.

8. Charles Maturin, *Melmoth the Wanderer* (Harmondsworth: Penguin Books, 1977).

9. Mary Shelley, *Frankenstein*, ed. James Kinsley and M. K. Joseph (Oxford: Oxford University Press, 1980). This text was prepared from the 1831 version of the novel; subsequent citations are noted parenthetically in the text.

10. For a reading of the "unspeakable" in *Frankenstein*, see James R. Kincaid, "'Words Cannot Express': *Frankenstein*'s Tripping on the Tongue," *Novel* 24 (1990): 26–47.

11. A successful cinematic play with frames is Woody Allen's *The Purple Rose of Cairo* in which a character leaves the screen to try to live in the world of the audience. A reverse of this device occurs in Michael Ende's novel *Die unendliche Geschichte (The Neverending Story)* (1979) in which the characterized reader must enter the book he is reading to save the fictional universe from ruin.

12. Roland Barthes, *S/Z*, trans. Richard Howard (New York: Hill and Wang, 1974), 89.

13. Fundamentally, my division of the text follows the order of the first edition's three volume publication. By imposing the first edition divisions onto the 1831 text, we would end volume 1 with chapter 8 and volume 2 with chapter 18. For a modern edition of the 1818 text, see James Rieger, ed., *Frankenstein*, by Mary Shelley (Indianapolis: Bobbs-Merrill, 1974).

14. See *Frankenstein* (87) for Justine's account of her confession. For an insightful reading of Justine's narrative function, see Beth Newman's study of the novel, in which she comments: "What finally condemns Justine is precisely her inability to counter [the story of her guilt] with a coherent narrative of her own" ("Narratives of Seduction and the Seductions of Narrative: The Frame Structure in *Frankenstein*," *ELH* 53 [1986]: 148).

15. J. Hillis Miller, *Fiction and Repetition: Seven English Novels* (Cambridge: Harvard University Press, 1982), 2–3.

16. The history of the De Lacey family presupposes many and scattered narrating acts by the De Laceys themselves, which the Creature summarizes and connects for the purpose of his narration. Commenting on the significance of Safie's "unreproduced letters," Joyce Zonana writes that "Safie's letters constitute the novel's inaccessible center, the locus where Mary Shelley's narrative movement inward ... can come to a conclusion" ("'They Will Prove the Truth of My Tale': Safie's Letters as the Feminist Core of Mary Shelley's *Frankenstein*," *The Journal of Narrative Technique* 21 (1991): 171). Zonana goes on to argue that we can read into the suppression of these letters by a trio of male narrators a "fundamental feminist message identical to a key premise in Mary Wollstonecraft's *A Vindication of the Rights of Woman*: that women have rational souls" (ibid.).

17. Peter Brooks, "Godlike Science/Unhallowed Arts: Language, Nature, and Monstrosity," in *The Endurance of "Frankenstein": Essays on Mary Shelley's Novel*, ed. George Levine and U. C. Knoepflmacher (Berkeley and Los Angeles: University of California Press, 1979), 205–20.

18. Ibid., 213.

19. Miller, *Fiction and Repetition*, 61.

20. U. C. Knoepflmacher, *Laughter and Despair: Readings in Ten Novels of*

the Victorian Era (Berkeley and Los Angeles: University of California Press, 1971), 95.

21. Alan R. Brick, *"Wuthering Heights*: Narrators, Audience, and Message," in *A "Wuthering Heights" Handbook*, ed. Richard Lettis and William E. Morris (New York: Odyssey Press, 1961), 226.

22. Terence McCarthey, "The Incompetent Narrator of *Wuthering Heights,"* *Modern Language Quarterly* 42 (1981): 48–64.

23. Sandra M. Gilbert and Susan Gubar, *The Madwoman in the Attic: The Woman Writer and the Nineteenth-Century Literary Imagination* (New Haven: Yale University Press, 1979), 257.

24. David Cecil, "Emily Brontë and *Wuthering Heights,"* in Lettis and Morris, *A "Wuthering Heights" Handbook*, 43; and, G. D. Klingopolus, "The Novel as Dramatic Poem (II): *Wuthering Heights,"* *Scrutiny* 14 (1947): 273.

25. James Hafley, "The Villain in *Wuthering Heights,"* in Lettis and Morris, *A "Wuthering Heights" Handbook*, 187.

26. Ernest A. Baker, *"Wuthering Heights,"* in Lettis and Morris, *A "Wuthering Heights" Handbook*, 55.

27. Carl Woodring, "The Narrators of *Wuthering Heights,"* in Lettis and Morris, *A "Wuthering Heights" Handbook*, 166, 165.

28. Brick, "Narrators, Audience, and Message," 224.

29. Charlotte Brontë, "Preface," in Brontë, *Wuthering Heights*, 11.

30. John K. Mathison, "Nelly Dean and the Power of *Wuthering Heights,"* in Lettis and Morris, *A "Wuthering Heights" Handbook*, 143.

31. Hafley, "Villain in *Wuthering Heights,"* 187.

32. Gilbert and Gubar, *Madwoman in the Attic*, 291.

33. Knoepflmacher, *Laughter and Despair*, 96.

34. Bruce McCullough, "The Dramatic Novel: *Wuthering Heights,"* in Lettis and Morris, *A "Wuthering Heights" Handbook*, 64.

35. Knoepflmacher, *Laughter and Despair*, 87.

36. N. M. Jacobs, "Gender and Layered Narrative in *Wuthering Heights* and *The Tenant of Wildfell Hall,"* *The Journal of Narrative Technique* 16 (1986): 213, 216.

37. John T. Matthews, "Framing in *Wuthering Heights,"* *Texas Studies in Literature and Language* 27 (1985): 27, 28. Emphasis added.

38. Miller, *Fiction and Repetition*, 71.

39. Quoted in Winifred Gérin, *Emily Brontë: A Biography* (Oxford: Oxford University Press, 1971), 232. Winifred Gérin later notes Brontë's inhibitions about society and her writing: "Most inhibiting of all perhaps had been the act of publication itself. For in a girl of such singular reticence, to be exposed to the world ... was an appalling experience" (246).

40. Mieke Bal, "Notes on Narrative Embedding," trans. Eve Tavor, *Poetics Today* 2, no. 2 (1981): 46. Much has been written on "focalization"; for a good overview of the issue, see William Nelles, "Getting Focalization into Focus," *Poetics Today* 11 (1990): 365–82.

41. M. M. Bakhtin, "Discourse in the Novel," *The Dialogic Imagination*, ed. Michael Holquist, trans, Caryl Emerson and Michael Holquist (Austin: University of Texas Press, 1981), 312, 313.

42. Jacobs, "Layered Narrative," 207.

43. Margaret Homans, "Repression and Sublimation of Nature in *Wuthering Heights,"* *PMLA* 93 (1978): 10.

44. Ibid.

45. For a forceful reading of Lockwood's dream, see Carol Jacobs,

Uncontainable Romanticism: Shelley, Brontë, Kleist (Baltimore: Johns Hopkins University Press, 1989), 61–81.

46. Bakhtin, "Discourse in the Novel," 294.

47. Wolfgang Iser, *The Implied Reader: Patterns of Communication in Prose Fiction from Bunyan to Beckett* (Baltimore: Johns Hopkins University Press, 1974).

48. Albert B. Lord, *The Singer of Tales* (Cambridge: Harvard University Press, 1960), 13.

49. Matthews, "Framing in *Wuthering Heights*," 28.

50. As James Thorpe reminds us of actual text transmission: the "ordinary history of the transmission of a text, without the intervention of author or editor, is one of progressive degeneration" (*Principles of Textual Criticism* [San Marino, Ca.: The Huntington Library, 1972], 51).

51. C. P. Sanger, "The Structure of *Wuthering Heights*," in Lettis and Morris, *A "Wuthering Heights" Handbook*, 14; in this reprinting of Sanger's essay, chapter "IX" has been misprinted as "IV." See also A. Stuart Daley, "The Moons and Almanacs of *Wuthering Heights*," and "A Chronology of *Wuthering Heights*," in *Wuthering Heights: A Norton Critical Edition*, 3d ed., ed. William M. Sale, Jr. and Richard J. Dunn (New York: Norton, 1990), 336–48.

52. Mary Ann Caws, *Reading Frames in Modern Fiction* (Princeton: Princeton University Press, 1985).

53. "I" can be the most problematic of signifiers in narrative transmission because it can signify more than one subject of the speech act. A case could be made that in *Wuthering Heights* this crucial cross-gendered identification of Catherine with Heathcliff is actually a cover for the identification of Emily Brontë with Heathcliff. In such a reading, Heathcliff's feminized position on the margin of society and his resultant rage to destroy conventional society symbolizes the inner rage of Brontë herself as she metaphorically textualizes her own marginal existence.

54. One might add to this list Odysseus, Pechorin, Peter Quint, Clarissa, Pamela, etc.—all character names within document texts are potentially alien words, especially when the name is inscribed within the context of the other's discourse.

55. Bakhtin, "Discourse in the Novel," 276.

56. See note 48.

57. Bakhtin, "Discourse in the Novel," 276.

58. The "hereditary imperative" has been discussed by Joyce Carol Oates ("The Magnanimity of *Wuthering Heights*," *Critical Inquiry* 9 [1982]: 435–49), who sees Catherine and Heathcliff as arrested children, whereas the second generation achieves full maturity. This sense of the novel's ending is problematic in that if it is not ironic, Brontë has capitulated to happy-ending plot conventions that dilute the subversive force of her text and reproduce much of the patriarchal status quo Heathcliff and Brontë wanted to dismantle.

59. On the significance of this anecdote, see Beth Newman, "'The Situation of the Looker-On': Gender, Narration, and Gaze in *Wuthering Heights*," *PMLA* 105 (1990): 1029–41.

Works Cited and Consulted

The primary sources listed include only those works that receive significant attention or are quoted. Those works merely alluded to have not been listed. Unless otherwise noted, the English translations of foreign language works are the editions cited parenthetically in the text. The original language editions have been consulted whenever possible.

PRIMARY SOURCES

Atwood, Margaret. *The Handmaid's Tale*. Boston: Houghton Mifflin, 1986.
Austen, Jane. *The Novels of Jane Austen*. 3d ed. 5 vols. Edited by R. W. Chapman. Oxford: Clarendon Press, 1933.
Barbellion, W. N. P. *The Journal of a Disappointed Man*. London: Hogarth Press, 1984.
Barth, John. *Giles Goat-Boy or, The Revised New Syllabus*. Garden City, N.Y.: Doubleday, 1966.
———. *Letters*. New York: Putnam's, 1979.
Behn, Aphra. *Love Letters between a Nobleman and His Sister*. New York: Penguin–Virago, 1987.
Brontë, Anne. *The Tenant of Wildfell Hall*. Harmondsworth: Penguin Books, 1979.
Brontë, Charlotte. *Shirley*. Harmondsworth: Penguin Books, 1974.
Brontë, Emily. *Wuthering Heights*. 2d ed. Edited by William M. Sale. New York: W. W. Norton, 1972.
Butor, Michel. *L'emploi du temps*. Paris: Minuit, 1956.
———. *Passing Time*. Translated by Jean Stewart. London: John Calder, 1965.
Cervantes, Miguel de. *The Ingenious Gentleman Don Quixote de la Mancha*. Translated by Samuel Putnam. New York: Viking Press, 1949.
Collins, William Wilkie. *The Woman in White*. Oxford: Oxford Univ. Press, 1980.
Constant, Benjamin. *Adolphe; Le cahier rouge; Cécile*. Paris: Gallimard, 1951.
———. *Adolphe*. Translated by Leonard Tancock. Harmondsworth: Penguin Books, 1964.
Defoe, Daniel. *"Robinson Crusoe" and Other Writings*. Edited by James Sutherland. 1968. Reprint. New York: New York Univ. Press, 1977.
Delafield, E. M. *Diary of a Provincial Lady*. 1931. Reprint. Chicago: Academy Chicago Press, 1982.
Derrida, Jacques. "Envois." *La carte postale de Socrate à Freud et au-delà*. Paris: Flammarion, 1980.
Dostoevsky, Fyodor. *Notes from Underground*. Translated by Constance Garnett. In *The Norton Anthology of World Masterpieces: Continental Edition*, edited by Maynard Mack, Bernard M. W. Knox, John C. McGalliard, P.M. Pasinetti, Howard E. Hugo, René Wellek, Kenneth Douglas, and Sarah Lawall, 2: 846–934. 4th ed. New York: W. W. Norton, 1980.

Dujardin, Edouard. *Les lauriers sont coupés*. Translated as *We'll to the Woods No More* by Stuart Gilbert. New York: New Directions, 1938.

Fielding, Henry. *"Joseph Andrews" and "Shamela."* Edited by A. R. Humphreys. New York: Dutton, 1973.

Flaubert, Gustave. *Madame Bovary*. Paris: Garnier-Flammarion, 1979.

———. *Madame Bovary*. Edited and translated by Paul de Man. New York: W. W. Norton, 1965.

Fromentin, Eugène. *Dominique*. Paris: Garnier-Flammarion, 1967.

———. *Dominique*. Translated by Edward Marsh. London: Crescent Press, 1948.

Gide, André. *Les faux-monnayeurs*. Paris: Gallimard, 1925.

———. *"The Counterfeiters" with "Journal of 'The Counterfeiters.'"* Translated by Dorothy Bussy and Justin O'Brien. New York: Modern Library, 1927.

Gilman, Charlotte Perkins. *The Yellow Wallpaper*. Old Westbury, N.Y.: Feminist Press, 1973.

Gissing, George. *The Private Papers of Henry Ryecroft*. New York: Modern Library, n.d.

Gogol, Nikolai. "The Diary of a Madman." In *Dostoevsky and Gogol: Texts and Criticism*, edited and translated by Priscilla Meyer and Stephen Rudy, 3–20. Ann Arbor: Ardis, 1979.

Hawthorne, Nathaniel. "Fragments from the Journal of a Solitary Man." In *Tales and Sketches*, edited by Roy Harvey Pearce, 487–500. New York: Library of America, 1982.

Homer. *"The Odyssey" of Homer*. Translated by Richmond Lattimore. New York: Harper & Row, 1967.

Hugo, Victor. *Le dernier jour d'un condamné*. Translated as *Last Day of a Condemned* by Eugenia de B. 1894. Reprint. New York: Howard Fertig, 1977.

James, Henry. *The Turn of the Screw*. Vol. 12 of *The Novels and Tales of Henry James: New York Edition*. New York: Scribner's, 1908.

Joyce, James. *A Portrait of the Artist as a Young Man*. New York: Viking Press, 1982.

———. *Ulysses*. Edited by Hans Walter Gabler. New York: Random House, 1986.

Kingsley, Charles. *Alton Locke, Tailor and Poet: An Autobiography*. Oxford: Oxford Univ. Press, 1983.

Laclos, Pierre Choderlos de. *Les liaisons dangereuses*. In *Oeuvres complètes*, edited by Maurice Allem. Paris: Gallimard, 1951.

———. *Les liaisons dangereuses*. Translated by P. W. K. Stone. Harmondsworth: Penguin Books, 1961.

Lermontov, Mikhail. *A Hero of Our Time*. Translated by Vladimir Nabokov and Dimitri Nabokov. Garden City, N.Y.: Doubleday Anchor, 1958.

Lessing, Doris. *The Golden Notebook*. New York: Bantam Books, 1973.

Leven, Jeremy. *Creator*. New York: Coward, McCann and Geoghegan, 1980.

Mackenzie, Henry. *The Man of Feeling*. New York: W. W. Norton, 1958.

Maturin, Charles. *Melmoth the Wanderer*. Harmondsworth: Penguin Books, 1977.

Norton, Caroline. *Caroline Norton's Defense: English Laws for Women in the Nineteenth Century*. Chicago: Academy Chicago Press, 1982.

Poe, Edgar Allan. *Poetry and Tales*. Edited by Patrick F. Quinn. New York: Library of America, 1984.

Prévost, Abbé. *Manon Lescaut*. Paris: Gallimard, 1972.

———. *Manon Lescaut*. Translated by L. W. Tancock. Baltimore: Penguin Books, 1949.

Pynchon, Thomas. *V*. 1963. New York: Harper and Row, 1986.

Richardson, Samuel, *The History of Clarissa Harlowe*. 8 vols. 1902. Reprint. New York: AMS Press, 1970.

———. *Pamela, or Virtue Rewarded*. Edited by Peter Sabor. Harmondsworth: Penguin Books, 1980.

Rousseau, Jean-Jacques. *Julie, ou la nouvelle Héloïse*. In *Oeuvres complètes*, vol. 2, edited by Bernard Gagnebin and Marcel Raymond. Paris: Gallimard, 1961.

———. *La nouvelle Héloïse*. Translated by Judith H. McDowell. University Park, Pa.: Pennsylvania State Univ. Press, 1968.

Sand, George. *Leone Leoni*. Translated by George Burnham Ives. 1900. Reprint. Chicago: Academy Chicago Press, 1978.

Sartre, Jean-Paul. *La nausée*. Paris: Gallimard, 1938.

Shelley, Mary. *Frankenstein*. Edited by James Kinsley and M. K. Joseph. Oxford: Oxford Univ. Press, 1980.

Stendhal. *Le rouge et le noir*. Paris: Gallimard, 1972.

———. *Red and Black*. Translated and edited by Robert M. Adams. New York: W. W. Norton, 1969.

Stoker, Bram. *Dracula*. Toronto: Bantam Books, 1981.

Stuart, Francis. *The High Consistory*. London: Martin Brian and O'Keefe, 1981.

Swift, Jonathan. *Gulliver's Travels*. New York: New American Library, 1960.

Turgenev, Ivan. *Polnoye sobraniye sochineniy i pisem*. 5:178–232. Moskva-Leningrad, 1963.

———. "The Diary of a Superfluous Man." In *The Vintage Turgenev*, translated by Harry Stevens, 2:343–91. New York: Vintage, 1960.

Updike, John. *A Month of Sundays*. New York: Alfred A. Knopf, 1975.

SECONDARY SOURCES

Abbott, H. Porter. *Diary Fiction: Writing as Action*. Ithaca: Cornell Univ. Press, 1984.

Abrams, M. H. *The Mirror and the Lamp: Romantic Theory and the Critical Tradition*. London: Oxford Univ. Press, 1953.

Alter, Robert. *Partial Magic: The Novel as a Self-Conscious Genre*. Berkeley and Los Angeles: Univ. of California Press, 1975.

Altman, Janet Gurkin. *Epistolarity: Approaches to a Form*. Columbus: Ohio State Univ. Press, 1982.

Auerbach, Erich. *Mimesis: The Representation of Reality in Western Literature*. Translated by Willard R. Trask. Princeton: Princeton Univ. Press, 1953.

Austin, J. L. *How to Do Things with Words*. 2d ed. Edited by J. O. Urmson and Marina Sbisa. 1962. Reprint. Cambridge: Harvard Univ. Press, 1975.

Baker, Ernest A. *"Wuthering Heights."* In *A "Wuthering Heights" Handbook* edited by Lettis and Morris, 50–58.

Bakhtin, M[ikhail] M. *The Dialogic Imagination*. Edited by Michael Holquist. Translated by Caryl Emerson and Michael Holquist. Austin: Univ. of Texas Press, 1981.

Bal, Mieke. "Narration et focalisation: Pour une théorie des instances du récit." *Poétique* 29 (1977): 107–27.

———. *Narratology: An Introduction to the Theory of Narrative*. Translated by Christine van Boheemen. Toronto: Univ. of Toronto Press, 1985.

———. "Notes on Narrative Embedding." Translated by Eve Tavor. *Poetics Today* 2, no. 2 (1981): 41–60.

Banfield, Ann. *Unspeakable Sentences: Narration and Representation in the Language of Fiction*. Boston: Routledge & Kegan Paul, 1982.

Bann, Stephen, and John E. Bowlt, eds. *Russian Formalism: A Collection of Articles and Texts in Translation*. New York: Barnes & Noble, 1973.

Barth, John. "The Literature of Exhaustion." In *Surfiction* edited by Federman, 19–33.

———. "The Literature of Replenishment: Postmodernist Fiction." *Atlantic Monthly* Jan. 1980: 65–71.

———. "Tales Within Tales Within Tales." *Antaeus* 43 (1981): 45–63.

Barthes, Roland. *Image-Music-Text*. Translated by Stephen Heath. New York: Hill & Wang, 1977.

———. *S/Z*. Translated by Richard Howard. New York: Hill & Wang, 1974.

———. "Textual Analysis of a Tale by Poe." Translated by Matthew Wald and Richard Howard. In *On Signs*, edited by Marshall Blonsky, 84–97. Baltimore: Johns Hopkins Univ. Press, 1985.

———. "To Write: An Intransitive Verb?" In *The Structuralist Controversy: The Languages of Criticism and the Sciences of Man*, edited by Richard Macksey and Eugenio Donato, 134–45. Baltimore: Johns Hopkins Univ. Press, 1970.

Benjamin, Walter. "The Storyteller." Translated by Harry Zorn. In *Illuminations*, edited by Hannah Arendt, 83–109. New York: Harcourt, Brace, 1968.

Bennett, Tony. *Formalism and Marxism*. New York: Methuen, 1979.

Benstock, Shari. "At the Margin of Discourse: Footnotes in the Fictional Text." *PMLA* 98 (1983): 204–25.

———. "From Letters to Literature: *La Carte Postale* in the Epistolary Genre." *Genre* 18 (1985): 257–95.

———. "The Printed Letters in *Ulysses*." *James Joyce Quarterly* 19 (1982): 415–27.

Benveniste, Emile. *Problems in General Linguistics*. Translated by Mary Elizabeth Meek. Coral Gables: Univ. of Miami Press, 1971.

Black, Frank Gees. *The Epistolary Novel in the Late Eighteenth Century: A Descriptive and Bibliographic Study*. 1940. Reprint. Folcroft, Pa.: Folcroft Press, 1969.

Bloom, Edward, ed. "In Defense of Authors and Readers." *Novel* 11 (1977): 5–25.

Booth, Wayne C. *Critical Understanding: The Powers and Limits of Pluralism*. Chicago: Univ. of Chicago Press, 1979.

———. *The Rhetoric of Fiction*. 2d ed. Chicago: Univ. of Chicago Press, 1983.

Borges, Jorge Luis. *Borges: A Reader*. Edited by Emir Rodriguez Monegal and Alastair Reid. New York: Dutton, 1981.

Brick, Alan R. "*Wuthering Heights*: Narrators, Audience, and Message." In *A "Wuthering Heights" Handbook* edited by Lettis and Morris, 218–27.

Brooks, Peter. "Godlike Science/Unhallowed Arts: Language, Nature, and Monstrosity." In *The Endurance of "Frankenstein": Essays on Mary Shelley's Novel*, edited by George Levine and U. C. Knoepflmacher, 205–20. Berkeley and Los Angeles: Univ. of California Press, 1979.

———. *The Novel of Worldiness: Crébillon, Marivaux, Laclos, Stendhal*. Princeton: Princeton Univ. Press, 1969.

———. "Psychoanalytic Constructions and Narrative Meanings." *Paragraph* 7 (1986): 53–76.

———. *Reading for the Plot: Design and Intention in Narrative*. New York: Alfred A. Knopf, 1984.

Brown, Homer Obed. "The Errant Letter and the Whispering Gallery." *Genre* 10 (1977): 573–99.

Butor, Michel. *Repertoire II*. Paris: Minuit, 1964.

Calder, Angus. Introduction to *Old Mortality*, by Sir Walter Scott. Harmondsworth: Penguin Books, 1975.

Caserio, Robert L. *Plot, Story, and the Novel: From Dickens and Poe to the Modern Period*. Princeton: Princeton Univ. Press, 1979.

Cate, Curtis. *George Sand: A Biography*. Boston: Houghton Mifflin, 1975.

Cavell, Stanley. *Must We Mean What We Say?* Cambridge: Cambridge Univ. Press, 1976.

Caws, Mary Ann. *Reading Frames in Modern Fiction*. Princeton: Princeton Univ. Press, 1985.

Cecil, David. "Emily Brontë and *Wuthering Heights*." In *A "Wuthering Heights" Handbook*, edited by Lettis and Morris, 20–49.

Chambers, Ross. *Story and Situation: Narrative Seduction and the Power of Fiction*. Minneapolis: Univ. of Minnesota Press, 1984.

Chatman, Seymour. *Coming to Terms: The Rhetoric of Narrative in Fiction and Film*. Ithaca: Cornell Univ. Press, 1990.

———. *Story and Discourse: Narrative Structure in Fiction and Film*. Ithaca: Cornell Univ. Press, 1978.

———. "The Structure of Narrative Transmission." In *Style and Structure in Literature: Essays in the New Stylistics*, edited by Roger Fowler, 213–57. Ithaca: Cornell Univ. Press, 1975.

Cohan, Steven, and Linda M. Shires. *Telling Stories: A Theoretical Analysis of Narrative Fiction*. New York: Routledge, 1988.

Cohn, Dorrit. *Transparent Minds: Narrative Modes for Presenting Consciousness in Fiction*. Princeton: Princeton Univ. Press, 1978.

Coleridge, Samuel Taylor. *Biographia Literaria*. Edited by J. Shawcross. Oxford: Clarendon Press, 1907.

Corti, Maria. *An Introduction to Literary Semiotics*. Translated by Margherita Bogart and Allen Mandelbaum. Bloomington: Indiana Univ. Press, 1978.

Coste, Didier. *Narrative as Communication*. Minneapolis: Univ. of Minnesota Press, 1989.

Crecelius, Kathryn J. *Family Romances: George Sand's Early Novels*. Bloomington: Indiana Univ. Press, 1987.

Culler, Jonathan. *On Deconstruction: Theory and Criticism after Structuralism*. Ithaca: Cornell Univ. Press, 1982.

———. *The Pursuit of Signs: Semiotics, Literature, Deconstruction*. Ithaca: Cornell Univ. Press, 1981.

———. *Structuralist Poetics: Structuralism, Linguistics and the Study of Literature*. Ithaca: Cornell Univ. Press, 1975.

Daley, A. Stuart. "The Moons and Almanacs of *Wuthering Heights*"; and "A Chronology of *Wuthering Heights*." In *Wuthering Heights: A Norton Critical Edition*, edited by William M. Sale, Jr. and Richard J. Dunn, 336–52. 3d ed. New York: W. W. Norton, 1990.

Dällenbach, Lucien. *Le récit spéculaire: Essai sur la mise en abyme*. Paris: Éditions du Seuil, 1977.

———. "Reflexivity and Reading." Translated by Annette Tomarken. *New Literary History* 11 (1980): 435–49.

Davis, Lennard J. *Factual Fictions: The Origins of the English Novel*. New York: Columbia Univ. Press, 1983.

Day, Robert Adams. *Told in Letters: Epistolary Fiction before Richardson.* Ann Arbor: Univ. of Michigan Press, 1966.

De Man, Paul. *Allegories of Reading: Figural Language in Rousseau, Nietzsche, Rilke, and Proust.* New Haven: Yale Univ. Press, 1979.

Derrida, Jacques. "The Law of Genre." Translated by Avital Ronell. *Critical Inquiry* 7 (1980): 55–81.

———. "Living On." Translated by James Hulbert. In *Deconstruction and Criticism,* edited by Harold Bloom, Paul de Man, Jacques Derrida, Goeffrey Hartman, and J. Hillis Miller, 75–176. New York: Seabury Press, 1979.

———. *Of Grammatology.* Translated by Gayatri Chakravorty Spivak. Baltimore: John Hopkins Univ. Press, 1974.

———. "Signature Event Context." Translated by Samuel Weber and Jeffrey Mehlman. *Glyph* 1 (1977): 172–97.

———. *La vérité en peinture.* Paris: Flammarion, 1978.

Docherty, Thomas. *Reading (Absent) Character: Towards a Theory of Characterization in Fiction.* Oxford: Oxford Univ. Press, 1983.

Dolezel, Lubomir. "Truth and Authenticity in Narrative." *Poetics Today* 1, no. 3 (1980): 7–25.

———. "The Typology of the Narrator: Point of View in Fiction." In *To Honor Roman Jakobson: Essays on the Occasion of His Seventieth Birthday.* 1:541–52. The Hague: Mouton, 1967.

Duyfhuizen, Bernard. "Belles' Letters." *Novel* 16 (1982): 91–94.

———. "GeStencilde transmissies: Geschiedenis vertellen in *V.*" Translated by Annick Cuynen and Luc Herman. *Yang* 28 (1992): forthcoming.

———. "On the Writing of Future-History: Beginning the Ending in Doris Lessing's *The Memoirs of a Survivor.*" *Modern Fiction Studies* 26 (1980): 147–56.

———. "Questions of Authority and (Dis)Belief in Literary Theory." *New Orleans Review* 12, no. 3 (1985): 67–74.

———. "Toward a Comprehensive Point of View." *Papers on Language and Literature* 20 (1983): 218–23.

Eagleton, Terry. *The Rape of Clarissa: Writing, Sexuality and Class Struggle in Samuel Richardson.* Minneapolis: Univ. of Minnesota Press, 1982.

Eco, Umberto. *A Theory of Semiotics.* Bloomington: Indiana Univ. Press, 1976.

Eikenbaum, B. M. *Lermontov: A Study in Literary-Historical Evaluation.* Translated by Ray Parrott and Harry Weber. Ann Arbor: Ardis, 1981.

Erlich, Victor. *Russian Formalism: History—Doctrine.* 3d ed. New Haven: Yale Univ. Press, 1981.

Federman, Raymond, ed. *Surfiction: Fiction Now ... and Tomorrow.* Chicago: Swallow, 1975.

Felman, Shoshana. "Turning the Screw of Interpretation." In *Literature and Psychoanalysis: The Question of Reading: Otherwise,* edited by Shoshana Felman, 94–207. Baltimore: John Hopkins Univ. Press, 1982.

Field, Trevor. *Form and Function in the Diary Novel.* Totowa, N.J.: Barnes & Noble, 1989.

Fish, Stanley. *Is There a Text in This Class? The Authority of Interpretative Communities.* Cambridge: Harvard Univ. Press, 1980.

———. "With Compliments of the Author: Reflections on Austin and Derrida." *Critical Inquiry* 8 (1982): 693–721.

Flaubert, Gustave. *The Letters of Gustave Flaubert: 1830–1857.* Translated and edited by Francis Steegmuller. Cambridge: Harvard Univ. Press, 1980.

Flores, Ralph. *The Rhetoric of Doubtful Authority: Deconstructive Readings of Self-Questioning Narratives, St. Augustine to Faulkner.* Ithaca: Cornell Univ. Press, 1984.

Forster, E. M. *Aspects of the Novel.* New York: Harcourt, Brace, 1927.

Foucault, Michel. *Language, Counter-Memory, Practice: Selected Essays and Interviews.* Edited by Donald F. Bouchard. Translated by Donald F. Bouchard and Sherry Simon. Ithaca: Cornell Univ. Press, 1977.

———. *This Is Not a Pipe.* Berkeley and Los Angeles: Univ. of California Press, 1983.

Fowler, Roger. *Linguistics and the Novel.* New York: Methuen, 1977.

Freeborn, Richard, trans. "The Diary of a Superfluous Man," by Ivan Turgenev. In *"First Love" and Other Stories,* 27–72. Oxford: Oxford Univ. Press, 1989.

Friedman, Norman. "Point of View in Fiction: The Development of a Critical Concept." *PMLA* 70 (1955): 1160–84.

Fuger, Wilhelm. "'Epistlemadethemology' (*FW* 374.17): ALP's Letter and the Tradition of Interpolated Letters." *James Joyce Quarterly* 19 (1982): 405–13.

Gardiner, Judith Kegan. "The First English Novel: Aphra Behn's *Love Letters,* the Canon, and Women's Tastes." *Tulsa Studies in Women's Literature* 8 (1989): 201–22.

Gasparov, Boris. "The Narrative Text as an Act of Communication." Translated by D. E. Budgen. *New Literary History* 9 (1978): 245–61.

Genette, Gérard. *Figures of Literary Discourse.* Translated by Alan Sheridan. New York: Columbia Univ. Press, 1982.

———. *Narrative Discourse: An Essay in Method.* Translated by Jane E. Lewin. Ithaca: Cornell Univ. Press, 1980.

———. *Nouveau discours du récit.* Paris: Éditions du Seuil, 1983.

———. *Seuils.* Paris: Éditions du Seuil, 1987.

Gérin, Winifred. *Emily Brontë: A Biography.* Oxford: Oxford Univ. Press, 1971.

———. Introduction to *The Tenant of Wildfell Hall,* by Anne Brontë. 7–18.

Gilbert, Sandra M., and Susan Gubar. *The Madwoman in the Attic: The Woman Writer and the Nineteenth-Century Literary Imagination.* New Haven: Yale Univ. Press, 1979.

Glowinski, Michal. "On the First-Person Novel." Translated by Rochelle Stone. *New Literary History* 9 (1977): 103–114.

Goffman, Erving. *Frame Analysis: An Essay on the Organization of Experience.* New York: Harper & Row, 1974.

Gordon, Jan B. "Gossip, Diary, Letter, Text: Anne Brontë's Narrative *Tenant* and the Problematic of the Gothic Sequel." *ELH* 51 (Winter 1984): 719–45.

Graff, Gerald. *Literature Against Itself: Literary Ideas in Modern Society.* Chicago: Univ. of Chicago Press, 1979.

Greimas, A. J., and J. Courtés. *Semiotics and Language: An Analytical Dictionary.* Translated by Larry Crist and David Patte. Bloomington: Indiana Univ. Press, 1982.

Gwilliam, Tassie. "*Pamela* and the Duplicitous Body of Femininity." *Representations* 34 (1991): 104–133.

Hafley, James. "The Villain in *Wuthering Heights.*" In *A "Wuthering Heights" Handbook* edited by Lettis and Morris, 182–97.

Hapgood, Isabel F., trans. "*The Diary of a Superfluous Man*" *and Other Stories* by Ivan Turgenev. New York: Scribner's, 1923.

Hartman, Geoffrey H. *Criticism in the Wilderness: The Study of Literature Today.* New Haven: Yale Univ. Press, 1980.

Hass, Wilber A. "The Reported Speech of Valentin N. Volosinov." *Dispositio* 1 (1976): 352–56.

Hawkes, Terence. *Structuralism & Semiotics*. Berkeley and Los Angeles: Univ. of California Press, 1977.

Hirsch, E. D. *Validity in Interpretation*. New Haven: Yale Univ. Press, 1967.

Homans, Margaret. "Repression and Sublimation of Nature in *Wuthering Heights*." *PMLA* 93 (1978): 9–19.

Hunter, J. Paul. "News, Novelty, and the Novel." Div. on English III. SCMLA Convention. Biloxi, 26 Oct. 1984.

Ingarden, Roman. *The Cognition of the Literary Work of Art*. Translated by Ruth Ann Crowley and Kenneth R. Olson. Evanston: Northwestern Univ. Press, 1973.

———. *The Literary Work of Art: An Investigation on the Borderlines of Ontology, Logic, and Theory of Literature*. Translated by George Grabowicz. Evanston: Northwestern Univ. Press, 1973.

Iser, Wolfgang. *The Act of Reading: A Theory of Aesthetic Response*. Baltimore: Johns Hopkins Univ. Press, 1978.

———. *The Implied Reader: Patterns of Communication in Prose Fiction from Bunyan to Beckett*. Baltimore: Johns Hopkins Univ. Press, 1974.

———. "Indeterminacy and the Reader's Response in Prose Fiction." *Aspects of Narrative*, edited by J. Hillis Miller, 1–45. New York: Columbia Univ. Press, 1971.

Jacobs, Carol. *Uncontainable Romanticism: Shelley, Brontë, Kleist*. Baltimore: Johns Hopkins University Press, 1989.

Jacobs, N. M. "Gender and Layered Narrative in *Wuthering Heights* and *The Tenant of Wildfell Hall*." *The Journal of Narrative Technique* 16 (1986): 204–19.

Jakobson, Roman. "Closing Statement: Linguistics and Poetics." In *Style in Language*, edited by Thomas A. Sebeok, 350–77. Cambridge: MIT Press, 1960.

James, Henry. *Literary Criticism: Essays on Literature, American Writers, English Writers*. Edited by Leon Edel with Marc Wilson. New York: Library of America, 1984.

———. *The Notebooks of Henry James*. Edited by F. O. Matthiessen and Kenneth Murdock. New York: Oxford Univ. Press, 1947.

Johnson, Glen M. "Richardson's 'Editor' in *Clarissa*." *The Journal of Narrative Technique* 10 (1980): 99–114.

Jordan, Ruth. *George Sand: A Biographical Portrait*. New York: Taplinger, 1976.

Jost, François. "L'évolution d'un genre: Le roman épistolaire dans les lettres occidentales." In *Essais de littérature comparée*, 89–179. Urbana: Univ. of Illinois Press, 1969.

———. "Le roman épistolaire et la technique narrative au XVIIIe siècle." *Comparative Literature Studies* 3 (1966): 397–427.

Kamuf, Peggy. *Fictions of Feminine Desire: The Disclosures of Héloïse*. Lincoln: Univ. of Nebraska Press, 1982.

Kaplan, Sidney. "An Introduction to *Pym*." In *Poe: A Collection of Critical Essays*, edited by Robert Regan, 145–63. Englewood Cliffs, N.J.: Prentice-Hall, 1967.

Kauffman, Linda S. *Discourses of Desire: Gender, Genre, and Epistolary Fictions*. Ithaca: Cornell Univ. Press, 1986.

———. "Special Delivery: Twenty-first-Century Epistolarity in *The Handmaid's Tale*." In *Writing the Female Voice: Essays in Epistolary Literature*, edited by Elizabeth C. Goldsmith, 221–44. Boston: Northeastern Univ. Press, 1989.

Kellman, Steven G. *The Self-Begetting Novel.* New York: Columbia Univ. Press, 1980.

Kellogg, Robert. "Oral Narrative, Written Books." *Genre* 10 (1977): 655–65.

Kent, Leonard J. *The Subconscious in Gogol and Dostoevsky and Its Antecedents.* The Hague: Mouton, 1969.

Kermode, Frank. *The Art of Telling: Essays on Fiction.* Cambridge: Harvard Univ. Press, 1983.

———. *The Sense of an Ending: Studies in the Theory of Fiction.* New York: Oxford Univ. Press, 1967.

Kestner, Joseph A. "Linguistic Transmission in Scott: *Waverley, Old Mortality,* and *Redgauntlet.*" *The Wordsworth Circle* 8 (1977): 333–48.

———. *The Spatiality of the Novel.* Detroit: Wayne State Univ. Press, 1978.

Kincaid, James R. "'Words Cannot Express': *Frankenstein*'s Tripping on the Tongue." *Novel* 24 (1990): 26–47.

Klingopolus, G. D. "The Novel as Dramatic Poem (II): *Wuthering Heights.*" *Scrutiny* 14 (1947): 269–86.

Knoepflmacher, U. C. *Laughter and Despair: Readings in Ten Novels of the Victorian Era.* Berkeley and Los Angeles: Univ. of California Press, 1971.

Koelb, Clayton. *The Incredulous Reader: Literature and the Function of Disbelief.* Ithaca: Cornell Univ. Press, 1984.

Kristeva, Julia. *Desire in Language.* Edited by Leon S. Roudiez. Translated by Thomas Gora, Alice Jardine, and Leon S. Roudiez. New York: Columbia Univ. Press, 1980.

Lanser, Susan S. "Toward a Feminist Narratology." *Style* 20 (1986): 341–63.

———. *The Narrative Act: Point of View in Prose Fiction.* Princeton: Princeton Univ. Press, 1981.

———. "Stephen's Diary: The Hero Unveiled." *James Joyce Quarterly* 16 (1979): 417–23.

Lemon, Lee T., and Marion J. Reis, eds. and trans. *Russian Formalist Criticism: Four Essays.* Lincoln: Univ. of Nebraska Press, 1965.

Lettis, Richard, and William E. Morris, eds. *A "Wuthering Heights" Handbook.* New York: Odyssey Press, 1961.

Levenson, Michael. "Stephen's Diary in Joyce's *Portrait*—The Shape of Life." *ELH* 52 (Winter 1985): 1017–35.

Lévi-Strauss, Claude. "The Structural Study of Myth." In *Myth: A Symposium,* edited by Thomas Sebeok. Bloomington: Indiana Univ. Press, 1955.

Loesberg, Jonathan. "Allegory and Narrative in *Clarissa.*" *Novel* 15 (1981): 39–59.

Lord, Albert B. *The Singer of Tales.* Cambridge: Harvard Univ. Press, 1960.

Lotman, Jurij. *The Structure of the Artistic Text.* Translated by Gail Lenhoff and Ronald Vroom. Michigan Slavic Contributions, no. 7. Ann Arbor: University of Michigan, 1977.

———. "The Text and the Structure of Its Audience." Translated by Ann Shukman. *New Literary History* 14 (1982): 81–87.

Lucid, Daniel P., ed. and trans. *Soviet Semiotics: An Anthology.* Baltimore: Johns Hopkins Univ. Press, 1977.

Lukács, Georg. *The Historical Novel.* Translated by Hannah Mitchell and Stanley Mitchell. Lincoln: Univ. of Nebraska Press, 1983.

Lyons, John O. *The Invention of the Self: The Hinge of Consciousness in the Eighteenth Century.* Carbondale: Southern Illinois Univ. Press, 1978.

MacAndrew, Elizabeth. *The Gothic Tradition in Fiction.* New York: Columbia Univ. Press, 1979.

Macovski, Michael S. "*Wuthering Heights* and the Rhetoric of Interpretation." *ELH* 54 (1987): 363–84.

McCarthey, Terence. "The Incompetent Narrator of *Wuthering Heights*." *Modern Language Quarterly* 42 (1981): 48–64.

McCullough, Bruce. "The Dramatic Novel: *Wuthering Heights*." In *A "Wuthering Heights" Handbook*, edited by Lettis and Morris, 59–70.

McKay, Janet Holmgren. *Narration and Discourse in American Realistic Fiction*. Philadelphia: Univ. of Pennsylvania Press, 1982.

McKillop, Alan D. "Epistolary Technique in Richardson's Novels." In *Samuel Richardson: A Collection of Critical Essays*, edited by John Carroll, 139–51. Englewood Cliffs, N.J.: Prentice-Hall, 1969.

——. *Samuel Richardson: Printer and Novelist*. Hamden, Conn.: Shoe String Press, 1960.

Mainville, Stephen. "Language and the Void: Gothic Landscapes in the Frontiers of Edgar Allan Poe." *Genre* 14 (1981): 347–62.

Mallon, Thomas. *A Book of One's Own: People and Their Diaries*. New York: Ticknor & Fields, 1984.

Martens, Lorna. *The Diary Novel*. Cambridge: Cambridge Univ. Press, 1985.

Martin, Wallace. *Recent Theories of Narrative*. Ithaca: Cornell Univ. Press, 1986.

Matejka, Ladislav, and Krystyna Pomorska, eds. and trans. *Readings in Russian Poetics: Formalist and Structuralist Views*. Cambridge: MIT Press, 1971.

Mathison, John K. "Nelly Dean and the Power of *Wuthering Heights*." In *A "Wuthering Heights" Handbook*, edited by Lettis and Morris, 143–63.

Matthews, John T. "Framing in *Wuthering Heights*." *Texas Studies in Literature and Language* 27 (1985): 25–61.

Medvedev, P. N., and M. M. Bakhtin. *The Formal Method in Literary Scholarship: A Critical Introduction to Sociological Poetics*. Translated by Albert J. Wehrle. Baltimore: Johns Hopkins Univ. Press, 1978.

Mendilow, A. A. *Time and the Novel*. 1952. Reprint. New York: Humanities Press, 1972.

Mersereau, John. *Mikhail Lermontov*. Carbondale: Southern Illinois Univ. Press, 1962.

Miller, J. Hillis. *Fiction and Repetition: Seven English Novels*. Cambridge: Harvard Univ. Press, 1982.

Miller, Nancy K. *The Heroine's Text: Readings in the French and English Novel, 1722–1782*. New York: Columbia Univ. Press, 1980.

Mylne, Vivienne. *The Eighteenth-Century French Novel: Techniques of Illusion*. New York: Barnes & Noble, 1970.

Nehamas, Alexander. "The Postulated Author: Critical Monism as a Regulative Ideal." *Critical Inquiry* 8 (1981): 133–49.

Nelles, William. "Getting Focalization into Focus." *Poetics Today* 11 (1990): 365–82.

Newman, Beth. "Narratives of Seduction and the Seductions of Narrative: The Frame Structure in *Frankenstein*." *ELH* 53 (1986): 141–63.

——. "'The Situation of the Looker-On': Gender, Narration, and Gaze in *Wuthering Heights*." *PMLA* 105 (1990): 1029–41.

Oates, Joyce Carol. "The Magnanimity of *Wuthering Heights*." *Critical Inquiry* 9 (1982): 435–49.

O'Donnell, Patrick. *Passionate Doubts: Designs of Interpretation in Contemporary American Fiction*. Iowa City: Univ. of Iowa Press, 1986.

Olney, James, ed. *Autobiography: Essays Theoretical and Critical*. Princeton: Princeton Univ. Press, 1980.

Patterson, David, trans. *Diary of a Superfluous Man*, by Ivan Turgenev. New York: W. W. Norton, 1984.

Pearce, Richard. "Enter the Frame." In *Surfiction*, edited by Federman, 47–58.

Perry, Ruth. *Women, Letters, and the Novel*. New York: AMS Press, 1980.

Poe, Edgar Allan. *Essays and Reviews*. New York: Library of America, 1984.

Poirier, Richard. *The Performing Self: Compositions and Decompositions in the Languages of Contemporary Life*. New York: Oxford Univ. Press, 1971.

Pratt, Mary Louise. *Toward a Speech Act Theory of Literary Discourse*. Bloomington: Indiana Univ. Press, 1977.

Prince, Gerald. "The Diary Novel: Notes for the Definition of a Sub-Genre." *Neophilologus* 59 (1975): 477–81.

———. "The Disnarrated." *Style* 22 (1988): 1–8.

———. *A Grammar of Stories: An Introduction*. The Hague: Mouton, 1973.

———. "Introduction to the Study of the Narratee." In *Reader-Response Criticism*, edited by Tompkins, 7–25.

———. "On Readers and Listeners in Narrative." *Neophilologus* 55 (1971): 117–22.

Propp, V[ladimir]. *Morphology of the Folktale*. 2d ed. Translated by Laurence Scott. Edited by Louis A. Wagner. Austin: Univ. of Texas Press, 1968.

Raoul, Valerie. *The French Fictional Journal: Fictional Narcissism/Narcissistic Fiction*. Toronto: Univ. of Toronto Press, 1980.

Ricardou, Jean. *Problèmes du nouveau roman*. Paris: Éditions du Seuil 1967.

———. "The Story within the Story." Translated by Joseph Kestner. *James Joyce Quarterly* 18 (1981): 323–38.

———. "Time of the Narration, Time of the Fiction." Translated by Joseph Kestner. *James Joyce Quarterly* 16 (1978): 7–15.

Richardson, Samuel. *Selected Letters of Samuel Richardson*. Edited by John Carroll. Oxford: Clarendon Press, 1964.

Ricoeur, Paul. *Time and Narrative*. Vol. 1. Translated by Kathleen McLaughlin and David Pellauer. Chicago: Univ. of Chicago Press, 1984.

Rieger, James, ed. *Frankenstein*, by Mary Shelley. Indianapolis: Bobbs-Merrill, 1974.

Riffaterre, Michael. *Fictional Truth*. Baltimore: Johns Hopkins Univ. Press, 1990.

———. "Flaubert's Presuppositions." *Diacritics* 11, no. 4 (1981): 2–11.

———. "On the Diegetic Functions of the Descriptive." *Style* 20 (1986): 281–94.

Rimmon-Kenan, Shlomith. *Narrative Fiction: Contemporary Poetics*. London: Methuen, 1983.

Riquelme, John Paul. "Pretexts for Reading and for Writing: Title, Epigraph, and Journal in *A Portrait of the Artist as a Young Man*." *James Joyce Quarterly* 18 (1981): 301–21.

Romberg, Bertil. *Studies in the Narrative Technique of the First-Person Novel*. Translated by Michael Taylor and Harold H. Borland. Stockholm: Almqvist & Wiksell, 1962.

Rousset, Jean. *Narcisse romancier: Essai sur la première personne dans la roman*. Paris: Corti, 1973.

Rubin, Louis D. "One More Turn of the Screw." In *A Casebook on Henry James's "The Turn of the Screw*," 2d ed., edited by Gerald Willen, 350–66. New York: Thomas Y. Crowell, 1969.

———. *The Teller in the Tale*. Seattle: Univ. of Washington Press, 1967.

Sacks, Sheldon. *Fiction and the Shape of Belief: A Study of Henry Fielding, with Glances at Swift, Johnson, and Richardson*. Chicago: Univ. of Chicago Press, 1964.

Sand, George. *My Life*. Translated by Dan Hofstadter. New York: Harper and Row, 1979.

Sanger, C. P. "The Structure of *Wuthering Heights*." In *A "Wuthering Heights" Handbook*, edited by Lettis and Morris, 4–16.

Saussure, Ferdinand de. *Course in General Linguistics*. Edited by Charles Bally and Albert Sechehaye. Translated by Wade Baskin. New York: McGraw-Hill, 1959.

Scholes, Robert. *Semiotics and Interpretation*. New Haven: Yale Univ. Press, 1982.

———. *Structuralism in Literature*. New Haven: Yale Univ. Press, 1974.

Searle, John R. *Speech Acts: An Essay in the Philosophy of Language*. Cambridge: Cambridge Univ. Press, 1969.

Sedgwick, Eve Kosofsky. *The Coherence of Gothic Conventions*. Revised. New York: Arno Press, 1980.

Selden, Raman. *A Reader's Guide to Contemporary Literary Theory*. Lexington: Univ. Press of Kentucky, 1985.

Shklovsky, Victor. "Art as Technique." In *Russian Formalist Criticism*, edited by Lemon and Reis, 3–24.

Shukman, Ann. *Literature and Semiotics: A Study of the Writings of Yu. M. Lotman*. Amsterdam: North-Holland, 1977.

Singer, Godfrey Frank. *The Epistolary Novel: Its Origin, Development, Decline, and Residuary Influence*. 1933. Reprint. New York: Russell & Russell, 1963.

Sokolyansky, Mark G. "The Diary and Its Role in the Genesis of the English Novel." *Zeitschrift für Anglistik und Amerikanistik* 28 (1980): 341–49.

Spacks, Patricia Meyer. *Gossip*. New York: Alfred A. Knopf, 1985.

Spaulding, P. A. *Self-Harvest: A Study of Diaries and the Diarist*. London: Independent Press, 1949.

Spilka, Mark, and Caroline McCracken-Flesher, eds. *Why the Novel Matters: A Postmodern Perplex*. Bloomington: Indiana Univ. Press, 1990.

Stanzel, Franz K. *Narrative Situations in the Novel*. Translated by James P. Pusack. Bloomington: Indiana Univ. Press, 1971.

———. "Second Thoughts on *Narrative Situations in the Novel*: Towards a Grammar of Fiction." *Novel* 11 (1978): 247–68.

———. *A Theory of Narrative*. Translated by Charlotte Goedsche. Cambridge: Cambridge Univ. Press, 1984.

Steiner, Peter. "Three Metaphors of Russian Formalism." *Poetics Today* 2, no. 1b (1980): 59–116.

Steiner, Wendy. "Point of View from the Russian Point of View." *Dispositio* 1 (1976): 315–26.

Sternberg, Meir. "Proteus in Quotation Land: Mimesis and the Forms of Reported Discourse." *Poetics Today* 3, no. 2 (1982): 107–56.

Stevick, Philip. *The Chapter in Fiction: Theories of Narrative Division*. Syracuse: Syracuse Univ. Press, 1970.

Stewart, Philip. *Imitation and Illusion in the French Memoir-Novel, 1700–1750: The Act of Make-Believe*. New Haven: Yale Univ. Press, 1969.

Suleiman, Susan, and Inge Crosman, eds. *The Reader in the Text: Essays on Audience and Interpretation*. Princeton: Princeton Univ. Press, 1980.

Tanner, Tony. *City of Words: American Fiction 1950–1970*. New York: Harper and Row, 1971.

Thorpe, James. *Principles of Textual Criticism*. San Marino, Ca.: The Huntington Library, 1972.

Tobin, Particia Drechsel. *Time and the Novel: The Genealogical Imperative*. Princeton: Princeton Univ. Press, 1978.

Works Cited | 271

Todorov, Tzvetan. "The Categories of Literary Narrative." Translated by Joseph Kestner. *Papers on Language and Literature* 16 (1980): 3–36.

———. *Introduction to Poetics*. Translated by Richard Howard. Minneapolis: Univ. of Minnesota Press, 1981.

———. *Littérature et signification*. Paris: Larousse, 1967.

———. *Mikhail Bakhtin: The Dialogical Principle*. Translated by Wald Godzich. Minneapolis: Univ. of Minnesota Press, 1984.

———. *The Poetics of Prose*. Translated by Richard Howard. Ithaca: Cornell Univ. Press, 1977.

———. *Théorie de la littérature*. Paris: Éditions du Seuil, 1965.

Toliver, Harold. *Animate Illusions: Explorations of Narrative Structure*. Lincoln: Univ. of Nebraska Press, 1974.

Tompkins, Jane P., ed. *Reader-Response Criticism: From Formalism to Post-Structuralism*. Baltimore: Johns Hopkins Univ. Press, 1980.

Torgovnick, Marianna, Mark Spilka, Don H. Bialostosky, Bernard Duyfhuizen, and Richard Pearce. "Still Towards a Humanist Poetics? A Largely Positive Panel." *Novel* 18 (1985): 199–226.

Treichler, Paula A. "Escaping the Sentence: Diagnosis and Discourse in 'The Yellow Wallpaper.'" *Tulsa Studies in Women's Literature* 3 (1984): 61–77.

Uspensky, Boris. *A Poetics of Composition: The Structure of the Artistic Text and Typology of a Compositional Form*. Translated by Valentina Zavarin and Susan Wittig. Berkeley and Los Angeles: Univ. of California Press, 1973.

Volosinov, V. N. *Marxism and the Philosophy of Language*. Translated by Ladislav Matejka and I. R. Titunik. New York: Seminar Press, 1973.

Warhol, Robyn R. "Toward a Theory of the Engaging Narrator: Earnest Interventions in Gaskell, Stowe, and Eliot." *PMLA* 101 (1986): 811–18.

Warner, William Beatty. *Reading "Clarissa": The Struggles of Interpretation*. New Haven: Yale Univ. Press, 1979.

Watt, Ian. *The Rise of the Novel: Studies in Defoe, Richardson and Fielding*. Berkeley and Los Angeles: Univ. of California Press, 1957.

Wellek, René, and Austin Warren. *Theory of Literature*. 3d ed. New York: Harcourt, Brace 1956.

Whipple, E. P. *"The Tenant of Wildfell Hall* by Acton Bell." *North American Review*. October 1848. Reprinted in *The Scribner Companion to the Brontës*, edited by Barbara Evans and Gareth Lloyd, 382. New York: Scribner's, 1982.

Wilson, W. Daniel. "Readers in Texts." *PMLA* 96 (1981): 848–63.

Wimmers, Inge Crosman. *Poetics of Reading: Approaches to the Novel*. Princeton: Princeton Univ. Press, 1988.

Wolff, Cynthia Griffin. *Samuel Richardson and the Eighteenth-Century Puritan Character*. Hamdon, Conn.: Archon Books, 1972.

Woodring, Carl. "The Narrators of *Wuthering Heights*." In *A "Wuthering Heights" Handbook*, edited by Lettis and Morris, 164–70.

Woolf, Virginia. *A Writer's Diary*. Edited by Leonard Woolf. New York: Harcourt, Brace, 1953.

Würzbach, Natascha, ed. *The Novel in Letters: Epistolary Fiction in the Early English Novel, 1678–1740*. Coral Gables: Univ. of Miami Press, 1969.

Zavarzadeh, Mas'ud. *The Mythopoeic Reality: The Postwar American Nonfiction Novel*. Urbana: Univ. of Illinois Press, 1976.

Zonana, Joyce. "'They will Prove the Truth of My Tale': Safie's Letters as the Feminist Core of Mary Shelley's *Frankenstein*." *The Journal of Narrative Technique* 21 (1991): 170–84.

Index